# New Directions in Education

Selections from
Holistic Education
Review

# New Directions — in — in — Education

Selections from
Holistic Education
Review

Edited by Ron Miller

Holistic Education Press
39 Pearl Street
Brandon, Vermont 05733

# Acknowledgements

I would like to thank all the contributors to this volume for allowing me to reprint their articles from *Holistic Education Review*—and also for contributing their work in the first place. Special thanks to Kathleen Kesson-Hatley of Oklahoma State University for her insightful comments on my editorial essays. Thanks also to Bob Sharp, who supervised production of the first six issues of the *Review,* and to Charles Jakiela, who has coordinated production of every issue since, and to their talented and efficient typesetters, proofreaders, graphic designers, and ace printers. And of course, I want to thank my parents, as well as my wife, Jennifer, and our son, Justin, for their support and inspiration.

— Ron Miller

# Contents

# Introduction

## by Ron Miller

This book brings together some of the provocative and inspiring articles that have appeared in the journal *Holistic Education Review (HER)*. *HER* began publication in March, 1988, as a forum for the many alternative, person-centered movements that exist on the margins of modern education. Most educators, and many parents, have heard of Montessori schools, Waldorf schools, "free" schools, progressive and humanistic education, while terms such as "learning styles," "whole language" and "developmentally appropriate curriculum" are becoming more familiar. But few people—even educators within these movements themselves—have recognized that an emerging *worldview* links these approaches together into a fascinating global movement which speaks directly to the present crisis of our culture. The mission of *HER* has been to articulate this emerging holistic vision, and as the selections in this book will make evident, it is an inspiring and compelling vision. It is a vision we desperately need today.

Conventional education, in the form we know it today, was designed for an industrial-age culture which is now in decline. This culture, which took root in the United States in the early nineteenth century, has had a pervasive influence on the economic, social, and political trends of almost all modern nations. It is a worldview based on several fundamental assumptions about nature and human nature:

- It is essentially a *materialistic* worldview; in most aspects of our lives, success, achievement, and value are measured by objective, tangible, quantifiable standards—wealth and possessions, net profit, advanced degrees, public opinion polls, Gross National Product, SAT scores, and so forth.
- It relies on rational, analytical, scientific ways of knowing in order to transform natural resources into "wealth." It honors professional expertise and impersonal technology above artistic or spiritual inspiration, and sees the Earth and all its life as a resource to be exploited. This is a decidedly *reductionistic* attitude.
- It assumes that human beings are primarily economic beings, motivated by the desire for comfort, luxury and status. It sees society as a competitive marketplace in which there are inevitably winners and losers.
- It assumes that the divisions between groups of people, based on religion, language, occupation, gender, race, and nationality, are more real and enduring than our common humanity.

Conventional education serves to perpetuate this worldview. The curriculum, learning materials, styles of teaching, methods of administration, and approaches to discipline and assessment all reflect these industrial-age assumptions and serve to establish them ever more firmly. The educational "restructuring" movement of the past few years is primarily a desperate effort to reassert this worldview even as it is more obviously becoming obsolete. Our leading educators and policy makers are obsessed with the nation's lack of "competitiveness" in the global economy; every major commission that has reported on the decline of our schools emphasizes the *economic* far more than the *human* consequences of their failure.

But these efforts to "restructure" the schools, without confronting the obsolete worldview that conventional education serves, are akin to rearranging the deck chairs on the *Titanic.* The industrial age has outlived its usefulness and is coming to a close. The reductionistic, economic, competitive worldview of the past century and a half has brought the Earth's ecosystem to the brink of destruction and human civilization into moral and spiritual decline. The mounting toll of Chernobyls and Exxon spills shows how callously and stupidly our culture is exploiting the Earth. The growing epidemics of homelessness, drugs and alcoholism, and child abuse are clear indications that colossal impersonal institutions and national competition do not address the deeper needs of human development.

The holistic worldview is a comprehensive response to this cultural crisis, challenging each of the assumptions of the industrial age:

> • The holistic worldview seeks to integrate objective achievement with the subjective, personal, interior, spiritual aspects of life. It is essentially a *reverence for life,* and values material success only when this brings about genuine happiness, harmony, and peace. It recognizes that many of the supreme values of life—beauty, joy, love, compassion, personal wholeness—cannot be measured by any quantifiable standard, but must be honored nonetheless.
> • The holistic worldview sees the Earth—and all life upon it, including all human life—as essentially *sacred.* It seeks to understand the natural world with a sense of awe and reverence, not to dominate or control it. It is an *ecological* perspective which recognizes the delicate web of connections between all living and nonliving things, including ourselves.
> • Holism holds that human beings are essentially spiritual beings, individual expressions of a transcendent creative source that we do not fully comprehend. Our long, sorry history of violence, greed, and oppression reflects ignorance of our spiritual nature and its suppression, not an innate drive toward evil. Humanity's development is not finished and may never be; we are still evolving morally, culturally, and spiritually. The holistic approach strives to develop our latent capacity for cooperation and community, and asserts that there need not be "losers" in a just and caring society.
> • The holistic worldview is a global perspective, celebrating what is distinctly human in all cultures. It recognizes that group rivalries and national competition can lead, in the nuclear age, only to total destruction. The holistic approach welcomes the diversity that expresses our ultimate unity.

Holistic education is not any one technique or curriculum; it is the application of this post-industrial worldview to the challenges of raising children. It calls for more than fiddling around with the current curriculum, and it is not simply a "child-centered" approach to teaching. Holistic education is an effort to honor those intricate and subtle connections in human experience that the reductionistic worldview has sundered—connections between persons, between the individual and the community, between humanity and nature, between the material and the spiritual.[1]

Education may be described as holistic when it demonstrates these four characteristics:

1. Holistic education nurtures the development of the whole person; it is concerned with intellectual as well as emotional, social, physical, creative/intuitive, aesthetic, and spiritual potentials.

2. Holistic education revolves around *relationships* between learners, between young people and adults. The teacher-student relationship tends to be egalitarian, open, dynamic in holistic settings, rather than bound by bureaucratic roles or authoritarian rules. A sense of community is essential.

3. Holistic education is concerned with life experience, not with narrowly defined "basic skills." Education is growth, discovery, and a widening of horizons; it is an engagement with the world, a quest for understanding and meaning. This quest goes far beyond the limited horizons of conventional curricula, textbooks, and standardized exams.

4. Holistic education enables learners to critically approach the cultural, moral, and political contexts of their lives. It recognizes that cultures are created by people and can be changed by people if they fail to serve important human needs. In contrast, conventional education aims only to replicate the established culture in the next generation. Holistic education, then, is a radical endeavor.[2]

In the selections that follow, these themes will be expressed through a diversity of styles and approaches. Holistic education is not a new orthodoxy; it is a richly varied approach that honors the inherent creativity and uniqueness of individuals—and communities. It is my belief that the holistic worldview is the only paradigm inclusive and flexible and dynamic enough to meet the tremendous ecological and human challenges confronting us in the twenty-first century. Clearly, humanity is entering a new historical period, and the selections in this book represent the responses of educators who are on the cutting edge of this new culture.

---

1. These connections are described clearly in John P. Miller's classic work on holistic education, *The Holistic Curriculum* (Toronto: Ontario Institute for Studies in Education Press, 1988).

2. David E. Purpel spells out this radical imperative brilliantly in *The Moral & Spiritual Crisis in Education* (Granby, MA: Bergin & Garvey, 1989). See also Ron Miller, *What Are Schools For? Holistic Education in American Culture* (Brandon, VT: Holistic Education Press, 1990).

# Philosophical Foundations

# Philosophical Foundations

## Introduction

### by Ron Miller

The holistic paradigm emerged as a vibrant and coherent intellectual movement in the 1980s and has been expressed by thinkers in diverse fields—psychotherapy and medicine, physics and biology, religion and philosophy, economic and political theory.[1] But holistic thinking is not new; it is not synonymous with the "New Age" movement of the past decade, nor is it a product of the 1960s counterculture: it has deep roots in ancient spiritual traditions and cosmologies, which Aldous Huxley described as *the perennial philosophy*. When the so-called Enlightenment of the eighteenth century elevated analytical, scientific reason to near-total dominance in the West, this perennial wisdom—the recognition of humanity's intimate connection to the evolving cosmos—was relegated to a dissident movement labeled *romanticism*. Holistic education thus has its roots in the "romantic" educational theories of Jean Jacques Rousseau, Johann Pestalozzi, and Friedrich Froebel.[2]

These three figures, and other leading holistic educators of the nineteenth and early twentieth centuries including Bronson Alcott, Francis W. Parker, Maria Montessori, and Rudolf Steiner, emphasized the *spiritual* nature of the human being. Despite differences in terminology, emphasis, and educational technique, all of these educators asserted that the developing person unfolds from within, guided by a divine, creative, transcendent source. For them, education meant what its Latin root suggests: *a leading out* or *drawing forth* of life energies and personal potentials which exist within the individual. They all recognized that adults have a vital role in assisting this development—in other words, they were not simply "child-centered" educators—but they argued that our efforts to educate must follow children's natural development as it unfolds spontaneously through various stages.

In the twentieth century, most holistic educators have adopted the language of depth psychology in place of spiritual conceptions. They speak of "self-actualization," for instance, rather than "God's nature which is in you." But essentially they mean the same thing: The purpose of education is to nourish the growth of every person's intellectual, emotional, social, physical, artistic, and spiritual potentials. This is a radical departure from the conception of education now prevalent, which seeks to instill a culturally biased curriculum, rewarding those students who most obediently comply and labeling the rest "learning disabled" or "at-risk."

To put it another way, holistic education does not focus on determining which facts or skills adults should teach children, but on creating a learning community which will stimulate the growing person's creative and inquisitive engagement with the world. Holistic education is not concerned with "cultural literacy" ("what every American needs to know") so much as with nurturing healthy, whole, curious persons who can learn whatever they need to know in any new context. This different emphasis undermines the traditionally authoritarian role of the teacher, administrator, policy maker, and textbook publisher. And it suggests that we need to critically examine our culture and our social institutions to determine whether these are contributing to—or hindering—a nourishing learning environment for young people. It is beyond question, I think, that modern American culture is suffering from excessive levels of violence, hedonism, greed, and corruption; in many ways our society hinders more than it supports the healthy development of growing human beings. Yet the elitist motto of "cultural literacy" and the ritual calls for educational "excellence" completely fail to take our cultural malaise into account.

Holistic educators are not speaking of piecemeal reforms, nor even of "restructuring," as the term is currently used. They are speaking of a fundamental transformation of education. The holistic philosophy is a challenge to all educators—indeed to all people who care about the quality of human life—to reconsider the course of our cultural evolution. It asks us to take a hard look at how we have defined our humanness, our untapped potentials, and our relationship as individuals to the larger community, to the nation, and to the planet.

A holistic approach would redesign education from the bottom up. The foundational assumptions, the basic goals, the content of the curriculum, the design of the classroom and the school building, the respective roles of learner, teacher, and administrator—all would be drastically changed. The essays in this section explain the philosophical foundations upon which we should proceed.

David W. Brown's essay is a concise summary of the emerging holistic paradigm and its relationship to conventional educational assumptions, and so it is a good opening for this section. He expresses the view which underlies the holistic thinking represented in this book: The industrial age is coming to an end, and so our educational system must be transformed accordingly.

Ed Clark is probably the foremost theorist in holistic education today. Four of his articles have appeared in *Holistic Education Review,* and three of them are reprinted here. One of Dr. Clark's main contentions is that "all good education is environmental"; that is, holistic education emphasizes an ecological or *contextual* perspective. In these three essays, Ed Clark clearly spells out the holistic paradigm and its educational implications. I think everyone involved in education needs to confront the issues that he explores here, and I hope this section will bring some serious attention to his ideas.

Finally, Dave Lehman looks at some fundamental philosophical issues which have blocked the holistic approach up to now. He reviews the writings of several important educators in the radical humanist tradition to explore alternatives to the dominant worldview.

## Notes

1.  For a basic reading list on the emerging holistic paradigm, see Appendix B.

2.  The most comprehensive study of the historical roots of holistic education is my book, *What Are Schools For? Holistic Education in American Culture* (Brandon, VT: Holistic Education Press, 1990).

Incidentally, it should be made clear that the "perennial philosophy," as a spiritual and transcultural worldview, is hardly comparable to "perennialism" in education, which is culture-bound and highly conservative.

# Toward a Paradigm of Promise: Transformational Theory Applied to Education
## An Alternate View of Reality for Curriculum Development

### by David W. Brown

*David W. Brown is Assistant Professor of Elementary Education at USC Coastal Carolina College, in Conway, SC. He received his Bachelor's degree in Elementary Education from Oklahoma State University, his Masters in Elementary Education from Northeastern Oklahoma State University, and his Doctorate in Curriculum/Supervision from Oklahoma State.*

*He has four years of experience as a fifth grade public school teacher and six years of experience as an elementary principal in Tulsa, Oklahoma.*

For decades educational research has been driven by the demands for higher standardized test scores, more efficient teaching techniques, and means-ends prescriptions for learning. It is time to stop kicking this "dead horse" around and look at the child holistically as a productive, spiritual, and emotional human being instead of an end-product of pedagogical technology. The industrial/technological mentality is narrow in scope and mission, and when applied to the educational processes of humans, as it has been, it tends to delete or squelch much of our innate spirit and potential, leaving us frustrated and starved of motivation to learn.

However, an extremely exciting possibility is emerging for an emancipation from the binding ties of the technocratic model of education. It is something entirely new; it is a new way of viewing reality—a paradigm that has the potential to perhaps change the whole idea of education as we see it today. To envision this, I believe we must look to some of

This selection originally appeared in the Spring 1989 issue of *Holistic Education Review*, Vol. 2, No. 1.

the latest discoveries in science which have raised serious questions as to what our physical reality actually is in the universe. But, before this can be comprehended, it is important to look how we got where we are now in education.

The purpose of this paper is two-fold. First, I would like to examine this reliance upon science as a means of curriculum design and, second, to look at a possible alternative "paradigm" for curriculum development that may just be the near future for all educational thought—transformational theory.

## The dominance of the scientific model in education

The curriculum field in America has endured many profound influences during its relatively short existence. The schools have been looked to ameliorate international and political tensions and cure the ills of our ubiquitous societal woes since even before the birth of the curriculum field near the turn of the twentieth century.

Significant threats to the integrity of the American way of life, such as the industrial revolution, the launch of the Russian Sputnik satellite, the rise of the counter-culture of the 1960s, and the rise of the technological age have forced curricularists to crank out curriculum plans, models, and designs which could keep up with the everchanging demands of the times.

Because of this urgency to keep up, a form of control and efficiency had to be developed and followed. Curriculum developers look to science and the scientific method to attain the control and universality needed to achieve their goals. According to Elliot Eisner, the reliance upon scientifically based technology in educational practice, similar to techniques in agriculture, engineering, and medicine, was established from the very beginnings of curriculum development with E.L. Thorndike and John Dewey. Both of these men looked to science as the most reliable means for guiding educational practice and they helped to establish and legitimize a tradition that others such as Franklin Bobbitt, W. W. Charters, Henry Harap, and Ralph Tyler were to follow.[1] Tyler's work, much influenced by his predecessors, set the prototype for the dominant, rational, systematic approach to curriculum planning which is in use in the schools today. And, further, many influential educators and researchers of today had the opportunity to work with Tyler such as Robert Anderson, Ben Bloom, Lee Chronbach, Hilda Taba, Ole Sand, and John Goodlad. Like Tyler, these authorities can be characterized as basically scientific in their assumptions, systematic in their procedures, and means-end oriented in their view of educational planning.[2]

## Models versus paradigms

I contend that American education has virtually been enslaved to a scientific model which, according to Eisner, has all but excluded any other view of the way in which inquiry in education can legitimately be pursued. What is a model? A model is defined as "a standard or example for imitation or comparison."[3] This conception of the word "model" coupled with the veneration held for the creators (Thorndike and Dewey) by our present curricularists is, in Eisner's opinion, the reason for our situation today. The approach has been to follow model after model, replacing one with another if it fails to accomplish the missions of political activists and/or other influential reform groups. With each replacement comes a more stringent empirical, analytic demand for accountability, evaluation, and scientific supervision. The more technologically efficient the model is, the more successful and error-free the product will be.

Where does this end? When do we reach the ultimate model where all stops are closed and all outcomes predicted to precise specifications? The answer is: probably never! So why do we keep doing this? Is there a viable alternative that has not been discovered or explored? I believe there is, and I believe that the possible answer will come out of the discoveries in process in the field of the new physics or "quantum mechanics"; they provide the foundation of transformational theory— what I see as the paradigm of promise.[4]

The search for this alternative conceptualization begins with the work of Thomas Kuhn and his idea of "paradigm." The word *paradigm* has become a popular term to describe certain ways of looking at reality. Kuhn's concept is based upon the mutability of theories in natural science. He states that a paradigm "is an object for further articulation and specification under new or more stringent conditions"[5]; therefore it is not as rigid as a model. Also, a paradigm never does explain all the facts with which it can be confronted; it does not contain all the answers.

A model contains certain rules, guidelines, and stipulations which are to be followed in order to be successful. Schubert states that, "as applied to teaching, a model refers to a coherent method, approach, or strategy. A model should be able to be discussed in terms of assumptions, propositions, essential characteristics or attributes, supportive theory, research, and practical precedent."[6] On the other hand, rules, according to Kuhn, "derive from paradigms, but paradigms can guide research even in the absence of rules." Furthermore,"the lack of a standard interpretation or of an agreed reduction to rules will not prevent a paradigm from guiding research."[7] According to Kuhn "a paradigm 'shift' occurs when the conventional devices or remedies to problems fail to work in the present paradigm. A crisis evolves and new methods must be researched and tried to solve the crisis. This is the beginning of the rejection of the old paradigm (which no longer works), and the start of the new."[8] Capra defines paradigm shift as "a profound change in the thoughts, perceptions, and values that form a particular vision of reality."[9]

Hence, a paradigm allows the freedom to adopt ideas and concepts from other areas such as sociology, science, and history, without the

stringent guidelines and rules of models. Paradigms are loosely structured and flexible; they are fluid and essential for the acceptance of the
ideas and conceptions of a new reality.

## The heart of the new paradigm—quantum reality

"Determinism—the worldview that nature and our own life are completely determined from past to future—reflects the human need for
certainty in an uncertain world."[10] We, as humans, must be able to
project, predict, determine, and accurately measure our future. We deal
with educational matters in much the same way today; we have an
uncertain quantity—human beings—with which we attempt to virtually
determine their successes and failures, their strengths and weaknesses,
their careers and ambitions. To relate this phenomenon to the historical
progression of science, particularly classical physics, will clarify why I
believe a change in curriculum thinking is imminent.

Classical physics supported the worldview of determinism for centuries. Classical science or "Newtonianism" evolved in the seventeenth
and eighteenth centuries. Isaac Newton pictured a world in which every
event was determined by initial conditions that were, at least in principle, determinable with precision. "It was a world in which chance played
no part, in which all the pieces came together like cogs in a cosmic
machine."[11] Today, however, the "Age of the Machine" is screeching to
a halt. The decline of the Industrial Age forces us to confront the painful
limitations of the machine model of reality.[12] And further, early
nineteenth century thermodynamics challenged the deterministic view
of the universe. The second law of thermodynamics states that there is
an inescapable loss of energy in the universe (entropy) which, in effect,
means that the world machine is running down; one moment is no
longer exactly like the last as it is with Newtonian thought. Therefore,
according to this, we can no longer "determine" anything. "You cannot
run the universe backward to make up for entropy. Events over the
long term cannot replay themselves."[13]

This brings us to the notion of "quantum reality." According to Pagels,
quantum reality requires changing from a reality that can be seen and
felt to an instrumentally detected reality that can be perceived only
intellectually. The world described by the quantum theory does not
appeal to our immediate intuition as did the old classical physics. "Quantum reality is rational but not visualizable."[14] In other words, scientists
are understanding quantum concepts through experimentation but are
not yet able to conceptualize it as easily as they could with Newton's
machine model. Quantum theory is the opposite of Newtonian theory:
Newtonianism is based upon determinism—ends-means predictability;
quantum reality is based upon randomness—indeterminism, probability, guesswork. All of this stems from the discovery of atoms and how
they behave. The movement of atomic particles in space defies the laws
of classical physics—the laws under which the universe has been perceived and by which our total existence has been governed. Quantum
behavior, in a sense, is deviant behavior under the laws of classical

physics. Quantum theory will perceivably be the language of the future of science.

As discussed earlier, curriculum developers historically have relied religiously upon scientific methodology and the advancements within the natural sciences for developing pedagogical practice and techniques in the classrooms. To this point these techniques have been thought of as being successful because the end results could be analyzed and verified through testing much like that done in the scientist's laboratory. But what about now? According to the new physics, scientists are no longer able to verify experimental outcomes according to the classical methods. The machine theory simply doesn't fit. Atoms simply won't behave according to the plan.

I contend that since scientific thought is on the verge of a reconceptualization of reality, so too is education. Our conceptualization of learning, methodology, usefulness, and worth of education to individuals will change; it will change commensurate with changes in scientific thought to follow suit with the past.

### Dissipative structures

The only "rational" means of describing what this notion of quantum irreversibility, randomness, and indeterminism holds for the future of curriculum development is through a portrayal of Ilya Prigogine's theory of dissipative structures.

Imagine a spinning mass of energy surrounded by helical or braided bands that hold it together. This is an "open system." All living things and some nonliving things are open systems; they are involved in the continuous exchange of energy with the environment. All open systems, according to Prigogine, are dissipative structures. Their form is maintained by the continuous dissipation or "consumption" of energy. They are highly organized and always in process.

Converting this to educational thought, the educational system is a dissipative structure. It is very complex and continually in process, considering the changes historically brought about by a demanding society. It is an open system which consumes energy from the efforts of society.

The braided helical surroundings of this energy mass are connected at many points, signifying its level of strength and complexity. The more interwoven the braids, the more complex the system is.

Imagine our educational system as a very complex mass of interwoven braids connected at many points. This is due to continuous reform efforts over the years which have strengthened the system by creating layers upon layers of helical braids via a deterministic mentality.

Now, according to Prigogine, the more complex this structure becomes, the more vulnerable it is to change or what he calls "fluctuations." This is a paradoxical situation because the more coherent or intricately connected the structure, the more vulnerable it is. Increased coherence means increased instability. This very instability is the key to transformation or change.

The continuous flow of energy through the system results in fluctuations and, if these are minor, it rejects or "damps" them, and they do not alter the structural integrity (neither strengthens or weakens the braids). On the other hand, if the fluctuations reach a critical size, they "perturb" the system. "They increase the number of novel interactions within it. They shake it up. The elements of the old pattern come into contact with each other in new ways and make new connections. The parts reorganize into a new whole. The system escapes into a higher order."[15]

Imagine our educational system again under the new circumstances of instability. Our system, according to the theory, is now requiring massive amounts of energy from the environment because of its greater complexity, and it is now highly vulnerable to fluctuations. In other words, our reliance upon prespecification of learning outcomes, standardized testing, goals, objectives, means-ends oriented curriculum designs, and so on, have built a "goliath" of a dissipative structure which is on the verge of perturbation—a transformation.

I believe that our educational system is at the point where continual reform movements which demand tighter controls and scientifically based outcomes are simply being damped or rejected; they are not effectually changing the structural integrity of the system. They are merely "fluff" or "gimmicks" based on the same old scientific "stuff," and it doesn't work anymore.

I believe that we are at a virtual standstill; that we are in a state of "entropia." We have this great, complex, and very vulnerable open system just waiting for a fluctuation of a magnitude that will, in Prigoginian terms, bifurcate or shatter the integrity and organization of the scientific paradigm. This "giant killer" must be of an entirely nondeterministic origin to bring about a transformation of reality for curricular thought. Here is where I feel the discoveries in quantum physics will provide the direction, the schematic, and the vehicle. It is uncertain and almost mystical as to what this new reality will be for education, but so is it with every transformation of thought. Just imagine what the world thought when Copernicus, discrediting the ancient, venerated Biblical conceptualization, announced that the world was not the center of the universe but just a mere one of many minute planets orbiting the sun!

Through the study of transformational theory, curricularists may begin to see their way out of the impenetrable web of reliance upon classical scientific methods to guide research and practice. Before new methods, techniques, and curriculum plans can be developed which are free of this influence, a transformation of thought about reality and our existence within it needs to take place.

The literature on transformational theory is limited and transformational literature as pertaining to education is scarce at this point in time. Changes have been occurring in educational thought for some time, but emancipation from the shackles of classical scientific application and remedies has not quite manifested itself significantly enough to make a difference. The transformation is yet to come, but perhaps with the aid of a new pair of conceptual lenses with which to view reality, curricularists will begin to visualize the excitement, the opportunities, and the possibilities of a new Paradigm of Promise.

## Notes

1.   E. Eisner, *The Educational Imagination*. (New York: Macmillan, 1985).

2.   Ibid.

3.   *Random House Dictionary*. (New York: Random House, 1988), p. 1235.

4.   See M. Ferguson, *The Aquarian Conspiracy*. (Los Angeles: Tarcher, 1980), p. 26.

5.   T. Kuhn, *The Structure of Scientific Revolutions*. (Chicago: University of Chicago Press, 1988), p. 23.

6.   W. Schubert, *Curriculum: Perspective, Paradigm, and Possibility*. (New York: Macmillan, 1986), p. 249.

7.   Kuhn, p. 42.

8.   Ibid., p. 67.

9.   F. Capra, *The Turning Point*. (New York: Bantam, 1982), p. 16.

10.   H. Pagels, *The Cosmic Code*. (New York: Bantam, 1982), p. 67.

11.   A. Toffler, Foreword to Prigogine and Stengers, *Order out of Chaos*. (New York: Bantam, 1984), p. xiii.

12.   Ibid.

13.   Ibid., p. xix.

14.   Ibid., p. xiii.

15.   Ferguson, pp. 164 165.

# The Search For a New Educational Paradigm:
## The Implications of New Assumptions About Thinking and Learning

### by Edward T. Clark, Jr.

*Edward T. Clark, Jr., is the former Director of the Institute for Environmental Awareness and Professor of Environmental Education at George Williams College in Warrenville, Illinois. He is currently an educational consultant and author of the Contextual Thinking program for educational reform and staff development. Dr. Clark is a frequent contributor to* Holistic Education Review; *his article "The Search for a New Educational Paradigm" (Spring 1988) earned a merit award from the Educational Press Association. He is on the Steering Committee of the Global Alliance for Transforming Education.*

In 1962 Thomas Kuhn, in his book *The Structure of Scientific Revolutions*, introduced the concept of "paradigm shift" into the literature and, thus, into our ways of thinking about ourselves and the world. Since that time, much has been written concerning the paradigm shift that is occurring in various fields of endeavor.

For Kuhn, a paradigm shift occurs as the result of a shift in the underlying assumptions upon which science is based. As he makes clear, at a certain fundamental level, the basic assumptions of a discipline shape the research and results of that research. When the evidence begins to challenge these commonly accepted assumptions, anomalies appear. These anomalies create conflicts—conflicts which can only be resolved by acknowledging a new set of assumptions. As these new assumptions gradually gain acceptance, a dramatic shift occurs both in the nature of scientific inquiry and in our understanding of the role of science in society. To use a Biblical analogy, one cannot put new wine in old wineskins because, in time, the new wine, as it ferments and expands, will burst the old wineskins.

This selection originally appeared in the Spring 1988 issue of *Holistic Education Review*, Vol. 1, No. 1.

While much has been written about the need for educational reform, not enough attention has been paid to the fact that, in education, as in virtually every other area of our lives, a major paradigm shift is occurring. Although implicit in each of the many national reports that first officially recognized the current crisis in education, few educators seem to have explicitly identified the problems as resulting from a major paradigm shift.

At a macro level the paradigm shift represents a conflict between two worldviews. If we think of a worldview as a cultural mindset, it seems clear that *a technological worldview* has guided Western thought since the beginning of the Industrial Revolution. Based on the analytical perspective of Newton and Descartes, it reduces things to their smallest component parts in order to understand them. Its strategies are fragmenting, linear, and sequential. Its empirical logic discounts intuition and value-based perceptions and forces us into an "either/or" problem-solving and decision-making mode. This reductionist worldview is explicitly taught in our schools and forms the conceptual framework for most social decisions.

A systemic *ecological worldview* is now emerging. Crucial to much of science today, this systems view is a fundamental premise upon which the cutting edge of research in every major discipline is based. This new worldview is global, holistic, and integrative. Its primary mode of thinking is whole-brain thought, incorporating both inductive and deductive strategies, while integrating both rational and intuitive modes of knowing. Although it acknowledges that for certain purposes the concept of objectivity is useful, this perspective affirms that, at its most fundamental level, all knowledge and experience is subjective and value-laden. As a consequence, in our complex world, the best decisions are more often "both/and" rather that "either/or" choices. This emerging worldview acknowledges the importance of science and technology, but holds that these must be understood and applied within the context of a global, ecological perspective.

This changing worldview obviously represents a major shift in the context within which education is conducted. Since "context" is "the frame of reference that provides meaning," when the context changes, meaning changes. This contextual shift reflects, at a micro-level, a change in the basic assumptions that have shaped the purposes, goals, and methodologies of education since the early part of this century. This shift has resulted from research in the nature of intelligence, thinking, and learning, which has thrown a new light on the vast area of human potential. The research challenges both the way that the educational system is structured and the way that teaching and learning are perceived to take place. The purpose of this article is to examine both the conventional wisdom and the emerging assumptions and explore their implications for the four major arenas that are central to education: students, teachers, administrators, and the curriculum.

The approach seeks to provide a "big picture" perspective on the issues. Such a synthesis, by its very nature, depends upon generalizations. Those in this article are offered with the full knowledge that many can be challenged with details that seem to contradict the conclusions that are presented. However, in our concern for pragmatic accuracy and empirical solutions, we seldom examine the "big picture," and as a result, we treat symptoms while the underlying problem goes unattended. It is only when we explore the issues from this macro-perspective that we can identify the more fundamental problem. The hypothesis upon which this article is based is that the fundamental problem is one of unexamined assumptions. Once this issues is addressed, we can proceed with our task of designing an educational system that is appropriate to the requirements of a global information society.

## Students

Stated simply, the paradigm shift vis-à-vis students is the movement from an assumption that each student was born with a given, mathematically quantifiable, intellectual capacity, to the assumption that each individual student has an innate potential for thinking and learning whose boundaries defy quantification.

There are three areas in which the assumptions which shape our perception of students have changed.

**The nature of intelligence.** Traditional wisdom suggests that intelligence is a given, mathematically identifiable quotient. Since the introduction of intelligence tests in the early part of this century, educators have classified students by IQ scores based on their linguistic and logical-mathematical abilities. Such classification is based on the assumption that intelligence is a fixed amount which can be measured with a mathematical formula. Traditionally, students have been given IQ tests before entering school and, although there has been some recognition of the fact that these scores may be subject to change, most students carry their scores with them throughout life.

Studies by Howard Gardner of Harvard call this assumption into question. His studies suggest that there are at least seven, rather than just two, forms of intelligence. In addition to the traditional linguistic and logical-mathematical abilities, he identifies spatial, musical, bodily-kinesthetic intelligences, and two forms of personal intelligence: interpersonal and intrapersonal. While our culture has given precedence to, and, therefore, measured intelligence exclusively by the first two areas, Gardner concludes that none of these should have priority over the others. He suggests that it is quite possible that every child has the potential of becoming a genius in at least one of these areas.[1]

Because IQ scores seem to follow the distribution pattern of the bell curve, we have long assumed that student achievement would follow the same pattern. However, in his studies of Mastery Learning, Benjamin Bloom concludes that, given an appropriate learning environment, virtually all students have the potential for achieving above average grades.[2] Similar conclusions are implied by the Rosenthal studies, which suggest that student performance is more the result of teacher expectations than the so-called "given" abilities measured by an IQ score.[3]

**The nature of thinking.** Implicit in the current wisdom on teaching thinking skills is the assumption that children have to be taught the higher order thinking skills such as analysis, synthesis, critical thinking, problem solving, creative thinking, and decision making. As a result, we have a multitude of programs, each presenting a combination of discrete strategies by which these skills can be taught. These programs seem to be characterized by several features which reflect what seem to be outdated assumptions about the nature of thinking.

Many of them tend to emphasize the discrete functions of the right and left brain hemispheres. Creativity is considered to be the result of right hemisphere activity, while problem solving is considered to be a left hemisphere activity. In recognition of the dominant left-hemisphere orientation of the curriculum, many programs have been developed to train students to use their "right brain."

For the most part, the strategies introduced in these programs are linear and sequential and have been designed as "add-ons" to the curriculum. A typical program is recommended for use in two to five one-hour lessons per week for two to three years. We know now that higher order thinking is not a linear, sequential process.

Leslie Hart[4] and David Loye[5] have synthesized the tremendous amount of research that has taken place in the areas of thinking and learning. This research strongly suggests that all higher order thinking is whole-brain thinking, and is an innate rather than a learned capacity.

For example, David Loye describes how the brain functions in a problem-solving mode. There are essentially three, virtually simultaneous, steps. In the first step, the right hemisphere identifies the gestalt, the big picture, the context. Given this holistic perspective, the left hemisphere begins to sort out and arrange details and identify probable solutions. Based on the input from the two hemispheres, and with additional input from the senses and the intuition, the forebrain, acting in its executive role, evaluates the information and makes a decision.

The evidence is strong that all higher order thinking involves these three steps: context, content, conclusion. The difference between the diversity of thinking skills which are taught in current programs may well lie in the context which triggers higher order thought. Whether the context calls for a problem to be solved, an analytical critique, or a new way to evaluate learning, the fundamental brain process is the same. Though it takes many forms in response to specific situations, it seems appropriate to conclude that all higher order thinking is, at its most fundamental level, "creative problem solving." It is this capacity, which I call "contextual thinking," that distinguishes humans from other animal species. If these conclusions are sound extrapolations from the latest research, then our children do not have to be taught how to think. What is needed are strategies for triggering this innate higher cognitive function. An example will highlight the difference between the two approaches, each based on a different fundamental assumption about the nature of thinking.

A strategy for teaching elementary students how to summarize a story (synthesis) proposes the following steps:

1. Delete trivial material
2. Delete repetitious material
3. Substitute a general term for a list of specific terms
4. Combine a list of actions into a broader, single action
5. Select a topic sentence
6. Create a topic sentence.

Hart uses an analogy to demonstrate the futility of sequential learning strategies such as this. He hypothesizes teaching someone to ride a bicycle by sequentially teaching them how to steer, to pedal, to balance, to lean into a turn, and to stop. He concludes that it is the coordination of these that is the essential learning.[6]

Based as it is on outdated assumptions about thinking and learning, such linear strategies are counterproductive. Like many other models for teaching thinking skills, they tend to ignore context and focus almost exclusively on a linear mode of thinking when in reality, this mode represents only one part of whole-brain thinking.

I have found, in my work with elementary students, that a simple question like, "How would you tell the story in one sentence?" is sufficient to trigger the skill we refer to as synthesis. Indeed, my experience, and that of teachers in Contextual Thinking workshops, has been that any of the higher order thinking skills can be triggered by appropriate questions related to the subject matter under consideration.

This research does not deny the usefulness and necessity of what David Perkins calls "tactics" and "thinking frames."[7] Such a "bag of tricks" helps students organize their thinking in more productive ways. It would seem that many of the "thinking skills" that are currently being taught might better be called "thinking tactics" in order to distinguish them from the more fundamental higher level thinking. The danger is that by confusing these strategies with the more fundamental cognitive processes described above, we mistake one for the other. The result may be that the tactics we teach work in opposition with the natural way of thinking.

Research has now reinforced what every parent has known intuitively: The process we call higher level thinking is an innate capacity that begins to develop at an early age. I recently watched my two-year old granddaughter spend ten minutes trying to solve the problem of how to put on her diaper by herself. She laid it on the floor and tried lying on it. Then she tried sitting on it using a variety of postures. Next she carefully placed it in her rocking chair and tried to sit in it. She experimented with several other strategies, and although she never quite succeeded, the chances are she will try it again. Any parent who has tried to hide the cookie jar from a four-year old knows that young children may be the best problem solvers in our society. Yet, by the time they reach third or fourth grade, teachers have to "teach" them problem solving. What has happened to that innate capacity? Research reported in *The Leading Edge Bulletin* gives us a clue. This study found that "creativity scores invariably drop about ninety percent between ages five and seven."[8] One obvious conclusion, which teachers are quick to reach, is that, upon entering school, the child is programmed for linear, sequential thinking to the exclusion of a more holistic, integrated, innate process.

**The nature of learning.** The first question that most teachers ask when they begin to write a lesson plan is: What do I want the student to learn? The way the teacher answers this question reflects his or her assumptions about the nature of learning, and obviously will have a significant impact on both what is taught and how it is taught.

A generation of teachers have been trained to answer this question in terms of behavioral or instructional objectives. Such objectives represent, by definition, terminal behaviors on the part of the learner that are demonstrable and quantifiable. Behavioral objectives have two specific purposes: to identify the desired outcome and to measure the degree to which the outcome is achieved. Thus, two functions—goal setting and evaluation—are directly linked in a linear, causal relationship that moves from the end to the beginning rather than the usual direction from beginning to end. According to Mager,

> If you are interested in preparing instruction that will help you reach your objectives, you must first be sure your objectives are clearly and unequivocally stated. You cannot concern yourself with the problem of selecting the most efficient route to your destination until you know what your destination is.[9]

The assumption upon which behavioral objectives are based is that learning, like intelligence, can be quantitatively measured. Once we accept this assumption, we find ourselves in the same circular trap that we were in with our assumptions about the nature of intelligence. Once you assume that learning can be measured, you end up defining all learning by that which can be measured. Therefore, by using behavioral objectives in the way they were designed to be used, we: 1) identify an end result that is measurable, and 2) decide on what we will teach and how we will teach it in order to reach that measurable end result. The obvious choice is to teach that which is measurable. Once in this circular trap, our only option is to teach what we test. Indeed, in essence, that sums up both the purpose and method of behavioral objectives: how to teach what you test. Carl Rogers describes this circularity as an assumption that "Evaluation is education, and education is evaluation."[10]

The result of this way of thinking has been an attempt to reduce all learning to that which can be measured. To accomplish this, we have created an elaborate system of testing based almost entirely on those learnings that can be demonstrated and quantified. In so doing, we have reduced concepts like understand, know, appreciate, enjoy, and believe into measurable behaviors like write, recite, identify, list, compare, and contrast. Since the only learning that can be accurately measured without ambiguity is recall, we have, implicitly if not explicitly, reached the conclusion that the measure of recall is a measure of learning. As a consequence, virtually the entire teaching/learning process is centered around the presentation, memorization, and recall of facts.

Once these assumptions are accepted, it logically follows that learning can be made more efficient if enough time is spent on the task at hand. Thus, we have a current emphasis of *time on task*—all in the attempt to beef up test scores that are based primarily on the amount of material that can be quantified by a test.

## New assumptions

The new assumptions about the nature of intelligence, thinking, and learning stress that which is potential rather than that which is measurable. Acknowledging both the intuitive and the cognitive aspects of learning, these new assumptions recognize the fullness and richness of learning that can only be expressed through words like understand, appreciate, enjoy, know, and believe. Indeed, it is because of the multidimensionality of these experiences that behaviorists reject them as unmeasurable. But in rejecting what these words represent, we are in danger of rejecting both the multidimensionality and the potentiality of human learning.

It seems evident that human learning is far more complex than the behaviorists recognized. Even with a virtually infinite list of observable and quantifiable behaviors, it is impossible to determine the exact extent to which a student "understands" the causes of the Civil War, "appreciates" a symphony that was studied in a music appreciation class, or "knows" how a cell functions. As such, these learnings cannot be fragmented and reduced to specific behaviors which can be measured. Whenever we attempt this, we ignore the reality that the whole is greater than the sum of its parts and, therefore cannot be reduced to or comprehended from its parts.

Understandably, if we have to give grades, we must find ways to measure outcomes. As long as we recognize their limitation, namely that what we are measuring may be only a small part of what has been learned, behavioral objectives have an appropriate place in the evaluation process. However, their use should not extend to identifying what is to be taught and what learning outcomes are desirable. While the two functions of goal setting and evaluation are obviously related, to use behavioral objectives to identify learning outcomes is to let the tail wag the dog. The result is the worst sort of reductionism—reducing the full panoply of human learning to the drabness of what can be memorized and, therefore, measured.

What every teacher and parent wants most of all is for students to understand, appreciate, know, enjoy, and believe. When we acknowledge that this is the true goal of learning, then we are free to expand both the what and how of the teaching/learning process, opening the door to both intuitive and cognitive experiences that enable students to expand their own awareness and begin the process of exploring that untapped potential that lies within each of them.

Implicit in the empirical view of learning is the assumption that learning is objective. We now know without equivocation, that all learning is, at its most fundamental level, subjective in nature. Research by Anthony Gregorc and others makes this clear. While recognizing the individual nature of learning, their work suggests that there are four basic learning styles, or modes of learning.[11] Because all children do not learn the same way, these studies conclude that effective teaching must acknowledge and adapt to these differences. The next step is to acknowledge that because children learn in different ways, there is no standard test by which everyone's learning can be accurately and fairly measured.

The research related to whole-brain thinking reported above, also suggests that learning is deductive in nature. Because it is the context that endows anything with meaning, learning always starts with the context as a frame of reference within which the parts can be taught, understood, or deduced.[12]

A study conducted by Even found that 75 percent of all adult learners have right-brain preferences during the attention and arousal stages of the learning process. It further indicates that in these initial stages of learning the preferred learning mode is holistic, pictorial, and broad-based rather than focusing on separate single concepts.[13] In other words, the first stage of the learning process is similar to the first stage of the problem-solving or decision-making process—a search for context.

If we acknowledge the importance of context in providing meaning, then it seems logical to conclude that all learning begins with context. As Neustadt and May in their study of political decision making suggest, the first question is not, "What's the problem?" but rather, "What's the story?"[14]

This is in contrast with the inductive strategy of Cartesian thought that teaches that the first step in understanding things is to first reduce them to their smallest component parts. Based on this Cartesian assumption, facts have been taught as the building blocks of knowledge. As a consequence, almost our entire curriculum has been designed to be taught inductively. The implications of this anomaly alone are staggering. The differences between inductive and deductive strategies and the implications of each will be discussed in greater detail in the treatment of the curriculum.

**Summary.** Our analogies and metaphors often provide significant insights to our thinking. The primary metaphor for the old paradigm, based as it is on Newtonian and Cartesian thinking, is the machine. Newton thought of the universe as a giant clock. When extended to the way we think and learn, this metaphor suggests that the mind functions like a giant computer. Thus, we logically conclude that just as a computer or any machine must be programmed before it can function, so students must be programmed by the teacher who is then perceived as the master programmer.

And just as the potential capacity of a computer can be quantified by an appropriate number of bytes, so the potential of a child to learn can be quantified by a mathematical score. The underlying assumption is that only that which can be quantified and measured empirically is real. As an extension of this manner of thinking, we organize our schools like factories and emphasize the necessity of treating each child the same, as though they were interchangeable cogs. Through all of this, we expect children to be efficient learners and to produce that which is measurable and quantifiable. It is indeed one of the great ironies of our time that, having designed computers that can perform the function of information storage and retrieval better than any human, we continue to emphasize in our teaching and testing, information storage and retrieval.

The metaphors of the new paradigm are organic. Just as some scientists are now referring to the earth as the largest single, living organism we know, so an appropriate organic metaphor for children is a seed. Just as every acorn has within it the potential to be an oak tree, every child has the potential to be a genius. As Katharine Kersey suggests in the preface of her book, *Sensitive Parenting,* "They (children) come to us like a packet of flower seeds, with no pictures on the cover, and no guarantees. We don't know what they will look like, be like, act like, or have the potential to become." Pursuing this metaphor, she likens parents (the teachers) to a gardener whose job is to "give proper nourishment, love, attention, and caring, and to hope for the best. The gardener learns to be "tuned in" to the plant . . . . He knows that all plants are different, need varying amounts of care and attention, and grow at different rates of speed."[15]

Research is just beginning to explore the depths of human potential, in the areas of mind/brain and thinking/learning. Therefore, the evidence is not all in and many conclusions are tentative. However, there are two conclusions about which there is absolutely no doubt. The first is that many of the assumptions upon which education today is based are no longer valid. The second is that *each individual has an enormous untapped potential for thinking and learning which, at least at present, is beyond measurement.* If we are to adequately prepare children to live in the global information society of the twenty-first century, the first step is to acknowledge the paradigm shift that is occurring. Once this has taken place, we are ready to design the most creative strategies we can devise that will enable students to "tune into," explore, and tap their unrealized potential for thinking, learning, and creative problem solving. This then becomes the primary responsibility for teachers.

### Teachers

The paradigm shift vis-à-vis teachers is directly related to the shift in assumptions concerning the nature of intelligence, thinking, and learning. At its most fundamental level, it is a shift from the perception of the teacher as a technician to a recognition of the teacher as a professional.

**The old paradigm.** The national report, *A Nation At Risk*, recognizes that the teacher is not perceived as a professional when it states: "Individual teachers have little influence in such critical professional decisions as, for example, textbook selection." Before we can address the problem, we must explore the assumptions that underlie the current role of the teacher in the educational system.

Michael Bakalis, formerly Illinois Superintendent of Education, suggests that, like it or not, one of the major functions of schools in our society is custodial. The result is that the primary responsibility for most teachers is to be an effective caretaker of children, i.e., classroom manager. Responsibilities include such diverse elements as discipline, collecting lunch money, making announcements, keeping students busy with seatwork, grading essays, entertaining the students and lecturing. Above all, the teacher must keep the students quiet lest the principal walk in unannounced. While an increased emphasis on "time on task" has, perhaps, increased the amount of time given to the curriculum, the focus is still primarily on management.

Once we move beyond the classroom management function, teaching is perceived as being virtually synonymous with lecturing. Mortimer Adler suggests that one of the problems facing education today is the belief that "good teaching is didactic." John Goodlad estimates that as much as 85 percent of classroom time is spent by the teacher talking to students.[16] Although we have known for a long time that listening is the poorest way to learn, we still tend to equate good teaching with an interesting and entertaining lecture. Implicit in this perception is the assumption that the best teachers are those who are the best purveyors of knowledge. Because they are perceived as the "font of wisdom," many teachers discourage questions for which they may not have the answer, maintaining tight control on what content is studied and how it is addressed. It is not difficult then, to recognize the truth in Carl Rogers' belief that we tend to equate presentation with learning.[17]

Though they are trained as professionals, teachers have little voice in selecting what they will teach and, except within narrow limits, how they will teach it. In the words of one teacher, Patricia Dombert:

> We affect none of the key elements in our working lives. For example, we have no control over class size or the length of the school day and class periods. We have almost no input into the form and content of report cards. We do not select our schedules, grade levels, or the building in which we teach. Indeed, we do not even control the time within our own classrooms, for we are slaves to the P.A., to notes from the nurse, from guidance, the librarian, the main office.[18]

Another fundamental assumption explicitly accepted throughout the educational system is that teachers are primarily motivated by external rewards such as salary and career status. Most responses to the call for improvement of teaching have focused on these two issues. *Educational Leadership* devoted an entire issue to the topic, "Making Teaching More Rewarding."[19] Every major article discussed career ladders and salary scales. The single voice in the wilderness of external reward systems was that of Patricia Dombert, the only classroom teacher to contribute to the issue. Her conclusion, which is reinforced by my own experience with teachers, is unequivocal. If given a choice, most teachers would prefer to participate in the major decisions which shape their professional lives, rather than be "bought off" by financial remuneration. While this does not negate efforts to upgrade teachers' salaries, it does suggest that intrinsic personal and professional satisfaction is more important than extrinsic rewards.

**The new paradigm.** The fundamental assumption of the new paradigm vis-à-vis teachers is that the teacher is the professional. Someone has suggested that there are four qualities that characterize the professional: vision, training, responsibility, and accountability. I have found, as has Patricia Dombert, that most teachers have a vision. Having entered the profession for what she calls a "love of subject and students," teachers share common ideals about what constitutes good teaching and effective learning. In my workshops, I find that teachers know what good teaching is and describe the "ideal" classroom without hesitation. They do have a vision, and their outstanding frustration is their perceived inability to make that vision a reality. As Dombert says so eloquently, "The paradox of education as a profession is that it attracts people with visions into a system designed to frustrate those visions."

A second quality of a professional is training. While I have some major criticisms of much that goes on and does not go on in teacher education programs, my experience suggests that most teachers have acquired the fundamental knowledge and skills requisite for being a professional. In fact, I have found that most of them have knowledge and skills that haven't been used yet. For example, in my workshops, teachers design curriculum units which are always more appropriate for their students than the textbooks which they use.

Responsibility goes hand in hand with ownership. In fact, one of the fundamental precepts of our capitalistic democracy is that ownership provides the best motivation for success. A recent poll indicates that the "dream job" for 47 percent of women and 38 percent of men was to be head of their own businesses.[20] Professionally, ownership involves full participation in the decisions that influence one's work. Inherent in such participation is both the responsibility and accountability for implementing those decisions. Until teachers are allowed to assume the responsibilities of a professional, a genuinely professional system of accountability is not possible. Teachers resist merit pay plans because they know that in a system where their responsibilities are severely limited, good survival strategies are more often rewarded than are provocative teaching strategies.

Once we acknowledge a new set of assumptions regarding the innate capacities of students, we find a new role for the teacher emerging. From being a dispenser of information and knowledge, the teacher becomes a gardener whose responsibility is to nurture growing children so that the innate potential of each organism is allowed to blossom and bear fruit. Another provocative metaphor with which to describe the teacher's function is that of the whetstone. Just as a whetstone does not cut, but rather sharpens steel, so the teacher does not teach, but sharpens and hones the natural "edge" of the brain.

One currently popular response to the perceived need for improving teaching is "mentorship." In such programs, new teachers are placed under the supervision of more experienced teachers. While this idea has merit, I have found that one of the most productive ways to improve teaching is to provide time for teachers to think, plan, share ideas, and write with their grade level or subject area colleagues. Unfortunately, teaching is perceived as such an independent, isolated function, that few teachers expect, nor do schools provide them with, time to work cooperatively with colleagues. One of the comments that I hear most often from teachers following a Contextual Thinking workshop is how much they appreciated the opportunity to spend a weekend thinking, talking, and writing curriculum units with colleagues. Unfortunately, after the workshop they return to a system which allows no time for such professional development.

**Summary.** I am convinced that teachers represent the greatest untapped resource in education today. For one thing, they have a vision that relates specifically to the teaching/learning process. Second, most of them are proficient in the pedagogical skills of classroom management and know their subject matter. In addition, they know and care for their students and recognize, better than most, what their true needs are. As one high school teacher said on the first day of a workshop, "I am so frustrated because I see so much potential sitting out in front of me going to waste. I don't know what to do about it." Like her, they are eager to be given the primary responsibility to do the job that is required. Once they are treated as professionals, they will be willing to be accountable as professionals.

However, they, too, are victims of an educational mindset that goes against what many of them intuitively know. They feel powerless when, in fact, they have far more power than they know. One of the interesting results of Contextual Thinking workshops is the empowerment of teachers that takes place. By the end of the workshop, participants freely acknowledge that they have everything that is necessary to accomplish approximately 90 percent of what they always wanted to accomplish without additional permission, money, or time.

What has happened to empower them? First, they have been exposed to a set of assumptions about themselves and students which reinforce their own intuitive sense of what they are about. Second, their professional competence has been enhanced as they redesign their curriculum so that it is relevant to the needs of their students and the realities of our global information society. The one thing that they desperately need on a continuing basis, is a support network that provides them with ideas and the encouragement to try these ideas. This leads us to the next arena, the administration.

## Administration

At its most basic level, the shift in paradigm vis-à-vis the administration of our educational system is a shift from top-down management to bottom-up management. In a bottom-up school district, the major responsibility and accountability for decisions related to teaching and learning are in the hands of the classroom teacher.

**The old paradigm.** School administration, with few exceptions, is organized in a traditional, bureaucratic, hierarchical structure. The power is at the top. The school board and superintendent exert control and make most of the decisions concerning organizational structure, personnel, budget, curriculum, and classroom management. This model worked well when the stated purpose of education was to provide public education for the masses in a time when social change was relatively slow. It is questionable whether such a system is viable in a complex society where change and diversity are accentuated.

Yet, little has changed in the way our educational system is structured. Still very much a top-down organization, it is operated according to the traditional factory model. In spite of the current research related to organizational theory, and the impact of new management strategies in the private sector, that knowledge and experience has had little influence on how schools are organized and conducted. Although many superintendents are both conversant with and nominally supportive of this new approach to management, few seem ready to explore the implications of these theories for their own organizations.

**The new paradigm.** Stan Davis of Boston University calls for a new paradigm of management when he states that: "Just as farms were not appropriate models for factories, the factory organizational model is not an appropriate model for information age organizations."[21]

Schools, along with many other organizations, are in desperate need of new management models. Perhaps more than other organizations, schools should be dedicated to fulfill the organizational purpose set forth in an unpublished speech by Peter Drucker at the National College of Education. When we substitute the word "school" for "organization," we have one of the most challenging definitions of a school that I have ever seen.

> The (school) is a human, a social, indeed, a moral phenomenon . . . . The only meaningful purpose of (a school) as a social and human institution is to make the strengths of individuals productive and their weaknesses irrelevant.

One organizational model, designed for the express purpose described by Drucker, is particularly appropriate for schools. It is a systems model based on general systems theory. Described in detail in *How To Do More With Less: The Art of Systems Management*,[22] this model focuses on the two most controversial aspects of management: responsibility and accountability. The model is based on a philosophy and strategy which William Ophuls calls "macro-constraints and micro-freedoms."[23]

The essence of this model is that, beginning at the top, the school board establishes the macro-constraints within which the superintendent must function. These constraints are primarily four in number: goals, outcomes, time frames, and money. This means that the superintendent is expected to work towards goals established by the school board and achieve the requisite outcomes within a given time frame and with the designated resources. Within these parameters, he is given the responsibility and freedom to function as a professional. In this model, the school board does not become involved in the decisions which are the responsibility of the superintendent. His accountability is based on his ability to provide the leadership required for everyone to function optimally within this framework.

At the next level, the superintendent establishes the macro-constraints within which each principal functions: again, goals, outcomes, time, and resources. Within these constraints, each principal assumes responsibility for educational leadership, management style, and organizational structure within his or her school. Accountability is based on the principal's ability to create a productive learning environment. At this level, each principal identifies the macro-constraints within which classroom teachers will be held accountable. Within the broad constraints of district-wide goals, desired learning outcomes, time frames, and resources, teachers are allowed, and indeed encouraged, to decide on teaching methods, textbooks, curriculum structure, and classroom management. Their accountability is based on their ability to function effectively as professionals within the identified constraints.

When carried to its logical conclusion, this strategy is applied by the teacher in the classroom. The teacher identifies the macro-constraints within which students can freely explore their own potential for thinking and learning. Students know the goals, expected outcomes and other constraints that may be appropriate at this level, such as classroom discipline. Within these constraints, students, in order to freely explore their individual potential for thinking and learning, are expected to assume primary responsibility for their own learning.

This is a bottom-up model. Responsibility and accountability are perceived as interdependent and are built into the system. Individuals at each level are given appropriate responsibility and challenged to creatively approach their tasks in a manner and style best suited to their interests, knowledge, skills, and goals. Accountability at each level is based on the degree to which this responsibility is exercised. When applied in the classroom, this model places the primary responsibility for learning where it belongs—on the student. In such a classroom, each student is encouraged to develop the skills required to become a responsible, life-long learner.

**Summary.** It is questionable whether or not significant educational reform can take place without the system as a whole changing. The chances of this occurring seem, at first glance, slim. As one observer commented, "Schools are among society's most entrenched and obdurate organizations when it comes to institutional change—rivaled only, perhaps, by correctional facilities."[24]

On the other hand, the most hopeful feature of public education in America is its decentralized nature. Individual superintendents who recognize that a major paradigm shift is in the making in education as elsewhere, have the opportunity and freedom to work independently for change in their schools. One difficulty which they face is that there are few organizational and management models which reflect the assumptions of the new paradigm. Since the reward system reinforces traditional rather than risk-taking behavior, the tendency is for superintendents and teachers alike to take whatever new ideas come along and force them into the old structures. We forget that new wine requires new wineskins.

While many administrators and teachers disagree with the current sentiment at the federal level for voucher plans, I think that the competition of the marketplace *in some form* may be the salvation of public schools. For example, competition within a school district could be encouraged within the macro-constraints of the systems model described above. The principal and teachers in each school would be encouraged to design creative educational programs which reflect their unique knowledge, skills, and teaching styles. Such a plan would provide parents and students with a variety of options. The principal and teachers of each school would be responsible for implementing their program and held accountable for its success. Fundamental to that success must be a curriculum that is integrated, interesting, provocative, and relevant—in short, a curriculum that addresses both the opportunities and dangers of the global crises that are inherent in the "real" world described by physicist Fritjof Capra.

> Today, we live in a globally interconnected world in which biological, psychological, social and environmental systems are all interdependent. To understand this world appropriately, we need an integrated perspective which Cartesian thinking simply does not offer.[25]

## Curriculum

The paradigm shift vis-à-vis the curriculum is a shift from the fragmentation to the integration of thinking, teaching, and learning. The present status of the curriculum can be best summarized by an analogy.

Getting an education is like putting together an ever-expanding jigsaw puzzle. Students spend years memorizing the shapes, color, and sizes of as many pieces as possible. They learn to collect and sort the pieces into appropriate piles, each of which has a label—math, science, history, art. Occasionally they may fit a few pieces together. However, because they seldom receive more than a few hints as to what the puzzle is all about, they have no frame of reference for understanding how the individual pieces fit together. Without some context to aid their understanding, the pieces which they have collected are essentially meaningless and, therefore, useless.

This fragmentation of learning is the direct result of the analytical, reductionist perspective of the old paradigm. What is ignored by this perspective is that *it is the picture of the puzzle that helps one make sense of the pieces.* Apart from the context provided by the picture, there is nothing intrinsically valuable about any single piece of a jigsaw puzzle. I refer to this as the "peephole approach" to education.

Every child knows that the first step in putting together a jigsaw puzzle is to look at the picture *because it is the picture that tells you what to look for and how the pieces fit together.* The picture tells you whether the red piece is a part of a firetruck, a flower, a barn, or something entirely different. It is this integrated, holistic, systemic, contextual perspective of the new paradigm that I call the "picture window" approach to education. It is this perspective which is crucial for achieving the educational mission set forth by the Carnegie Foundation for the Advancement of Teaching:[26] *The goal of common learning is to understand the connectedness of things.*

When referring to the curriculum, we are discussing two basic issues. One is the way the content is organized or structured, and the other is the nature of the content itself. What we shall see is that these two factors, structure and content, are inextricably linked together and reflect some fundamental assumptions about the relationship between information or data, and knowledge. Since together these shape the methodology of teaching and learning, it is crucial that we explore the implications of both the old and new assumptions upon the structure and content of the curriculum.

**Curriculum structure.** To discuss the way curriculum content is organized and structured is to talk about the relationship between information (the pieces of the puzzle) and knowledge (the picture). Traditionally in Western thought, the primary starting point for structuring knowledge has been to begin with the smallest self-evident parts (information) and proceed from these parts to incrementally construct the whole (knowledge). This inductive approach is based on the Cartesian assumption that the whole is equal to the sum of its parts and thus can be predicted and extrapolated from the parts. Based on this assumption, it is logical to conclude that the parts have intrinsic value *in and of themselves,* and that the primary purpose of education is to provide students with as many pieces of the jigsaw puzzle as possible. As a consequence, we teach facts as the building blocks of knowledge.

Almost without exception, our curriculum is organized inductively. For example, every biology textbook begins with a study of the cell and concludes with a study of the ecosystem. As every student who has taken an introductory biology course knows, what you try and remember are facts, i.e., the parts of a cell, the parts of a frog, the parts of a flower. Because these facts are perceived as the foundation upon which any later learning will be based, it is assumed that both the science major and the liberal arts student, who is only surveying the sciences, must accumulate the same building blocks as a starting point for understanding biology.

This fragmented perspective has shaped our entire educational system. It is reflected in the division of knowledge into academic disciplines, each of which continues to be divided into increasingly discrete units. These units are divided into discrete classes where discrete facts are presented to be recorded and memorized for recall in cumulative fashion. As a result, when a high school history teacher makes reference to something from science, the typical response is, "What has that got to do with history?"

Because it is explicitly taught in our schools, this fragmented perspective forms the conceptual framework for most adult thinking. For example, in a recent workshop, a group of middle managers of a multinational corporation acknowledged that one of the most difficult problems they faced in their own corporation was the fragmented mindset that compartmentalized jobs and responsibilities so that no one—except *perhaps* the Chief Executive Officer—saw the entire picture. Because the way we think shapes the way we respond to the demands of our daily lives, we can only conclude that we are educating people to think in fragmented ways and, thus, to live fragmented lives in an increasingly fragmented world. This fragmented thinking may be the most devastating legacy of the Cartesian perspective.

## A holistic curriculum

There is a second starting point from which knowledge can be structured. The deductive approach is based on the assumption that "in order to understand anything we must have a sense of the fundamental connections which form the backdrop of all existence."[27] It begins with the whole which provides a context within which the parts, as they are learned, can be understood in relationship to each other and to the whole. From this perspective, it is clear that the whole is greater than the sum of its parts so that, without an understanding of the whole as a context to endow them with meaning, the parts are essentially worthless. As Professor I. K. Taimni puts it:

> A mass of unrelated and unconnected facts is a mere rubbish heap. Discover the underlying principle which connects those facts and it becomes valuable material which can be utilized in innumerable ways.[28]

This deductive strategy for organizing information follows what appears to be the natural mode of thinking and learning, which always *starts with the context as a frame of reference within which the parts can be taught, understood, or deduced.* Described earlier, this process seems to involve a movement from right hemisphere (context), to left hemisphere (content, i.e., details), to the forebrain (conclusion, i.e., evaluation and decision making). Thus, in the new paradigm, emphasis is given to context as a frame of reference for understanding content. Alvin Toffler recognized that this was one of the major characteristics of the new paradigm. He wrote: "We are moving from a culture that studies things in isolation from one another to a . . . culture that emphasizes contexts, relationships and wholes."[29]

What should be clear is that the way knowledge is structured determines the nature of the content of what is studied. Hilda Taba provides us with a taxonomy of knowledge that helps us understand the relationship between structure and content.[30] She identifies four levels of knowledge:

THOUGHT SYSTEMS
CONCEPTS
BASIC IDEAS
FACTS

When this taxonomy is viewed inductively, facts, as the building blocks of knowledge, are the starting point of learning. When viewed deductively, the starting point is the thought system, i.e., the "big picture." From this big picture, concepts, basic ideas, and facts which are relevant to the topic at hand can be deduced. If we compare the structure of knowledge with the structure of a house and think about building knowledge like we build a house, this difference in perspectives becomes clear.

THOUGHT SYSTEMS = BLUEPRINTS
CONCEPTS = FRAMING: JOISTS AND STUDS
BASIC IDEAS = WALLS AND ROOM DIVIDERS
FACTS = FURNITURE

The blueprint provides the big picture, the overview that shows how all of the parts fit together. The blueprint literally provides more knowledge with less information. One does not build a house without a blueprint. But, once one has seen the blueprint, one can deduce where the joists and studs belong. And, once the framing has taken shape, the walls and room dividers become evident. *Only then* does one select the furniture.

This analogy suggests that even inductive thinking assumes a blueprint or plan. One does not take a pile of bricks and, willy-nilly, begin to build. There is always at least a mental image or plan of what one wishes to build. In reality, the present emphasis on facts as the building blocks of knowledge, without some context to provide meaning is, at best, a spurious representation of genuine inductive thinking.

**Curriculum content.** In a world where the amount of available information is estimated to double every five years, one of the most significant and controversial questions facing educators is the question: "What should all students learn?" If the response to this question is based on the Cartesian paradigm, they are caught in an almost intolerable double-bind. Forced to choose from the virtually infinite amount of facts and information, educators invariably select math and science and eliminate music, art, and environmental education, *not because the latter are perceived as being unimportant, but because schools can't teach everything.* As long as curriculum content decisions are based on the old assumptions which highlight the importance of facts, educators will be forced to make either/or choices among a smorgasbord of subjects, each of which is rightly considered by someone to be of primary importance.

When the question of what all students need to know is addressed from the perspective of the new paradigm and its assumptions, one reaches a different conclusion. Students need to know the "big picture" as the context within which relevant facts can be selected, organized, and used for understanding, problem solving, and decision making. It is this knowledge which enables one to turn facts into valuable knowledge which can be utilized in innumerable ways.

Taba's taxonomy provides us with an answer to our question. Students need to know the underlying principles and concepts that make up the structure of thought systems and help us make sense out of the world. Because a concept is often worth a thousand facts, through an understanding of these fundamental concepts and principles students can literally "know more with less" information.

This is not new. Twenty-five years ago Jerome Bruner identified the need for teaching the structure of knowledge and insisted that students could be taught the structure of a subject, i.e., its fundamental concepts, in some form, at any age. His proposal of a spiral curriculum was based on such a structure.[31] Research has made it clear that when concepts are taught first, *as a structure for learning,* retention of detail is 80 percent higher than when facts are presented in the more traditional way.[32] On the other hand, when concepts are taught as additional facts to be memorized for recall rather than perceived as cognitive structures for understanding "the connectedness of things," their usefulness is severely limited.

In Contextual Thinking workshops, teachers are provided with models and strategies for identifying and teaching structure as the context within which relevant facts can be learned. One high school social studies teacher designed a curriculum unit on the Great Depression that was organized around four interdependent concepts that are fundamental to social studies as a discipline: political, social, economic, and ecological. After identifying additional subconcepts that were relevant to each of these four major concepts, he found that he had designed a basic structure based on 25 concepts which could be used to study any period in any society or culture. Once the students understood these basic concepts, they had the framework and tools with which to select, organize and analyze, compare, contrast, or synthesize the facts which were relevant to the particular social studies topic or issue that was being studied. One might presume that when students who were taught like this are ready to vote, they will be better prepared to make mature decisions because they recognize and understand the interdependent nature of all political, social, economic, and ecological systems. In short, they "understand the connectedness of things."

**Summary.** One thing can be said about the curriculum without danger of contradiction. If it is not inherently interesting, substantive, provocative, and relevant, effective learning will not occur. No amount of money, training, classroom management skills, organizational strategies, teaching methodologies, or external reinforcements can lead to effective learning without a curriculum that stimulates the interest and captures the imagination of the students, and, not so incidentally, of the teachers. Many studies verify the fact that most students and many, if not most, teachers are bored, frustrated, and often angry about having to "put in time" when nothing of significance takes place. On the other hand, when students and teachers are both genuinely interested in the subject matter, external factors take on secondary significance.

The key to designing a curriculum that meets this criterion is integration and context. Inherently, a curriculum that focuses on the learning of facts without a context to give them meaning, is neither interesting, substantive, provocative, nor relevant. Most curricula are based on textbooks which, because they reflect the assumptions of the Cartesian paradigm, focus on facts. The irony is that while there seem to be few educators who really like the available textbooks, they complain but do nothing to change it.

I believe that what is needed more than anything else is a curriculum that will stimulate the imagination of both students and teachers, and challenge them to think deeply and become profoundly involved in some of the significant issues in life. This is why we encourage teachers to design curriculum around "questions worth arguing about." Using Contextual Thinking models and strategies, one private school redesigned its entire K-8 curriculum around the "question worth arguing about": *What does it mean to grow up in a global information society?*[33] The curriculum for various age and grade levels was designed around such questions as *How am I a member of many families?* (K-1); *What are the patterns that make communities work?* (2,3); *How do humans and cultures evolve and change?* (4,5); and *How does one live responsibly as a member of the global village?* (6-8). Each of these questions was explored from various perspectives—the humanities, the natural sciences, the social sciences, and, because it was a private school, the religious. Vertical articulation was based on ten fundamental concepts which spiraled through the entire curriculum.

## Conclusion

The traditional purpose of education in any culture has been to transmit to each succeeding generation the stored knowledge of that culture. In our nation of immigrants, the goal of mass public education was to build a common storehouse of meaning based on shared knowledge. Given this context, the assumptions that shaped our educational system were appropriate to its mission. Needless to say, that mission was highly successful.

But, almost without our knowing it, the primary mission of education has changed. Today, there is common agreement that the mission of education is to provide students with the knowledge and skills required for "learning how to learn." What has not been recognized is that this new mission requires both a new content and a new process for education. And because content and process are so interdependently woven together, they cannot be addressed in the former, fragmented, piecemeal fashion. In short, what is needed is a new curriculum and a new teaching/learning/managing methodology based on a new set of assumptions about human potential. Instead, what we have done in the name of educational reform has been to take a few exciting new programs based on a new set of assumptions and force them into the old mold. The result is that the new programs are either watered down or soon dropped because they don't work. It's the reform movement of the 1960s all over again. We keep trying to pour our new wine into old wineskins.

The first step in addressing the new mission is to acknowledge the emergence of a new paradigm for education. Contrary to much that has been written about the inadequate preparation of teachers, my experience with thousands of teachers suggests that most of them are open to new ideas and ready for substantive change. For the most part, they have the training, experience, qualifications, and desire to design and teach a curriculum that will address the new mission of education. They require two things. The first is administrative leadership and support structures that not only recognize the need for change, but encourage the teachers to assume both responsibility and accountability for what happens in the classroom.

Second, they require integrated, holistic, contextual models and strategies with which to turn their present curriculum into one that is integrated, interesting, substantive, provocative, and relevant to the real world described above. As a teacher at one of our state's most prestigious high schools said to me, "Everyone out here is talking about curriculum integration but no one knows how to do it."

A simple strategy for change involves four steps: 1) Strong initiative by the superintendent and a willingness to provide the management and support structures that are required; 2) The recognition that the key to quality teaching and learning is the teacher, and that ownership is the best motivator for professional development; 3) Providing the training required for teachers to design a curriculum that is integrated, interesting, substantive, provocative, and relevant; and 4) Keeping the focus at the individual building level.[34] The cost is low and the potential impact is great.

A major paradigm shift is taking place. The chances are that by the year 2000 we will have a vastly different system for educating our children. If this is to occur, however, we must explore both the old and the new assumptions relating to every facet of the educational process. Only then can we determine those which are most appropriate to the needs of young people who will spend most of their lives in the twenty-first century.

### Notes

1.  Howard Gardner, *Frames of Mind* (New York: Basic Books, 1984).

2.  Benjamin Bloom, "The Search for Methods of Group Instruction As Effective As One-To-One Tutoring," *Educational Leadership*, May 1984.

3.  Richard Rosenthal and Lenore Jacobson, *Pygmalion in the Classroom: Expectations and Pupils' Intellectual Development* (Irvington, 1986).

4. Leslie A. Hart, *Human Brain and Human Learning* (New York: Longman, 1983).

5. David Loye, *The Sphinx and the Rainbow* (Boulder: Shambhala, 1983).

6. Hart, *Human Brain*.

7. David Perkins, "Creativity By Design," *Educational Leadership*, September, 1984.

8. Niles Howard, Untitled article. *Leading Edge Bulletin*, 28 September 1981.

9. Robert F. Mager, *Preparing Instructional Objectives* (Palo Alto: Fearson, 1962).

10. Carl Rogers, "The Facilitation of Significant Learning," In *Instruction: Some Contemporary Viewpoints*, Laurence Siegel, ed. (New York: Chandler, 1967)

11. Anthony Gregorc, *Style Delineator* (Maynard, MA: Gabriel Systems, 1982).

12. Edward T. Clark, Jr., "Making a Difference." Unpublished manuscript, 1985.

13. Mary Jane Even, "The Functions of Brain Lateralization in the Process of Adult Learning." Paper presented at the National Conference on Research in Adult and Continuing Education, 1981.

14. Richard Neustadt and Ernest May, *Thinking in Time: The Uses of History for Decision Makers* (New York: Free Press, 1986).

15. Katharine Kersey, *Sensitive Parenting* (Washington: Acropolis, 1983).

16. John Goodlad, *A Place Called School* (New York: McGraw-Hill, 1984).

17. Rogers, "Facilitation."

18. Patricia Dombert, "The Vision of an Insider: A Practitioner's View," *Educational Leadership*, November 1985.

19. *Educational Leadership*, November 1985.

20. Kenneth E. John, "Dream Jobs," *The Washington Post Weekly Edition*, 30 June 1986.

21. Stanley M. Davis, "The Case of the Missing Management Model," *The Review*, January/February 1982.

22. Edward T. Clark, Jr., "How To Do More With Less: The Art of Systems Management." Unpublished manuscript, 1982.

23. William Ophuls, *Ecology and Politics of Scarcity* (San Francisco: Freeman, 1977).

24. Kenneth A. Sirotnik, "Let's Examine The Profession, Not The Teachers," *Educational Leadership*, November 1985.

25. Fritjof Capra, *The Turning Point* (New York, Bantam, 1982).

26. Ernest Boyer and Arthur Levine, *A Quest For Common Learning* (Washington: Carnegie Foundation for the Advancement of Teaching, n.d.).

27. Jonas Salk, *Anatomy of Reality* (New York: Columbia University Press, 1983).

28. I.K. Taimni, *Man, God and the Universe* (Wheaton: Theosophical Publishing House, 1969).

29. Alvin Toffler, *The Third Wave* (New York: Morrow, 1980).

30. Hilda Taba, *Curriculum Development: Theory and Practice* (New York: Harcourt, Brace and World, 1982).

31. Jerome Bruner, *The Process of Education* (New York: Vintage, 1960).

32. Laine I. Gurley, "Use of Gowin's Vee and Concept Mapping Strategy To Teach Responsibility for Learning in High School Biological Sciences." Ph.D. Thesis, Cornell University, 1982.

33. "What Does It Mean To Grow Up In A Global Information Society?" Statement of Curriculum, Beaver Dam, WI, Unified Catholic Parish School, 1987.

34. Edward T. Clark, Jr., "Making A Difference."

# Environmental Education as an Integrative Study

## by Edward T. Clark, Jr.

After almost fifteen years of obscurity, environmental education seems to be on the verge of a comeback. This should come as no surprise to those who follow social trends. In *Cycles of American History*, Arthur M. Schlesinger, Jr., identifies a cyclical rhythm in our national life that oscillates between "public purpose" and "private interest."[1] If this rhythm continues, the 1990s will see public purpose move to the forefront of American political life once again. When Schlesinger wrote in 1986, the values and goals of "privatization" seemed to dominate every aspect of our social, economic, political, and environmental decisions, and there was little evidence of a return to public interest in the near future. But, as he points out, true cycles are self-generating, driven by their own internal rhythms. Each phase flows naturally from the conditions of the previous phase and, in turn, creates the conditions that call forth the next recurrence. One evidence of this ebb and flow is the recent, rather sudden recognition of the increasing threat to our planetary life support systems that has resulted from the free reign of private interest during the past decade. In the minds of many, environmental degradation has reached a crisis point, so that Schlesinger's prediction of a return to public interest seems appropriate.

It is significant that Schlesinger prefers the concept of "spiral" to that of "cycle," because there does seem to be an evolutionary direction involved in the process. The spiral nature of these cultural rhythms suggests that the attention to be paid to environmental concerns in the next decade may be both more dramatic and more enduring than previous efforts. The increasingly serious nature of the global environmental crisis reinforces this possibility. The warning signals are everywhere: overpopulation; resource depletion; air, water, and solid and toxic waste pollution; drought; desertification; famine; and the greenhouse effect. For the first time in a decade, environmental issues have begun to move higher on the political agenda of every industrialized nation. This shift in

This selection originally appeared in the Fall 1989 issue of *Holistic Education Review*, Vol. 2, No. 3.

significance was graphically reinforced when *Time* magazine depicted "Endangered Earth" smothered with plastic and bound with chains as "The Planet of the Year."[2] With this increased awareness, there is a slow but growing recognition that we can no longer take what is euphemistically called "the environment" for granted.

For some at least, this growing awareness includes the recognition that education must play a major role in reshaping our thinking and attitudes toward the world in which we live—a process that Robert Ornstein and Paul Ehrlich call "reprogramming."[3] I suggest that the primary vehicle for this kind of reprogramming will be environmental education. However, if environmental education is to meet the challenge of reshaping the thinking and attitudes of the next generation of adults, it must have a different focus and a different form than most environmental education programs that have survived the educational reform movement of the past five years. For the most part, existing programs have become the victim of three fundamental misconceptions, each of which stands as a major barrier against any effective resurgence of environmental education.

The first misconception is that environmental education is a separate subject that must be added to an already overcrowded curriculum. Because there is no room in the curriculum for a new subject, what passes for environmental education is usually tacked on to an introductory science course where it is presented as a unit on ecology, usually at the tail end of freshman biology. The placement of environmental education as an appendage to science reflects the second misconception, namely, that environmental education is the same thing as science education. Both of these misconceptions reflect a third, perhaps even more fundamental misconception that the environment is something "out there," and is just another word for "nature." This misconception is reflected in the commonly accepted assumption that environmental education and outdoor education are synonymous.

Individually or collectively, these three misconceptions shape the dominant mind-set of the great majority of educators as well as the public in general. Thus, the first step in considering what environmental education "should be" is to change that mind-set. A new mind-set requires a new and different conceptual framework—one more appropriate both to the nature of the environmental problems we face and to what we now know about the nature of thinking and learning. The purpose of this article is to suggest such a conceptual framework.

## A brief history of environmental education

Before World War II, most children received their "environmental education" as a part of growing up. Because the majority were raised either on farms or in small towns, there was a high level of awareness of and sensitivity to the natural cycles that governed much of their lives. The farmer was a confirmed "weather watcher" who needed no computerized "forecast" to tell him what was happening outside. Children learned firsthand about plants and animals, life, birth and death, often developing a deep, intuitive appreciation for the rhythms of the natural world. Few believed that milk came from a bottle or eggs from a box. It was only with the movement to cities during and following the war that the majority of children grew up without this experiential knowledge. As a result, when the intensive economic and industrial growth of the 1950s and 1960s left us with substantial problems related to pollution—smog in Los Angeles, a "dead" Lake Erie, an abandoned "Love Canal"—environmental programs seemed to be the logical educational response. The early 1970s became the heyday of environmental education.

The initial emergent programs had a solid conceptual base. Sidney Marland, then U.S. Commissioner of Education, provided a unifying focus for what was considered by many to be a major new field of study. Marland suggested that environmental education could become the key to true interdisciplinary education, because it started with humanity and moved into every area of life. With this single insight, Marland challenged each of the above misconceptions. The environment is not "out there" but is everywhere. Environmental education is not solely or even primarily science education, nor is it a separate subject to be studied in isolation from other subjects. The U.S. Office of Environmental Education added a crucial element to this integrative perspective when it defined environmental education as "educational processes dealing with man's relationship with his natural and man-made surroundings." This definition went on to identify with some specificity the relevance of these relationships to each of the various subjects taught in school.

Unfortunately, education was not ready for these integrative themes. Most administrators and teachers were still struggling with the aftermath of well-conceived but often poorly understood and thus inadequately executed innovative programs of the 1960s. When environmental education became a mandated program, as it did in many states, educators responded as they usually do to such mandates—pragmatically. They fit this new program in wherever they could and continued business as usual. When the inevitable cutbacks came, environmental education was often the first victim. Today, most remaining programs exist only because of a single teacher or an occasional principal whose interest and commitment kept environmental education alive—almost as an underground movement. In the process, the misconceptions that shaped these first environmental programs continued to dominate the thinking of most educators.

Although the integrative themes that dominated the environmental philosophy of the 1970s had a limited impact on the actual emergent programs, their power and relevance are undiminished, and they remain as appropriate to today's need as they were to the need of their time. Indeed, they stand as a benchmark for what environmental education must become if it is to meet the challenge presented by today's substantively more serious environmental threats. To summarize these themes: environmental education is about the *fundamental relationships* that exist between humans and the world in which we live. To use the words of Noel McInnis, environment is "nature, culture, technology, people, ideas and feelings."[4] In short, environmental education is about "everywhere" and "everything." As such, its concerns are relevant to and must become an integral part of every academic subject taught from kindergarten through graduate school. What is required is a conceptual framework that reflects the integrative nature of environmental education and provides teachers and students alike with a new way of understanding the world.

## A new look at environmental education

Unfortunately, the universal relevance of environmental education is difficult for most educators to understand, primarily because of the fragmented conceptual framework that dominates education as a whole. Perhaps the best way to explain this is through analogy. Let us think of education as learning to put together a jigsaw puzzle. The pieces represent all of the data, information, and knowledge that we have about the world. Each subject studied in school focuses its attention on a specific collection of pieces. To pursue our analogy, let's say that the natural sciences study the green pieces, the social sciences study the blue pieces, the humanities study the orange pieces, and math studies the red pieces. When we subdivide the pieces by shades of color, each shade of green could be said to represent a different science—biology, geology, physics, chemistry. Because the nature of the scientific method is reductionist, its primary focus is on the individual piece of the puzzle in isolation from the rest of the parts. Pursuing the analogy, the primary goal of education becomes one of providing students with as many pieces of the puzzle, that is, as much information, as they can possibly retain. The unstated assumption is that, given enough information, students will understand how the pieces of the puzzle fit together and thus will be able to determine what the picture looks like.

The trouble with this view of education is that the underlying assumption is false. It does not reflect what we now know about the way thinking and learning take place; namely, thinking and learning are contextual in nature. As research has made clear, all thinking and learning begins with the context as a frame of reference for providing meaning. In short, without the picture, the pieces of a puzzle are meaningless. This is why no one tries to put together a jigsaw puzzle without first looking at the picture. Even young children know that. I once tried to play a joke on my four-year-old granddaughter. I gave her a plain paper bag full of jigsaw puzzle pieces. She dumped them on the floor and after a moment of puzzled silence, she turned and asked, "Granddaddy, where's the picture?" I am suggesting that *because its perspective is comprehensive and global, environmental education can provide education with the "big picture," which enables us to make sense out of our jigsaw puzzle world.* Because it focuses on the relationships that exist between nature, culture, technology, people, ideas, and feelings, environmental education can become the integrative component that enables us to understand how the data and information *we already have* can be fit together to make a healthy, safe, and productive environment. In short, environmental education can provide an integrative, global frame of reference as a context to help us better understand all of the other subjects taught in school.

## The goals of environmental education

The bottom line outcome for any effective environmental education program is to change behavior. The first step in achieving this goal is to change the way a person thinks about something—what I call their mind-set. The way we think influences the way we act.[5] To change the way we live in the environment, we must first change the way we think about the environment. Thus, a primary focus of any environmental education program must be to *change the way people think about their relationship to the world in which we live.* As John Helfrich writes, we must "change enough people's perception of the world (if we are) to save it."[6] Unfortunately, one of the great illusions of the so-called information age is that the way to change people's thinking is to give them more information. The truth is that information, per se, seldom changes thinking. Indeed, the process is just the opposite. The way we think determines what information we take in and how we interpret and use that information. For example, the naturalist sees the last stand of virgin timber as a resource to be protected, while the lumberman sees the same trees in terms of profit to be gained. No amount of information is going to change either of these perceptions, precisely because it is the mind-set that shapes perception and behavior. In order to change the mind-set of a generation raised with little personal experiences of the "environment," we need a new way of conceptualizing or thinking about the world and our relationship to it. Fundamental to this new way of thinking is what the Carnegie Foundation for the Advancement of Teaching refers to as "understanding the connectedness of things."

The most effective method I have found to change people's mind-sets is to expand the context within which they perceive something. In this case, the expanded context is global in nature and is symbolized by the photograph of Earth from space. This powerful visual image has encouraged some scientists to consider Earth as the largest single living organism we know. Whether one accepts this concept as a literal or merely a metaphorical description of our planet, it seems clear that this image contains powerful new insights that will in time have a tremendous impact on the way we think about ourselves and our relationship with the planet. In 1948, astrophysicist Fred Hoyle wrote these prophetic words: "Once a photograph of the Earth, taken from the *outside,* is available . . . a new idea as powerful as any in history will be let loose."[7] This idea must form the core of environmental education as it evolves in the next decade.

One facet of this powerful new idea is the recognition that the planetary ecological system is essentially a *single, integrated life support system.* We are as tied to and dependent upon the life support system as the scuba diver is tied to and dependent upon the life support system she carries on her back. This analogy represents a major reconceptualization of what is meant by "the environment" and the problems related to maintaining that environment. It is as though we are all scuba divers—totally dependent upon a fragile supply of oxygen for survival. To inject pollutants into the air we breath is precisely the same as injecting pollutants into a scuba diver's oxygen tanks. Once we understand the full implications of this analogy, we will be able to develop an environmental education program that shapes not only the way we *think* about the environment, but also the way we live in the environment.

Another facet of this new idea, which is implicit if not explicit in the image of Earth from space, is the recognition that all of our natural and cultural systems are interconnected and interdependent. Given this insight, it seems obvious to conclude that all of our cultural systems are subsystems of a single planetary ecological system *in exactly the same way that the heart and lungs are subsystems of the human body.* In short, all cultural systems are themselves ecological systems! Every academic discipline and professional field of work is, at some fundamental level, ecological in character. Sociology is the ecology of social groups. Political science is the ecology of collective decision making. Economics is the ecology of finance and exchange. Business management is concerned with the ecology of organizations. Physics, chemistry, and geology are studies of the ecology of physical matter, while mathematics is the ecology of numbers and their relationship to physical matter. Reading and writing are fundamental expressions of the ecology of language and communication, while art, music, drama, and dance reflect other forms of the ecology of communication. This insight provides the rationale by which environmental education can become the integrative component in the entire curriculum. Precisely because it focuses on the relationships that exist among all physical and cultural systems that make up the single planetary ecological system, we can say unequivocally, *all good education is environmental.*

Implicit in the above discussion is the recognition of what general systems theory refers to as the isomorphic nature of all ecological systems—both natural and cultural. This means that, regardless of their many differences, all natural and cultural systems share certain fundamental organizational characteristics. Just as the organizing principles that govern the health of the human body as a whole apply equally to each individual organ (subsystem) of the body, the fundamental principles of a healthy planetary ecological system are equally relevant to the health of all cultural subsystems. In other words, the same principles that apply to the planetary ecological system can be applied equally to all academic disciplines and fields of professional study. By incorporating these principles into its fundamental structure, environmental education will become the vehicle by which the integrative, relational principles of ecological systems can be applied to all of our cultural systems and the academic disciplines to study these systems.

Once we understand that all physical and cultural systems *and the thought systems by which we know and study them* are ecological in nature, we can begin to build a cognitive structure that will serve as a comprehensive and integrative frame of reference within which a rich diversity of environmental education programs can be designed. The base for such a structure is provided by ecology, which is by definition "a study of the relationships between living things and their environments." Although "ecology" is not synonymous with "environment," ecological principles and concepts provide an appropriate conceptual framework for environmental education. The relationship between ecology and environmental education can be clarified if we look at the etymology of the word *ecology*. Derived from the Greek root word *oikos* meaning "household," ecology is the study of how "Household Earth" works. Environmental education thus becomes a study of the relationships that exist among *everything that is a part of our planetary ecological system, that is, "Household Earth."*

## Operating principles for ecological systems

General systems theory suggests that all ecological systems are structured to function in essentially the same way. Over the past fifteen years, my studies of ecological systems suggest that there are seven distinctive functions intrinsic to all living systems.[8] Each reflects a unique yet necessary functional component of a system. These seven are fundamental because they seem to incorporate all other such functions. On the basis of our understanding of how ecological systems function, each of these functions is characterized by an ecological principle. Because each of these principles reflects a different facet or aspect of the connectedness of things, together they provide us with a conceptual framework appropriate to environmental education as described above. By extrapolation, they are relevant to all subjects taught in school and therefore can provide the basis upon which to organize an entire curriculum. A graphic model of such a curriculum might resemble a seven-strand helix. A brief discussion of each of the seven principles and their functional relevance follows.

1. **Carrying capacity.** Every system must have a resource base to provide the raw materials upon which the system depends for survival. Thus every system is finite and must exist within limits prescribed by its resources. In ecology, these limits are characterized by the concept of carrying capacity. By definition, *carrying capacity* identifies the maximum number of individuals of a given species that can be maintained for an indefinite period of time in a specified area by the resources in that area. As such, carrying capacity defines population limits imposed by available resources. For example, if it takes one acre of an oak forest to provide the resources needed by a single squirrel, then the carrying capacity of a hundred-acre oak forest would be one hundred squirrels. This number will remain relatively stable for an indefinite period of time, unless some outside influence changes this balance of nature. If someone were to cut down some of the trees, then the carrying capacity of the forest would be diminished accordingly. Over the vast period of evolutionary history, plants and animals have adapted to their

resource requirements so that territorial needs are closely correlated to available resources. Over time, this amount of space becomes psychologically necessary for both plants and animals. If further crowding occurs, then the result is disease or starvation.

Every system requires a resource base to determine its carrying capacity. A home has a carrying capacity; so does an office, a schoolroom, a nation, and the planet. When the limits prescribed by that resource base are exceeded, there is trouble. For example, crowding in an office inevitably cuts down on productivity. Crowding in a classroom always has negative consequences on learning. Crowding in our cities produces physical hazards (ranging from joblessness, homelessness, disease, and crime) to more subtle psychological hazards (such as loneliness, stress, depression, anger, frustration, and helplessness).

One of the fundamental realities in American society is that the concept of limits seems to have no place in our lexicon. Collectively, we prefer to believe in an infinite horizon and a limitless frontier. As a result, we operate both politically and economically on the assumption that there are enough resources for everyone in America, if not in the world, to have a standard of living that lacks for nothing.

**2. Interdependence.** Interdependence is the unifying principle operative in all systems. As the "queen" principle of ecology, it defines the nature of the relationships that exist among the individual parts of a system and between those parts and the system as a whole. Because we are programmed to think in polarized, either/or terms, the concept of interdependence is difficult for many people to understand. Substantively, it is a relationship in which the success of the system as a whole depends upon the success of each part, while the success of each part depends upon the success of the system as a whole. In ecology, this relationship is illustrated best by the relationship that exists between an ecological community and the individual niches which make up that community. Each niche represents a functional slot in the ecology of a community. In a food chain, for example, each species represents an often highly specialized function: providing food for a predator species and at the same time acting as predator for the species on which it feeds. If a particular species is wiped out by disease, then the entire ecological community is threatened. Thus, the success of each species depends upon the success of the community as a whole, while the success of the entire community depends upon the success of each individual species.

Interdependence is a universal characteristic recognized as being fundamental to the success of all social, economic, and political systems. As an integrative concept it can be applied with equal appropriateness to a work of art and the study of a galaxy; to writing a sentence and learning a language; to computer science and the engineering of a spaceship; to the sociology of a family or of a multinational corporation. Because of its comprehensive relevance, interdependence can become a powerful unifying strand in the broad tapestry of thinking and learning. Once a child understands this concept, he or she is able, through the transfer of learning, to operationalize the concept in a virtually limitless number of applications.

**3. Diversity.** Diversity is the foundation upon which the stability of any system is dependent. The more diverse any system is, the more stable it becomes. For example, an oak forest with its rich diversity of life is far more stable than a cornfield, which is essentially a monoculture. A natural forest is more stable than a manmade forest of Douglas firs planted by a lumber company. Stability in cultural systems requires similar diversity. The diversity of ethnic and cultural backgrounds is one of the strengths of our nation. In spite of our envy of Japan's success, her major weakness is the lack of ethnic diversity. What appears to be strength may in time prove to be a fundamental, unmitigated weakness. It is ironic that both Japan and Germany, the two aggressor nations in World War II, were both in essence ethnic monocultures— highly susceptible to ideologies based on ethnic superiority. Such ideologies could never be effective in the United States because, if they appealed to one group, at the same time they would be rejected by many other groups. In all human organizations, diversity is necessary to maintain stability. This is especially important in our age of narrow specialization.

**4. Change, adaptation.** Change is a universal principle that reflects the impact of time on all systems. But the concept of change alone is meaningless without some understanding of the way that systemic change takes place. The fundamental principle that describes change in natural and cultural systems is adaptation—a short-term form of evolution. Adaptation is the process by which a system (e.g., a human body, a forest, an organization, an entire society) responds to the vicissitudes of a constantly shifting external environment. Because of their ability to adapt to the incursions of civilization, animal species such as deer and coyotes have been far more successful than larger predators such as mountain lions and bears. Primitive cultures that have been able to adapt to the intrusion of technology on their lives have survived, while the most rigid ones have not. One advantage that small businesses often have over larger ones is their ability to adapt more readily to rapidly changing demands of the market place. The inability to adapt eventually results in extinction—for an animal species, for a business, or for a national government. The ability to adapt successfully to a changing environment results in creativity and diversity, the hallmark of a successful system.

**5. Competition/cooperation.** All systems are characterized by the twin impulses of competition and cooperation. These two powerful drives ideally function in a unique reciprocal relationship much like centrifugal and centripetal forces. When a balance between the two is achieved, the dynamic of adaptive change results in both stability and creativity, each of which is crucial to the success of all living systems.

Competition is one of the most misunderstood of all ecological concepts. It seems to be believed almost universally that unbridled competition is the fundamental driving principle in the natural world. Extrapolating from this interpretation of natural principles, there is a powerful bias in our country toward unrestrained competition in human economies. The irony is that (a) there is no such thing as unrestrained competition in nature, and (b) no one believes in unrestrained economic competition. In natural systems, competition within species is always constrained by cooperative strategies such as territoriality and dominance hierarchy. Competition between species is controlled by factors such as adaptive modifications, which often result in two similar species utilizing entirely different food sources. In cultural systems, the most vocal defenders of unrestrained economic competition are the first to exploit political means to protect themselves from the very competition that they defend. Even the most voracious of the robber barons sought the cooperation of government to protect their rights to exploit their competitors.

In short, competition apart from cooperation is essentially a meaningless concept. Even in so-called competitive sports, successful competition requires some form of cooperative behavior. If one compares the number of cooperative transactions with the number of competitive transactions that take place during a typical professional football game, it is obvious that there is far more cooperation that competition. Indeed, one cannot conceive of a game without rules, whether it be the "game of life" as played in nature, or the economic game as played either in capitalist democracies or in communist dictatorships. Just as socialist countries are beginning to recognize the need for more economic competition, so capitalist countries will be forced to acknowledge the need for more explicit cooperative economic strategies. The ideal is neither unlimited competition nor absolute cooperative agreement, but a dynamic balance between the two. Competition apart from cooperative constraints is not only meaningless but will ultimately lead to annihilation.

The need to reconceptualize our understanding of the function of competition in both natural and cultural systems is crucial if we are to achieve some viable form of global economic cooperation. For too long we have allowed the outdated and poorly understood concept of "survival of the fittest" to dominate our thinking in political and economic arenas. Significant insights to help rethink our understanding of competition are found in *The New Biology* by Robert Augros and George Stanciu.[9]

**6. Cycles.** There are two kinds of cycles in natural and cultural systems. One is the rhythmic fluctuations that occur over time, such as the seasons and life cycles. The other refers to the physical recycling of materials—the flow and exchange of atoms and molecules of matter through physical systems, such as the planetary ecological system and the human body—or money as a symbolic substitute for materials through cultural systems. Cycles in living systems are never static. Rather, as "rhythms of change" they reflect the ongoing adaptive processes of a system. Because of their dynamic nature, their function in living systems can be described best in cybernetic terms as feedback loops. For example, the recent trend toward warmer summers can be interpreted as systemic feedback regarding the overall health of the planetary ecological system. In the same way, the presence of strontium 90 in mothers' milk or DDT in eagles' eggs provided us with feedback concerning the health of the larger system of which we are a part. Just as urinalysis provides feedback concerning health of the human body, the quality of our planetary water supply provides us with feedback concerning the health of our ecological systems. I began this article with a reference to Arthur Schlesinger's provocative book, *Cycles of American History*, in which he points to the lessons learned from a study of various historical cycles. In a similar manner, cycles are relevant to every subject studied in school and every arena in life.

7.   **Energy flow.**   All living systems are open systems and as such are dependent upon an external energy source for survival. Just as our planetary ecology is dependent upon the energy from the sun, all plants and animals are dependent upon an external energy source in the form of food. If we were able to think of food as energy, we would learn to be as careful about the food we take into our bodies as we are about the quality of gasoline we use in our automobiles. Cultural systems depend for their survival upon some form of external energy—in the form of human energy or mechanical energy, and usually a combination of both. Since the first law of thermodynamics tells us that energy can be neither created nor destroyed but only transformed, and the second law tells us that it can be transformed only one way—toward a dissipated state—every energy exchange produces waste or dissipated energy no longer available for work. The measure of this unavailable energy is entropy. The more energy we use, the greater the entropy. Jeremy Rifkin points out that pollution is merely another name for entropy.[10] Once we understand this, it becomes clear that the increasing levels of pollution are the direct result of high levels of energy usage. The greenhouse effect is the result of an accumulation of high levels of wasted energy. For the short term, the principle of energy flow can be summed up in the well-known phrase, "there's no such thing as a free lunch." For the long term, it reflects the ultimate bottom line—"nothing is forever." All ecological systems will, in time, die. While there is nothing we can do to prevent the long-term death of the universe, in the short term, it becomes clear that the immediate consequences of our high levels of energy transformation result in dangerously high levels of pollution. The only way to reduce pollution will be to use less energy and to rely as much as possible on low entropic forms of energy, the so-called natural energy sources such as solar, wind, and water.

## Ecology and economics: A special case

One of the greatest conceptual barriers to effective environmental education in American society is our understanding of the relationship between ecology and economics. Until this relationship is clarified, environmental education will never be truly successful. This is a great irony, because the appropriate relationship between the two should be obvious once we understand the relationship between the two words, ecology and economy. As I have already pointed out, *ecology* is derived from the Greek word for household and is the study of how Household Earth works. *Economics* is derived from the same word and was considered to be the study of how to manage Household Earth. On the basis of this etymological association, it seems almost simple-minded to suggest the obvious: If one wishes to manage the household, one must first understand how the household works. That this is not the case is evident.

Adam Smith, the father of our market-oriented "capitalistic" economic system, understood this relationship well. A close and astute observer of nature, he used "nature's economy" as a model for his economic ideas. Unfortunately his model was contingent upon two false assumptions, neither of which was particularly significant at the time. First was the assumption of an unlimited resource base—certainly a reasonable assumption in the late eighteenth century. The second was an assumption that competition was the sole driving force behind the survival of species and individuals—again an understandable oversimplification of the way natural systems maintained their balance. However, because these two assumptions have for the most part gone unquestioned, today we are trapped in an economic system that ignores the fundamental relationship between ecology and economics implicit in their definitions. Ignoring the constraints imposed by "carrying capacity," our global economic system is dependent upon ever increasing consumption, which in turn is dependent upon ever increasing exploitation of the resources that constitute our planetary life support system.

An illustration of how the relationship between economics and ecology has become distorted is provided by economist and Nobel Laureate Milton Friedman. He discusses this relationship in terms of a cost/benefit analysis by posing the question: How much pollution can the economic system afford? In his words,

> The real problem is not "eliminating pollution," but trying to establish arrangements that will yield the "right" amount of pollution: an amount such that the gain from reducing pollution a bit more just balances the sacrifices of the other good things— houses, shoes, coats, and so on—that would have to be given up in order to reduce the pollution. If we go further than that, we sacrifice more than we gain.[11]

If we return to the analogy of the scuba diver and apply the same cost/benefit analysis to her experience, the more fundamental issue becomes clear: If someone is willing to pay me $1000 to pollute my oxygen tank by ten percent, and $5000 for polluting it twenty percent, or $25,000 for polluting it thirty percent, then I should determine the "right" amount of pollution by first deciding the gains, i.e., how much money I want to get from the transaction. (Note: in considering such a transaction, it is worth remembering that any pollution is soon dispersed throughout the entire tank so that one can't adjust for it merely by cutting the time spent under water by ten or twenty percent.) Given this perspective it seems obvious—even to a novice scuba diver—that the real cost/benefit question is the opposite of Friedman's question.

The operative question is *How much consumption can the ecological system afford?*

If we are to reconceptualize the meaning and purpose of environmental education, it is necessary that we understand the true nature of the relationship between ecology and economics. Although George Bush during his election campaign proclaimed, "There is no conflict between the economy and the environment," the reality is otherwise. It is expressed best in the mathematical principle that one cannot maximize two variables in the same equation. In this case the equation is:

$$\text{Economy} + \text{Ecology} = \text{Healthy Life Support System}$$

As already illustrated, few economists recognize this relationship or have any substantive understanding of how our ecological life support systems work. As a result, primarily due to this conceptual barrier, we continue to destroy our life support system at an alarming rate—all in the name of a growth economy. In short, the environmental problems we have created have not been caused by evil men but by ignorant men. We simply do not understand what we are doing! A first step toward correcting our problems would be for economists to gain an understanding of the seven systemic ecological principles described above.

## Conclusion: Ecological principles in education

Perhaps the most appropriate synonym for "environment" is "context." Just as good education is environmental, it is also contextual. As such, environmental education should provide the integrative context or framework within which any subject can be understood more completely. In this sense, environmental education is about the "big picture," which gives meaning and relevance to the various pieces of our jigsaw puzzle world. From this perspective, environmental education is truly an integrative study.

Each of the ecological principles described above illustrates characteristics that are relevant to all natural and cultural systems and thus are relevant to every subject that is taught in school. They are intended as a conceptual framework for understanding how the world works. In my workshops, I have found that once teachers are introduced to a concept and its ecological implications, they have no difficulty in identifying specific applications in their own subject areas. Because of their universal applicability, when used collectively these principles provide a powerful conceptual tool for organizing a curriculum whose purpose is to teach "the connectedness of things." The teachers in one K–8 school designed their entire curriculum around a set of ten concepts including the above. Each concept was addressed in some form in every unit at every grade level. In the earlier grades, the concepts were presented in concrete terms through experiential activities and simple explanations. As the child advanced, each concept was fleshed out with increased understanding. The concepts became powerful bridges across which the transfer of learning occurred on a regular basis, because once a concept was learned in one subject it could be applied in five, or ten, or a hundred other areas. The result was an example of Jerome Bruner's spiral curriculum in which teachers and students "revisit these basic ideas repeatedly, building upon them until the student has grasped the full formal apparatus that goes with them."[12]

A brief word about the role of concepts in education. Having worked with teachers for more than twenty years, I have concluded that most do not understand the function of concepts in thinking and learning. In our fact-oriented educational system, the importance of concepts in the retention of information and the transfer of learning is still largely ignored, because it is not understood. Thus the tendency in environmental education—as elsewhere in the curriculum—is to provide students with lots of facts about the various environmental issues and assume that this will lead to better understanding and eventually to a change in behavior. I suggest that we have the cart before the horse. The first step is to provide students with the conceptual framework as a context for understanding the facts. To paraphrase the well-known Chinese proverb: A concept is worth a thousand facts. The facts have their place, but they are not the starting point of learning.

In July 1980, the first international conference sponsored by the World Future Society chose as its theme, "Think Globally, Act Locally." This theme could well become the theme for what I think of as the "new" environmental education. We now recognize that virtually all of the environmental problems are global in nature, and that solutions which do not take into account this global context are doomed to failure. Ultimately, the goal of environmental education is to change the thinking of an entire generation of people. The first step toward thinking globally is for those of us who consider ourselves environmental educators to provide a comprehensive, integrated, conceptual framework that is appropriate to the task.

## Notes

1. Arthur M. Schlesinger, Jr., *Cycles of American History* (New York: Houghton-Mifflin, 1986).

2. *Time* (January 2, 1989), p. I.

3. Robert Ornstein and Paul Ehrlich, *New World, New Mind: Moving Toward Conscious Evolution* (New York: Doubleday, 1989).

4. Noel McInnis, *You Are an Environment: Teaching/Learning Environmental Attitudes* (Evanston, IL: The Center for Curriculum Design, 1972).

5. See Edward T. Clark, Jr., "The Role of Mindset in Global and Peace Education," *Holistic Education Review* 1, no. 4 (Winter 1988).

6. John Helfrich, "The Legacy of Edward Abbey," *Lake and Prairie* 30, no. 3 (May/June 1989).

7. Quoted in *The Home Planet*, edited by Kevin W. Kelley (Reading, MA: Addison Wesley, 1988).

8. Edward T. Clark, Jr., and John W. Coletta, "Ecosystem Education: A Strategy for Social Change," in *Quest for a Sustainable Society*, edited by James C. Coomer (New York: Pergamon Press, 1981).

9.  Robert Augros and George Stanciu, *The New Biology* (Boston: Shambala, 1988).

10.  Jeremy Rifkin, *Entropy* (New York: The Viking Press, 1980).

11.  Milton Friedman and Rose Friedman, *Free to Choose* (New York: Harcourt Brace Jovanovich, 1980).

12.  Jerome S. Bruner, *The Process of Education* (New York: Vintage Books, 1960).

# Holistic Education:
# A Search for Wholeness

## by Edward T. Clark, Jr.

In the Winter 1989 issue of *Holistic Education Review*, Editor Ron Miller defined *holistic education* by identifying what he considers to be four essential principles to the practice of this emerging educational approach.* While I agree that each of these principles represents a significant facet of holistic education, I question whether they or any such group of terms are the *sine qua non* of holistic education. This list of "essentials"—like any such list—is actually based upon a more fundamental and, I believe, far more profound assumption about the nature of the world: an assumption that everything in the universe is fundamentally interconnected. I suggest that this assumption represents the true essence of holistic education in all of its manifestations. Furthermore, I believe that the essence of holistic education lies at a deeper level of insight and experience than any selective list of principles, as appropriate as those principles may be. While this essence is implicit in each of Miller's principles, it is not explicit in any. Like the soil that nurtures a plant, this essence cannot be taken for granted but must be actively cultivated if the plant is to grow and thrive.

To use another metaphor, this essence serves as the foundation and unifying principle upon which the edifice of holistic education rests. Since there are many components to any edifice, any attempt to develop a definitive characterization of holistic education, either by selectively identifying those facets which have personal appeal or by trying to add incrementally all of these parts together, is bound to raise controversy. Each of us lives in a different part of the edifice and therefore has a different perspective on the whole. Even those who share the same apartment will often perceive the details of the shared space somewhat differently.

This makes for significant diversity among holistic educators, which in itself is quite positive. We know, for example, that in ecological systems diversity makes for stability. Every cultural system, including edu-

This selection originally appeared in the Summer 1990 issue of *Holistic Education Review*, Vol. 3, No. 2.

*These four principles or characteristics are described in the Introduction to this volume.

cation, is in some fundamental ways ecological in character (see "Environmental Education as an Integrative Study"); therefore, the greater the diversity in any cultural system, the more stable the system becomes. The more diverse holistic education is, the more stable it will be as a movement for change in education. However, if diversity is to be recognized as a strength rather than perceived as a basis for endless debate about what is or is not holistic education, we must identify our fundamental commonalities.

Unfortunately, as long as we focus on our differences, our commonalities will continue to elude us. The preoccupation with differences is a consequence of our culture's almost single-minded commitment to analysis as the exclusive skill required to understand anything. We have become equally adept at identifying the parts and either ignoring the whole or taking it for granted. To use the still useful cliché, we can't see the forest for the trees. Debates about differences will continue ad nauseam until we can identify some more fundamental criterion that is broad enough to enable us to honor our unity while we celebrate our diversity.

The foundation is what gives integrity to any building. It represents the unity out of which emerges the diversity which Miller addresses so eloquently. Until we can recognize and acknowledge this unity, we face the danger of endless debate concerning the shape, size, and relative significance of the various rooms (e.g., the four principles identified by Miller, each of which merely represents one facet of our multifaceted edifice).

## The first principle

I would suggest that, like all cultural systems, the foundation of holistic education consists of certain fundamental assumptions about the nature of the world. While there are many such assumptions, at what may be the deepest level of one's understanding there is a single "first principle" upon which all other assumptions rest and from which all other assumptions emerge. Much as the structure of a building is shaped by its foundation, the structure of one's thinking and experience is shaped by this fundamental first principle. And, just as we often take building foundations for granted, we also tacitly accept the correctness of this fundamental assumption about the nature of reality. In our pragmatic world, we take for granted that the way we experience the world is the way it "really" is, rarely considering the existence, much less the relevance, of such assumptions. In short, we make no distinction between the shapes of our cognitive maps and the territories described by those maps.

At this deepest level of understanding, each of us selects, either consciously or by default, one of two alternative "first principles" as the foundation upon which we base our lives. This decision is crucial because the alternatives provide fundamentally different shapes for the mental models that mold our behavior. One's life is shaped by either an *assumption of separateness* in which the essence of reality is fragmentation, or an *assumption of wholeness* in which the essence of reality is unity.

Even the earliest human experiences recognized a fundamental dualism implicit in the nature of things—yin/yang, you/me, right/left, light/dark. However, all so-called primitive cultures and all of the world's great religions have been based on an assumption of wholeness. Although they had an infinite diversity of perspectives, interpretations, and expressions, they shared the insight that underlying all of the explicit dualisms is an implicit, fundamental unity. On the other hand, Western civilization has been dominated from its beginnings by an assumption of separateness. This assumption was given philosophical legitimacy by the either/or alternatives of Aristotelian logic and theological legitimacy by Augustine, whose distinction between the "city of God" and the "city of man" has become a cardinal point of faith in the Christian world. With the advent of modern science and its analytical perspective, this assumption was given pragmatic validity. Through the application of the scientific method, it was possible to demonstrate empirically that, at its most fundamental level, reality was no more than a set of irreducible building blocks, each of which could be characterized by its precise definition and empirical description. In the process of verification, the cognitive map (i.e., the analytical process), became so confused with the territory that today few recognize the difference. The result is that culturally we have become what Frank Tipler has called "ontological reductionists."[1] The essence of this perspective is the tacit assumption that the world actually is the way science has described it: a fragmented collection of jigsaw puzzle pieces in search of a picture. The consequence of this fragmentation on our thinking and thus our behavior is personal, social, and global competition, conflict, confusion, and exploitation.

That this reductionist assumption is the foundation of our present educational system should be obvious to even the casual observer. Why wouldn't it be, since this reductionist assumption provides the philosophical foundation for the Newtonian-Cartesian paradigm upon which our entire social structure is built? As Miller rightly notes, "The holistic approach represents a new paradigm. In essence, it is the educational approach of a new culture...."

Holistic education—and the emerging paradigm—is based on the single assumption that, at some fundamental level, "everything is connected to everything else." Physicist David Peat referred to this assumption as "the law of the whole."[2] If this assumption is valid, then it follows that nothing can be truly understood apart from this global context. Thus, holistic education reflects an attitude, a philosophy, a worldview that challenges the fragmented, reductionist, mechanistic, nationalistic assumptions of mainstream culture and education. Because there are many synonyms for wholeness, there are many ways to characterize this perspective: holistic, ecological, evolutionary, spiritual, integrative, global. Whichever term one prefers, the ultimate purpose of holistic education is to transform the way we look at ourselves and our relationship to the world from a fragmented perspective to an integrative perspective. Any curriculum content, classroom methodology, or organizational structure that reflects this fundamental assumption of wholeness falls legitimately within the rubric of holistic education. Given this perspective, the primary criterion for evaluating any educational practice is the following: *Is there an implicit, and preferably explicit, assumption of wholeness, that is, a recognition that in some fundamental sense everything is connected to everything else?*

One of the barriers to any conceptualization of wholeness is the set of mental models or cognitive maps—what I call mind set—that shapes our thinking and consequently our behavior. Because all of us have been programmed to be "ontological reductionists," most of our personal, professional, and social behavior reflects this fragmented perspective. The first step in changing our behavior is to embrace a new mind set based on the assumption of wholeness (see my essay "The Role of Mindset in Global Education," *Holistic Education Review*, Winter 1988). The following sections present both a rationale for the assumption of wholeness and appropriate reinforcing mental models. If it is true that at some profoundly fundamental level the ultimate nature of reality is unity, then the assumption of separateness, though often pragmatically useful in our everyday world, is nevertheless an illusionary one and, in a world with nuclear weapons, a highly dangerous one.

## Puzzle pieces, or unity?

Consider this analogy: Life is like putting together a jigsaw puzzle. We spend most of our lives collecting and sorting pieces of the puzzle and, on occasion, putting a few pieces together. Occasionally in our effort to make sense out of the process of playing around with these pieces, we ask, "What do these pieces mean?" At such times, we find ourselves wondering if there is a "big picture" somewhere that could help us understand the pieces we have collected.

In all likelihood, we are too busy collecting and sorting pieces to spend much time speculating about meaning. Still, in the dark recesses of our innermost being, we intuitively feel that there must be some "big picture" somewhere. (As my four-year-old granddaughter said upon being given a plain paper bag full of jigsaw puzzle pieces: "Where's the picture, grandpa?") But we aren't strong on trusting our intuition anyway, and, since rational logic says that "what you see is what there is," we tend to dismiss these intuitive feelings as relics of a simpler era dominated by superstition and myth.

The *assumption of separateness* posits that there is no "big picture," no ultimate purpose or meaning to existence. Therefore, all meaning must reside either in the individual pieces of the puzzle themselves, or in whatever meaning we, as isolated individuals, choose to invest in those pieces. If this is true, then the only sensible goal of life is to collect as many pieces of the puzzle as possible and create what meaning we can from "our" particular pieces.

The *assumption of wholeness* posits that there is an ultimate *unity* to the universe from which meaning is derived. In the same way that each individual cell carries the DNA of the entire body, each person is an individual expression or representation of the wholeness. This unity is recognized in the ecological principle that "everything is connected to everything else." Using this insight, it becomes clear that at some profound level we are all working on the same jigsaw puzzle. Implicit in the assumption of unity and wholeness are meaning and purpose. Indeed, the only philosophical basis for belief in a purposeless universe is the assumption of separateness.

Now try this thought experiment: Imagine you are going to make a jigsaw puzzle. First imagine a picture of an Earth-like planet. Then draw this image, replicate it onto a piece of heavy cardboard, and, finally, with a giant cookie cutter, cut it into pieces of many shapes and sizes.

Now, imagine yourself taking an Alice in Wonderland trip in which you become small enough to enter and actually become one of those puzzle pieces. You take on its shape and characteristics, and it takes on your shape and characteristics. Now imagine that, as soon as you have done this, you forget that this was just a thought experiment, so that where you are now is the "real" world. From your new perspective, the world is an apparently random assortment of individual "pieces" or "persons" and "things."

In your efforts to make sense of all this, you spend a great deal of time and energy collecting as many pieces as you can, protecting your pieces and fending off others who seem to be grabbing for pieces you want. You figure that the only way you can make any sense out of your situation is to accumulate as many pieces as possible. After all, "The one who dies with the most puzzle pieces, wins," and those who seem to know what life is all about have said that "winning is everything." The only logical assumption is that meaning comes from winning. So you work all the harder to collect more pieces, hoping that eventually you will "win"—whatever that means.

Then one day you begin to wonder about what you're doing. You suddenly think, "Maybe there is a bigger picture of which I am a part." The next thing you begin to wonder is, "If there is a larger picture, how do I (my pieces) fit into it?" So, instead of trying to collect more pieces, you begin to look for patterns, connections, and relationships. One day, you suddenly remember (i.e., put together again)—in a flash of insight—how it was before you imagined yourself as this particular piece of the puzzle. You remember that there was a big picture and you realize that intuitively you knew all along that everything was connected to everything else.

The conclusion to the thought experiment is that each of us is like a jigsaw puzzle piece endowed with consciousness. In order to find where we belong, that is, our meaning and our particular connections and relationships, we have to start by intuiting and then imagining the whole. While the assumption of separateness seems to be rational and logical, the assumption of wholeness is intuitive and imaginative, reflecting what Joseph Chilton Pearce called the "intelligence of the heart."[3] Although rational logic is a powerful tool, it must be superseded by imagination and intuition because, ultimately, things aren't what they appear to be on the surface.

The object of this thought experiment is to suggest that the universe is, as its name implies, an indivisible whole that is manifested as multiplicity and which gives meaning to the parts. To function effectively, we need to understand the nature of both the underlying unity and the manifested multiplicity that we perceive on the surface of things. *This unity is the basic principle of the universe.*

Now try another thought experiment: Imagine yourself in space traveling toward a distant star. As you approach the star, it begins to appear round, and soon takes on the color of a big blue marble. As you approach, you begin to differentiate other colors, predominantly green, brown, and white.

As you begin to circle that ball, you can distinguish water and land. As you get closer, you can distinguish forests and plains and deserts and rivers and lakes. Then you get close enough to identify individual trees, buildings, and vehicles. Finally you are close enough to distinguish people. The closer you get, the more detail you see and the more you become aware of the individual parts, each a different piece of the whole planet.

When you land, you discover that everyone on this planet thinks of himself as a separate, unconnected, individual, isolated entity. The ethic of this planet is based on the principle, "Take care of Number 1, because, if you don't, no one else will." This ethic is manifested by each individual grabbing as much of everything as possible and then holding onto it for dear life. In large social groups this ethic is manifested in guns, tanks, bombs, submarines, and even laws designed to "protect" the "things" that belong to a particular person or group.

After living on this planet, you begin to take on its characteristic thought patterns and behavior. You begin to think of yourself as a separate, unconnected, individual, isolated entity and act accordingly. You forget the image that you once had of this planet from space: a single whole in which everything was connected to everything else. As your perspective changed, your reality changed to one of separateness, fragmentation, and isolation.

Now imagine yourself entering your spaceship for your return to outer space. As the ship takes off, you see trees turn into forests and forests turn into undifferentiated patches of green, which then become large land masses. As the planet fades into the distance, it changes into four colors, brown, green, blue, and white, until it becomes only a small blue marble floating in apparent nothingness. Finally, it is no more than a single point of light in the blackness of space. Then you "re-member" the parts into the whole. And you understand that separateness is an illusion born of a single, very limited perspective. And you know that separateness or unity is a matter of perspective and that it's all in your mind. Because you can change your mind, you are able to change your perspective by making simple thought experiments.

## The voyage of consciousness

When a child is born, she emerges from a universe of wholeness. Call it God, unity, cosmic consciousness, life force, universal energy. Whatever the name, the reality is that of *one, wholeness, unity, totality.* The child's consciousness was once, and still is, a part of that unity. As she emerges from the womb, she becomes Consciousness manifest. Her first task in life is to explore her new environment, an experience that results in a general awareness that she is apparently separate from her environment. As we know, one of the earliest developmental tasks of infancy is learning to differentiate between self and the outside world. This is a dawning, emerging awareness which moves from undifferentiated wholeness to a recognition of separateness.

Soon the child's consciousness becomes so programmed by her experiences of the separateness of things that separateness becomes her "reality." This reality is reinforced by the assumptions, beliefs, interpretations, attitudes, actions, thoughts, and feelings of those around her. She quickly forgets the unity from which she emerged, namely, her *Source.* She "buys into" the illusion of separateness and becomes as self-serving, as competitive, as self-protective as everyone else. And yet, deep within her being—perhaps buried in the genetic code itself—is the intuitive knowledge of wholeness.

When this knowledge of wholeness is reinforced by her bond first with her mother and her family and, as she develops, with the natural world, she is able on occasion to remember that wholeness intuitively. As she grows older, she learns the great myths of human cultures that were designed to help her remember her origins of wholeness. Thus, because the truth of wholeness is firmly embedded within her whole being and reinforced by her experiences, on occasion she is able to see intuitively, as through a glass darkly, the wholeness beneath the shadow of separateness. The more she is willing to use imagination and intuition to get in touch with this wholeness, the more she realizes that the separateness is only on the surface of things and is thus an illusion. Through thought experiments, she is able once again to get in touch with that experience of coming from wholeness and, in time, return to the Source of that wholeness.

She learns that, just as her imagination is able to manifest separateness, her imagination can manifest wholeness. As she touches this wholeness again, she finds power and energy beyond any she had ever known. Its source is cosmic, and she is able to tap into the waves of energy that surround her as readily as she can turn on a TV or radio.

What she may discover is that consciousness is the ultimate high energy field and that her mind, manifested as a physical body, is in reality a combination "tuner" and "transformer" with which she can tap that *cosmic energy* and channel that energy into the world. She learns that when she tunes in to the appropriate channel, cosmic energy flows through her and becomes manifested in countless ways so that, if the need arose, she could literally move mountains. Indeed, she begins to understand that her primary task in this reality is to be a channel for this flow of energy which will in time transform the Earth.

## New paradigms in science

In 1948, astrophysicist Sir Fred Hoyle predicted, "Once a photograph of the Earth, taken from the *outside*, is available ... a new idea as powerful as any in history will be let loose."[4] In 1984, astronaut Rakesh Sharma of India, traveling about in Soyuz T-11, wrote, "My mental boundaries expanded when I viewed the Earth against a black and uninviting vacuum, yet my country's rich traditions have conditioned me to look beyond manmade boundaries and prejudices. One does not have to undertake a space flight to come by this feeling."[5] And in 1985, Saudi astronaut Sultan Bin Salman al-Saud, traveling aboard Discovery 5, shared his experience: "The first day or so we all pointed to our countries. The third or fourth day we were pointing to our continents. By the fifth day we were aware of only one Earth."[6]

Quantum physics now recognizes that the basic substance of the universe is energy. Thus, every "thing" in the universe is a temporary manifestation of energy in "physical" form. We are literally "star stuff." Indeed, the universe itself, in Thomas Berry's words, is "a single gorgeous celebratory event."[7] One of my colleagues was more prosaic. He would hold up a rock and proclaim, "This is a rock festival." Just as the universe is "a single, multiform event," so, Berry reminded us, "Everything from subatomic particles to galactic systems are energy events." Or, to use physicist David Peat's words, "Indeed, the whole universe could be thought of as unfolding or expressing itself in its individual occurrences."[8] In short, every event is a representation, a part of the fundamental unity that is the cosmos. Carl Sagan said it simply: "We are the universe contemplating itself."

Once we acknowledge this perspective, we can recognize that the boundaries which divide the sacred from the secular, the spiritual from the material, mind from matter, the individual from the larger community, and one nation from another are all arbitrary boundaries. Though they have been created for the sake of convenience and are thus not only important but absolutely necessary, these boundaries do not reflect the nature of reality. As Peat suggested, "The more analytical types of explanation ... play an important role, but [only] within the general context of a more global description."[9]

## Conclusion

There are a number of significant principles for holistic education to be extrapolated or deduced from this fundamental assumption of wholeness. For me, these principles take on substantively more significance once I understand them in the context of the "law of the whole." In his editorial, Miller has identified four which he considers to be essential. But there are other principles of equal significance. For example, once holistic educators understand the implications of what the Carnegie Foundation for the Advancement of Teaching referred to as "the connectedness of things,"[10] we are faced with a much broader spectrum of interdependent relationships than most of us usually consider. For example, there are the relationships that exist within an individual, such as those between the ego and the shadow and the very subtle relationships that exist between the mind and the body. Then there are interpersonal relationships between parents and children, among children, and between adults both in the family and in the larger community. Within the community there are the group relationships that exist between the school, the home, and the community and between the larger social, economic, and political systems that shape our lives in powerful ways.

At least three relationships tend to be taken for granted and are just being recognized as having significant influence on the way we live our lives in the so-called information age. One is our relationship to and understanding of time. In his book, *Time Wars*,[11] Jeremy Rifkin pointed to the subtle but profound impact that is occurring with our changing concept of time. A few generations ago our ancestors measured time in seasonal cycles, but today it is not unusual for certain critical factors to be measured in nanoseconds. This significant relationship cannot be ignored if education is to be considered holistic. Then there is our relationship to information itself, that ubiquitous reality which has the capacity both to enslave and to enlighten us. We ignore this relationship at our peril. Finally, perhaps the most fundamental of all relationships is the relationship between humans and the planet Earth, a relationship that ideally serves as the model for understanding the myriad relationships implied in that profound ecological statement, "the connectedness of things."

This universal application is appropriate because, as Miller recognizes, at the fundamental level holistic education is "an overarching philosophy of life." Implicit in this philosophy is the insight that holistic education has the potential for transforming the world. Indeed, I would suggest that the ultimate goal and therefore virtually limitless potential of holistic education is nothing short of transformation—personal, social, and global. I say transformation because this holistic perspective ultimately requires a new relationship among people and our planetary home, the Earth. If William Wordsworth was able to recognize "the universe in a grain of sand," how much more of the universe is potentially visible in the eyes of a newborn babe or in the eyes of every human being on Earth—or, not so incidentally, in a rock, a tree, a bird, a mountain, or a sunset. This is the transformative quality of the assumption of wholeness. Anything less is not enough.

I affirm Miller's conviction that holistic education is fundamentally spiritual in nature. Indeed, I have concluded that any search for wholeness, regardless of its form, is a spiritual search or a "remembering": an innate desire to "arrive where we started and know the place for the first time."[12] Thus it seems appropriate to close this essay with an excerpt from the "Theosophical World View." This statement incorpo-

rates certain fundamental propositions that are common to the "perennial wisdom" of all ages. As such, it provides us with what I consider
to be an appropriate and comprehensive statement of the rationale,
purpose, philosophy, and mission—the essence—of holistic education:

> 1. The universe and all that exists within it are one interrelated and interdepen-
> dent whole.
> 2. Every existent being—from atom to galaxy—is rooted in the same universal
> life-creating Reality. This Reality is all-pervasive, but it can never be summed up
> in its parts, since it transcends all its expressions. It reveals itself in the purposeful,
> ordered, and meaningful processes of nature as well as in the deepest recesses of
> the mind and spirit.
> 3. Recognition of the unique value of every living being expresses itself in rever-
> ence for life, compassion for all, sympathy with the needs of all individuals to find
> truth for themselves, and respect for all religious traditions. The way in which
> these ideals become realities in individual life are both the privileged choice and
> the responsible act of every human being.[13]

I can think of no better way to describe the foundation and unifying
principle of holistic education. If we agree on this, then with the French,
we can celebrate our diversity by proclaiming loudly and vigorously,
*Vive la difference!"*

## Notes

1.  In Frederick Turner, *Beyond Geography: The Western Spirit Against the Wilderness* (Camden,
NJ: Rutgers Univ. Press, 1983).

2.  F. David Peat, *Synchronicity: The Bridge Between Matter and Mind* (New York: Bantam,
1987).

3.  Joseph Chilton Pearce, *The Magical Child Matures* (New York: Bantam, 1986).

4.  Kevin W. Kelley, *The Home Planet* (Reading, MA: Addison Wesley, 1988).

5.  Ibid.

6.  Ibid.

7.  Thomas Berry, *Dream of the Earth* (San Francisco: Sierra Club, 1988).

8.  Peat, *Synchronicity.*

9.  Ibid.

10.  Ernest Boyer and Arthur Levine, *A Quest for Common Learning* (Washington, DC: The
Carnegie Foundation for the Advancement of Teaching, no date).

11.  Jeremy Rifkin, *Time Wars* (New York: Holt, 1987).

12.  T.S. Eliot, "Little Giddings," in *The Complete Poems and Plays: 1909–1950* (New York:
Harcourt, Brace, 1952).

13.  *The American Theosophist.* A bimonthly publication of The American Theosophical
Society, Wheaton, Illinois.

# Authority, Aggression, and Building Community in Alternative/Free Schools

## by Dave Lehman

*Dave Lehman, Ph.D., is principal and a teacher at the Alternative Community School, a public middle and high school in Ithaca, New York. He has served as a consultant on staff development, human relations training, and science education for a number of school districts and organizations, and has written for, as well as edited, a variety of educational publications. Dave is active in state and national alternative education networks.*

Most of us entered alternative education or free schools because we strongly disagreed with the heavily authoritarian, centrally controlled, nonhumanistic "schooling" which predominates in education even today. We also freely chose to work in alternative schools because we believed that students could learn to work cooperatively in a nonviolent community, and that the things learned and experienced by our students would be transferable to their later adulthood, resulting in positive changes in society. Certainly these were true for myself and remain so today. Yet, all too rarely have we really eliminated authoritarianism in our schools or developed genuinely democratic, nonviolent school communities. That these are still crucial and timely issues is evident in an article from a recent issue of *Skole*, the journal of the National Coalition of Alternative Community Schools, in which Alan Parachini interviewed Herb Kohl and referred to elements in Kohl's various books:

> He [Kohl] still faithfully applies the principles he developed.
>
> The movement [alternative/free school movement], he says, took the philosophical position that the traditional authoritarian structure of schools, with students the lowest class, was counterproductive . . . . There would be discipline, but it should be developed from within a group of children, not imposed.
>
> "In an authoritarian classroom, annoying behavior is legislated out of existence," Kohl wrote in *The Open Classroom*. "In an open situation, the teacher tries to express

This selection originally appeared in the Summer 1989 issue of *Holistic Education Review*, Vol. 2, No. 2.

what he feels and to deal with each situation as a communal problem. It is important
not to equate an open classroom with a 'permissive environment.'"[1]

In order to get at these essential issues, I will first briefly trace the
history of the concepts of *freedom* and *authority* in the development of
our alternative/free schools. Then, I will look at three key factors in the
broader cultural context of our Western society which powerfully con-
strain those of us working in such schools—the concepts of "original
sin," "Social Darwinism," and "innate human aggression." Finally, I
will draw on several recent sources, as well as my own experiences with
the Alternative Community School in Ithaca, New York, to suggest three
specific activities to address these issues in helping alternative/free
schools toward the fuller development of nonauthoritarian, nonviolent,
democratic, "free" school communities.

## Historical background on freedom and authority

The concept of freedom is surely central to our nation and its creation,
as is the word happiness, so clearly expressed in the Declaration of
Independence," . . . certain inalienable rights . . . life, liberty, and the
pursuit of happiness." It was Thomas Jefferson in particular, along with
Ben Franklin, who, largely because of their experience with the Iroquois
Indians of the Northeast, influenced the inclusion of such phrases.
According to Bruce Johansen,

> Jefferson believed that the freedom to exercise restraint on their leaders, and an
> egalitarian distribution of property, secured for Indians in general a greater degree
> of happiness than that to be found among the superintended sheep at the bottom
> of European class structure . . . . Jefferson's writings made it evident that he, like
> Franklin, saw accumulation of property beyond that needed to satisfy one's natural
> requirements as an impediment to liberty.[2]

Thus, the very roots of our nation are embedded in the rich soil of the
ideas of freedom from authority and each individual's right to personal
and societal well-being. These are two essential themes in the history
of alternative/free schools. As Joel Spring points out clearly in his *Primer
of Libertarian Education*, "Radicals have searched for an educational system and a process of child rearing that will create a non-authoritarian
person who will not obediently accept the dictates of the political and
social system and who will demand greater personal control and
choice."[3] [Hopefully the term *radicals* is not a stumbling block; clearly
this is to be taken as the word originally intended by the Latin root,
*radix,* meaning "to go to the root of"—and is in the noble tradition of
Jefferson, Franklin, Paine, and others from our own "revolutionary"
past.]

Early alternative or free school efforts, such as those of William God-
win in England in the late eighteenth century, were reactions against
an educational system which was concerned primarily with the development of citizens loyal to the new nation states.[4] Again, in the late
nineteenth century, in response to the system's emphasis on producing

trained workers for the new industrial revolution, Francisco Ferrer founded the "Modern School Movement" in Spain and it spread rapidly to the United States with such educational pioneers as the Hutchinsons at Stony Ford School in New York and the Dicks at the Stelton School in New Jersey.[5] Thus, words such as the following have a familiar ring.

> . . . Freedom in education meant freedom from the authority of the teacher as well as the church and state. Under the prevailing system, argued Ferrer, the teacher was merely an agent of the ruling classes, training his charges "to obey, to believe, to think according to the social dogmas which govern us." Like the soldier and policeman, he was always imposing, compelling, and using violence; the true educator is the man who does not impose his own ideas and will on the child, but appeals to its own energies.[6]

Another important figure in the alternative tradition was the novelist Leo Tolstoy, who conducted a school in Russia in the mid-nineteenth century. Tolstoy believed that "the school should practice non-interference, with students left free to learn what they wanted to learn . . . . A non-compulsory school was one without a planned program where teachers could teach what they wanted and their offerings would be regulated by the demands of the students." Earlier, the French philosopher Jean Jacques Rousseau made an appeal in *Emile* to reason rather than authority, particularly in the education of the young child, and he was followed by the German Max Stirner who ". . . essentially agreed with Rousseau that the method of education should allow for individual choice of belief."[7] Out of such educational philosophies, these early radical educators developed their views on conduct in the classroom, also familiar to us today at least in theory, as described by Avrich:

> Godwin, who recognized that boisterous activity was often a mere outlet for energy, criticized teachers who favored "the sober, the dull, the obedient lads that have no will and no understanding of their own." For Stirner, too, a certain amount of disorder was inevitable in the school. He believed that the qualities of obstinacy and intractability in a pupil were mere expressions of the "natural strength of the will," from which conventional teachers defended themselves with "the convenient rampart of authority."[8]

Likewise, these early efforts were followed more recently with twentieth century efforts such as the free school movement and A.S. Neill's Summerhill, to create either nonauthoritarian schools or to reject the concept of schooling altogether. Spring describes these schools as follows:

> The free school movement was an attempt to establish an environment for self-development in a world that was considered overly structured and rationalized . . . as an oasis from authoritarian control and as a means of passing on the knowledge to be free.[9]

But, what is "authoritarian control" and "nonauthoritarian freedom"? Here, Erich Fromm's introductory words to A.S. Neill's *Summerhill* are most instructive:

> The basic principle of . . . self-determination was the replacement of authority by freedom, to teach the child *without the use of force* by appealing to his curiosity and

spontaneous needs, and thus to get him interested in the world around him . . . .
To discuss this matter clearly we must first understand the nature of freedom; and
to do this we must differentiate between *overt authority and anonymous authority.*

Overt authority is exercised directly and explicitly. The person in authority frankly
tells the one who is subject to him, "You must do this. If you do not, certain
sanctions will be applied against you." Anonymous authority pretends that there
is no authority, that all is done with the consent of the individual . . . . Overt
authority used physical force; anonymous authority employs psychic manipulation . . . . Parents and teachers have confused true nonauthoritarian education with
*education by means of persuasion and hidden coercion.*

Later, Fromm describes how nonauthoritarian education, as practiced
at Summerhill, is based on respect.

*Freedom does not mean license.* This very important principle, emphasized by Neill,
is that respect for the individual must be mutual. A teacher does not use force
against a child, nor has a child the right to use force against a teacher. A child
may not intrude upon an adult just because he is a child, nor may a child use
pressure in the many ways in which a child can.[10]

As Fromm indicates, one of the points Neill strongly emphasized was
the destructive role of *guilt* in binding the child to the authority of
adults. At Summerhill, personal relationships were based on an honest
give and take rather than guilt and fear.

This kind of twentieth century radical educational change was paral-
leled by the development of "humanistic education," which also spoke
to the concepts of freedom and authority. Specifically, the humanistic
psychologist/educator Carl Rogers described a self-actualizing, student-
centered teaching which could result in an environment in which " . . . a
young person can find him or herself respected, can make responsible
choices, can experience the excitement of learning, can lay the basis for
living as an effective concerned citizen, well informed, competent in
knowledge and skills, confident in facing the future."[11] This concept of
personal, psychological freedom has been an important concept in the
development of alternative and free schools, as noted by Spring:

Ownership of self is an important concept in radical theories of education because
it extends the idea of freedom, taking it beyond its usual meaning of political
liberty and equality before the law, and emphasizing control over one's beliefs and
actions. Political liberty has little meaning if an individual's actions are guided by
an internalized authority from which there is no escape . . . . Certainly one of the
goals of most educational systems has been the internalization of beliefs and the
development of a conscience that will give unquestioned support to the existing
social structure.[12]

In describing these twentieth century alternative and free schools,
Jonathan Kozol, probably the most outspoken contemporary educational
critic, rewrote his book, *Free Schools* (1972), ten years later with a new
title, *Alternative Schools: A Guide for Educators and Parents.* In the introduction to this revised edition, he proposes the following explanation which
seems to describe well our current struggles:

That struggle addressed, above all else, the question of the role of adults in the
lives of children. The tension between egalitarian and open avenues of inquiry for
children and the natural seemingly inevitable authority of well-informed adults

was at the heart of all our efforts, all our disagreements (frequently quite painful), and all of our real success . . . . Beyond the issues of equality and justice, the ultimate question still remains the same: How does a teacher dare to teach, impose, intrude, provoke, inspire, and instruct, while also striving to excite the curiosity, autonomy, and moral spontaneity that can empower children to grow up to be compassionate and competent adults?[13]

## Social Darwinism, original sin, and innate human aggression

Central to the alternative/free schools of the past and present, as an active counter to authoritarianism, has been the principle of democratic self-governance. This is certainly true of Summerhill as it was of its forerunner in England, "The Little Commonwealth," as well as "The Gorky Colony" in the early twentieth century in Russia,[14] and it is a central feature of many such schools today. Yet, this simple idea, although it is so basic to our democratic nation which is founded on the belief that people can live together cooperatively and nonviolently, is yet to become reality either in our schools or our society. One of the factors influencing this has been the kind of thinking which took the concepts of Charles Darwin and twisted them into a view of humankind as continually engaged in a dog-eat-dog and competitive fight for survival. Thomas Huxley and other Social Darwinists put forth this view strongly in the late nineteenth century. (See "The Struggle for Existence in Human Society," 1888, as reprinted in Kropotkin's *Mutual Aid*). They influenced much of the Western world's view of humankind, including educational philosophy.

In the 1960s and '70s this view was actively represented with supposedly "new" research findings from the studies of animals, particularly other primates. Ashley Montagu described these writers as the "innate aggressionists"—Konrad Lorenz, Niko Tinbergen, Robert Ardrey, Desmond Morris, Anthony Storr, and others. In *The Nature of Human Aggression*, Montagu summarized the key components of their ideas: that aggressiveness is an inherited genetic trait with little hope for amelioration; that humans are naturally killers; that it is through weapons that prehuman creatures developed into human beings; that aggressive energies, tied to territorial instincts, are irresistible and need to be discharged periodically, in some fashion or another. Montagu then went on to point out how crucial this matter is:

This is important, . . . for what is involved here is not simply the understanding of the nature of man but also the image of man that grows out of that understanding . . . for the image we hold of man, of ourselves, is the image that will largely influence our individual and collective behavior toward ourselves and toward our fellow man.[15]

I believe this is a pervasive part of our present mindset about humans and specifically about young people and how we expect them to act, and if this is how we expect them to act, then we ought not be surprised when they indeed act this way.

Another powerful cultural factor which I believe has, almost unconsciously, constrained teachers and the parents of students in alternative/free schools (and still does!) from constructively countering authoritarianism and aggression in ourselves, our students, and our schools is the concept of *original sin*. Our Western culture is predominantly Judeo-Christian, and this concept is as old as these two pervasive religions. And, even though many people working with alternative/free schools may not be actively involved in either of these religions, I believe, as Elaine Pagels has written, that it has pervaded our present Western mindset. In her recent book *Adam, Eve, and the Serpent,* Pagels traces the historical roots of original sin and its subsequent impact on the development of our culture's sexual and political beliefs.

> Most Jews and Christians had agreed that God gave humankind in creation the gift of moral freedom, and that Adam's misuse of it brought death upon his progeny. But Augustine went further: Adam's sin not only caused our mortality but cost us our moral freedom, irreversibly corrupted our experience of sexuality (which Augustine tended to identify with original sin), and made us incapable of genuine political freedom . . . . Augustine's theory of original sin not only proved politically expedient, since it pursuaded many of his contemporaries that human beings universally need external government—which meant, in their case, both a Christian state and an imperially supported church—but also offered an analysis of human nature that became, for better or worse, the heritage of all subsequent generations of western Christians and the major influence on their psychological and political thinking.[16]

## Humankind as cooperative

I suggest that we need to strip ourselves of the oppressive burden of this baggage of Social Darwinism, innate human aggression, and original sin. We need a "new," more accurate mindset which sees humankind as essentially nonaggressive and cooperative by nature, with the freedom of moral choices, and that we build on such a mindset in restructuring our educational institutions, beginning with our alternative/free schools which have the greatest likelihood of initially accomplishing such a goal. Fortunately, there are several who have already developed cogent arguments for such a mindset. Just as Elaine Pagels has helped us understand more clearly the political basis of original sin (not having anything to do with any actual teaching of Jesus!), so too Peter Kropotkin—Russian scientist, philosopher, educator, and writer of the turn of the century—wrote a wonderful response to the early Social Darwinists in 1902, *Mutual Aid: A Factor of Evolution,* in which he noted:

> We have heard so much lately of the "harsh, pitiless struggle for life," which was said to be carried on by every animal against all other animals, every "savage" against all other "savages," and every civilized man against all his co-citizens—and these assertions have so much become an article of faith—that it was necessary, first of all, to oppose to them a wide series of facts showing animal and human life under a quite different aspect. It was necessary to indicate the overwhelming importance which sociable habits play in Nature and in the progressive evolution of both the animal species and human beings: to prove that they secure to animals a better protection from their enemies, very often facilities for getting food (winter provisions, migrations, etc.), longevity, and therefore a greater facility for the development of intellectual faculties; and that they have given to men, in addition to the same advantages, the possibility of working out those institutions which have enabled mankind to survive in its hard struggle against Nature, and to progress, notwithstanding all the vicissitudes of its history.[17]

Three recent books have corroborated this early work of Kropotkin—Ashley Montagu's *Learning Non-Aggression: The Experience of Non-Literate Societies* and *The Nature of Human Aggression,* and Shirley Strum's *Almost Human: A Journey into the World of Baboons.* In his introduction to *Learning Non-Aggression,* Montagu points out:

> Many human societies cannot be characterized as aggressive . . . . Most people in civilized societies get involved in wars not because they feel aggressive toward the socially defined "enemy," but because their leaders—who themselves are seldom motivated by aggressive feelings—consider it necessary to make war. Such considerations have nothing to do with feelings, universals or instincts, but usually mainly with political constraints.[18]

Strum has recently turned the primate behaviorists on their heads with her more than ten years of study of baboons, believed to be our closest relatives, with the following startling findings:

> Watching the baboons convinced me to take a new stance on the place and importance of aggression in the lives of animals. Aggression might be just *one* option instead of the *only* option that an individual could choose when he needed to defend himself or to compete with others. Furthermore, with alternatives possible, aggression suddenly would become less inevitable . . . . My shocking discovery was that males had no dominance hierarchy; that baboons possessed social strategies; that finesse triumphed over force; that social skill and social reciprocity took precedence over aggression . . . . Baboons were "nice" to one another because such behavior was as critical to their survival as air to breathe and food to eat . . . .
>
> The implications were breathtaking. I was arguing that aggression was not as pervasive or important an influence in evolution as had been thought, and that social strategies and social reciprocity were extremely important. If baboons possessed these, certainly the precursors of our early human ancestors must have had them as well.[19]

No longer can educators look at young males fighting and simply say, "Boys will be boys." No longer is it defendable to say that competition is what counts, and that the educational goal is to develop winners in the aggressive combat for survival. For clearly aggression is a learned behavior in humans, and thus humans can also learn to be unaggressive. As Montagu has said,

> Whatever humanity's potentialities for aggression may be, and we know that such potentialities exist, it is clear that their expression will largely depend upon the environmental stimulation they receive. If this is so, then there is every reason for optimism, for if we understand the conditions that produce aggressive behavior, there is some hope that by changing those conditions we may be able to control both its development and expression.[20]

All of this is significant and related to the earlier discussion of authority and freedom in our alternative schools, because if we are to develop schools without arbitrary force, then it is important to realize that nonviolent, nonaggressive, democratic, cooperative behavior is of greater survival value for our species. Thus, the teaching and learning of such behavior is at least one viable alternative to the learning of aggression and authoritarianism.

## Developing democratic school communities

In a recent summer workshop our staff at the Alternative Community School spent three lengthy sessions at a two-day retreat working on these issues. We began by looking at "authority" and "freedom" and sharing our personal reflections on what these had meant, and presently do mean, for us in our alternative school teaching. From this sharing we extracted an understanding of *authoritarian* as stifling, cutting off of relationships (e.g., between teacher and student), and abusive. We then came to describe an opposite teaching style as *authoritative*, which is nurturing, builds relationships, is nonabusive, constructive, and shares responsibility for teaching/learning—where everyone has a right to be listened to, to learn, to be in a safe environment, and to be respected. From here we worked on various ways we could continue developing such a teaching style in our school. One summary of our goal is that which follows (by Don Kesselheim, from a staff workshop done on the same topic at the former Shanti Alternative High School in Hartford, Connecticut) as "Criteria for a Healthy Authority Relationship":

> I am incomplete and growing toward completeness, and we both know this.
>
> You are incomplete and growing toward completeness, and we both know this.
>
> I have experience/knowledge/skills/competence that will help you in your growth.
>
> You have experience/knowledge/skills/competence that will help me in my growth.
>
> My self-image is sufficiently strong and positive so that I can respond to direction from you without feeling diminished by doing so.
>
> Your self-image is sufficiently strong and positive so that you can respond to direction from me without feeling diminished by doing so.*
>
> I wish to maximize your individual autonomy as an ultimate goal, and we both know this.
>
> You wish to maximize my individual autonomy as an ultimate goal, and we both know this.

Thus, I believe strongly that the *first activity* for alternative/free school educators trying to develop nonauthoritarian, nonviolent, democratic classrooms and school communities is to get in touch with their own, personal sense of authority and freedom, and to do some shared reading, reflecting, and discussing of their own cultural history around such issues as Social Darwinism, innate aggression, and original sin. From this foundation and shared perspective, a staff could then move toward specific means of implementing their own approach to issues of freedom and responsibility.

---

*It is important to note here that, with many of our young people, this is particularly difficult because their self-image is not yet "sufficiently strong and positive." Therefore, a precondition to their development of "healthy authority relationships," and a task for us to work on with them, is, I suggest, the development of such a self-image.

In a recent outstanding article on "Education for Democracy and Empowerment," Miami University education professor Henry Giroux states that

> Progressive education reforms attempted, with some success, to democratize America's system of education. Where those who implemented these changes failed, however, was in their blind endorsement of a romantic notion of personal freedom.

He then goes on to analyze why he feels this occurred.

> Part of the reason . . . was that they [early progressive educators] had endorsed a type of moral relativism that seemed to imply that it was wrong to "impose" any particular set of opinions. Instead, they felt that a truly democratic education would emerge simply from the interpretations that students gave to their own experiences. The resulting education neither empowered students politically nor did it provide them with the knowledge and understanding necessary to function in the world of work.[21]

I feel that many of us alternative/free school educators, still today, fall prey to these same failings. We, also, often seem to lack the conviction of our stated philosophies, and are quietly skeptical that we can ever teach young people "mutual respect" because they are simply too self-centered. As Pearl Oliner put it in an interview in the *Noetic Sciences Review*: "A large portion of social science research is based on the assumption that people don't behave out of any motivation except their own self-interest."[22] Yet, in the recent book by her and her husband, Samuel, entitled *The Altruistic Personality: Rescuers of Jews in Nazi Germany*, they have presented encouraging evidence for an opposite viewpoint, which emphasizes the "prosocial" motives of individuals. Here, the important thing for alternative/free school educators is to look, with the Oliners, at what can be done to develop young people who will care about others and who would even risk their lives for other people as the rescuers did. Specifically, they recommend the following which has clear implications for those of us who would like to develop "caring, democratic communities" in our alternative/free schools:

> The kinds of relationships you have are more important than personal autonomy. Western tradition has always emphasized autonomy and independence of thought . . . . We suggest that autonomy is only one style for moral courage. Most people develop such behavior through relationships with other people. This suggests, therefore, that if you're going to promote altruism, in schools for example, you have to create an environment which supports these varying styles [of altruism]. We can't just teach moral principles. We need to provide opportunities for people to develop empathy. We need to create institutions which are caring—which model care and communicate the message that caring is important.[23]

Thus, the *second activity* for moving alternative/free schools further in building democratic communities is to create schools where individual actions count, where students not only are taught about historical individuals who have made profoundly positive changes in their communities, but where students and staff (and parents) are regularly engaged in constructive social action and community service.

Here at the Alternative Community School, we have developed a number of schoolwide structures and processes which form the matrix of our democratic self-governance. At the heart of these are the shared values of mutual respect and trust. At a recent workshop at the Fall symposium of the Coalition of Essential Schools* in Providence, Rhode Island, Judy Codding—now principal of Pasadena High School in California, former principal of the Scarsdale Alternative High School in New York, and protege of the late Lawrence Kohlberg and his efforts at Harvard to develop "just-community schools"—described the following five structures as essential ingredients of genuinely democratically run schools where students and teachers have a real voice in what happens:

1) A forum for noncurricular issues and decision making; at ACS, we conduct weekly "All School Town Meetings";

2) Small (8-12 ideally) advisory or core groups for nurturing; we have "Family Groups";

3) Student court or a "fairness committee" for sharing in rule enforcement; we use a "Student Review Board";

4) Moral dilemma discussions; part of several of our social studies courses and sometimes part of our Family Groups; and

5) Community service projects; done at ACS in a variety of group, individual, and whole school settings.

Likewise Tom Gregory and Gerry Smith, in their book on *High Schools as Communities: The Small School Reconsidered*, make the case for building truly caring communities in high schools:

> But why community? It may help people feel good about themselves, but what does it do beyond that? For one thing, it provides a unifying force; it increases commitment among students and teachers; it lessens alienation and improves motivation, it gives teachers greater autonomy and harnesses the human potential that is in every social situation; and it gives students a greater stake in a school and increases their identification with it. Without community, school is just a place to get through as painlessly as possible; with community, it is *our* school, a place in which to live and find meaning.

They describe the essential ingredients of such caring, democratic communities as follows, "The characteristics that define communities as having a strong sense of wellness are caring, commitment, and trust, which build strong bonds between individuals in the community; and physical, mental, and emotional support, which enable individuals to risk, succeed, and grow."[24] Thus, a *third activity* for the development of democratic schools is the creation of specific structures and processes that will regularly, daily, actively involve students and staff (and parents to the degree that their time permits) in the real decisions affecting the teaching/learning in the school.

---

*We are one of ten alternative schools in this national group of 54 high schools experimenting with the development of nine "essential" principles, originally developed by Ted Sizer of Brown University.

Finally, in closing, none of this is easy! It all takes time, rigorous intellectual and emotional work, and a recognition that change and conflict are essential to growth. And it may not be for everyone! Yet, it seems to me that for alternative/free school educators, this is our most crucial work; it is also the most essential thing we can do for (and teach) our future generations.

## Notes

1. Alan Parachini, "Alternative Education Not Dead Yet, Leader Insists: Herbert Kohl Says Revival in the Cards" *Skole* 4, no. 1 (Summer, 1988), pp. 59-64. (Reprinted from *The Oregonian*, 19 August 1987).

2. Bruce Johansen, *Forgotten Founders: How the American Indians Helped Shape Democracy* (Boston: Harvard Common Press, 1982).

3. Joel Spring, *Primer of Libertarian Education* (New York: Free Life Editions, 1975), p. 14.

4. Spring, *Primer*, p. 24.

5. Paul Avrich, *The Modern School Movement: Anarchism and Education in the United States* (Princeton, NJ: Princeton University Press, 1980), p. 239; Charlotte Winsor (ed.), *Experimental Schools Revisited: Bulletins of the Bureau of Educational Experiments* (New York: Schocken, 1973), pp. 73ff.

6. Avrich, *The Modern School Movement*, p. 9.

7. Spring, *Primer*, pp. 48-49, 38.

8. Avrich, *The Modern School Movement*, p. 13.

9. Spring, *Primer*, pp. 54-55.

10. Erich Fromm, Foreword to A. S. Neill, *Summerhill: A Radical Approach to Child Rearing* (New York: Hart, 1960), pp. x-xi, xiii.

11. Carl Rogers, *Freedom to Learn for the '80's* (Columbus: Merrill, 1983), p. 2.

12. Spring, *Primer*, pp. 33.

13. Jonathan Kozol, *Alternative Schools: A Guide for Educators and Parents* (New York: Continuum, 1982), pp. 8-9.

14. E. T. Bazeley, *Homer Lane and the Little Commonwealth* (New York: Schocken, 1969); A. S. Makarenko, *The Road to Life: An Epic of Education*, vols. 1 and 2 (Moscow: Progress Publishers, 1951).

15. Ashley Montagu, *The Nature of Human Aggression* (New York: Oxford University Press, 1978), p. 7-8, 300-301.

16. Elaine Pagels, *Adam, Eve, and the Serpent* (New York: Random House, 1988), p. xxvi.

17. Peter Kropotkin, *Mutual Aid: A Factor of Evolution* (Boston: Sargent/Extending Horizons, 1914), pp. ix, xvi.

18. Ashley Montagu, *Learning Non-Aggression: The Experience of Non-Literate Societies* (New York: Oxford University Press, 1978), p. 4.

19. Shirley Strum, *Almost Human: A Journey into the World of Baboons* (New York: Random House, 1987), pp. 147, 157-158.

20. Montagu, *Learning Non-Aggression*, p. 6.

21. Henry Giroux, "Education for Democracy and Empowerment" *Tikkun* 3 no. 5 (September/October 1988), pp. 30-33.

22. Samuel and Pearl Oliner (interviewed by Barbara McNeill), "The Risk of Caring: Rescuers of Jews in Nazi Europe" *Noetic Sciences Review* (Summer, 1988), p. 5.

23. Oliner and Oliner, "The Risk of Caring," p. 7.

24. Thomas Gregory and Gerald Smith, *High Schools as Communities: The Small School Reconsidered* (Bloomington, IN: Phi Delta Kappa Educational Foundation, 1987), pp. 57, 53.

# A Global-Ecological Perspective

# A
# Global-Ecological
# Perspective

## Introduction

### by Ron Miller

The major challenge of our time is to find a path toward a lasting peace. Given the incredibly sophisticated and deadly power of nuclear, biological, and chemical weapons, and the ominous potentials of genetic engineering and artificial intelligence, it is imperative that humankind find alternatives to its millenia-old fascination with conquest and warfare. The building of a global community living in peace is as much an educational task as it is a political and economic one; the roots of human conflict are in our relationships with each other, with our children, with the natural world, and within ourselves, and it is within these relationships that the seeds of peace must be sown.

A holistic understanding of peace involves a new worldview that is global, ecological, and spiritual. This perspective is a celebration of life in all its aspects. Only when we have truly learned to celebrate life will we be unwilling to destroy life for the sake of ideology, territory, or economic gain. A "global" perspective does not imply the establishment of some sort of monolithic, authoritarian "one-world government," as some critics fear. In the holistic view, it is not government—"one-world" or otherwise—that will turn humanity away from war, but the cultivation within persons of all cultures of a deep sense of reverence and love for life. This is a primary task of an education conceived holistically.

In this section, Phil Gang's essay captures the essence of this worldview and places it in historical perspective. Dr. Gang is a leader of the holistic education movement who has worked with educators and built networks around the world. In "Ecological Literacy," David Orr reminds us that humanity's relationship to the natural world is seriously out of balance today. It may even be said that humankind is at war with the Earth, and is, unfortunately, winning. Ecological literacy is a first step in healing our relationship with the Earth and its life.

Donna and Jerry Allender focus on human relationships between people from different cultures. Their reflections on the essence of humanistic education as it is practiced in several cultures lead to a greater appreciation for our common humanity even as this is expressed through great diversity. Sonnie McFarland's "Holistic Peace Education" covers the many levels of relationships underlying true peace. As she indicates, the great holistic educator Maria Montessori was deeply concerned with achieving peace and believed strongly that nurturing children's healthy development was a vital part of this task. Finally, Linda Macrae Campbell describes an emotional meeting between American and Soviet youths and the powerful insights into global problems which they attained together.

# The Global-Ecocentric Paradigm in Education

## by Phil Gang

*Phil Gang, Ph.D., is an author, international lecturer, educational consultant, and contributing editor to* **Holistic Education Review,** *as well as a member of the Soviet-American Education Project of the Association for Humanistic Psychology. Currently the Director of the Institute for Educational Studies, he is the developer of the "Our Planet, Our Home" global-ecological learning system based on the Gaia model. Phil is deeply committed to developing a sense of "Earth consciousness" among young people and has created "Transforming Education . . . and Ourselves" Workshops to help parents and teachers deal with these issues. These workshops are held in cities around the world. He is on the steering committee of the Global Alliance for Transforming Education.*

> A man said to the universe
> "Sir, I exist!"
> "However," replied the universe,
> "The fact has not created in me
> A sense of obligation."
> —*Stephen Crane*
> *1899*

Have you ever gazed at a full moon against a star-studded black sky? Have you ever paused by the ocean's shore and listened to the sounds of life and felt the soft breeze caressing your cheek? Have you ever walked through a pristine forest breathing and smelling the gentle, clean, and natural air? When was the last time you experienced the innocent laughter of children, or saw the glowing hues of a rainbow reaching from earth to sky, or witnessed a breathtaking sunset?

Some three to five billion years ago the earth was totally barren, a fiery caldron of gases and molten lava: no atmosphere, no wind, no water, no rainbows, and no life. Through the processes of time and the unconscious will of the universe there emerged one event after another to take this planet along an evolutionary path that is unique in the

This selection originally appeared in the Spring 1990 issue of *Holistic Education Review,* Vol. 3, No. 1.

history of the cosmos. Our earth is truly a miraculous set of unfolding circumstances that many of us take for granted.

Today, at a very deep level, we are beginning to unmask creation's web, where all has purpose and all has meaning. Throughout human history there have been individuals who were connected in an unconscious, spiritual way to the wholeness of life and its profound relationship to an evolving earth. However, during the last hundred years, scientific discoveries have provided the rest of us with a view of life that has the potential to transform our understanding of humanity's relationship to the whole. If we look carefully we can see how each life-form has a role, a task so to speak, and how each animal and plant has a specific range of functions that enables it to live and to contribute to the harmony of the whole.

Many of us have yet to comprehend what that role is for humanity. However, if we take an analytical view of the history of humankind, some strong patterns emerge—patterns that give us a better understanding of the human experience. It is through this analysis that new and definitive ways can be explored for educating the rising generation. (See Figure 1.)

## Humanity In Nature

Ever since human beings came into existence and began the process of understanding the environment, we have sought to uncover the mysteries of our world and universe. Unlike any other member of the animal kingdom, we have been given the power to observe and then to reflect upon that observation. We have used this power to understand the phenomena that occur in both macrocosm and microcosm. We have reasoned that such understanding will lead us to live in closer harmony with ourselves and our universe.

And so, in each epoch, humans have developed a relationship to the environment that was consonant with the latest theories concerning the unknown. From the very beginning we have sought to discover the essential nature of all things. To grasp the essence of the early human observer, all one has to do is to look closely at an infant. As we watch an infant's attempt to grasp a finger held before his or her eyes—and indeed grasp understanding—we are witnessing the early human observer. The infant is becoming aware of the subtle division between self and the outside world.

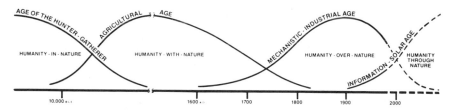

*Figure 1.* PARADIGM SHIFTS: Schematic depiction of rising and declining cultures throughout history.

Consciousness is born out of one's ability to separate "out there" from "in here." Hunting and gathering tribes functioned at the level of the infant-explorer. They lived "in" nature because they were subjected to the whims and vicissitudes of their environment. They experienced a direct connection between their own welfare and the natural order as evidenced by their total dependence on variations in weather patterns, animal migration, and vegetation cycles. Theirs was a time of being in nature and of trying to make meaning out of relationship.

A darkening sky warned tribal people to seek protection, but it also provided certain clues about where game might be found. Repetitive patterns in nature began to give early human groups a deeper understanding of their place in the world. It was a life directly connected to the environment, and there was little differentiation between "out there" and "in here." Humanity and nature were one.

During this age education was informal, consisting of the young imitating the examples of their elders. We might say it was the simplest form of experiential education. Leonard explains,

> Hunting bands have no government, courts or laws, no formal leadership, no social classes, no full-time economic specialists or trades. Labor is divided on the basis of age and sex. Rights to the band's territory are collective. Society is based on kinship ties and is egalitarian. Trade consists of reciprocity in goods, favors and labor. There is no warfare as we know it. . . . For members of the hunting band there is the Creation followed by a continual social equilibrium. Each individual life thus partakes of this mythic.[1]

That social equilibrium was disturbed and uprooted some 10,000 years ago when, commensurate with the retreat of the last ice age, a new paradigm evolved as the agricultural revolution began.

## Humanity With Nature

When the ice age diminished in intensity, our ancestors, who had been battling the elements for centuries, suddenly found themselves surrounded by flowering ground and an abundance of animals. They were instantaneously propelled into a new kind of life. In the words of Leakey, ". . . Agriculture was invented simultaneously in many different places and it diffused out from these foci to revolutionize life in much of the world in less than four hundred generations. Such is the power of cultural evolution."[2]

Among the new vegetation that appeared as the ice age came to a close was a hybrid form of wheat. A series of genetic accidents produced a variety of wheat called "bread wheat" whose ears were too tight to break up in the wind and replant itself. "Suddenly, man and the plant came together. . . . For the bread wheats can only multiply with help; therefore, man must harvest the ears and scatter their seeds; and the life of each, man and the plant, depends on the other."[3]

In the same way, human beings domesticated animals, and the agrarian society evolved. With the birth of this new life-style came the development of civilization and the expansion of knowledge—both scientific and political. Human beings began to work with nature, forming a reciprocal partnership. According to Leonard, "[The early farmer] is aware of the energy of the universe and shares the tingling connectedness of earth, sky and sun, night and day, animal and plant. He remains in the mythic of time and space.[4]

The age of Humanity With Nature was directly tied to the land. In all agricultural civilizations, land was the basis of the economy, life, culture, family structure, and politics. Human beings were no longer dominated by nature but were in the process of learning how to blend as equals with the natural environment. Education was basically informal as children learned to partake in the society by observing and experiencing. However, as civilization evolved, formal tutorial education was instituted to teach the very few who were to become priests and leaders.

When the early Greek philosophers came onto the scene, consciousness took a giant leap forward. The Greeks sought to discover the causes of natural phenomena and in so doing became the first scientific observers of the universe. During the sixth century B.C., when science, philosophy, and religion were not separated, the aim of philosophical inquiry was "to discover the essential nature or real constitution of things which they called physis."[5] Physis is the root of our word *physics*, thus, the study of the nature of things evolved in the early days of civilization. For the Greeks, logic and cause and effect ruled philosophical and scientific inquiry. This was the apex of Humanity With Nature.

Science and technology rapidly expanded until the end of the sixteenth century when new advances resulted in the industrial revolution breaking over Europe and unleashing a wave of planetary change. A new paradigm emerged.

## Humanity Over Nature

> Three hundred years ago . . . an explosion was heard that sent concussive shock waves racing across the earth, demolishing ancient societies and creating a wholly new civilization. This explosion was the industrial revolution. And the giant tidal force it set loose on the world collided with all institutions of the past and changed the way of life of millions.[6]

The architects of this new age were Francis Bacon, René Descartes, and Isaac Newton. Together they created a model of the universe that was all-knowing and all-encompassing. A new spirit of inquiry evolved that urged the scientist to be critical, to use logic ruthlessly, and to analyze everything by taking everything apart. The dominant philosophy was espoused by Descartes when he said, "Cogito ergo sum" ("I think, therefore I exist.") This Cartesian "mind over matter" philosophy formed the basis of scientific inquiry until the new physics evolved early in this century, and its residue is still felt in modern-day institutions and thought.

Prior to the time of Bacon, the goal of scientific inquiry had been wisdom: understanding the natural order and living in harmony with it; the period of Humanity With Nature. It was a *yin* or integrative purpose, and the basic attitude of the scientist was ecological. In the seventeenth century this attitude changed from *yin* to *yang*, from integration to self-assertion. For 300 years after Bacon, the goal of science was knowledge that could be used to dominate and control nature.

But it was Newton who became king of the mechanistic age. Newton's universe is a system of perfect, clearly definable order. It runs like a gigantic machine in which everything from the animate and inanimate is explainable, for everything can be broken down to basic building blocks. All is predictable and all is knowable. Newton incorporated these ideas into a new reality in his *Principia*, where he sets forth his immutable laws of motion. Leonard explains: "The world of the 'Principia' was a world of fixed measurements, objective space and time, a world of isolated cases within an all-encompassing system, and a world without angels or smells."[7]

Combined with Bacon and Descartes' framework, Newton's world of physics established the foundation for the mechanistic industrial age. All three viewed the world as a perfectly ordered giant machine that operated ad infinitum. This set the pattern for social and political institutions as well as human relationships. It was a period of Humanity Over Nature because throughout this time institutions were established that sought to define, order, and control the forces of nature. This is evidenced by the lack of environmental concern and the life-threatening deteriorating conditions that exist in our rivers, lakes, forests, oceans, and atmosphere. It is also clearly seen in the proliferation of weaponry and the nuclear arms race. More has become better, even if more means enough bombs to destroy the earth seven times over!

Nowhere is the mechanistic industrial age more conspicuous than in the field of education, where knowledge is separated into fixed categories and is parceled out in assembly-line fashion. The school favors competition over cooperation and achievement over integration. Modeled after the factory, mechanistic-age schools have a covert curriculum in punctuality, obedience, and rote repetitive work. Compulsory education throughout the world was instituted during the latter part of the nineteenth century at the height of Humanity Over Nature. It was a hierarchical-autocratic model with the teacher and school as supreme authorities.

Industrial society began to crack during the twentieth century, and this process continues today. It was predicted in the early 1900s when Western science made startling breakthroughs in two different directions: an exploration of the macrocosm to discover the origins of the cosmos, and an exploration of the microcosm to discover the intimate nature of reality. Both lines of inquiry have revealed truths about our existence and are reshaping our worldview, setting the course toward a new paradigm shift. Another crippling blow to the mechanistic age was the realization of the inevitable depletion of its energy basis; that is, if the irreplaceable fossil fuels of coal, gas, and oil continue to be used at the current rate, then they will disappear before the middle of the next century.

## Humanity Through Nature

This century has become the stage for new revelations in science, thought, and values. The authors of the drama are the physicists who paved the way for an understanding of a new reality, and all of us are the players.

Ten thousand years ago, human beings were not consciously aware of the emerging agricultural paradigm; 300 years ago, farming communities were similarly unaware of the slow shift to an industrial society. These changes occurred over very long periods of time. Today we have the capability and the knowledge to perceive the changes that are occurring because change now takes place in a matter of decades. This gives us the possibility of contributing and participating in the transition.

Although much of the scientific evidence that has given birth to this new era has been known since early in this century, it has taken some eighty years for these realizations to seep into the mainstream. Gribbin explains, "Science doesn't always progress in an orderly flow. A discovery made today may have to wait years, or decades, for its significance to be appreciated and slotted into place."[8]

The first inkling of difficulty with the Newtonian worldview came when physicists began studying elementary particles. According to Zukav, "It was the study of elementary particles that brought physicists nose to nose with the most devastating discovery: Newtonian physics does not work in the realm of the very small! The impact of that earth-shaking discovery still is reshaping our worldview."[9]

As physicists began to explore the microcosmic world, they found that classical physics could no longer explain certain phenomena. It all began when Max Planck discovered that the energy of heat radiation is not emitted continuously but in "energy packets" which Albert Einstein later called "quanta." This discontinuity of energy emission shattered the Cartesian model of the Great Machine.

The story of "quantum mechanics"—the study of the motion of quantities—is a story wrought with contradictions and inexplicable occurrences. Every time the physicists asked nature a question in an atomic experiment, nature answered with a paradox; and the more the physicists tried to clarify the situation, the sharper the paradoxes became. In their struggle to grasp this new reality, scientists became painfully aware that their basic concepts, their language, and their whole way of thinking were inadequate to describe atomic phenomena.

Out of this nebulous experience of inadequate answers evolved a new view of nature—one that merges the observer with the observed, is based on probabilities, synthesizes energy and matter, and ultimately describes the oneness of the universe. Capra tells us:

> In contrast to the mechanistic Cartesian view of the world, the world view emerging from modern physics can be characterized by words like organic, holistic, and ecological. . . . The universe is no longer seen as a machine, made up of a multitude of objects, but has to be pictured as one indivisible, dynamic whole whose parts are essentially interrelated and can be understood only as patterns of a cosmic process.[10]

In 1929 a discovery was made that is still reshaping our reality. It proved to the Western mind what some of our religious traditions and mystics had already "experienced" and "known." Throughout history these and other spiritual people have described the existence of a unifying principle in the universe. They discovered this through direct experience, while Western science allows us merely to conceptualize it. In 1929 Edwin Hubble made measurements with a very high-powered telescope and discovered that distant galaxies were moving farther and farther apart at "speeds up to a sizable fraction of the speed of light."[11] The consequence of this discovery was the realization of an expanding universe in juxtaposition with the dominant worldview of a fixed universe.

An expanding universe! Expanding from what? The most immediate connotation is that it must be expanding from a singular origin. That is, the universe had a common beginning, and all of us and everything we see, touch, smell, and know are further articulations of an explosion that occurred some 15 to 20 billion years ago. We are all one! Western science has followed in the footsteps of the Eastern mystics-psychologists and paved the way for a truly unified worldview—one that is leading us out of the mechanistic age and into the information age, into interdependence and cooperation. It is an era when humanity, realizing its role in the ever-unfolding cosmos, should begin to awaken to its personal responsibility to protect the earth from further deterioration and to become participants in the evolution of the cosmos. It is a knowing participation in nature, realizing nature through human nature. It is the age of Humanity Through Nature, a humanity that embraces nature and reclaims the innocence of Humanity In Nature.

Humanity Through Nature is a giant shift in consciousness from Humanity Over Nature. It requires individuals to "see the whole picture." Humanity Through Nature is transformative, intuitive, and beyond the mind. It is all the things that Eastern philosophers and mystics knew about consciousness. As part of Humanity Through Nature, the people of the twentieth and twenty-first centuries have several responsibilities: We need to live, by conscious choice and design, within the ecological and resource limits of the planet. We need to develop effective alternatives to our current patterns of violence, particularly war. We need to develop social, educational, and political institutions that acknowledge, appreciate, and incorporate four guiding characteristics of the emerging paradigm: democratic, experimental, humanistic, and holistic.

## The global-ecological paradigm in education

Education is the single most important of these institutions and therefore requires our immediate and direct attention. Healthy education embodies the principles of unity and potentiality. The child should be viewed as the perpetuator of humanity, in whom rests the potential for positive global transformation. Teachers then have a responsibility to help each child achieve his or her own potential. This can be accomplished in an atmosphere that fosters self-confidence and self-esteem, integrates academics with experience, and develops a sense of community among students and adults. Three individuals have made a direct impact on my thinking with regard to a new evolving form for education.

Robert Muller, recently retired assistant secretary-general of the United Nations, lectures around the world on the need for a global education. The basis of his World Core Curriculum is spelled out in his book, *New Genesis*. In it he poses the question: "How can our children go to school and learn so much detail about the past and so little about the world, its global problems, its interdependencies, its future and its international institutions?"[12] For Muller everything in the universe has meaning and importance, and he insists on giving this knowledge to children.

The founder of the Waldorf School movement, Rudolf Steiner, asserted that the basis for all pedagogical work is an insight into the living, including the nature of humanity and the world. He laid this out in great detail in his science of the spirit called Anthroposophy. His is a child-centered pedagogy taking aim at the spirit and will of the child. "Our highest endeavor must be to develop free human beings who of themselves are able to give purpose and direction to their lives," he wrote.[13]

Maria Montessori diligently applied her resources to help humankind understand, through the child, the implications and responsibilities for becoming Humanity Through Nature. By creating educational environments that meet the physical, psychological, intellectual, and spiritual needs of young people, Montessori schools all over the world support that effort.

The contributions of Muller, Steiner, and Montessori are under-recognized in the current educational climate that grasps for a return to the past. However, growing numbers of individuals and groups are emerging as catalysts for educational change. Collectively there is enough insight available to create a new conceptual framework for education; Table 1 highlights the principles and goals of such a framework.[14]

*Table 1.* **A New Framework for Education**

| Principle | Goal Summary |
|---|---|
| Democratic | To give learners a sense of their responsibility to one another and to the planet |
| Experiential | To incorporate meaningful activity into the learning experience and to relate academics to the real world |
| Humanistic | To heighten self-esteem and to allow the whole personality of the learner to develop in affective ways |
| Holistic | To provide for an integration of subject matter and to give the learner a sense of humanity's relationship to the whole, incorporating the knowledge of how everything on earth and in the universe is interdependent and interrelated |

## Application of the global-ecocentric paradigm

During the 1988-1989 school year I worked with teachers and children in Australia, New Zealand, Finland, Sweden, the Soviet Union, and the United States. My dialogue with adults centered on the need for planetary change, especially in reforming industrial age education. The children and I discussed the current state of the environment and how people can take responsibility for making this a healthier planet.

Children today possess an impressive amount of knowledge about our planet. As young as age eight or nine they discuss such complicated issues as the greenhouse effect, acid rain, holes in the ozone layer, and toxic waste. Not only are they knowledgeable about the problems, but they have the capacity to talk about the technical aspects of them. This is an accomplishment, considering that at the beginning of this decade most people were unaware of environmental issues.

Anyone who has been exposed to the media has received an exponential increase in descriptions concerning the deterioration of the environment. We have been inundated through newspapers, books, and magazines. All of the messages we receive are in the form of warnings and descriptions of impending doom. I maintain that, if we truly are going to take our human responsibility seriously, then we must not only report the current state but also offer the ingredients for recovery.

For example, the rain forests are being depleted at a rate equal to one football field per second, and this dramatic reduction is accelerating the warming of the planet from the greenhouse effect. Why, then, do we continue to cut down the rain forests? What can you and I do about a problem of this magnitude? Are multinational corporations abusing these forests for their own self-interest? If so, shouldn't we know who they are? Would foreign aid help teach less developed nations the techniques of intensive agriculture so that they would not need to eliminate more of their rain forests? With answers to questions like these, we would be empowered to act according to the needs of our planet.

And what are the earth's needs? Today we know more than we have ever known about our planet. In the 1970s James Lovelock and Lynn Margulis shared a new scientific paradigm with the world. This paradigm was given the name *Gaia*, from the name of the mythical Greek goddess, Mother Earth. The Gaia hypothesis explains that the organic and inorganic matter on earth conspire to make this a fit planet for life and that the earth is a total living system.[15] In the past decade, the Gaia hypothesis, which addresses the concept of the "living planet" has leaped from the scientific subculture to the everyday language of those who understand that humanity is part of the interconnected web of earth systems.

To demonstrate these concepts I have developed a learning system called Our Planet, Our Home. It is a series of laminated pictures and arrows that depicts all of the components of Gaia and how they work together in an interdependent system of relationships. Its purpose is to help people understand that human beings must take active responsibility for restoring the earth to a healthy condition.

During a lesson in a Moscow public school, I asked a group of nine-year-olds what was needed for life. They responded by saying water, air—then a little girl stood up and said, "mir" (peace). I believe this answer demonstrates the deep-seated desire of children to grasp a sense of the whole, a sense of what it means to take responsibility for the whole.

By describing the needs of the planet, we describe Gaia's needs: water, air, sunlight, and soil, together with living systems (plants and animals). Our Planet, Our Home details how all of these have worked together in perfect harmony for millions of years until rather recently, according to geological time. However, during the past 400 years, humanity has indulged itself and has abused our planet's resources.

This was not an intentional abuse. We really did not know any better. We did not have enough data to determine that our actions were not in the best interest of planetary health. Today, however, our numbers are growing at such a rate that the problems are rapidly becoming catastrophic. In 1900, after 3½ million years of human existence, the earth's population was 2 billion. According to the latest reports, today's population is 5 billion, and within the next 35 to 40 years that number will soar to 10 billion.

If we do not begin to live in harmony with our environment, if we continue to accumulate non-recyclable wastes, destroy the rain forests, dump pollutants into the air and water, Gaia will eventually eliminate us, and the earth will restore itself to a natural and healthy state. It is true, this complicated, interconnected system of relationships on earth would operate perfectly well without human beings. This is a lesson in humility that can be easily understood when one studies the ramifications of Gaia.

With Our Planet, Our Home we can construct a web of life that starts with plants and animals and humanity. An arrow from plants to animals/humanity shows the flow of oxygen to the atmosphere and then to people. A return arrow shows the flow of carbon dioxide. Then the children say that plants also give us food, shelter, and clothing. These picture cards are placed in the web with arrows from plants to people. At this point the children take the laminated circles of earth, water, and sunlight and show the needs of plants with directional arrows. Now, one by one, the following questions are raised: Will this web work without sunlight? No! Without earth? No! Without air? No! Without water? No! Without people? No! Then, after a moment of silence, another voice says, Yes! And suddenly there is a flurry of "yes" voices as the children discover that the earth does not need people. It is the people who need the earth!

So we have some choices. We can persist on our current path, or we can begin to act consciously to make the earth a fit place for humanity. The message I share is basic and relatively simple: Humanity created the current crisis and humanity has the potential to turn it around. Each of us must move from knowledge to action, from thinking in a new way to being a new way. This is the essence of the new global-ecocentric approach to living and learning in today's world.

## Notes

1.  G. Leonard, *The Transformation* (New York: Dell, 1972), p. 51.

2.  R. Leakey and R. Lewin, *People of the Lake* (New York: Doubleday, 1978), p. 257.

3.  J. Bronowski, *The Ascent of Man* (Boston: Little, Brown, 1973), p. 68.

4.  Leonard, *The Transformation*, p. 59.

5.  F. Capra, *The Tao of Physics* (New York: Shambhala, 1976).

6.  A. Toffler, *The Third Wave* (New York: Morrow, 1980), p. 37.

7.  Leonard, *The Transformation*, p. 144.

8.  J. Gribbin, *In Search of the Big Bang* (New York: Bantam, 1986), p. 55.

9.  G. Zukav, *The Dancing Wu Li Masters* (New York: Morrow, 1979), p. 46.

10.  F. Capra, *The Turning Point* (New York: Simon and Schuster, 1982), p. 77.

11.  Gribbin, *In Search of the Big Bang*, p. 55.

12.  R. Muller, *New Genesis* (New York: Doubleday, 1982).

13.  R. Steiner, *Education As Art* (New York: Multimedia Publishing, 1979).

14.  The conceptual framework summarized in Table 1 is fully developed in my book, *Rethinking Education* (Atlanta: Dagaz, 1989).

15.  J. Lovelock, *Gaia: A New Look at Life on Earth* (Oxford: Oxford Univ. Press, 1979) and *The Ages of Gaia* (New York: Norton, 1988).

# Ecological Literacy:
## Education for the Twenty-First Century
### by David W. Orr

*David Orr is Codirector of the Meadowcreek Project in Fox, Arkansas, an ecological education center that he founded in 1979. He is also Associate Education Editor of* Conservation Biology *and has written or edited more than thirty-five articles and three books, including* The Global Predicament: Ecological Perspectives on World Order *(1979, with Marvin Soroos). He holds a Ph.D. in International Relations from the University of Pennsylvania and taught college for eight years.*

A century ago, or even fifty years ago, humankind was a relatively insignificant force in nature. In recent decades, however, we have become an increasingly disruptive agent on a planetary scale. Human actions are now disturbing critical natural thresholds and balances. No part of the planet remains unaffected by human actions. Acid rain is changing the flora and fauna of large areas of the Northern Hemisphere. According to the Brundtland Commission report, we are turning 23,000 square miles into desert each year, while another 42,453 square miles are deforested.[1] The destruction of rain forests is contributing to the rapid extinction of plant and animal species. Of life forms now extant, fifteen to twenty percent will be gone by the year 2000. Carbon dioxide from the combustion of fossil fuels is warming the earth's climate, and human actions are now known to be the cause of the sharp decline in atmospheric ozone. In Lester Brown's words: "Never have so many systems vital to the earth's habitability been out of equilibrium simultaneously."[2]

One response to this situation is to launch a major scientific campaign, a kind of global Manhattan Project, to solve what is perceived to be a "crisis of crises."[3] Concealed within proposals of this sort that regularly come from government and universities are assumptions that:

1. This crisis of crises consists of discrete problems that are solvable, not dilemmas which, though avoidable, are not solvable.

---

This selection originally appeared in the Fall 1989 issue of *Holistic Education Review,* Vol. 2, No. 3.

2. The analytical tools and methods of reductionist science, so useful for taking things apart in order to dominate nature, can be adapted to the tasks of restoration and healing.
3. Solutions consist of value-neutral remedies that will not create even worse secondary or tertiary effects.
4. Solutions, therefore, originate at the top, from governments and corporations, and are passed down to a passive citizenry in the form of laws, policies, and technologies.
5. Hence, the public need not be ecologically literate or competent.
6. The results would be socially, ethically, politically, and humanly desirable.
7. The will to live and to sustain a humane culture can be preserved in a technocratic society.

Clearly, some part of the crisis of crises can be described accurately as problems. Some of the crises can be solved by technology, particularly those that require increased resource efficiency. The mistake, however, in proposals of this sort is the belief that we can technologize our way out of the crisis, that is, that science and technology will rescue us from the consequences of stupidity, arrogance, and ecological malfeasance. This is asking too much. Used wisely, however, they can buy us time. But time for what?

The crisis originates in the widening gulf between humankind and its natural habitat, and no science can heal this breach. At issue are the assumptions and values underlying our science, technology, economy, politics, and education. It is education, I think, that holds the key to transforming the others. If so, we must rethink both the substance and the process of education at all levels and the way we define knowledge. What will we need to know to heal the widening gulf between people and their natural habitat? What does it mean to prepare persons to live sustainably, in the words of Aldo Leopold, to go from "conqueror of the land community to plain member and citizen of it"?[4]

Against this challenge it is no small concern that young people are increasingly ecologically illiterate and alienated from natural systems. Their world is shaped by shopping malls, freeways, television, and computers. Fewer and fewer have the opportunity for regular experience with nature. They view nature as through a rearview mirror receding in the haze.

While many critics of education worry about our ability to compete with the Japanese, it is at least equally worrisome that students will not know, or care to know, that they are only a "cog in an ecological mechanism," as Leopold put it, whose well-being is ultimately dependent on the stewardship of natural systems. Most students now complete their formal schooling without any such comprehension. And why should it be otherwise? Few educational institutions have related the challenges of building a sustainable society to the learning process.

## Foundations

Earth-centered learning rests on seven propositions. The first is the recognition that *all education is environmental education.* By what is included or excluded, emphasized or ignored, students learn that they are a part of or apart from the natural world. Through all education we inculcate the ideas of careful stewardship or carelessness. Conventional education, by and large, has been a celebration of all that is human to the exclusion of our dependence on nature. As a result, students frequently resemble what Wendell Berry has called "itinerant professional vandals," persons devoid of any sense of place or stewardship, or inkling of why these are important.[5]

Second, *environmental issues are complex and cannot be understood through a single discipline or department.* Despite a decade or more of discussion and experimentation, interdisciplinary environmental education remains an unfulfilled promise. The failure occurred, I submit, because it was tried within discipline-centric institutions. A more promising approach is to reshape the larger institutional structure to function as an interdisciplinary laboratory that includes components such as agriculture, solar technologies, forestry, land management, wildlife, waste cycling, architectural design, and economics.[6] Part of the task of interdisciplinary education is the study of interactions across the boundaries of conventional knowledge and experience.

Third, *the study of place is a fundamental organizing concept for education.* To a great extent formal education prepares students to reside, not to inhabit. The difference is important. The resident is a temporary and rootless occupant who mostly needs to know where the banks and stores are in order to plug in. The inhabitant and a particular habitat cannot be separated without doing violence to both. The sum total of violence wrought by people who don't know who they are because they don't know where they are is the global environmental crisis. To reside is to live as a transient and as a stranger to one's place and inevitably to some part of self. The inhabitant and a place mutually shape each other. The resident, shaped by forces beyond himself, becomes that moral nonentity: a "consumer" supplied by invisible resource networks that damage his and others' places. The inhabitant and the local community are parts of a system that meets real needs for food, materials, economic support, and sociability. The resident's world is a complicated system that defies order, logic, and control. The inhabitant is part of a complex order that strives for harmony between human demands and ecological processes. The resident lives in a constant blizzard of possibilities engineered by other residents. The life of the inhabitant is governed by the boundaries of sufficiency, organic harmony, and the discipline of paying attention to minute particulars. For the resident, order begins from the top and proceeds downward as law and policy. For the inhabitant, order begins with self and proceeds outward. Knowledge for the resident is theoretical and abstract. Its purpose is control.

For the resident, education is akin to training, the overdevelopment of one part of self. For the inhabitant, education aims toward wholeness.

Fourth, *for inhabitants education occurs in part as a dialogue with a place and has the characteristics of good conversation.* Formal education happens mostly as a monologue of human interest, desires, and accomplishments that drowns out all other sounds. It is the logical outcome of the belief that we are alone in a dead world of inanimate matter, energy flows, and biogeochemical cycles. But true conversation can occur only if we acknowledge the existence and interests of the other. In conversation we define ourselves, but in relation to another. The quality of conversation does not rest on the brilliance of one or the other person. It is more like a dance in which the artistry is mutual.

In good conversation, words represent reality faithfully. And words have power. They can enliven or deaden, elevate or degrade, but they are never neutral, because they affect our perception and ultimately our behavior. The use of words such as *resources, manage, channelize, engineer, produce* can determine whether we are engaged in a conversation or monologue with nature. The language of nature includes the sounds of animals, whales, birds, insects, wind, and water: a language more ancient and basic than human speech. Its books are the etchings of life on the face of the land. To hear this language requires patient, disciplined study of the natural world. But it is a language for which we have an affinity.

Good conversation is unhurried. It has its own rhythm and pace. Dialogue with nature cannot be rushed; it is governed by cycles of day and night, the seasons, the pace of procreation, and the larger rhythm of evolutionary and geological time. Human sense of time is increasingly frenetic, driven by clocks, computers, and revolutions in transportation and communication.

Good conversation has form, structure, and purpose. Conversation with nature has the purpose of establishing, in Wendell Berry's words, "What is here? What will nature permit here? What will nature help us do here?" The form and structure of any conversation with the natural world is the discipline of ecology as a restorative process and healing art.

Fifth, it follows that *the way education occurs is as important as its content.* Students taught environmental awareness in a setting that does not alter their relationship to basic life support systems learn that it is sufficient to intellectualize, emote, or posture about such things without having to live differently. Environmental education ought to change the way people live, not just how they talk. This understanding of education is drawn from the writings of John Dewey, Alfred North Whitehead, J. Glenn Gray, Paulo Freire, Ivan Illich, and Eliot Wigginton. Learning in this view best occurs in response to real needs and the life situation of the learner. The radical distinctions typically drawn between teacher and student, between school and community, and between areas of knowledge are dissolved. Real learning is participatory, experiential, and interdisciplinary, not just didactic. The flow can be two ways between teachers, who function best as facilitators, and students who are expected to be active agents in defining what is learned and how.

Sixth, *experience in the natural world is both an essential part of understanding the environment, and conducive to good thinking.* Experience, properly conceived, trains the intellect to observe land carefully and to distinguish between health and its opposite. Direct experience is an antidote to indoor, abstract learning. It is also a wellspring of good thinking. Understanding nature demands a disciplined and observant intellect. But nature, in Ralph Waldo Emerson's words, is also "the vehicle of thought," a source of language, metaphor, and symbol. Natural diversity may well be the source of much of human creativity and intelligence. If so, the simplification and homogenization of ecosystems can only result in the lowering of human intelligence.

Seventh, *education relevant to the challenge of building a sustainable society will enhance the learner's competence with natural systems.* For reasons once explained by Whitehead and Dewey, practical competence is an indispensable source of good thinking. In Alfred North Whitehead's words, "It is a moot point whether the human hand created the human brain or the brain created the hand. Certainly, the connection is intimate and reciprocal."[7] Good thinking proceeds from the friction between reflective thought and real problems. Aside from its effects on thinking, practical competence will be essential if sustainability requires, as I think it does, that people take an active part in rebuilding their homes, businesses, neighborhoods, communities, and towns. Shortening supply lines for food, energy, water, materials, while recycling waste locally, implies a high degree of competence not necessary in a society of residents dependent on central vendors and experts.

## The aim: Ecological literacy

If these can be taken as the foundations of good education, what can be said of its larger purpose? In a phrase it is ecological literacy, a quality of mind that seeks out connections. It is the opposite of the specialization and narrowness characteristic of most education. The ecologically literate person closely resembles the "educated man" described by J. Glenn Gray who "has fully grasped the simple fact that his self is fully implicated in those beings around him, human and non-human, and has learned to care deeply about them."[8] Gray implies that the educated person has the knowledge necessary to comprehend interrelatedness and an attitude of care or stewardship. The definition also implies a minimum level of practical competence in order to act on the basis of knowledge and feeling. Competence can be derived only from the experience of doing, and the mastery of what Alasdair MacIntyre describes as a "practice."[9] Knowing, caring, and practical competence constitute the basis of ecological literacy. I think it no accident that these are also the core of the ancient Greek concept of *paideia.*[10]

Ecological literacy, further, implies a broad understanding of how people and societies relate to one another and to natural systems, and how they might do so sustainably. As Garrett Hardin defines it, ecological literacy ("ecolacy") culminates in the ability to ask "what then?"[11] It presumes both an awareness of the interrelatedness of life and the knowledge of how the world works as a physical system. To ask, let alone answer, "what then?" presumes understanding of concepts such as carrying capacity, overshoot, Liebig's Law of the minimum, thermodynamics, trophic levels, energetics, and succession. Ecological literacy presumes that we understand our place in the story of evolution. It is to know that our health, well-being, and ultimately our survival depend on working with, not against, natural forces. The basis for ecological literacy, then, is the comprehension of the interrelatedness of life grounded in the study of natural history, ecology, and thermodynamics. It is to understand that: "there ain't no such thing as a free lunch"; "you can never throw anything away"; and "the first law of intelligent tinkering is to keep all of the pieces." It is also to understand, with Leopold, that we live in a world of wounds senselessly inflicted on nature and on ourselves.

A second stage in ecological literacy is to know something of the speed of the crisis that is upon us. It is to know magnitudes, rates, and trends of: population growth, species extinction, soil loss, deforestation, desertification, climate change, ozone depletion, resource exhaustion, air and water pollution, toxic and radioactive contamination, resource and energy use—that is, the vital signs of the planet and its ecosystems. To become ecologically literate is to understand the human enterprise for what it is: a sudden eruption in the enormity of evolutionary time.

Ecological literacy requires a comprehension of the dynamics of the modern world. The best starting place is to read the original rationale for the domination of nature found in the writings of Francis Bacon, René Descartes, and Galileo. Here one finds the justification for the union of science with power and the case for separating ourselves from nature in order to control it more fully. To comprehend the idea of controlling nature, one must fathom the sources of the urge to power and the paradox of rational means harnessed to insane ends portrayed in Christopher Marlowe's *Doctor Faustus*, Mary Shelley's *Frankenstein*, Herman Melville's *Moby Dick*, and Fyodor Dostoyevsky's "Legend of the Grand Inquisitor."

Ecological literacy, then, requires a thorough understanding of the ways in which people and whole societies have become destructive of the natural world. The ecologically literate person will appreciate something of how social structures, religion, science, politics, technology, patriarchy, culture, agriculture, and human cussedness combine as causes of our predicament.

The diagnosis of the causes of our plight is only half of the issue. But before we can address solutions there are several issues that demand clarification. "Nature," for example, is variously portrayed as "red in tooth and claw," or like the film *Bambi*, full of sweet little critters. Economists see nature as natural resources to be used; backpackers see it as a wellspring of transcendent values. We are no more clear about our own nature, whether we are made in the image of God, or merely a machine or computer, or animal. These are not trivial, academic issues. Unless we can make reasonable distinctions between what is natural and what is not, and why that difference is important, we are liable to be at the mercy of the engineers who want to remake all of nature, including our own.

Environmental literacy also requires a broad familiarity with the development of ecological consciousness. The best history of the concept of ecology is still Donald Worster's *Nature's Economy*.[12] It is unclear whether the science of ecology will be "the last of the old sciences, or the first of the new." As the former, ecology is the science of efficient resource management. As the first of the new sciences, ecology is the basis for a broader search for pattern and meaning. As such it cannot avoid issues of values and the ethical questions raised most succinctly in Aldo Leopold's "The Land Ethic."

The study of environmental problems is an exercise in despair unless it is regarded as only the preface to the study, design, and implementation of solutions. The concept of sustainability implies a radical change in the institutions and patterns that we've come to accept as normal. It begins with ecology as the basis for the redesign of technology, cities, farms, and educational institutions, and a change in metaphors from mechanical to organic, industrial to biological. As part of the change we will need alternative measures of well-being, such as those proposed by Amory Lovins (least-cost end use analysis),[13] H.T. Odum (energy accounting),[14] and John Cobb (index of sustainable welfare).[15] Sustainability also implies a different approach that gives greater priority to technologies that are smaller in scale, less environmentally destructive, and rely on the free services of natural systems. Not infrequently technologies with these characteristics are also highly cost-effective, especially when subsidies for competing technologies are leveled out.

If sustainability represents a minority tradition, it is nonetheless a long one, dating back at least to Thomas Jefferson. No student should be considered ecologically literate until he or she has read Henry David Thoreau, Pyotr Kropotkin, John Muir, Albert Howard, Alfred North Whitehead, Mohandas Gandhi, Albert Schweitzer, Aldo Leopold, Lewis Mumford, Rachel Carson, E.F. Schumacher, and Wendell Berry. There are alternatives to the present patterns that have remained dormant or isolated, but not because they did not work, were poorly thought out, or were impractical. In contrast to the directions of modern society, this tradition emphasizes democratic participation, the extension of ethical obligations to the land community, careful ecological design, simplicity, widespread competence with natural systems, sense of place, holism, decentralization or whatever can best be decentralized, and human-scaled technologies and communities. It is a tradition dedicated to the search for patterns, unity, and connections among people of all ages, races, nationalities, and generations, and between people and the natural world. This is a tradition grounded in the belief that life is sacred and not to be expended carelessly on the ephemeral. It is a tradition that challenges militarism, injustice, ecological destruction, and authoritarianism, while it supports all actions that lead to real peace, fairness, sustainability, and the people's right to participate in decisions that affect their lives. Ultimately, it is a tradition built on a view of ourselves as finite and fallible creatures living in a world limited by natural laws.

The contrasting Promethean view, given force by the success of technology, holds that we should remove all limits, whether imposed by nature, human nature, or morality. Its slogan is found emblazoned on the advertisements of the age: "You can have it all" (Michelob Beer), or "To know no boundaries" (Merrill Lynch). The ecologically literate citizen will recognize these immediately for what they are: the stuff of epitaphs. Ecological literacy leads in other, more durable directions toward prudence, stewardship, and the celebration of the Creation.

## Notes

1.  World Commission on Environment and Development, *Our Common Future* (New York: Oxford University Press, 1987), pp. 1–23.

2.  Lester Brown, *State of the World: 1987* (New York: W.W. Norton, 1987), p. 18.

3.  The phrase is John Platt's, "What We Must Do," *Science* (28 November, 1969).

4.  Aldo Leopold, *A Sand County Almanac* (New York: Ballantine, 1966), p. 240.

5.  Wendell Berry, *Home Economics* (San Francisco: North Point Press, 1987), p. 50.

6.  On the structure of environmental education, see Lynton K. Caldwell, "Environmental Studies: Discipline or Metadiscipline," *The Environmental Professional* (1983), pp. 247–259.

7.  Alfred North Whitehead, *The Aims of Education* (New York: Free Press, 1975), p. 51.

8.  J. Glenn Gray, *Rethinking American Education* (Middletown: Wesleyan University Press, 1981), p. 39.

9.  Alasdair MacIntyre, *After Virtue* (South Bend: Notre Dame University Press, 1981), pp. 168–189.

10.  See Werner Jaeger, *Paideia: The Ideals of Greek Culture* (New York: Oxford University Press, 1945); also Lewis Mumford, *The Transformations of Man* (New York: Harper Torchbooks, 1972), pp. 169–192.

11.  Garrett Hardin, *Filters Against Folly* (New York: Penguin Books, 1985), pp. 53–69.

12.  Donald Worster, *Nature's Economy* (San Francisco: Sierra Club Books, 1977; reissued by Cambridge University Press, 1985).

13.  Amory Lovins, *Soft Energy Paths* (Cambridge: Ballinger, 1977).

14.  For the best discussion of energy accounting, see Charles Hall et al., *Energy and Resource Quality* (New York: Wiley and Sons, 1986) pp. 3–151.

15.  John Cobb, et al., "An Index of Sustainable Welfare" (1988), unpublished.

# Humanistic Education:
## Exploring the Edge

### by Jerome S. Allender
### and Donna Sclarow Allender

*Jerome S. Allender is professor of education at Temple University in the Psychoeducational Processes Program. He coordinates the initial undergraduate teacher-training course and teaches seminars in humanistic education and re-search, mental imagery, and the nuclear threat. Co-editor of* Real Learning: A Sourcebook for Teachers, *his writings have appeared in the* Journal of Humanistic Psychology, *the* Journal of Humanistic Education, *the* Confluent Education Journal, *the* Review of Educational Research, *and the* Encyclopedia of Educational Research.

*He is past president of the Association for Humanistic Education and a member of the second and fourth AHP delegations to the Soviet Union. He is most pleased when he is making some contribution toward a more humanistic world, and skiing with his family.*

*Donna Allender is co-founder and Educational Coordinator of Project Learn School in Philadelphia. She has had more than 25 years of experience in teaching, curriculum development, school organization, and educational consulting worldwide. She was a member of the fourth AHP delegation to the Soviet Union, and the coordinator of a joint US/Soviet educational seminar in Moscow. She is a longtime member of the Association for Humanistic Education and an active member of Educators for Social Responsibility.*

Our experiences on a recent visit to the Soviet Union have triggered new thoughts about humanistic education. We began to recall other vicarious and personal incongruous examples of humanistic education. We remembered our feelings in the 1960s the first time we read about Summerhill, a small residential school in rural England.[1] Just recently we were stunned and charmed by *Totto-chan*, a book about a Summerhill-like school that existed in Tokyo in the period before World War II.[2] Our

---

This selection originally appeared in the Spring 1988 issue of *Holistic Education Review*, Vol. 1, No. 1.

We want to express our appreciation to the many people who were an integral part of the projects we describe here. Special thanks to the Southeast Asia travel team, our hosts in Japan, and the members of the Soviet planning team, in particular, Fran Macy. We also appreciate the generous support of the Temple University Research and Study Leave Committee and the Project Learn School Community. One last thank you to Gene Stivers who thought to bring us the book *Totto-chan* from Japan.

own experiences with humanistic education in Japan a few years ago, and in a Thai open school a few years before that also came to mind. Reflecting on this spectrum of cross-cultural education, we noticed some telling differences within it and with our experiences as American humanistic teachers. Naturally, there are cultural differences, but there seems to be something more. We found ourselves wondering about the meaning of humanistic education. What is it really?

In general, we've not been satisfied with the occasional attempt to produce a neat and tidy definition. The 1987-1988 National Board of the Association for Humanistic Education (AHE), under the leadership of board member Mary Blankenship, produced an outline of the basic tenets of humanistic education, which included four focuses: the individual, the planet, the learning environment, and the future. A few years ago, the National Coalition for Democracy in Education, with helpful leadership from Howard Kirschenbaum, published a flyer entitled "What Humanistic Education Is and Is Not." One of the major aims was to clarify for the public how ultra-conservative accusations about the dangers to society were unfounded. Arthur Combs, who had a significant influence on the formation of AHE, succinctly outlined the parameters in an article in *Phi Delta Kappan*.[3] He related them to humanity's pressing problems, the inner life of students, and learning as an affective process. All of these definitions are helpful, but there is an arbitrariness about them that doesn't capture the spirit of their endeavors—each one different from the other as it reflects the point of view of the author. Over the last ten years, the *Journal of Humanistic Education*, appropriately, has voiced a cacophony of opinions. The article "Affective Education" in the *Encyclopedia of Educational Research* distinguishes a dozen viewpoints that might be identified as humanistic education.[4]

We have shied away from offering yet another better mousetrap and instead have simply described in a series of letters to each other the work we do in Philadelphia at Temple University and the Project Learn School. Oddly, the original letters were published in the Japanese journal, *Seito Shido*, but they were later republished in English in the *Confluent Education Journal*.[5] We covered effective learning environments, cognitive and affective learning, group processes, and issues of freedom and limits—all from the point of view of theory and practice. Many influences are evident. The contributions of Dewey, Maslow, and Rogers stand out, as well as the ferment of the 1960s and the plethora of literature that it produced.[6] Brown's concept of confluent education, and its underlying Gestalt theory, were particularly influential and helpful.[7] Even today two writers who were part of that early influence, Carl Rogers and Herb Kohl, have given us up-to-date versions of practical applications of humanistic education.[8] Today we would also focus on exploration of the untapped powers of human learning that are revealed by the literature on how the human mind functions.[9]

There are persistent and common themes in this literature that can be used to create a picture of humanistic education. There is concern for individual needs and concern for person-to-person connectedness that are meant to come before stressing achievement. Rogers' emphasis on realness, acceptance, and empathy is central. The need for balancing affective and cognitive learning is recognized. Without losing sight of this balance, the critical importance of intellectual challenge has finally come to light. Somewhat less salient, but present, is an understanding of the need to expand the powers of the human brain through such avenues as mental imagery techniques.

The problem of definition is not apparent when we are working within our own context. There are many good ideas to draw upon, and our students have shared their appreciation for our innovative efforts. The picture changes when we attempt to put our work in perspective. Cremin, in his classic book *The Transformation of the School*, describes how many achievements of progressive education were incorporated into the mainstream of educational practice and are no longer identified as progressive.[10] Ironically, or maybe quite logically, these changes in American education were finally in place about the time, the middle 1950s, that the Progressive Education Association folded. It's easy to see that what once was called progressive can eventually become traditional, and it is likely that a definition of humanistic education will not remain static either.

Teachers do not have to identify themselves as humanistic educators to apply the variety of possibilities that others have found useful and helpful, but the question persists for us. *The Lives of Children: The Story of the First Street School* is a good example of why.[11] To our knowledge, this small school of 23 children existed for only a few years in the middle 1960s. When we went to visit it in the early 1970s, it was already out of business. As one of the initial experimental free schools, its educational philosophy was aimed at maximizing freedom for growth and learning, and it served to provide an alternative for repressive conditions that its children had experienced in other schools at the time. The mark of the First Street School was *energy*. Teachers and students were involved in a high energy system that gave nearly everyone a new spark for teaching and learning. Its philosophy was incomplete when compared with our current attempts to define humanistic education, but the school felt right in its place and in its time. We are slowly coming to realize that *the meaning of humanistic education is contextual*. Our thinking about innovative schools in other cultures has helped to make the picture clearer.

### England

Neill's *Summerhill* provided us with a vivid vicarious experience. At the time, along with so many other educators, we saw in Summerhill the answer to the big problems of education. Here was a school, although small, that truly strived to give equality to students, teachers, and administrators. In weekly town meetings, everyone had one equal vote—from the youngest child to the oldest adult. "Ridiculous," some thought, and yet the school had already existed for 40 years. Students only came to class if and when they wanted. It didn't matter how they were taught, said Neill, because by choosing to learn, they were highly motivated, ready, and eager.

The message almost everyone sees in the description of the school is freedom. It was a response to methods of upbringing that created the repressed child. Even now, most of our students still see this same message in Neill's philosophy of education. Upon analysis, though, it is not difficult to understand that it was a reciprocal structure of relationships that made Summerhill work. The structure was largely carried by Neill's charisma, but it had strong roots in Freudian psychology and in a wonderful common sense. Lots of time was taken to help youngsters work through their problems, and there was a keen ability to anticipate students' needs, often before they were expressed. Achievement clearly took second place to personal growth, and because Summerhill was a residential program, there were many opportunities for the development of a strong community.

Our feeling is that the underlying foundation was *trust*. Neill was able to see tremendous potential in each child. He conveyed this belief in his words and actions. The children felt his trust and responded in kind—enough to make the program viable and exciting. Neill's attitude made it possible to work through the many difficult problems that were constantly occurring.

In some important ways, Summerhill was not a humanistic school. "With Freud as its grandfather?," Maslow and Rogers, whose theories developed in opposition to Freudian psychology, would wonder. And it certainly doesn't seem practical. Yet, it gave birth to important elements of our humanistic thinking. We think it is the climate of trust that is central.

## Japan I (Tokyo)

Discovering that there was also a "Summerhill" in Japan in the 1930s was quite a surprise. Its headmaster, Mr. Kobayashi, was not a writer, nor did he want publicity, so it took a long time for the story of Tomoe to reach us. One of his very appreciative young students, Tetsuko Kuroyanagi, is now a famous television personality in Japan. In his honor and his memory, she has written a book about the school—partly from an adult and partly from a child's view. In its original Japanese, it has sold millions of copies, and it is now available in English translation. The title, *Totto-chan: The Little Girl at the Window* includes Kuroyanagi's childhood nickname and the Japanese expression "that referred to people being 'over by the window,' meaning they were on the fringe or out in the cold."[12] Totto-chan's mother had found her way to Tomoe because her daughter had been expelled from first grade. The book is a charming account of a "free school," Japanese style.

Actually, Tomoe differed greatly from Summerhill. It is curious that Neill had acquired two old railway cars in which his students were permitted to bash about and that Mr. Kobayashi had actually set up his school in six such abandoned coaches. But this is where the similarity mostly ends. Mr. Kobayashi was much more focused on providing exciting educational alternatives for his students as the way to help them deal with their repressed nature. And for him, student achievements were very important. He believed that they built self-esteem.

At Tomoe, the teachers were encouraged to use innovative teaching methods. Mr. Kobayashi had spent many years studying the art of teaching in Japan and throughout Europe. He was particularly skilled in music and he brought to the school the methods, known as eurythmics, of the Swiss teacher and composer, Emile Jacques-Dalcroze. Rhythm was important and so were the lessons of nature in general. These concepts affected the teachers' approach to the curriculum as a whole. Mr. Kobayashi did not have a preconceived notion of success, but he did want his students to determine goals for themselves. He insisted that their achievements be ones for which they would feel inner pride. From intuitive knowledge, he and his teachers found ways to challenge each student in personal, growthful ways.

Reading *Totto-chan*, we feel the school's energy and we sense the great trust that exists between the teachers and the students, but somehow they do not seem to be the key. The significance of Japanese culture is not lost at Tomoe, and we see the spirit of the school carried in an atmosphere of *mutual respect*. Integral to Japanese culture, yet expressed in such an open way, this is how the teachers and the students create an environment for themselves that facilitates a high quality of teaching and learning. Most of all, one can feel the deep respect that Mr. Kobayashi has for each of his students.

## Japan II (Yokohama, Kyoto, Kobe)

We ourselves have visited Japan on two occasions and have spent time working with Japanese teachers and students. During our last visit in 1983, we met with members of the Japanese Association for Humanistic Education (JAHE), facilitated a teacher education workshop, and taught elementary school students English lessons as part of a cross-cultural study of mental imagery techniques. At the time, we had not yet read *Totto-chan*, and we did not visit any of today's Japanese humanistic schools. In fact, if there were any, none was notable enough to be brought to our attention in our talks with JAHE members. Consistent with the popularity of *Totto-chan*, however, there was great interest in humanistic education.

Professor Ito from the Department of Humanistic Education at Yokohama National University is a major source of energy for the humanistic education movement in Japan. Under his leadership, the University sponsored the International Meeting on Confluent Education in 1982. For our visit, he organized a brief afternoon conference for us and twenty JAHE members. There was an excellent interchange of ideas as we discussed our thoughts about humanistic education and the work we do in our respective countries. Certainly there was evidence of the role that respect plays for them in education that we subsequently noted in *Totto-chan*, but it was not a major feature of our discussions. Clearly, the modern-day Japanese educators with whom we spoke had a high regard for tradition, but they were now looking for new possibilities that might be built upon the old. It was as if they were searching for respectable, new traditions that could be used to modernize and improve the quality of education in Japan. What was striking was their *openness and excitement about new ideas.*

We had also been invited to give a teacher education workshop at the Kyoto University of Education. In a day-long meeting, we asked teachers-in-training and college professors, ten people in all, to participate in an experiential presentation on teacher-student interaction and the use of mental imagery techniques for classroom teaching. There had been warnings that the norms of Japanese culture would interfere with our usual highly interactive workshop designs. At one point, quite unsure of ourselves, the group was asked to form pairs and to spend four or five minutes each telling positive traits about themselves. Such bragging is contrary to normal polite behavior. Maybe it is because it is also impolite not to follow teachers' instructions that they, timidly at first, but finally, energetically engaged in this activity. What followed was a series of activities that emphasized and demonstrated the power of a here-and-now focus for teacher-student relationships. Photographs of the workshop reveal the same kind of intense interactions that we find in our work with Americans. The participants were not members of JAHE, yet it was clear from the concluding discussions and from the feedback that they were also excited about the new possibilities that had been opened up for them.

For us the most fascinating part of this visit to Japan was the opportunity to teach elementary school children in the area around Kobe. In all, we worked with 69 children in two schools in six different classrooms over a period of a week. With the help of our colleague and translator, Yoshia Kurato, we were able to make arrangements to collect data on the practical usefulness of mental imagery techniques that we had designed. Our students for the week, who had very little, if any, experience with humanistic approaches to teaching, were clearly delighted with the exercises we used for teaching them English lessons: writing with their eyes closed, learning words by their shape, turning meanings into pictures, associating new words with the feeling of textures, guided fantasies, and others. Their teachers assured us of the students' progress; they seemed to have gained some new tools for learning as well. Even with the burden of translation, it was possible to establish the magical rapport that sometimes comes in teaching. The children had been as open to us as had the adults with whom we had worked.

In these three instances, the highlights of this trip to Japan, we see another kind of humanistic education. It was not so much the definition that our traveling road show conveyed but the common response of each audience. For the Japanese teachers and students, their adventure came by virtue of their openness to what we offered. We suspect that humanistic education in Japan today is developing along this dimension.

## Thailand

Ten years earlier, on our first trip to the Far East, we had the opportunity to spend a week at an open school in a rural northeastern part of Thailand. With a team of six, including a photographer and a translator, we were visiting schools in Southeast Asia. Contacts at Chulalongkorn University in Bangkok encouraged us to include this school in our itinerary and gave us a letter of introduction. Connected with Khon Khaen University, the school was directed by the head of the Department of Education, Dean Saisuree Chutikul. She had been educated at the University of Indiana during the 1960s and, upon returning home, had managed to set up a model open school in Khon Khaen.

If that seems strange and unusual, you can begin to imagine how the Thais felt. As in Japan, tradition is very important in Thailand. Thai schools, although without ancient historical roots, have always looked like other schools everywhere in the world: neat rows of desk-chairs facing the teacher's desk in a rectangular room with little space to spare. Here in Khon Khaen was a beautiful campus with each class located in its own separate building. Covered walkways connected the classroom buildings with each other to form an indoor/outdoor school. There were a variety of spaces within each building, including, of course, a large classroom. But the desk-chairs and teachers' desks were absent. Tables, benches, corners, walls, and spaces on the floor offered many different activity centers. There was movement from large group to small group learning and sometimes the instruction was highly individualized.

We don't mean to imply that everything happened smoothly. The Thai teachers indicated to us in taped interviews that they had their share of difficulties making this new American model work in their culture. The teachers, the children, and the parents, too, had been placed in a world which was missing many of the normal rules that make smooth social interaction possible. Even so, the teachers expressed their optimistic commitment to what they considered an important educational experiment. Our observation of, and occasional participation in, classroom activities consistently revealed a highly supportive and challenging educational environment. There was no doubt that the children were enjoying learning, and though there was much more freedom than in their traditional schools, the students were usually busily working on their studies.

Dean Saisuree thought that the school was not as foreign as many Thais would have themselves believe. The regular Thai schools had followed and copied the development of Western notions of schooling. Her model, she said, was much more consistent with the way education had taken place in Thailand in the temple courtyards for centuries before the advent of the "modern" school. She suggested that these, the *watt* schools, were the real model for the open classroom. She felt that this provided an historical perspective that partly accounted for the program's success.

Upon reflection, it is not energy, trust, respect, even openness, or any such value that comes to mind when thinking about this school. In our opinion, the change from the Thai traditional school to the open school is mostly a matter of form. A humanistic school, from our cultural perspective, is primarily concerned with freedom for personal growth and the development of greater interpersonal responsibility. These were not the salient issues. All around us in rural Thailand, we felt a strong sense of self and nurturing social connections—among and between ages—which we attributed to a more traditional way of life. Making school freer seemed to impose very little demand for a psychological shift in the nature of the learning environment. In fact, the interviews showed that the teachers' behaviors and attitudes were not fundamentally different from when they were teaching in traditional schools. What stands out here is the concern for simply finding new ways to help children do their regular school work more effectively.

It is reasonable to wonder in what way the school is an example of humanistic education. We remember feeling how wonderfully effective the learning environment was and how many of the values expressed matched our own. The feeling appears connected with our hunch that *school* learning in and of itself is an *adventure* for these Thai students. Worthwhile achievement in their culture is often related to the fulfillment of the roles in life that traditions define. School learning, in contrast, seems to be taking these Thai children beyond what is normally expected of them. Humanistic education would be defined as teachers helping students to discover their connections with a world that is outside of their own sphere—beyond their town and maybe beyond their country. An autobiographical story of a Thai woman who grew up in an isolated village, who became a teacher, and who eventually learned English, conveys this message.[13] Intellectual knowledge serves as the critical stimulus for fostering personal and social growth. The need for the development of self and the creation of connections, in this case, is on a different frontier than it is for us.

The strength of our conjecture is supported by an observation we made of a traditional classroom in an even more rural Laotian school a few hundred miles north of Khon Khaen. In an ordinary sized classroom, 80 children sat bunched together on benches in front of long desks. Without any of the commotion that one would expect under such crowded conditions, they sat beaming as they alternately listed and recited lessons about letters, numbers, and words. For these children, the particular structure of the educational environment is not of great importance. Although the school and daily life in Khon Khaen were more modern, the feeling was similar. Indeed, as a freer school environment, one might imagine that it fostered even more excitement for the journey that these teachers and students were taking together into the unknown. From our worldview, so much of the program was focused on what we ordinarily call achievement. From another view, the daily school activities could be perceived as challenging students to broaden their concepts of self and as an opportunity for making new and responsible connections with others.

## Soviet Union I (Moscow)

We were surprised that we even considered going to the Soviet Union. To say the least, it was not on our list of the top ten places to go looking for an interesting example of humanistic education in another culture. Given our kindred backgrounds, we were particularly bothered by how the Soviet government treats refuseniks—Jews who are refused permission to emigrate. We are, however, active members of Educators for Social Responsibility (ESR), the Association for Humanistic Psychology (AHP), and AHE. As a result, we have participated in a host of activities centered on working for world peace. Given our professional interests, it was natural for Fran Macy, the director of AHP's Soviet Education Project, to ask us to form an American team that would plan with the Soviets, for the fall of 1986, a small conference on humanistic education. Macy had had long talks with Alexei Matyushkin, the director of the Institute of General and Educational Psychology of the Moscow Academy of Pedagogical Sciences. Matyushkin wanted a two-day seminar focused on such issues as creativity, teaching, research, and psychological services from a humanistic point of view. The conference was one part of the itinerary for a 30-person American delegation of humanistic psychologists and educators who would visit the Soviet Union for two weeks as citizen diplomats. Adventurous spirits that we are, although feeling a little foolish, we accepted the invitation and the responsibility.[14]

The difficulty of planning the conference proved to reveal yet another view of humanistic education. The conference actually had two parts for the Soviets. In the first part, members of the Institute met with Carl Rogers a few weeks before we arrived. For the second part, the common Soviet/American goal was to design a seminar built on Rogerian concepts and thinking. To accomplish this goal effectively, the American planners, five of us altogether, insisted that the design itself had to be a model of humanistic educational process. Initial correspondence led us to believe that Matyushkin and his colleagues understood and agreed with this premise.

We proposed that the conference would include our delegation and an equal number of Soviets—60 in all. There would be six small groups, again with equal membership from both countries, each with a translator or two (a combination of ours and theirs). The task of the small groups would be to discuss informal presentations by three or four members on agreed-upon themes. In an effort to build a close working relationship, the plan provided that these groups would meet for at least four two-hour-long work sessions. We would assign a process person to each of the small groups who would assist the group in two tasks: to hear each other carefully and to bring productive material to the plenary sessions. Plenary meetings for the beginning and end of each day were planned as process-only sessions. This would be a time for expressing expectations, exploring differences, problem solving, and sharing the accomplishments and questions that resulted from the work of the small groups. Given the professional experience of the planning team, we were prepared to lead the large group with structured activities that have a high probability for creating conditions that would facilitate real dialogue. It was our hope to demonstrate in action, through the work of the small and large groups, what we meant by humanistic education. Achieving some understanding and common meaning with the Soviets was one of our goals, but the process of how we worked together was of greater importance to us.

Good theory. It wasn't so much that the Soviets disagreed; they had to contend with their own agenda. Besides correspondence and telephone, there were three critical planning meetings: in Washington, in Helsinki, and in Moscow. All along there was marvelous good will on both sides, but the negotiations seriously brought into question whether this would be a humanistic conference. Most important for the Soviets was not to have a series of papers read and translated. That, they knew, would be deadly. Matyushkin, however, insisted that we had to allow for as many people as wanted to participate, maybe three hundred. He was under a lot of pressure after Rogers' presentation not to exclude any members of the Academy who wanted to be there. Furthermore, plenary sessions had to be formal presentations. He wanted everyone to hear about the Project Learn School, an action research design for changing school climate, and our views on future scenarios. Technical problems reduced the time for the small groups and their number to four. Agreement on the content, interestingly enough, had evolved easily: humanistic teaching, humanistic research, creativity, and psychological assistance.

Despite these difficulties, the negotiations begun months before accomplished our goals. A couple of paragraphs from the planning team report tell the story:

> What finally became of this seminar for which we had so excitedly planned during the summer months is intriguing. Our interactions with the Soviets had already resulted in some close relations. The translators on both sides were caring, involved professionals; they added an important dimension and depth to the dialogue that had already begun. As we talked with Professor Matyushkin the day before the meeting, we could see that he was very excited about this seminar and felt it was a radical endeavor. He was committed to the idea that presentations should involve all those present and that papers should not be read. This, it seemed, was a radical departure from the usual Soviet seminar. He was excited about our being there and was clear about what he considered important for the success of this endeavor: an open exchange of ideas was the essence. In this exchange, we began to understand one important element of humanistic education. Matyushkin recognized the cutting edge of his own culture.

> The small groups . . . provided opportunities for stimulating discussions for 30 to 60 people each day. For some, the Soviets had prepared presentations, and in others, the Americans presented. In all of them, there was thoughtful interaction among those present.

The plenary sessions with two hundred people in attendance were as different from our preconceived ideas as night and day . . . . Following the presenters' directions, the Soviet audience was more than willing to move around and form small groups. In fact, they moved into small groups as if they had done this all their lives and didn't seem to mind the inconvenience of the room or the extra time it took . . . . Our experience in Moscow showed us that, like us, many Soviets were responding to a universal human need that creates the energy for making education more humanistic. Our vision of a humanistic seminar and the Soviet vision interacted to produce an experience far richer for us all than either one by itself could have achieved.[15]

Our experience in Moscow was mind boggling. After the effort we had made in reframing our thinking to understand how the open school in Khon Khaen, Thailand, is an example of humanistic education, one might imagine oneself prepared to recognize how preconceptions block seeing the world of others. With hindsight, we now know that the differences between ourselves and the Thais is simply cultural. "Simply" we say because there is no underlying psychological tension between us that marks us as potentially mortal enemies. Between ourselves and the Soviets, there was a strong commitment to think differently. Because of the tension, we reminded ourselves constantly that we are not alike in important ways.

There is good reason, then, to appreciate the unique results of this small conference. Throughout this travelogue, we have shown how looking at education in other cultures is an opportunity for expanding our horizons and our vision. Here, though, special risks were taken. For the Soviets, the key to humanistic education was an open exchange of ideas. They negotiated with us in a spirit of real dialogue because of their commitment to this. It is no small risk in a country where one's commitment to ideology is under close scrutiny. Humanistic education in this instance turned out to be an exploration by Soviets and Americans, together, of very troublesome ground. How we might grow personally and socially in peace, in fact, is the ultimate humanistic planetary question. In a tribute to the memory of Carl Rogers, John Vasconcellos remembered him saying after his return from Moscow,

The Soviet Minister of Education invited me to Russia to consult on individualizing instruction and fostering creativity. I asked him, "Isn't it somewhat dangerous to be doing that in a collective society?" and he replied, "Yes, but not as dangerous as not doing it."[16]

Negotiation in a climate where there is truly an open exchange of ideas is yet another view of humanistic education.

## Soviet Union II (Tblisi)

Our last stop on this educational world tour is Tblisi, Georgia, in the Soviet southwest. This is a city of a million people nestled in a horseshoe valley among high mountains not far from Turkey. Its character is more Mediterranean than Russian, and the delegation had come here to broaden its impressions of the Soviet Union. The feeling is not the same as Moscow. The climate is warmer, the food is middle-eastern, the people initially are more expressive. Even the language is different. Among themselves, Georgian is spoken, not Russian.

Our big surprise here was Experimental School Number One. Our itinerary had included schools in Moscow, Leningrad, and Tblisi. Because the others we visited were also called experimental, our impression was that all Soviet schools must be very traditional. Innovation referred to equipment and architecture, subject specialties, and the education of faculty. But from the moment we entered this building, we knew it was unusual; the feeling was familiar.

Throughout the school, there was a constant bustle of activity. We were immediately reminded of Project Learn School in Philadelphia.[17] The halls were lined with children's paintings. In these same halls, with and without the presence of teachers, students were engaged and involved in small group activities such as language-learning games, art projects, chess, and others. The structure of the classrooms did look quite traditional, but the interaction level was bouncy and energetic. As part of their learning activities, students interacted with each other as well as with the teachers. Small groups had created a record of their class work in books they themselves made. Included was everything from stories, academic projects, and art work to baby pictures. Each book was a unique history of the group over the years. There were other opportunities for self-expression, and even in large group lessons, the teachers were particularly sensitive to individual differences. Some aspects of the teacher-student relationship were formal, but they were coupled with an ease on the part of the students and caring on the part of the adults. The high priority that was placed in the school on relationships was palpable as we watched administrators and teachers relating to students, teachers with other teachers, and students with other students.

The school's founder and director is Dr. Amanashvili, who is also head of an educational research institute in Tblisi. His charismatic leadership was immediately obvious. He first introduced himself to us by teaching language and math lessons to a first year class. He demonstrated his skill as a master teacher using innovative methods with games, problem solving, imagery, chanting, whispers, movement, and touch. It was a joy to watch how delighted the children were as Amanashvili moved hurriedly from child to child, their eyes shut, folding the number of fingers they held up to let them know that an answer to an arithmetic problem was correct—quietly changing their fingers if they had a different answer. Teachers in other classrooms demonstrated similar skills.

Later in the day, through dinner and late into the evening, we had a chance to talk at length with Amanashvili about the school's program. It was particularly startling to find so many similarities with Project Learn when we recognized at the outset that the alternative school in Philadelphia has only 65 students and Experimental School No. One has 2500! In both places, it is assumed that quality education first of all depends upon *connections* between everyone involved: children, teachers, administrators, parents, and whoever else might have a role. We found that we agreed on the importance of affective learning, especially as a balance for the attention that is always given to cognitive learning in each of our cultures. We also agreed on the need for teachers and students to develop common meaning, the value of cooperative planning, and the responsibility that education has to help create a more peaceful world. Because we knew it was essential to the accomplishment of these goals, neither program emphasizes tests. Unusual for the United States, and unheard of in the Soviet Union, in neither school do students receive grades.

Finding so much in common with the Soviets was disquieting. We have unresolved personal concerns and, more remote but equally troublesome, constantly brewing political tensions. In Moscow, we had good *talks* about humanistic education, and we found areas of agreement that offer promise for continued work together. That is the general expectation for citizen diplomacy; more camaraderie is suspect. It was beyond our ken to imagine we would find humanistic concepts not only endorsed, but active in a real live school. Further, the contextual key element in Tblisi required no new perspective for it to be understood. It took some doing to appreciate what humanistic education meant for the conference in Moscow. Not so for our understanding in Tblisi; it literally could have gone without saying. One has to reframe the concept of a climate for negotiation to understand how that is an example of humanistic education, but connected relationships are sine qua non.

Don't let our exuberance be misleading. Experimental School No. One is as unusual in the USSR as it would be in the USA. It doesn't seem to be so "over by the window," as Kuroyanagi would say, but it in no way represents mainstream Soviet educational theory or practice. From our discussions with Amanashvili and others, we learned that he is part of the educational and political establishment. It is reasonable to believe that no educational innovation could survive in the USSR unless it were connected with the power structure. The reason for Project Learn's viability in our country is quite different. Put these reasons aside; it is more important to think about the role that both of these schools play in their respective societies.

## Exploring the edge

What role does humanistic education play in any society? The memory of our personal experiences as children growing up with the faults of American education sometimes gives our work as humanistic educators a missionary zeal. There is an urge to review all of the different definitions we have encountered and to combine them into one grand plan. It is appealing, too, to invent some broad concepts that will encompass the experiences we have told of humanistic education in cultures that are so different. "See," we might say, "look at these common problems and pay attention to the universal human need that is being expressed." It is tempting to clearly raise a flag and argue and fight for what one believes is right. This response is all too human, but it is not creative.

A few minds are changed, and a few comrades are won to one's side. It is a dance that mirrors all of mankind's problems, and it is woefully inept. It seems more insightful for us to focus on the differences that have been highlighted. In every instance, there is a glint in the beholders' eyes that tells us that quality education is in progress. You can't miss it. The differences tell us something, and we need to ferret out the message.

In the beginning we noted the National Coalition for Democracy in Education's flyer, "What Humanistic Education Is and Is Not." For the Coalition, "humanistic education is an educational approach." It teaches a wide variety of skills, it is humane, and it deals with basic human concerns. Included are the teaching of basics, values education, and the goals and involvement of parents. Humanistic education is considered essential preparation for democracy, and years of research support are cited. Some troublesome "nots" are also mentioned like religion and psychotherapy. The description is quite comprehensive yet agreeably argues that humanistic education is not the only valid approach to schooling. The wording is assertive, specific, clear, and fair. It may well be that all or most of our international examples could be fitted into this broad view. But something gets missed by doing so. Humanistic education, in these terms, is just another educational method. It becomes one more variation after progressive schools, Steiner schools, Montessori schools, alternative schools, open schools, etc. Something is missing when we look at humanistic education in this way.

Metaphorically, we think of our examples as gems to which we, rather than comment from the distance on their overall beauty, need to come up close and notice which facets are reflecting special light. In each country, special problems are being addressed which insightfully reflect relevant educational issues, and the issues are related to the larger cultural context. The meaning of each of these approaches to education is only understandable within its context. When the context shifts, so does the meaning of humanistic education.

At the First Street School, Summerhill and Tomoe, there is a specific focus which is responsive to a matching need. The mission of the First Street School was to release blocked energy. The teachers felt that the children suffered primarily from the repressive conditions of their earlier school experiences. An educational environment that removed these repressive conditions released energy that could be focused and utilized for the joy of learning. At Summerhill, Neill was primarily concerned with the children's belief in their self-worth which he felt was undermined by general child-rearing practices. Repression played its part in his theorizing, but it isn't the key. Offering what seemed to be unlimited amounts of trust shook children loose from the self- concepts with which they arrived at the school. Its democratic process, of one vote for every person of whatever age, powerfully demonstrated Neill's belief and trust in every student. Tomoe too had its mark. Mr. Kobayashi turned Japan's traditional high regard for respect into self-respect. He would not imagine that the children should be encouraged to disrespect or disregard their cultural mores. For him, one simply must nurture the budding natures of children and help them to appreciate their own unique achievements. He successfully broadened his students' worldview so that there was more room for them to grow.

To understand our personal experience in Japan, at the open school in Thailand, and at the conference in Moscow required significant shifts in our own worldviews. Japanese teachers and students alike responded to humanistic educational experiences with an openness that initially we believed was uncharacteristic of their culture. But they showed themselves capable of suspending their need for tradition and allowed themselves to become fully engaged in our activities and exercises. Our experience at the Thai school was much different. The school's program at first looked mostly like changes in form. Only from a broader cultural view was it possible to see how the encouragement of greater academic achievement was the program's mark as a humanistic endeavor. The more informal classroom structure was less important than the educational need to balance cognitive and affective learning. In this case, it was the intellectual pursuits that needed bolstering as a means to personal and social growth. Shifting our perspective in Moscow was even more difficult. As Americans, the cultural significance we attribute to negotiation and the open exchange of ideas is second nature to us. We don't normally think of an emphasis on them as a humanistic endeavor. The problems in Moscow are substantially different. We found people in the Soviet Union today who are striving to achieve a new balance of cognitive and affective learning in education. Humanistic education means allowing for an honest struggle between collective ideology and personal growth. The people we met in Moscow are aware that their views of both have to be modified.

Just as we had grown accustomed to finding such telling differences everywhere, we discovered an alternative school in Tblisi, Georgia, USSR that reminded us of home. The key characteristic, for us, of Experimental School No. One and Project Learn School is connection. Reciprocal relationships exist between teachers and students, as well as among teachers and students themselves, that reflect an understanding of each others' needs, mutual caring, and a respect for each others' power—the rightful power of the teachers and the rightful power of the students. The usual tension that is often present when the exercise of power only goes in one direction is absent. These learning environments, like all others, are not utopian, but they do have a noticeably higher level of enjoyable and productive interpersonal interaction. Visitors usually see it immediately and comment on it frequently—just as we did during our short visit to Experimental School No. One. There is an easier chance for mutually satisfying goals aimed at personal and social growth.

We see these experiences as exploring the edge of yet uncharted possibilities in their specific cultural context. There is a frontier in view, and these examples of humanistic education, each with its own mark, are evidence of exploration. If the work of these educators is a response to an underlying universal need, it is surely some force that impels us to explore the edge. Without a doubt, there is a complementary force that draws on us to maintain traditions. Peddiwell's *The Saber-Tooth Curriculum* vividly comes to mind. The pressure of tradition on education is cleverly satirized in his example of a curriculum that requires learning how to scare away saber-tooth tigers after they are already extinct.[18] Despite excesses, the maintenance of tradition and the exploration of edges are fundamental aspects of any culture. Survival and growth depend upon these processes; they are a symmetrical pair of universal needs. The role of humanistic education, we feel, is to explore the edge for new educational possibilities—when that edge is likely to nurture personal and social growth.

What happens in schools mirrors what is happening in cultures in general. The same forces interplay on science, religion, art, and probably all of humankind's arenas. There is an enormous quantity of discussion, for example, on how science impedes its own progress as it stimulates exciting discoveries. Kuhn shows how both tendencies are an integral part of scientific inquiry.[19] Recognizing the need for both tendencies in education is equally important. Our examples from England, Japan, Thailand, the Soviet Union, and our own country are obviously on the side of exciting new discoveries. We see this function as the role of humanistic education. It is really a question of balance. Education is rarely without numerous advocates for its traditions. Humanistic education is a force within schools that stimulates growth in the educational culture and potentially in the culture as a whole. This is a force to redress the balance that is needed when traditions in education are pulling too strongly in the direction of the past.

This view of humanistic education helps each of us to recognize our personal possibilities for acting as empowered and responsible educators. It discounts thoughts of educational practices as mainly governed by the swinging of a pendulum in each historical period. We are discouraged by notions that the effect of our actions are overridden by current philosophies, methods, and fads. We discourage ourselves when we discount our inner knowledge in the face of others' theory and research. We heighten our vulnerability when we uncritically accept the abiding pessimism of other teachers and students. There are many reasons why a humanistic educator can feel frustrated, and the difficulties are aggravated when we view ourselves as simply trying to apply another method. Empowerment comes from knowing that our job is to explore for possibilities that work in our own given context. Sometimes in growing, we feel that we are constantly facing the same old problems and that helpful solutions are beyond our creative abilities. There is no better reason for finding a new edge to explore—one that offers some other fantasies that indeed are within our power to make real.

It is most important to strive for an understanding of our own personal educational context. We aren't responsible for changing the world. The long-range effect of what each of us does is unknown; there is always the possibility that the ripples of our individual efforts will make waves.

Sometimes we wish that we hadn't made waves. Our vicarious and personal travels have made us aware of many new possibilities. For all of us, these are possibilities for finding effective avenues for personal action as humanistic educators.

## Notes

1.  A.S. Neill, *Summerhill: A Radical Approach to Child Rearing* (New York: Hart, 1960).

2.  T. Kuroyangi, *Totto-chan: The Little Girl at the Window,* trans. D. Britton (Tokyo: Kodansha International, 1981; 1982).

3.  A.W. Combs, "Humanistic Education: Too Tender for a Tough World?" *Phi Delta Kappan,* 62, 1981, 446-449.

4.  J.S. Allender, "Affective Education," in H. E. Mitzel, ed., *Encyclopedia of Educational Research,* 5th ed. (New York: Free Press, 1982).

5.  J.S. Allender and D.S. Allender, "Real Learning: A Series of Letters," *Confluent Education Journal,* 18, 1984, 1-42.

6.  J.S. Allender, "Affective Education," M.L. Silberman, J.S. Allender and J.M. Yanoff (eds.) *Real Learning: A Sourcebook for Teachers* (Boston: Little, Brown, 1976).

7.  G.I. Brown, *Human Teaching for Human Learning: An Introduction to Confluent Education* (New York: Viking, 1971).

8.  C.R. Rogers, *Freedom to Learn for the 80's* (Columbus: Merrill, 1983); H. Kohl, *Growing Minds: On Becoming a Teacher* (New York: Harper & Row, 1984).

9.  J.C. Pearce, *Magical Child: Rediscovering Nature's Plan for Our Children* (New York: Bantam, 1977); L.V. Williams, *Teaching for the Two-sided Mind: A Guide to Right Brain/Left Brain Education* (New York: Simon & Schuster, 1983).

10.  L.A. Cremin, *The Transformation of the School: Progressivism in American Education, 1876-1957* (New York: Vintage, 1961).

11.  G. Dennison, *The Lives of Children: The Story of the First Street School* (New York: Vintage, 1969).

12.  Kuroyangi, p. 18.

13.  P. Thirabutana, *Little Things* (Godalming, Surrey, Great Britain: Fontana/Collins, 1971).

14.  J.S. Allender, D.S. Allender, and L.B. Miller, "Humanistic Education Goes to Moscow," *Celebrations,* 12(4), 1987, 1-2; D.S. Allender, J.S. Allender, et al., "Humanistic Education: What Is It? Where Is It?" *AHP Perspective,* Nov. 1987, 4-5.

15.  D.S. Allender, J.S. Allender, et al., "Humanistic Education: What Is It?"

16.  J. Vasconcellos, [A tribute in memory of Carl Rogers]. *AHP Perspective,* May, 1987, 7.

17.  J.S. Allender and D.S. Allender, "Real Learning."

18.  J.A. Peddiwell, *Saber-tooth Curriculum* (New York: McGraw-Hill, 1939).

19.  T.S. Kuhn, *The Structure of Scientific Revolutions* (2nd ed.) (Chicago: University of Chicago Press, 1970).

# Holistic Peace Education

## by Sonnie McFarland

*Sonnie McFarland received a B.S. in Sociology from Brigham Young University and went on to receive Montessori certification from the American Montessori Society in 1969. She and her husband founded and directed the Shining Mountains Center for Education and Consciousness in Pueblo, Colorado (a Montessori school, adult education and yoga center) from 1972 to 1980. In 1980 Sonnie moved to the Montessori School of Denver, where she currently teaches. During this time she has served as the President of the Montessori Teachers' Association of Colorado, a consultant for the American Montessori Society, and a consultant for the Rocky Mountain Montessori Teacher Training Program.*

*In addition to her work with Montessori activities, she and her husband do parenting classes and co-direct the First Divine Science Church School in Denver. They have two children, Christian 23 and Jeannie 18.*

There is much talk and concern about the lack of peace and harmony in the world today. We as a culture are beginning to examine the possible causes of such unrest and violence throughout the world as we face ever-growing challenges to find some answers and solutions that might turn the course of destruction around. From one corner we hear the cry, "No Nukes!"; from another corner we hear the need for conflict resolution skills; from another corner we hear the cry for greater awareness and appreciation of other people and cultures; from still another corner we hear pleas to take care of the environment; others are advocating stricter discipline and law enforcement; while still others are calling to "look within" for peace. Wherein lies the answer?

I began asking myself this question some 25 years ago as I was entering the adult phase of my life and doing all I could to discern life's meaning and my purpose in it. I was at the peak of frustration with this question when I picked up a book by Maria Montessori in which she beautifully stated that the children are the hope of peace for the world and that we must learn to educate them in such a way that they will be able to develop their fullest potential as human beings and reveal to us the "spiritual embryo" of humankind. She stated over and over that the children will show us the way and that we, as adult teachers and guar-

This selection originally appeared in the Winter 1988 issue of *Holistic Education Review*, Vol. 1, No. 4.

dians, need to serve them sincerely. This message burned deeply within my soul as I read it and, as a result, I dedicated my life's work, both as a parent and educator, to the children—our hope of peace.

My earliest spiritual training instilled within me the belief that all people are divine, so as I went on to pursue my educational training, I was most comfortable with the Montessori philosophy of respect for children. Basic to this philosophy is the conviction that the child is divine and that there is a oneness and unity within everything in the Universe. Maria Montessori called this "cosmic education," which in today's terms could just as well be termed holistic education or peace education.

As my work continued, it was enriched by my experiences of becoming a mother; working on my own personal growth through various workshops, seminars, and classes; studying such persons as Carl Rogers, Abraham Maslow, Martin Buber, Carl Jung, and Rudolf Steiner; and becoming a student of yoga and meditation. Each of these experiences added significantly to the holistic dimension of my work with children over the years.

As I have come to see it, holistic education is education that recognizes and encourages the unity and harmony of all elements of the Universe. It further recognizes the full depth of all existence and sees at its core divinity, love, goodness, or peace. It seems to me that as we begin talking about the importance of peace education, we need to talk about learning to understand this core of peace within ourselves, and then move out into the world in proper relationship to the peace within all others and all elements of the Universe.

Peace education is much more than weapons control, conflict resolution, environmental awareness, discipline, cultural exchanges, etc. These are all part of peace education, but without a proper understanding of the true essence of our inner nature, peace, we will not use these techniques effectively and will not reach our goal of world peace. First we must begin our peace work by learning to understand the inner workings of ourselves. We must learn how to "purify our heart and render it burning with charity . . . ."[1] so we can recognize the essence of peace within another and relate harmoniously outside ourselves. The words to a familiar song say it clearly, "Let there be peace on earth, and let it begin with me."

Of course, this peace or inner illumination is not accomplished overnight; it is a continual process of self-observation, discrimination, and purification until one is able to experience true peace. Peace then becomes our inner teacher, our guide, and our inspiration that allows us to move out into the world in harmonious relationship with everyone and everything. Within the context of education (holistic or traditional), there needs to be peace education or education of the heart.

In a most illuminating article on "Educating the Whole Child," Dr. Edwina Hartshorn states that,

> our goal as educators must be to help our children reach their full potentials by providing both inner and outer education—to help them learn about and develop

the skills necessary to live in the world but also to help them become aware of their inner being and to understand themselves on all levels.[2]

This inner education that Edwina talks about is assisting children to understand the various functions of their body, mind, emotions, and spirit so they can consciously manage them and relate effectively to their external environment. The outer education is providing an appropriate environment, experiences, and knowledge that encourage the children to explore, discover, understand, master, and appreciate the external world of beauty. All too often in education, we focus entirely on the life without and fail to educate ourselves or others about the life within. Peace education, to me, is educating the "life within" and learning how to relate harmoniously to the "life without."

Willis Harman, President of the Institute of Noetic Sciences, further illuminated my ideas of peace when he suggested that there are three kinds of peace: (1) *enforced peace* that is gained through terror, threat, and fear; (2) *practical peace* which comes by changing the environment, developing conflict resolution skills, negotiation, disarmament, etc.; and (3) *real peace* which is the true, lasting inner peace. This peace takes a long time and is a process of dealing with self and relationships.

When we speak of peace education, we need to be aware of which level of peace we are focusing on. In my work, I am focusing primarily on the third level of peace education—that process of understanding the levels of inner self and the process of relating harmoniously to everyone and everything within one's consciousness. Over the years I have worked in the context of a Montessori environment and have added various ideas and activities that I feel have brought about greater awareness, appreciation, and expression of peace and harmony in the children. For the sake of this discussion I will be focusing primarily on the specific ideas that have contributed to this awareness in the classroom. These activities can be applied at various levels depending on the age group and can be applied effectively to most teaching styles.

I will present my ideas under four main areas:

1. Setting the Stage. This section includes preparation of the teacher, staff, environment, and the children.

2. Peace: Individual Awareness and Centering. This section includes ideas and thoughts to give the children greater awareness and mastery of their bodies, minds, and emotions so that their spirit or full potential might be more easily manifest.

3. Harmony: Interrelationships and Community. This section includes various ideas and thoughts to give the children greater awareness and mastery of the elements necessary to relate effectively outside themselves. This is based on Jack Gibb's TORI model of community (Trust-Openness-Realization-Interdependence).

4. Cultural Awareness: Global Vision of Peace and Harmony. This section includes various ideas and activities to expand the children's awareness and appreciation of other people and cultures so they can more easily apply the principles of peace and harmony globally.

While these ideas appear in an outlined sequential form, it is not necessary to use them in this systematic order. Over the years I have used all of them at various times successfully and find it useful now to present them in this particular context.

## Setting the stage

Before beginning our work in peace education, it is important to make specific preparations—to set the stage for our star, peace, to appear. This phase includes the preparation of self, staff, environment, and the children.

**Preparing self.** Maria Montessori made a statement that has been a support and strength for me throughout my years of working with children.

> The first essential is that the teacher should go through an inner, spiritual preparation—cultivate certain aptitudes in the moral order. This is the most difficult part of her training, without which all the rest is of no avail . . . . She must study how to purify her heart and render it burning with charity towards the child. She must "put on humility," and above all, learn how to serve. She must learn how to appreciate and gather in all those tiny and delicate manifestations of the opening life in the child's soul. Ability to do this can only be attained through a genuine effort towards self-perfection.
>
> This first thing, then, the would-be teacher has to acquire is what one might call a "spiritual technique." And to attain it she will have to experience something akin to a religious conversion, for it will involve a "transvaluation of values."[3]

Several ideas that stand out to me are the idea that there must be a willingness on the part of teachers to go through a "refiner's fire" to purify oneself for the sacred task of "appreciating and gathering in the tiny and delicate manifestations of the opening life in the child's soul." We, as teachers, need to go through a continual process of observing ourselves, understanding the source of our disturbances, removing the seed cause of disturbance through nonattachment, and learning how to consciously tune into our center of peace within our hearts. From this center of peace we act with love, allowing, encouraging, and appreciating the unfoldment and manifestation of peace within the children. Our work becomes that of selfless service as we act for something greater than ourselves, as we become an instrument of love.

As we become more and more in tune with this center of peace within us, we are guided by intuition and creativity. Our work becomes spontaneous, pure joy.

Some of the techniques I have used successfully to assist me in this self-preparation include the following:

1) Breath awareness. If there is one technique that has helped the most over the years, it is breath awareness. Breath and mind are close friends and each has a great effect on the other. By learning to slow down and control breath, one can quiet and center the mind. By calming the mind, one simultaneously affects the emotions in a constructive way.

> To the extent we can be fully aware of our breath and keep it even and steady, our behavior will be appropriate to the present situation, rather than determined by our unconscious emotional structures and conditioning.
>
> —Edwina Hartshorn[4]

One simple exercise is to begin breathing from the diaphragm, consciously lengthening the inhalation and the exhalation by one or two counts. Keep the inhalation and exhalation even and smooth. Practice this at all times. Observe its effect.

2) Relaxation. Being tense or stressed is the opposite of being peaceful. It is important to find some activity that releases tension and relaxes the mind and muscles each day. These might include stretching, running, golfing, swimming, hot baths, Tai Chi, yoga, etc. Learning to do total deep relaxation is most helpful. This can be done by laying with back on the floor, arms to the sides, palms up and legs about one foot apart. Begin by taking several deep, slow, even breaths. Consciously begin at the top of the head and ask each muscle group to relax. Proceed through each group systematically to the toes. Breathe deeply several more times and come back up the body relaxing. Enjoy the peace!

3) Meditation-Silence. Taking time daily to find a quiet spot where everyday concerns can be put to rest and one can communicate with the deeper peace within is one of the most healing and strengthening activities one can choose. By practicing meditation or silence we are able to consciously study the internal workings of our body, mind, emotions, and spirit so that we can have greater self-mastery. The greater the mastery of our body, mind, and emotions, the brighter our inner soul of peace can manifest itself in life and the greater will be our ability to facilitate this in others.

4) Self-acceptance. It is important to appreciate oneself, treat oneself kindly and affirm oneself continually. Remember that we are all in process and life is our teacher. We are here to learn and grow. Mistakes are part of the game. The important thing is to learn from everything and everyone we encounter. It is taking a potential stumbling block and using it for a stepping stone.

5) Love the children unconditionally. In a lecture, Dr. Gerald Jampolsky, director and founder of the Center for Attitudinal Healing, was asked what he would teach the teacher. His answer was, "I would teach *love*. I would have less school and more experience of love." He went on to state that the children represent unconditional love, the only peace there is and that to be fully alive we need to live by our hearts, rather than our eyes. We must be filled with forgiveness and give ourselves away in love. One specific exercise that has helped me be open to the possibility of unconditional love is to take some time before greeting the children to visualize them as whole and beautiful (especially those I might be having difficulty with). I see my love surrounding them and I see all of our love coming together in a mandala. I consciously offer myself as an instrument to serve the children in their journey to self-discovery and self-mastery.

6) Be a student. Remain humble and teachable in all situations and appreciate each child, person, or experience as having something to share. There are in reality no teachers or students, rather there is mutual sharing and learning. We are all a vital part of a community of learners.

One final word about preparing ourselves as teachers of children. What we are will ring louder than what we say. Our role model teaches more than any materials can. We must be manifesting peace to help others manifest peace.

**Preparing staff.**   Other adults in the classroom are a vital part of the environment. They, too, model behavior that influences the children; they, too, have something of value to offer the class. I have found that the more I appreciate my staff, utilize their talents, and honestly care about their growth and development, the more they feel comfortable to take the risk to open up and manifest the greater self within them.

**Preparing the environment.**   Just as a seed must have carefully prepared soil in which to reach its maximum potential, so must the children have a carefully prepared environment to reach their maximum potential. Following are a few specific ideas that have assisted me in creating beautiful learning environments for the children.

1) Energy spots. When establishing an environment, sit quietly in the space and get a sense of where specific activities would best take place. Where is the center of energy in the room? Where is the best spot to give group lessons? Where is a quiet spot for a library or for a peace corner? Where is a spot conducive to creative activity? Proceed to build the environment around these main areas.

2) Child's viewpoint. As the environment unfolds, keep in mind the child's point of view. Make sure that all furniture fits, pictures are at the child's eye level, shelves are the proper size, and materials are displayed simply and attractively. Sit in the middle of the floor and see the environment through the eyes of the child.

3) Provide attractive materials. Materials for the children need to be of fine quality and complete. Glass and natural wood are preferred when possible as the child's aesthetic taste is keen. If the child is given poor quality, what incentive is there to respect or care for the materials? The extra touch of matching colors, adding a piece of felt to an exercise for aesthetics, or displaying the activity in a unique basket or tray draws the child to the work.

4) Use concrete symbols. Children respond so beautifully to the use of concrete symbols to illustrate more abstract concepts. One example is to have a white peace dove in the classroom as a symbol of peace. When the children are peaceful, allow the dove to sit outside its cage and watch the children. Another symbol might be a peace candle or birthday candle that is lit at special times. Having a specific shelf to keep these "sacred" objects is ideal. This shelf with its special objects that have significant meaning to the children becomes a classroom altar that the children revere and respect. This symbolic representation is extremely powerful for the children.

5) Sensorial impression. Be aware of the overall sensorial impression of the environment. How does it look? How do the colors used affect how I feel? What is the texture of the room? How does it smell? What are the sounds upon entering? (Relaxation music playing softly has

added much to the tone of my classroom.) How does the general tone of the environment feel?

It is important that the classroom environment reflect a feeling of love, respect, and peace if we are to encourage the manifestation of peace within the children. The environment potentially facilitates as much, or more, learning for the children as the teacher. Much care, thought, and love needs to go into its preparation.

**Preparing the children.**   When I begin a new year with the children, I emphasize a few specific ideas that help set a tone of peace and awareness among them.

1) Focus on the peace within the child. There is a beautiful book entitled *Something Special Within*[5] that I read each year to the children. It illustrates vividly the idea that within each person is a lovelight. It explains what kinds of things make it bright and what kinds of things make it become dim. Several ideas are given to make the light grow brighter when it becomes dim. We refer often to our lovelight throughout the year as it becomes a concrete symbol of inner peace. We have a specific lovelight candle that sits on a table in our peace corner as a reminder of the inner light within each of us. Children can use this peace corner when they feel a need to center, rekindle, or enjoy their inner peace.

2) Focus on the purpose of their being in school. Help the children understand that their purpose for being in the classroom is to allow their lovelight or peace to shine and to learn how to understand and relate harmoniously to others and life around them.

3) Establish ground rules from a position of peace. Present the ground rules as agreements necessary to show respect for other's peace. We talk softly so others can concentrate. We walk rather than run in the classroom so we don't disturb other's work, etc.

4) Encourage cooperation. It is important to encourage and appreciate instances where the children cooperate and share. There are many opportunities to use these words and express joy when seeing cooperation and sharing.

5) Show respect for everything in the environment. This means that it is important to help the children develop respect for the animals, plants, and materials in the classroom. Grace and courtesy lessons help to focus this awareness. Sincere appreciation on the teacher's part for the smallest of gifts received sets a tone of appreciation and respect among the children.

6) Introduce the Silence Game. Just as it is important for children to learn how to move properly, it is equally as important for them to learn how to "be still." To focus on this, we make silence every day before going to work. This consists of sitting with legs crossed, hands on knees, back straight, and closing our eyes for a few seconds to listen to the sounds, feel inner peace, or listen for their name to be whispered. This activity, done daily, increases the attention span and concentration of the children significantly.

By doing some initial groundwork with these ideas, the children are more receptive and comfortable in the classroom. As their comfort level increases so does their willingness to risk to reach out, to attempt new challenges, and to let their light of peace shine.

## Peace, individual awareness, and centering

After "setting the stage," some specific activities to help the children become more aware of how their body, mind, emotions, and spirit operate are useful as they begin to realize that they have some control over themselves and their lives.

**Body.** Since we can see, feel, and touch the body on a material level, it is probably the easiest place to begin as we assist children in understanding its functions and being able to consciously use if effectively.

We might begin our study by focusing on simple body parts for a preschool age group. Having them work with body part puzzles and cards helps them learn the names of some of the more obscure parts. Having them trace their own body and label the parts is exciting as are records and games such as "Simon Says." Along with this study, it is important to stress the importance and use of each part. After having focused on the body parts, the call to Silence becomes more real as you suggest the possibility that the children make each part be still.

Other areas of focus for all age groups are the organs and various internal systems of the body. This might include the stomach and digestive system, the lungs and respiratory system, and the heart and the circulatory system. As each area is presented, emphasize the interworkings of the parts to the whole and how the proper care of each will bring about greater health, happiness, and peace. For example, when talking of the stomach, emphasize how different foods affect the body; when discussing the lungs, emphasize how the breath affects the brain and the emotions (this is a great time to add breath awareness to the Silence Game); with the heart, emphasize its need for exercise and relaxation. As children can visualize the inner workings of themselves, they will more consciously care for themselves.

The skeleton of the body is always fascinating. Learning about the bones, joints, and vertebrae are helpful as the children can visualize what allows them to move. One important area to focus on is the spinal column. Through this study, children become aware of the spinal cord that is the transmitter of the messages to the brain. The importance of posture and sitting with straight back in silence can be emphasized at this time.

Finally, the muscles can be explored. Children can develop appreciation for how their bodies move and the importance of aerobic as well as stretching exercises. Introducing them to both types is important. Developing awareness of tensing and relaxing muscles is excellent. (I have incorporated some stretching and relaxing every day prior to the Silence Game.)

In summary, as the children become conscious of the importance and interaction of the various aspects of body, they begin to develop more appreciation for it, as well as learn that they can have some control over their mental and spiritual states through conscious care and use of their body—an empowering realization, indeed.

**Mind.** To understand the function and power of mind is a lifelong study. We can, however, begin to give the children some idea of how the mind operates and how they can begin to creatively and consciously work with it.

One of the most dramatic demonstrations of mind is to focus on the senses, emphasizing that the mind gets its messages from the senses. This is particularly fun for the preschool age children, but it can be enjoyed at higher levels by older children. Various exercises that require them to discern through one of the five senses illustrates how important the senses are in knowing what is in the external environment. This introduces a study of basic nerves that carry messages to the brain.

Thoughts are powerful and affect what we feel, say, and do. It is important to help children understand that their thoughts trigger their emotions. Illustrate through various ways the power of negative, as well as positive, thoughts on feelings. Begin working with children to be aware of their thoughts and to examine them. Help them realize they can change the thoughts they have of themselves or others and can, thereby, change their feelings. Having the children repeat positive affirmations periodically can be useful, i.e., "I am a special person," or "I am strong and healthy." It is important to remember how powerful words are and realize we can make a difference in a child's life just by what we communicate to them about themselves. We need to take every opportunity to affirm the beauty of the children with whom we work.

Emotions are a direct result of how our mind operates. Assisting children to recognize them, name them, and talk about them is vital. Learning to accept, understand, and channel emotion is empowering.

Willis Harman spoke beautifully of imagination when he said, "Children can imagine so much more because they haven't been taught what isn't possible. They can believe."[6] Lots of opportunity for imagination is imperative. Appreciating and encouraging all variety of creative activity will give the children a deep sense of self-worth as well as a powerful tool to express their center of peace. I find symbols of peace (rainbows, doves, suns, for example) appearing more frequently in the creative expressions of the children as we focus on peace in the classroom.

The strength of visualization is being talked about by many people. There are those who claim that we have the power to create our reality by what we visualize. While it may not be quite so simple as this, visualization is a powerful tool and we need to give children the opportunity to practice it. *Meditating With Children*[7] is a book that gives some good ideas to start working with guided imagery. I have found it helpful to do relaxation with the children prior to a creative visualization. It can be effectively used in conjunction with specific lessons. In the study of the Native American plains culture, I have the children go on a guided visualization to seek their own Indian name.

Finally when speaking of the use of mind, it is vital that we provide learning experiences that touch both hemispheres of the brain. There are some specific exercises that can be taught children that link both hemispheres simultaneously. This comes from yoga and educational kinestheology.[8]

While the mind is always active in these and other ways, it is important for the children to have daily experience in the silence of the mind. They need to learn how to observe and control the thoughts of the mind through control of the breath so they can become aware of the deeper aspects of mind—intuition and inner peace!

**Spirit.**   When I speak of the Spirit of the child, I am referring to the deep abiding love or peace within the child's soul. Our ultimate purpose, as I see it, is to become one with this peace and manifest it in all aspects of life to fulfill our greatest potential.

I have found that as we talk about this peace and work with it in so many varied ways in the classroom, the children become more sensitive to its existence and desirous of its presence. A new consciousness of peace grows among the children, creative ideas spring from this consciousness, sharing happens more naturally, cooperation is more frequent, and love is expressed more freely. Children begin to listen to the "inner teacher," and we begin to tune in to one another on a higher level of knowing. Spontaneity and joy abound among the children as they are freed to express the peace within themselves.

We have enjoyed several activities that have reinforced these feelings of love and peace. One such activity the children do each year is give away one toy of their own to the Native American children at the Pine Ridge Indian Reservation. We, of course, talk about the "give away" principle and read *The Legend of Blue Bonnet*[9] and the Native American legend of "Jumping Mouse"[10] to illustrate this principle.

Another set of fascinating books is the Shahastra books, *The Missing Energy of Earth*[11] and *The Magical Rainbow Man*.[12] These books tell a beautiful tale of how the earth is saved by the manifestation of love. We ended up writing and doing a play based on this story.

Celebrations and rituals become very important expressions of the spirit of love and peace. Holidays and seasonal cycles present perfect opportunities to celebrate the special place within—peace. One of the most successful celebrations we have had is an annual Children's Festival of Peace—Through the Arts. Here the children have an opportunity to work with various artists in the community to express their vision of Peace. This is set up so that the children come together in the beginning to share peace songs, poems, and stories and then they go to the workshops of their choice for the morning and afternoon. At the end of the day, there is a re-gathering and the various artistic expressions of peace are shared.

## Harmony: Interrelationships and community

Peace and harmony represent, to me, a cosmic dance. I see individual peace centers reaching out and relating to other individual peace centers. If there is realization of the peace within self and the peace within another, then this relationship can be called harmony. Oppositely, when the individual is not aware of this inner peace in self or another, relationships, too often, are based on superficial, selfish, individual desires. This creates disharmony.

Martin Buber talks about two kinds of relationship attitudes, "I-It" and "I-Thou." The "I-It" type relationship comes from the individual seeing others as objects and relating to them as separate and different from self. "I-Thou," on the other hand, recognizes the peace or inner soul within self and in another and relates with total being to another's total being in a genuine meeting.

According to Buber,

> The primary word I-Thou can be spoken only with the whole being. Concentration and fusion into the whole being can never take place through my agency, nor can it ever take place without me. I become through my relation to the Thou; as I become I, I say Thou. All real living is meeting.[13]

While Buber referred primarily to relationship between human beings, I see the possibility of expanding the definitions to include animals, plants, and objects of all creation. I believe as we each become closer to our center of peace, we will more easily recognize and respect it in everyone and everything we encounter. The more peace we experience within, the more likely we are to enter into an I-Thou relationship without.

While "I-Thou" can't be forced or manipulated, one can hold oneself open to its appearance and can do some inner work to prepare oneself to receive it. Jack Gibb, a humanistic psychologist, has created a model of relationships and community that I have found very helpful, personally and professionally, over the years. He calls his model TORI: T(rust), O(penness), R(ealization), I(nterdependence). He states that as one begins to relate with trust, rather than fear, one feels more comfortable and can become more open; as one opens up, one can begin to realize more completely one's true inner nature; the realization of the inner nature of self and another creates spontaneous interdependence or community. He sees this process as a spiral repeating itself to deeper and deeper levels, ending up in "genuine meeting."[14]

It is my experience that, just as children benefit from naming, focusing, and consciously working on various aspects of finding inner peace, they benefit by consciously focusing on learning how to relate effectively outside themselves. Over the years I have followed the TORI model. While many of the techniques and ideas can be randomly applied, I feel it is helpful to have a specific unit of attention on each of the four areas.

**Trust.**    Trust is that attitude of love that is willing to take a chance and risk opening up to the possibility of union with life. It is the opposite of fear which creates barriers, negates, and destroys. Fear is our greatest enemy. Gerard G. Jampolsky, M.D. in his book, *Love Is Letting Go of Fear*, states:

> as we help ourselves and each other let go of fear, we begin to experience a personal transformation. We start to see beyond our reality as defined by the physical senses, and we enter a state of clarity in which we discover that all minds are joined, that we share a common Self, and that inner peace and Love are in fact all that are real . . . .[15]

Some experiences that can be used in the classroom include having the children take Trust Walks where one child is blindfolded and another is trusted to guide them. For older children you can do the Trust Circle where one person stands in the center of the circle and falls to the outside circle. This person must trust the group to catch him/her and pass him/her to others in the circle. The Trust Fall is good and can be demonstrated with one adult falling into the arms of another. With these exercises it is important for the children to be able to process their impressions through group discussion.

Animals in the classroom are wonderful to use to illustrate the importance of trust as they usually become nervous when children tease or otherwise disrespect them and cause the animal to lose trust. (Even the plants grow better in a climate where they feel cared for.) The story of "Hortense the Elephant" who sat on an egg because she said she would and "an elephant can be trusted 100%" is a great story of trust.

One can also focus on several other principles that are directly related to trust. They are non-harming, non-stealing, non hoarding, and non-lying. Each of these principles when applied, builds trust. Their opposites, harming, stealing, hoarding, and lying create suspicion, doubt, and distance.

Of course, the most powerful teacher of trust is deep unconditional love for the children. By feeling this in the classroom they will spontaneously begin to experience trust and respond joyously to it.

**Openness.** As we and the children develop trust and feel comfortable, we do begin to share ourselves more with others. We desire to communicate our thoughts and feelings. This is an excellent time to focus on communication skills such as active listening, "I" messages, and conflict resolution. It is a time to help children express their emotions in clear and concise ways. An excellent book on this and other peace activities is *Teaching Peace* by Ruth Fletcher.[16]

Being a model of authenticity is of major importance. As adults we need to be willing to share ourselves, to be real, to relate to the children person to person. By having a clear example of openness, the children will begin demonstrating it in their activities.

A poem, entitled "Lost Star," written by Dr. James C. McFarland illustrates the beauty of openness.

> A long lost star blinks dimly in the night.
> We wandered here, strangers from another sphere,
> A longing soul seeking to go home.
> We need not that any man should show the Way.

Rivers return eternally to the seas that gave them birth.
To think and scheme, to cling and grasp,
Draws curtains on the Light, making beggars of us all.
Not discovery, but recovery of the Center is the Way.
The divine within grows brighter—returning to the Source.
As we empty our cup, revealing our whole, becoming as a Child—
The core of creativity is opened wide.

**Realization.**    Abraham Maslow, a pioneer of the humanistic psychology movement, talked about the goal of education:

> the goal of education, the human goal, the humanistic goal, the goal so far as human beings are concerned—is ultimately the "self-actualization" of a person, the becoming fully human, the development of the fullest height that the human species can stand up to or that the particular individual can come to.[17]

This "self actualization" that Maslow refers to, is, to me, that state where one has conscious realization of inner peace and has harmony in all relationships. Of course, this is a life-long process of discovery, and at times we catch glimpses of this reality. (Maslow refers to these glimpses as "peak experiences.")

As we work with the children it is important that we take time to honor and respect the beauty within each one. Displaying their creative work, providing opportunities for them to perform and develop talents, and facilitating their sharing important things in their lives—all add to building their sense of self-esteem. One specific activity that the children enjoy is "Happy Hour." Once a week or so, one child's name is drawn from a basket. This child is the center for Happy Hour and literally sits in the center of the group of children. The group is asked to become silent and focus on some special quality of this selected child. Each child then shares what he/she appreciates or admires in the special child. Recording the sentiments is a nice touch so that the child has a memory to take home.

Another aspect of Realization is to give the children the concept of an inner teacher that will guide them. Encourage them to be still and listen for the ideas to come from within. This can be done nicely when asking children to select their individual work activities. Explain to them that the inner teacher is their peaceful nature sharing thoughts and that it is easiest to understand these ideas when they are silent.

**Interdependence.**    The happier we are with ourselves, the more likely we are to be able to reach out, share, and cooperate with others. As confidence in self rises, so does interdependence.

Providing opportunities for the children to be involved in activities such as feasts, hikes, programs, and projects develops cooperation and interdependence. It is important to involve the children as much as possible in the planning and execution of the activities so they can experience the process of interdependence.

Interdependence can be felt and described as community or the ability to relate effectively. From a sense of community or interdependence we catch a glimpse, on a micro scale, of the unity of all peoples. From this experience perhaps, our level of trust will move up a little higher and we will spiral to greater heights of openness, realization, and interdependence ad infinitum. We will gradually see the unity and oneness of all—the goal of holistic peace education.

## Cultural awareness: Global vision of peace and harmony

The natural outcome of peace within and without must eventually become worldwide peace. While this may take many years to accomplish, we can prepare the children to be open to and appreciate people of different cultures.

This can be done effectively by beginning with the study of the basic needs of all people—physical needs of food, clothing, shelter, tools, transportation, health and communication; spiritual needs of culture, adornment, and religion and ritual. From this perspective we can study cultures in relation to how the environment around them determines and influences the manner in which they meet these basic needs. Study of the Native American culture areas lends itself beautifully to this concept.

Participating in rituals and celebrations from other cultures helps develop a sense of connection. Creating and appreciating symbols of peace throughout the world is powerful and healing as is the frequent singing of peace songs.

## Conclusion

If our hope of peace is in the children, then our education must include holistic peace education. That is education that focuses on both the inner and outer education of the child. True peace will only come when we as a people know the true source of peace and can consciously have access to this source as we interact in all phases of our lives. It has been said that the children will lead us in this journey. In conclusion, I would like to share an insightful story written by Tara Bardeen, age 6:

> This Indian is taking the peace dove for his tribe. His tribe will take the peace dove to the other tribe of Indians. The Lord said that if you had a peace dove around you could not fight. So they went and they showed the tribe the peace dove. They had no war but they had peace.

> They picked up their teepees and went close to the tribe that took the peace dove to them. They lived happily. After they had seen the peace dove for a while they let him go. The Indians put a tag on him that said "Indian tribe peace dove."

## Notes

1.   E.M. Standing, *Maria Montessori: Her Life and Work* (New York: Mentor/New American Library, 1957), p. 298.

2.   Edwina Hartshorn, "Educating the Whole Child," *Dawn* 7, no. 2, (1987), p. 35.

3.   Standing, *Montessori,* p. 298.

4.   Hartshorn, "Educating," p. 36.

5.   Betts Richter, *Something Special Within* (Calif: DeVorss, 1978).

6.   Lecture given by Willis Harman in San Francisco, 1986.

7.   Deborah Rozman, *Meditating With Children: The Art of Concentration and Centering* (Calif: University of the Trees Press, 1975).

8.   Paul E. Dennison and Gail E. Dennison, *Brain Gym* (Calif: Edu-Kinesthetics, 1986).

9.   Tomie DePaola, *The Legend of Blue Bonnet* (New York: Putman, 1983).

10.   Hyemeyohsts Storm, *Seven Arrows* (New York: Ballantine, 1972), pp. 68-85.

11.   Shahastra, *The Missing Magical Energy of Earth* (Calif: Shahastra Creations, 1982).

12.   Shahastra, *The Magical Rainbow Man* (Calif: Shahastra Creations, 1981).

13.   Martin Buber, *The Way of Response* (New York: Schocken, 1966), p. 48.

14.   Jack R. Gibb, "Meaning of the Small Group Experience," in *New Perspectives on Encounter Groups*, Lawrence N. Solomon and Betty Berzon, eds. (San Francisco: Jossey-Bass, 1972), pp. 1-12.

15.   Gerald G. Jampolsky, *Love is Letting Go of Fear* (New York: Bantam, 1970).

16.   Ruth Fletcher, *Teaching Peace* (San Francisco: Harper & Row, 1986).

17.   Abraham H. Maslow, *The Farther Reaches of Human Nature* (New York: Viking, 1971), pp. 168-169.

# And the Children Shall Lead the Way

## by Linda Macrae-Campbell

*Linda Macrae-Campbell is the Director of New Horizons for Learning based in Seattle, WA and Director of Teacher Certification, Antioch University-Seattle. Her areas of expertise include comprehensive public school reform, global education, and the application of educational research to the improvement of instruction.*

Mother Earth has suffered greatly from human insensitivity. Not only are we rapidly depleting her resources and fouling her air, land, and water with pollution, we also waste our own financial resources on destructive expenditures. Current global environmental trends reveal the unhealthiness of our host planet and human priorities:

- One species a day is becoming extinct. This rate is expected to accelerate to one species every fifteen minutes by the year 2000.[1]
- Air pollution and its damage to the protective ozone layer will most likely increase world temperatures, melt the polar ice caps, raise the ocean levels, cause widespread skin cancer, and interrupt natural food chains.[2]
- In 1987 alone $900 billion were spent by the nations of the world for military purposes.[3]
- Every year fourteen billion pounds of trash is dumped into the oceans. Oil spills, industrial wastes, agricultural chemicals, and human pollution relentlessly choke our oceans and marine life to death.[4]

Such statistics are frightening and depressing. It is obvious that humanity must immediately work together to achieve peace, not only with each other, but with the world itself. Achieving peace between nations and achieving peace with the environment was the intent of American and Soviet children who met in Moscow, in April 1988. At this first youth summit, 200 Soviet and American students between the ages of 10 and 18 addressed serious environmental issues while building bridges of friendship and trust between these world superpowers.

This selection originally appeared in the Winter 1988 issue of *Holistic Education Review*, Vol. 1, No. 4.

Fifty of the 200 students attending the youth summit were American. They came from all over the United States, as citizen diplomats, ready and excited to meet the Soviet people and to encounter Soviet culture. The two-week trip to the Soviet Union was organized by Youth Ambassadors of America, based in Bellingham, Washington. This is an organization that has earned the praise not only of those who have attended its tours but also of both Ronald Reagan and Mikhail Gorbachev for its work in establishing trust between the two nations through citizen and educational exchanges.

Since 50 American children were traveling to the USSR, it was originally planned for them to work with 50 Soviet children at the summit. However, the excitement about the world's first youth summit literally spread like wildfire throughout the entire Soviet Union on the airwaves of Radio Moscow. Fifty Soviet students from Moscow did attend the four-day event with 100 additional Soviet children traveling from all corners of the world's largest country to participate in the summit as well. The Soviet sponsor for the summit was the Velikov Fund for the Survival and Development of Humanity. Mr. Velikov is Gorbachev's nuclear affairs advisor, an avid proponent of peace well known in the United States as well as his homeland. His wife Natalie also helped coordinate the tour and Natasha, their daughter, was one of the Soviet students participating in the summit.

While the hundred additional Soviet children were traveling by train to reach Moscow, our band of American students and adults first landed in Helsinki for a two-day rest to adjust to a new time schedule, bond as a group, and learn about the Soviet Union and its culture. My associate Micki McKisson and I were responsible for orienting the students to the USSR, as well as planning and facilitating the youth summit in Moscow. We wanted our American students to know much about the USSR before they arrived. In our previous travels to the Soviet Union, we became immediately aware of how much the Soviets know about us and felt it was important to take time to learn about these people and their nation as well. Through games, discussions, songs, scavenger hunts, and other processes our American students quickly learned about the geography, the government, the arts, education, history, and youth groups of the Soviet Union.

At the Leningrad airport, we were promptly whisked through customs and were met by our Sputnik guides and the Soviet children and adults who had all arranged their schedules to be with us the entire time. We spent five glorious days in Leningrad, making Soviet friends, enjoying Soviet cuisine (many of us were vegetarian and we were delighted with our excellent meals), visiting the world famous Hermitage museum, visiting Soviet schools, and adjusting to being a media event! The youth summit, we learned, was a major national event in the Soviet Union. For our television session in Leningrad about 20 Soviet children were met by 20 of our students at the studio. We were informed that the half hour television program would be broadcast to millions of Soviet homes.

We sang songs together before air time and when the show started, the children from both countries were asked to spontaneously paint a mural together that symbolized friendship between our two nations. None of the adults knew what to expect, but the children knew what they wanted to draw. What quickly emerged was a large heart, one half of it the Soviet flag and the other half, the American flag. The Soviet children painted the American flag with great care and respect. The American children, with equal care and skill, painted the Soviet flag. Around the large and beautiful heart, flowers, doves, rainbow, and poems to friendship and peace appeared. So did a few tears as we watched the children from both nations paint their desire and wishes for world peace.

Tears also flowed when one of the American students, a 17-year-old boy, was interviewed about why he wanted to come to the Soviet Union. Jeff eloquently explained that he had been sent to the USSR by the Starlight Foundation, a foundation that grants terminally ill children a wish to be fulfilled. Jeff's wish was to visit the country that so many in the US had viewed as a nation to be feared and mistrusted, and to share words of friendship, love and peace with the Soviet people.

We had so many delightful experiences in Leningrad that many of us openly stated how impossible it would be for Moscow to surpass what we had already experienced. We soon learned we had no idea what we were talking about!

We took the all-night train to Moscow. The adults did the best we could to remind our young troupe that they needed to be well rested for the summit which was a day away. Our gentle admonitions were quietly and even respectfully ignored. Everyone, adults and students alike, found too much to talk about to sleep. A huge welcome awaited us in Moscow; 150 Soviet students, teachers, friends, and well wishers greeted us as we stepped off the train.

I have often wondered about the immediate affinity that develops between Soviet and American people as soon as we meet. I feel that the instantaneous friendships form due to an unbounded curiosity for each other and a common and deep desire to replace fear with love among the citizens of both nations. I have also repeatedly found the Soviets to be so gracious, polite, charming, generous, and sincerely excited to be with us that we Americans cannot help but enjoy ourselves and our visits with newfound Soviet friends.

After we had checked into our hotel rooms, rested, and ate, we were scurried to Radio Moscow where a huge gathering and celebration had been prepared in our honor. Television cameras recorded official greetings from many well-known Soviet leaders as well as American senators. We were royally entertained with ethnic dancers, singers, Soviet rock n' roll, circus acts, and songs written and performed by students just for the opening of the youth summit. The Soviet people demonstrated their interest and support for the summit by sharing themselves, their culture and talent, and warm words of welcome.

## The youth summit

The next morning, the youth summit officially began. The summit, entitled Our Only Earth, would enable the 50 American students and the 150 Soviet students to discuss and find ways to resolve serious global problems. This summit, the first event of its kind, had three goals: to nurture citizen diplomacy between the youth of the world's two superpowers, to engage the students in meaningful dialogue about serious global problems, and to encourage them to take action. Considering the current state of affairs on the planet, Mother Earth needs the wisdom of all of her children, young and old alike. And much wisdom was revealed through the results the children achieved.

The students were organized by interest areas into committees comprised of both Soviets and Americans. Committee topics included air and ocean pollution, the destruction of tropical rain forests, endangered species, Soviet-American relations, drug and alcohol abuse, and the responsibility of educational systems for informing and preparing students to effectively address global concerns. In all, seven committees met for four days, each participating in a seven-step global problem-solving process developed by my associate Micki McKisson and myself.[5]

The students worked in their committees for four afternoons sharing information, learning more about their topics, brainstorming, evaluating, laughing, getting to know each other, going on field trips, and for some, jointly recording a song at a Soviet studio. This song, written by Soviet students, was originally performed for us at the gala Radio Moscow celebration of the summit. The opportunity arose for about 20 Soviet and American students to record the song. It is beautifully sung together in English and Russian, and the lyrics follow:

### A Slice of Heaven

Please look around.
See how wonderful the world is.
Life is ahead
And faith is all we need.

When people call
Peace will be there for us.
If you are alone,
Then peace can never be.

Now, we can throw away our fears.
Sing and in friendship let the world get closer.
Our song will fly
Over land, sea and universe,
Our love will return
Wrapped in this melody.

Give us your hand.
Open your hearts to us.
Know and believe world peace is possible.

Now, we can throw away our fears.
Sing and in friendship let the world get closer.
Now.

The final step of the youth summit process was a sharing by all committees of their plans to improve international relations and to enhance the well being of life on our planet. Through skits, songs, poems, art work, and presentations, the 200 students revealed how they planned to better their world. They felt that there was much they could do to improve the quality of life for humanity and for our gracious host planet. They also made personal commitments to turn their ideas into reality.

To heal our bodies and prevent drug abuse, the students committed themselves to four different activities:

• They felt it was critically important to discover their own talents, explore their own potential, and learn how important their lives can be to extinguish the desire to use drugs or alcohol.
• Some students planned to work to create a retreat for drug abusers and nonabusers so that positive relationships could be established in a drug-free environment.
• Others will attempt to appear on a television talk show and suggest their proposals to end drug abuse.
• Still others want to establish a variety of clubs and organizations so that young people can have many enjoyable activities to choose from in their leisure time.

Many other students at the summit addressed healing Soviet-American relations in a variety of ways:

• Some students plan to ask their schools to teach about each other's country in positive ways and to also teach about times of peace in the world with less focus on wars.
• Others want to encourage their peers to participate in youth exchanges.
• Many students wanted to learn Russian just as the Soviets begin learning English in second grade.
• A novel request some students plan to make is the dismantling of 50 Soviet and American missiles. They intend to melt the metal from the missiles and turn it into peace jewelry. This jewelry could be sold in both the USSR and the USA to raise funds for children's peace projects.

Still other students addressed the healing of Mother Earth. They felt there was much they could do to improve the environment.

• They could first learn about environmental toxins and write letters opposing their usage.
• Some students will request that each of their hometowns create a tree preserve.
• Others want to establish an animal congress to create and protect animal rights.

• Many students planned to make presentations to church and community groups about environmental problems to raise the awareness level of the general public.

The students did not stop with their committee work, however. In addition to their action plans generated at the summit, the students authored The Youth Declaration for the Future (see below). They intend to send this document to all nations on earth, signifying new priorities for a world that will soon, in another ten to twenty years, be under new management, the management of our youth of today.

With their summit committee work and presentations complete, it was time to celebrate, and celebrate we did. There was a large and generous dinner on our last evening together with a floor show provided

---

## The Youth Declaration for the Future

We, the children of today, and the future adults of the twenty-first century, desire to make a positive difference in our world and secure the survival of all life on the planet. We request that governments, in their role as representatives of the people, establish political and social priorities to enhance the welfare of all kingdoms of life. As Youth Ambassadors of the Soviet Union and the United States, we worked together in Moscow for the world's first youth summit. For four days we met to discuss how we envision our future and how we can work together to create a better world for today and tomorrow. Seven committees of students from 10 to 18 years of age declare that:

1) The youth of the world desire more avenues for communication with one another.

2) Educational systems must prepare everyone for the twenty-first century by creating a strong foundation for peace.

3) Opportunities should be provided that enable youth to develop their full potential so that substance abuse will be eliminated.

4) Individuals must take responsibility for caring for the earth that supports us.

5) Increase the love within families and communities.

6) Cultural exchanges be established to increase international trust and understanding.

7) Replace global competition with global cooperation.

This declaration is submitted by the youth of the world to every government on earth, requesting adult support in carrying out our visions for our future. We acknowledge our relationship to our planet and each other and we want all people to work together to improve the world we share, today and tomorrow.

by the Soviets and a dance that followed for everyone. The next morning we were off to the airport for a long flight home. Many of the Soviets joined us at the airport to share tearful good-byes and wishes for return visits. All of the experiences of our two-week journey would soon be memories, but the implementation of the summit projects would begin shortly. What I could not foresee was that within two or three short months after their arrival home, students would make presentations to the United Nations, be featured on television and in newspapers, do presentations to their church groups and schools, and engage in other activities making their commitments and dreams from the summit a reality.

I reflected on the work of the children during the world's first youth summit. What immediately struck me was the students' undaunted energy and enthusiasm when given meaningful tasks to address. They learned about real life problems and much more. They generated solutions and action plans to implement. They learned how to solve problems and how to resolve conflicts that arose due to language barriers, differing belief systems, or strong personal opinions. They stepped into each other's cultures for a brief period of time without judging, but acknowledging differences and similarities. And they learned that inside all people everywhere is the hope for a better life and the universal desire to personally contribute to making life better.

The adults who accompanied the students to their summit learned many things as well. We found that when adults provide children with access to information and a problem-solving process, the children will provide us with solutions to world problems that are filled with the wisdom of both head and heart. We learned that the youths' vision of the future is one full of hope, confidence and, from what we observed, great competence. It is evident that children from the United States and from the Soviet Union and, I am certain, from every nation on earth, are eager to assume important responsibilities. We, as adults, must provide them with opportunities to make meaningful contributions at all ages. Too often their eagerness dries up or gives way to cynicism when their wisdom and enthusiasm are not tapped. As adults, we can encourage children to participate in solving real life problems. When we do, we discover that the children *know* what to do and that they are capable of leading the way to the healing of our bodies, the healing of relationships between nations, and the healing of Mother Earth.

### Notes

1. Dr. Norman Myers (Editor), *Gaia: An Atlas of Planet Management* (New York: Anchor, 1984), pp. 154-155.

2. Walter Corson, ed., *Citizen's Guide to Global Issues* (Washington: Global Tomorrow Coalition, 1985), pp. 123-132.

3. Lester Brown and Edward Wolf, "Reclaiming the Future," *In Context: A Quarterly of Human Sustainable Culture*, August, 1988, pp. 8-13.

4. "Plastic in the Sea," *Nature Scope* 4, no. 2, 1988, p. 59.

5.  For six books on current global affairs for children see *Our Only Earth: A Global Problem-Solving Series* by Linda MacRae-Campbell and Micki McKisson, Zephyr Press (P.O. Box 13448-G, Tucson, AZ 85732-3448). For more information on Soviet-American Adult and Youth Exchanges, contact Youth Ambassadors of America, 119 Commercial St. Suite 440, Bellingham, WA, 98225. 206/734-6132.

# Rethinking Some
# Old Problems

# Rethinking Some Old Problems

## Introduction

### by Ron Miller

It seems that Americans have never been entirely happy with their public schools. From the time of Horace Mann through the Progressive Era to the critics of progressive education in the 1950s to the commission reports of the 1980s, some segment of the public has usually complained bitterly about how schools are run or what they teach (or, more often, what they fail to teach). Every 20 or 30 years, a major "reform" movement takes place; the furniture is rearranged, new textbooks are brought in, new credentials and more objective measurement devices are instituted. But since the establishment of mass public education in the 1830s, there has been virtually no genuine transformation of the fundamental aims and purposes of public schools, and so the cycle of discontent and reform continues.

Public education, precisely because it is public, will always be a forum for social and political conflict.[1] The overriding mission of public schooling is to ensure the perpetuation of the present culture by instilling a particular intellectual and social discipline in each aspiring generation. The stakes are high because whichever ideological or economic interests control the schools will (presumably) determine the future course of the social order. But holistic educators envision an entirely different purpose for education; as the great educator Pestalozzi put it,

> It is far from our intention to make of you men [and women] such as we are. It is equally far from our intention to make of you such men [and women] as are the majority of [people] in our time. Under our guidance you should become men [and women] such as your natures—the divine and sacred in your nature—require you to be.[2]

It is the mission of holistic educators to follow the principles of human development, to nurture the delicate unfolding of young life. To be sure, human development will always be intertwined with the process of enculturation, and this necessarily involves ideological cross-purposes; holistic educators need to recognize this fact more explicitly than they usually do. Nevertheless, I believe they are entirely correct in asserting that there are universal principles of healthy development, as well as a common spiritual essence, which to a great extent lie beyond the scope of enculturation.

Consequently, the effort to serve human development to the best of our understanding is an effort that unifies more than divides us. We can agree on fundamental principles—on core elements essential to healthy growth—and still differ in specific techniques; the colorfully diverse holistic education movement, with its Montessori and Waldorf and progressive and "free school" approaches coexisting under similar basic principles, is living proof of this. If public education can be freed from its service to the dominant culture, and be reconstrued as an aid to healthy human development, then public schools too can offer a wonderful diversity of educational approaches, satisfying diverse groups of parents and students. The critical barrier is not diversity; it is the reductionist urge for uniformity.

Given this holistic perspective, educators are rethinking the traditional problems of public education in the United States, for example, literacy, assessment, discipline, and cultural diversity. As the following section makes clear, holistic approaches offer fresh solutions to these problems. For an overview, the section begins with Mitchell Sakofs and David L. Burger's critique of the contemporary educational paradigm; in the form of a dramatic dialogue between two fictional characters (loosely based on the film, *My Dinner With Andre*), their essay explores the current obsession with "excellence" and professional technique, arguing that these overused concepts actually hinder the development of a genuinely humane education.

Then we turn to the central problem of literacy and reading instruction. Mary Lou Breitborde-Sherr points out that how we define "literacy" will affect the nature of the entire curriculum, and she argues for a critical rather than a reductionistic fact- or skill-oriented conception. Once we determine that literacy is a critical faculty—that is, a meaning-seeking and meaning-producing activity—we will demand non-reductionistic methods for teaching reading. The whole language approach answers this need directly, as Connie Weaver explains in her article. The whole language movement is a promising development in public education that could pave the way for a genuine transformation of educational thought and practice. At least four additional articles on whole language have appeared in *Holistic Education Review* since Dr. Weaver introduced our readers to it.

Next, this section examines conventional assumptions underlying measurement and evaluation of learning. Charles Hargis and Marge Terhaar-Yonkers argue that so-called "learning disabilities" are not, for the most part, inherent deficiencies in learners but a direct result of the high-pressure, one-dimensional competition set up by traditional grading practices. They call for an education which is truly individualized, one which represents the diverse talents and abilities that children bring to the classroom.

Another persistent problem in traditional schooling is the management of classrooms—or, put more accurately, the control of behavior. Given an authoritarian adult-centered model of education, children's divergent learning styles, interests, need for physical activity, and emotional conflicts are conveniently interpreted as "misbehavior." Historically, educators have attempted to suppress undesired behavior by taking advantage of their superior size and strength and inflicting violence on children. Corporal punishment is an anachronistic practice which, as Robert Fathman explains, is still used only in some parts of the United States and a handful of other nations. It is time to call it what it is—child abuse—and it is time to get rid of it. Steve Harlow's reflection on "hyperactivity" and its suppression with drugs is likewise a call to rethink the entire structure of our classrooms. Granted that some few children suffer from organic "attention deficit disorder" and genuinely need help, a much larger problem is that standard educational approaches are not flexible enough to accommodate the multiple intelligences, learning styles, and activity cycles of our children. This comes back, I would argue, to their reductionistic abhorrence of diversity.

If behavioral diversity has threatened educators, ethnic and cultural diversity has posed an even more serious threat to the policy makers whom I call the "guardians of culture." Since the early days of the republic, cultural uniformity has been a major—if not the major—aim of public education leaders. A reading of the social history of American education leaves little doubt that education policy makers have been preoccupied with the task of preserving national and cultural identity— as they define it.[3] Here, Yvonne and David Freeman discuss the unfortunate consequences of American educators' insensitivity toward minority cultures. It is significant that they recommend a whole language approach as an alternative—one which Lois Bird describes later in this volume. Donald Murphy and Juliet Ucelli, responding to the provocative writing of Lisa Delpit, attempt to understand the racial problems of urban education in a new context; educators, they argue, need to recognize that our educational system represents a social order that is perceived as oppressive by minority communities. The problems of urban education are cultural as much as they are pedagogical.

Finally, Mary Ellen Sweeney (co-editor of *Holistic Education Review* in its first two years) writes on the topic of alternative schools. Given present educational assumptions, "alternative" generally means special programs for dissatisfied, alienated, and so-called "at risk" youth; in effect, problematic students are siphoned off so that nonalternative schools can get on with their business. But holistic educators seek a *comprehensive* alternative to mainstream educational practice. We cannot blame the problems of modern education on "at-risk" kids; we must rather examine our deepest assumptions about teaching and learning; we must ask why we have put so many young people at risk in the first place. It is, I would argue, because modern education is too caught up in efforts to control behavior and homogenize thinking to address the true developmental needs of our children.

## Notes

1. For an excellent discussion of this problem, see Stephen Arons, *Compelling Belief: The Culture of American Schooling* (New York: McGraw-Hill, 1983).

2. J.H. Pestalozzi, 1809. Quoted in Kate Silber, *Pestalozzi: The Man and His Work*, 2nd ed. (London: Routledge and Kegan Paul, 1965), p. 213. A century later, Rudolf Steiner, founder of the Waldorf School movement, spoke at length about the "threefold social order"—the distinct spheres of politics, economics, and humanistic culture. Education, he insisted, must be guided by the third sphere rather than the first two, as it is now.

3. See Ron Miller, *What Are Schools For? Holistic Education in American Culture* (Brandon, VT: Holistic Education Press, 1990), chapters 1-3.

# Thoughts on Educational Excellence, Technique, and School Structures

## by Mitchell Sakofs and David L. Burger

*Mitchell Sakofs is currently the Director of Education and Research for Outward Bound USA. He is the former Executive Director of the Association for Experiential Education and a former member of the graduate faculty of the University of Colorado at Boulder, where he received his Ph.D. and served as a research associate and coordinator of a resident teacher program for the university's School of Education. Mitchell received his M.S. Ed. from Northern Illinois University in 1978 and a B.S.E. from SUNY at Cortland in 1975.*

*David L. Burger is currently involved with an innovative experiential program designed for preservice teacher training at the University of Colorado School of Education, Boulder, where he is a doctoral candidate. David has had many years of experience with teaching and adventure programming with private and public schools. David earned his Master's degree from the University of Colorado, Boulder, School of Education, 1978, and earned his B.A. from Western State College of Colorado in 1976.*

"Thoughts on Excellence" is an imaginary discourse between two university faculty members. Although sometimes light-hearted and whimsical in its format, the discussion presents ideas and concerns focusing on excellence in education and the social implications of the embrace of technique in schools. Moreover, the discussion explores how the pursuit of excellence and the embrace of technique have affected the structure of schools, as well as ideas on how schools might be restructured to become more humane and effective within the context of a new definition of the role of teacher.

This selection originally appeared in the Spring 1989 issue of *Holistic Education Review*, Vol. 2, No. 1.

*It is 7 a.m. Andrew, a university professor of some national distinction, watches the sun rise from his third floor office window. Though the sky is ablaze, he is lost in thought and therefore sees nothing. Wally, a diligent young colleague whose arms are filled with computer printouts, rushes by Andrew's door. Andrew turns.*

**Andrew:** *(Shouting)* Wally, I am concerned about the direction our public schools are moving.

**Wally:** *(In a most convivial manner)* Isn't everyone!

**Andrew:** No, Wally, I'm serious. I'm concerned. I'm concerned about public education, but perhaps what concerns me even more is how people are reacting to issues related to education and schooling. Do you know what I mean? Most people are concerned with the poor job our public schools are doing. They are concerned with the fact that teachers are not our country's best and brightest; they are concerned with gifted and talented programming; they are concerned with their children getting upwardly mobile jobs. Wally, to be perfectly honest, my concern with these issues is rooted in everyone else's hyper-concern with these issues, and their overreaction to them.

**Wally:** *(A bit taken back and with an air of seriousness)* Excuse me, Andrew. You've seen the research. You've read the reports.

**Andrew:** *(With an air of sadness and fatigue)* Yes, Wally, I've seen the research and read the reports. But it seems to me that there is a national hysteria overtaking the field of education—a hysteria which is propelling us down a road which I have grave concerns about. In many ways, I'm feeling like our teachers are being scapegoated for some serious social problems, and that the solutions which school systems are being asked or pressured to design and implement are, in fact, pathological, not curative, as they are rooted in and thus perpetuate the pathology. In fact, schools are only following those conventional mythic structures and belief systems of our culture which have proven themselves to be problematic and maladaptive.

**Wally:** *(Sensing the importance of Andrew's point)* Andrew, perhaps we better back up a bit. I feel like I'm missing some of the background, some of the things you've been thinking about since we last talked.

**Andrew:** *(With intensity)* Okay, Wally. Perhaps this will help . . . . I have three main concerns. The first centers around the idea of "excellence," the second around the idea of "technique," and the third around the hysteria which I sense exists from the interaction of the pursuit of excellence and technique, which, by the way, is intimately tied to the search for security and certainty.

**Wally:** Okay Andrew, what about excellence?

**Andrew:** Well, to begin with, who could ever have a problem with the concept of excellence? People have always pursued excellence in the things which were important to them, and the pursuit of excellence has always existed both in form and content in the schools. Granted, for some reason it feels like excellence in education appears as islands in some great sea of educational bureaucracy; however, I sense that my use of the word *excellence* differs markedly from the definition of the word which is currently unstated yet in vogue today. Moreover, I sense that the bureaucracy of public education, the system which now hungers for excellence, is responsible for the decline in excellence. In a sense, I am reminded of Pogo's statement, "We have met the enemy and he is us." The system has reduced us all to the lowest common denominator, so we do need excellence, Wally, yet what is being asked for and programmed for in the school's pursuit of excellence is simply a sophisticated form of more of the same.

**Wally:**   You've lost me.

**Andrew:**   O.K., Wally. Let me get back to the idea of excellence real briefly. To be perfectly honest, I find today's use of the word obnoxious, trite, and all hype; sure it's the word of the times—but I fear the word is being misused, for in reality the word has become the banner around which people will rally and create programs which will ultimately accelerate the demise of true education. I fear the definition of the term which schools embrace *confuses excellence with the pursuit and mastery of skills applicable to the acquisition of a well paying job in various technological fields.* Simply put, today's pursuit of excellence is directed at the mastery of concrete, objective skills, and not the integration of knowledge with insight. In a sense, Wally, the focus of our schools has become training and not education.

**Wally:**   Come on, Andrew. Granted there is some hype surrounding this issue of excellence, but it is much more than pursuit of a job. It is the pursuit of high levels of academic performance. Teachers need to demand more of their students. Teachers need to encourage their students to pursue, for example, the sciences and math, for these subjects represent high order thinking skills which essentially constitute survival knowledge for the future. Moreover, they have to encourage their students to achieve in these areas. The pursuit of excellence is a recognition that schools are places of learning and that we can't allow schools to accept the kind of rinky-dink courses which were being taught in schools during the sixties.

**Andrew:**   Wally, that was well handled rhetoric, but is it a clear, whole picture, or a reaction to modern pressures? Those so-called rinky-dink courses were much more than courses devoid of content. Wally, they were courses which spoke of values embraced by our society at that time. They were courses which encouraged students to think for themselves; they were courses which encouraged students to be human and humane. And Wally, they were courses concerned with relationships—people-to-people relationships. In my mind, Wally, when I think of survival knowledge for the future, I can't think of a more important thing to consider than knowledge of how to get along with others in this finite world. Moreover, some of those '60s courses taught kids to seek knowledge, whereas today's pursuit of excellence tends to teach kids to seek the "right" answer. And perhaps just as important as seeking the right answer, today's pursuit of excellence, at some deep and very profound level, holds as one of its highest goals the pursuit of a high paying, high tech job.

**Wally:**   *(Silence)*

**Andrew:**   What is it, Wally?

**Wally:**   Granted, the human values which were on the surface during the 1960s are not as apparent these days; however, that's no reason to blame the schools for their push for excellence. Nor is there anything wrong with wanting to get a good job when you're done with school.

**Andrew:**   You are right, Wally. There is nothing wrong with wanting a good job. We all do. However, when the overwhelming thrust of schools becomes professional training for higher salaries, absent of the questions of why and what makes a good job, then I do have a problem with it. *As you know, schools are more than simply the training grounds for industry. Schools are where people cultivate an appreciation for the world while nurturing a sense of personal and social responsibility.* The purpose behind the pursuit of excellence is what is in question. I am convinced that the intentions of educators are good, yet the purpose of education is getting lost in the limited way we approach the purpose. In short, to have an operating premise that says only objectivity works, is to limit our potential of reaching any true excellence. Wally, let me move on to my next point, for it's intimately tied to what we've been talking about. Today's pursuit of excellence, Wally, is narcissistic, and this self-serving orientation, in turn, is reinforced and fueled by the form lessons take.

**Wally:**   What do you mean by that?

**Andrew:**   Well, Wally, social evolution and human productivity have been fueled by human intellect. And perhaps the most overwhelming product of this intellect has been the development and refinement of *techniques;* in essence, techniques are the product of human intellectual activity and have enabled us to systematize functions to maximize efficiency. Thus techniques, the refinement of techniques, and the layering of techniques upon techniques, are the foundation upon which society, culture, and industry are now built. Moreover, techniques constitute the fluid superstructure upon which humanity and humane behaviors are built.

**Wally:**   *(Silence)*

**Andrew:**   There is no doubt that technique is one concept that has enabled us to begin to master the physical world. Yet despite all that technique has enabled and continues to enable us to do, I must tell you, Wally, there is something very unsatisfying and ominous about our dependency on it. There is something unsettling about how technique has infiltrated every aspect of our lives, and although there is nothing inherently evil in technique, its all-pervading nature frightens me, and the love of technique disturbs me. Moreover, when I think of teachers embracing techniques to make the pursuit of excellence efficient, I can't help but think we have missed the boat somewhere.

**Wally:**    To be honest, Andrew, I'm not sure where you are going with this. My sense is that the discovery, if you will, of various instructional technologies, have improved many teachers' abilities to teach. So what's wrong with improvement?

**Andrew:**    Nothing is wrong with improvement; however, I have several concerns. First and foremost, I am concerned that educators have arrived at the solution to the wrong question. More specifically, they have asked the question, "How can we teach better?" and answered it with 'techniques.' Unfortunately, however, no matter how satisfying the answer of technique is, it is the answer to the wrong question. Better questions to ask are: "How can we help students learn?," "What is worth learning in the long run?," or "What helps the evolution of the entire community?" So, as you can see, Wally, I have some grave concerns about the foundation upon which these improvements have been developed. I also have some serious concerns about the impact of technique on the educational process. Stay with me on this, Wally, because it can get somewhat confusing. When I think of pure technique, I think of machines—mindless, artless entities performing techniques—procedures, if you will, without wisdom. *And thus when teachers begin to see techniques as an end to ensure a desired outcome rather than a means to ensure that outcome, they have been transformed into machines; they have lost their humanity and have become trainers, not educators, and in essence they have become teaching machines,* that is, extensions of technique.

**Wally:**    Extensions of technique?

**Andrew:**    Yes, Wally, extensions of technique. If you think of it, an effective technique emerges out of a context which brings to bear an individual's creative, personological, intellectual, and physical resources to the solution of a problem. And from this contextual interaction of circumstance and humanity the individual develops a technique as a solution to a problem. More than likely, the technique which emerges from this interplay of context and humanity is an intuitive expression of the individual in that context, thus technique can be considered *contextual inspiration.* When people start to apply the techniques of others to disassociated situations, the technique is taken out of context and they then become extensions of the technique. And when that happens, Wally, when the technique is taken out of context, the technique may even get in the way of the desired outcome, for it moves from a creative part of a process to become the object of pursuit. It moves from a tool to an outcome. It becomes an end rather than a means. Moreover, such a situation may even squelch those intuitive or creative dimensions which each and everyone of us have, and thus block us from developing our own contextual and personologically appropriate techniques. *Thus, the possible is put out to pasture, and we begin to comply with a limited vision of what learning is all about, with the result that we even ask our teachers for compliance, confusing it with commitment.* The idea of commitment has become a measure of whether or not a person complies with the techniques in vogue.

**Wally:** But, Andrew, do you really think that teachers blindly follow techniques, that they no longer infuse their lessons with a bit of themselves?

**Andrew:** Of course, Wally, some teachers still do. However, I am afraid that this push for excellence is accompanied by an administrative, top-down push for standardization of procedures to ensure success. Thus administrators and supervisors are now watching for a standard procedure, that is, a technique. And Wally, I have seen this more times than I care to mention. I have seen administrators observing teachers, and during the follow-up conferences the administrators' criticisms generally focused on the teachers' inconsistencies related to the implementation of a technique. And you know, Wally, the demand for a 'right' technique is bad enough, but when it is compounded with this idea of consistency I have some serious concerns, for consistently in the dark or wrong is no solution. Few educators ask the question, "Is this method congruent with our valued outcomes?" Mainly, it is just the teacher's ability to comply with the technique that is questioned by many administrators; for to comply with a technique is equated with the acquisition of the desired educational outcome.

**Wally:** O.K., Andrew, I understand what you're saying; however, there is clear research evidence to demonstrate that certain teaching techniques are better than others. So why shouldn't we push for an acceptance of these superior techniques?

**Andrew:** To be honest, Wally, I'm not sure. However, let's try to see the whole picture instead of questioning in a simple either-or context. In the short run, there are either-or questions that may have "right" answers. But a more profound question is, "Does our present system work in the long run?" Some techniques work well, but do they work in all situations, with all teachers, with all students, with lasting efficacy? Is the pursuit of technique an attempt to cure the illness or does it simply treat a symptom of a profound illness?

A machine, Wally, a physical expression of pure technique, does not have the capacity to think and thus make itself relevant to variations. Sure, machines can be programmed with various options; however, they are preprogrammed options and thus rigid alternatives. Schools and teachers must constantly remain fluid in their options in order to address each student's needs. What I'm feeling is that administrators and parents of school children must begin to trust teachers more and empower them. *Empower them, Wally, with the freedom to be human, artful, and imperfect and thus legitimize their transcendance of technique to humanity.* Empower them with the knowledge that the success of a school is contingent upon a complex network of social, familial, genetic factors, teaching and learning styles, and thus the burden of the students' success does not fall solely on any one set of shoulders. Teachers could be given license to be professional role models of a knowledgeable learner, or an inquiring mind—a fallible human thirsting for knowledge who can impart information as well as demonstrate effective learning processes. Students and administrators (and for that matter, parents) could be seen in the same light for they can all serve as role models for learning. The point I'm making, Wally, is that although the research may show certain techniques are better than others in promoting information acquisition in the minds of students, the sole focus on statistically significant gains realized by the imposition of technique may exact the high price of our humanity.

**Wally:**   Whatdayamean?

**Andrew:**   What I mean is that a teaching technique is only one of many factors which influence a child's learning potential; I'm not convinced that the increases in a student's achievement scores, which may result from the imposition of technique upon the teachers and the students, is worth the price of the implicit lesson of the unquestioning use of technique. Remember McLuhan's point about the media being the message? Well, don't forget that my definition of pure technique is a machine, and thus the message of technique is that teachers, students, and even administrators do not count. *Humanity does not count.* Thus a strong argument can be made that our wholehearted embrace of technique speaks to our general distrust of each other, ourselves, and our humanity.

**Wally:**   Well, what do you suggest?

**Andrew:**   Trust begets trust, freedom begets freedom, limits beget limited performance, and standardizing objectivity begets a limited range of options. What we need, Wally, are educators who do not believe in objectivity as our deity. *Education needs a new mythic structure which celebrates learning, achievement, diversity, and a higher vision of our humanity.* But I've gotten off track a bit, Wally. You asked for some suggestions. Well, to begin with, we should take some of the pressure off our teachers to pursue a narrow definition of excellence and replace it with a reaffirmation of their service to the community as role models of an inquiring mind. I would suggest that we invest more time, money, and energy in revitalizing their creative spirit, while simultaneously providing them with opportunities to become learners again. This last point would reacquaint them with the frustrations their students may be having as they try to explore the world and learn, which in turn would add empathy to our schools and vision to humanity. In addition, it will broaden their scholarly understanding of various academic topics, and thus make them better informed educators as well.

Further, Wally, I would look to make changes within the power structures which exist in schools, and create organizations free from hierarchy. Think of the stress of always being on top, where the right answer is relentlessly required. Let us restructure the administrative bureaucracy to encourage and support teachers rather than functioning as another layer of demands, as a police force which further breaks the teaching spirit and distracts us from our roles as educators. For example, I would encourage school administrators to see their faculty in another light. Perhaps they could trust and coach rather than measure their faculty against standards of technique and conformity. Administrators must understand that this whole aspect of human nature can be nurtured; nurtured through trust and empowerment. Administrators must trust and encourage their teachers to invest themselves in their teaching and to discover their inner resources, their personality-appropriate techniques, if you will, for excellent or simply good enough teaching. For administrators to accomplish this goal, I would ask them not to place another layer of bureaucracy on their teachers, to not insist upon techniques, for another layer of bureaucracy will only continue to smother the creativity of teachers and further defeat their spirit. Rather, I would suggest that they encourage effective and meaningful teaching by stripping away these layers of bureaucratic requirements, and thus free teachers to find their intrinsic motivations and professional skills to be educators.

Administrators must recognize and validate diversity, subjectivity, objectivity, and creativity in teachers; let us not give up the gains in objectivity and in teacher-directed techniques that have been realized, but let us mature past these elements and integrate them into a larger, more complete picture. As long as administrators ask only for objectivity, they will get only a small part of the teacher's potential. And, Wally, in this version of reality we will never realize the full potential of our humanity, and thus we will continue to function as jail keepers of uninspired lives. Think of it. What if we cooperatively tightened up our picture of values, and loosened up the structures? What if we treated each other in a way that we would prefer to be treated, if we were in the other roles?

**Wally:** *(Nodding his head to indicate understanding and agreement)*

**Andrew:**   Furthermore, I think administrators ought to look more closely at their own ways of being, and look to transcend techniques in their job roles. *They, too, must transcend technique, and reprimand, encourage, critique, and support their faculty from the heart, not the technique.* Words spoken from the heart go directly to the heart and thus move people to change. In many ways, administrators must move beyond policy to humanity. Now, Wally, I know this kind of procedure costs money and takes more time in the short run; however, the implicit human lesson taught to everyone is worth the price, and in the long run is the least expensive road to travel. Humanity is at stake, not prestige, not professionalism, not hype. We must create a complete picture of success and direct our efforts toward bringing it to fruition. Otherwise, we will all remain prisoners of the obstacles to which we surrender our power. Wally, let us use these obstacles as opportunities, as complements rather than enemies.

# Teaching the Politics of Literacy
## Notes from a "Methods" Course

### by Mary-Lou Breitborde Sherr

*Mary-Lou Breitborde Sherr, Ed.D., has been an elementary and high school teacher, an administrator and program developer, and a consultant on urban desegregation programs. She has published and presented papers in the areas of peace education, whole language, literacy, and empowering teachers. Dr. Sherr received her graduate degrees in Humanistic and Development Studies at Boston University, and she is currently Assistant Professor of Education at Salem State College in Massachusetts. She is on the Executive Council of the Society for Educational Reconstruction and is active in local community educational issues.*

Most of the time in public schools is taken up by the teaching of reading. Those of us concerned with transforming schools into places of personal and social liberation would do well to look closely at what notions of self and society are conveyed through reading instruction. In the minds of my education students and their cooperating teachers, what is important in the classroom is not so much what teachers think but what they do about reading in the way of providing lessons that are effective, interesting, and palatable. No amount of proselytizing from the podia of "foundations" courses about the need to teach toward self-actualization or liberation or holism will survive the onslaught of the minute-to-minute concerns of a teacher confronted with 25 students and their parents, a building full of colleagues and supervisors, and a plethora of books, games, and ideas for reading instruction. Rather than assume that discussions about the liberating power of education in Philosophy of Education will stay with them to inform their decisions about what and how to teach once they enter the culture of a school, we must show them directly how particular methods and materials support or negate those important goals.

I begin my course in Methods of Teaching Reading by addressing the philosophical, social, and political assumptions behind competing no-

This selection originally appeared in the Spring 1990 issue of *Holistic Education Review*, Vol. 3, No. 1.

tions of literacy. Any approach to reading assumes a particular conception of literacy. Any outcry about "illiteracy in America" or "declining reading test scores" is based on some taken-for-granted notion of what it means to be "literate." Rather than attempt to find the one true definition of the concept, my students and I recognize that there exist several competing ones. We examine these concepts with respect to what they assume about the nature of the learner and the role of school in society. We understand them as giving rise to very different teaching practices. Moving beyond the superficial treatment provided in chapter one of every reading text, we spend time articulating our definitions of literacy and relating these to the decisions we make about methods and materials. My aim is to use the notion of literacy to convince my students that they, as teachers, have the potential to empower children to read, think, and act critically in their own lives and in the world. I will describe three notions of literacy and evaluate each with regard to its potential for liberation and in terms of its manifestation in current teaching practice.

## Cultural literacy

One conception of literacy is presented in the best-selling book by E.D. Hirsch, *Cultural Literacy*.[1] In Hirsch's view, the literate or educated person is familiar with a determinable number of words, terms, and ideas, taken together as a common stock of knowledge. The degree to which the reader understands these words, terms, or ideas is not as important as the reader's ability to "place" each term and to communicate with the confidence of a full member of the dominant culture. Mortimer Adler delineates a tripartite curriculum that would accomplish this cultural literacy. His proposal for a program leading to *paideia*, or general education, begins with the student's acquisition of the "organized knowledge" in traditional subject areas by means of lectures and textbooks. The student develops "intellectual skills" such as reading, writing, calculation, and problem solving through drill and practice so as to decipher the textbooks and understand the lectures. The hard work of amassing information and honing cognitive skills pays off when finally (during adolescence and in college) the student can engage in Socratic dialogue toward "an enlarged understanding" of the fundamental ideas and values of our government and social institutions, contained in the basic subject matters and in "a certain number of books" and documents that reflect our common intellectual tradition.[2]

Education for cultural literacy would produce informed citizens able to communicate in a common language within the framework of a common intellectual and cultural tradition. Such a goal recalls J.H. Newman's rationale for the liberal-arts college. The educated person "is at home in any society. He has a common ground with any class. . . he is able to converse, he is able to listen. . . he is a pleasant companion, and a comrade you can depend upon."[3]

A reading program directed toward the goal of cultural literacy emphasizes content: books, stories, poetry, essays. It cares more that all children receive the benefit of exposure to a common content, and less that reading experiences be adapted to individual students' needs. It is characterized by lists of books, such as that offered recently by former U.S. Secretary of Education William J. Bennett,[4] recommended as representing the best of our traditional stock of knowledge. Bennett's reading list for the idealized "James Madison Elementary School" has been criticized for omitting many books that express contemporary multicultural experience in favor of some archaic, less relevant literature.[5]

I do believe that the cultural literacy approach has much merit. It exposes children to a wealth of human experience conveyed in literature of good quality, and it presents excellent models of the linguistic expression of human experience. It does not go far enough, though, in considering either the experiences of the student or the context of society. Cultural literacy commits teachers and children to arbitrary standards imposed on human experience in the past and in the present. It leaves little room for individual interpretation or for critical analysis of the historical, social, and political contexts of literature. Nor does it allow for the creative expression of the student's own life experience. It assumes that knowledge of one's cultural traditions is sufficient to convince students that reading is a meaningful expression of lived experience. It also assumes that familiarity with the traditional stock of knowledge will enable students to live intelligently in the world. It confuses confidence with power.

## Mechanical literacy

A second concept of literacy, more limited and more mechanical in nature, treats literacy as a collection of skills which, applied separately or together, allow a person to "decode" words, sequence events, draw inferences, compare and contrast, find the main idea, and so on. In this approach, student achievement is continually measured against some grade-level norm. A literate person is one who reads at a "fourth grade level" or an "eighth grade level," who can "decode" enough to survive in a supermarket, on the job, and on the road. This concept of *mechanical literacy* purports to be content-free, and, to my mind, is most destructive. It is represented by programs that are worksheet- and workbook-based, where correct responses never require a full sentence of explanation. In such programs, students do not read good literature nor read it well. Books are peripheral and rarely discussed; their value is determined only by the number of stars on the class chart or free pizzas they bring. Reading is a quantifiable experience: its value to the child is in the number of pages read or in the number of error-free worksheets completed. Such an approach clearly alienates the reader not only from what is read but also from his or her own interests—from the full context of the reader's life.

Treating the ability to read as distinct from what is read leaves us with a public that reads, believes, and votes by *Reader's Digest* and *People* magazines; that fails to look past product packaging to the ingredients; that receives news information from headlines flashing across the screen behind nightly television anchors; and that bases hard-won presidential votes on articles about the candidates' spouses in the *National Enquirer*. In 1970, 75% of the available reading material in the United States was read by less than 5% of the population.[6] It is no accident that, while national assessments show improvement in basic decoding and recall skills, scores on tests of higher order reading comprehension, where thought is linked to print, are disappointing.[7] I believe that the reading ability of the nation suffers from content-less, skills-based reading programs which do not teach children to read for information or for enjoyment, nor establish in children patterns and habits of purposeful or meaningful or enjoyable reading. The problem with this mechanistic approach to literacy training is that it is training only, and training is easily lost. Democracy is indeed endangered when its citizens, alienated from or victimized by print, do not have the power to gather the information necessary to broaden their views, weigh alternatives, and make decisions on any basis other than immediate experience.

## Critical literacy

In contrast, the liberationist educators Paulo Freire and Donald Macedo offer a third, very different conception of literacy, one that includes the context of the reader's experience. For Freire and Macedo, literacy is a *critical* reading of "the word and the world."[8] The literate person understands the deeper social and political meaning of what he or she reads, and thus has the knowledge that makes it possible to liberate self from unexamined, perhaps unjust, life conditions. For example, a person able to read and fill out a loan application from an agency charging exorbitant interest rates is not literate in Freire's view. The literate applicant reads the high interest rate and understands its context—the motivation of the lender, the potential consequences to the borrower, the relative economic and political power of each, the implications of this relationship for the borrower's work-life, lifestyle, future economic status, and he or she understands the alternatives to this loan. According to this definition, even those of us who "decode" well are probably illiterate in some areas. (Certainly my own illiteracy surfaces every time I endorse an auto repair bill.) There is, then, the possibility of multiple literacies, much as psychologists now talk about "multiple intelligences."[9] More broadly, Freire's conception of *critical literacy* assumes that we have the power to examine all aspects of our lives; whether we in fact exercise this power (as in the auto repair shop) is our own conscious choice.

Embedded in critical literacy is the belief that we are actors in the world and actors in the educational process. A reading program based on this concept would be oriented toward language experience or "whole language," using any method that considers meaning-making on the part of the reader as central to the reading project and puts the reader in control. This approach treats children's experiences as content of educational value, worth sharing, and worth writing books about. It views children as active learners, not just in the sense of using hands-on materials to learn, but as actively making meaning of the printed word. Sylvia Ashton-Warner's "key work" technique[10] and the more current whole-language and "writing-to-read" programs[11] exemplify this approach. Skills are taught as needed, but always in the context of linguistic meaning. Added to the emphasis on personal meaning, though, is the importance of guiding students to look critically at every text. Teachers help readers place the text in a context appropriately historical, social, political, or economic. Understanding the author's frame of reference is essential. Sexist literature is read and discussed critically, as are more balanced alternatives. Mark Twain's *Huckleberry Finn* provides a wealth of discussion, not as a historical anomaly, but as a vehicle for reflecting social relationships and students' own experiences. Because language comprises meanings peculiar to certain people or certain experiences, dialect becomes a respectable means for conveying thought and experience.

Because of my own social philosophy and philosophy of learning, this last conception of literacy is the one that I espouse and which grounds both my teaching practice and my reading. But in my reading methods classes, I leave open to discussion the definition of literacy and the consequent selection of methods. We begin the semester with lively debates about literacy, adding newspaper and journal articles and government reports to the fray. We leave the question unanswered, for it comes up continually as we proceed through the semester and learn about different methods and materials. I ask my students to read the introductions to teachers' manuals, and compare and evaluate their underlying assumptions about literacy and the nature of the reading process. I ask them to give a written rationale with every lesson plan and unit along with their skills objectives. I ask them to justify everything they do, and I do not accept pragmatic reasons such as "It works" (What does it do?), "The kids love it" (They also love Kool-Aid), and "It's fun" (So are arcade games). I try to link my students' reading assignments to Freire's principles, to the students' own experiences, and to the implications for the lives of their students. I work toward the impossible goal of educating my students to be well versed in all reading methods, yet aware that some are terrible ways to ensure a truly literate public. They should be able to deal with system-mandated programs and modify them according to their beliefs about literacy, learning, and the purpose of education. They should be able to select materials and methods that best serve their students' needs, given not just reading achievement scores, but the whole context of their lives. I ask questions such as these: Can you justify a solely skills-based approach with children who do not have at home many printed examples of the connection between spoken and written language? (Why should these children not have an impossible time learning to read by such a contrived method?) Can you justify a totally basal reader-based program? Given the choice, what materials should your students read? Write about? Talk about and translate into written language? Why? How will you respond to their nonstandard English? *Why?* In my students' answers I expect to hear a reference to the link between reading instruction and the students' lives.

Any reading method, even one grounded in a liberationist ethic, as I believe whole language is, can be subverted into a tool of oppression. Without attention to the philosophical and political assumptions behind the method—without continually reflecting on our reasons for what and how we teach—we fall victim to educational practices that are mindless at best, and which at their worst negate our professed beliefs about the nature of the learner and the ultimate social and political goals of education. Critical theory should ground our educational goals, which in turn should ground our methods. Too many teachers end up doing it backwards for the sake of entertaining students or responding to administrative and parental demands. We need to begin with theory and belief and then translate these into effective teaching practice. The teaching of reading—of literacy—is the most important context for this endeavor, and we ought to understand what we mean by it. Does literacy mean teaching students to crack a code? Does it mean allowing students access to a common culture? Or does it mean enhancing their potential for individual freedom, social change, and responsible world citizenship?

## Notes

1.   E.D. Hirsch, *Cultural Literacy: What Every American Needs to Know* (Boston: Houghton-Mifflin, 1987).

2.   M. Adler, *The Paideia Proposal* (New York: Macmillan, 1982), pp. 22-33.

3.   J.H. Newman, *The Idea of a University* (New York: Longman, Green, 1947), Discourse VII.

4.   W.J. Bennett, *James Madison Elementary School: A Curriculum for American Students* (Washington, DC: U.S. Department of Education, 1988).

5.   S. Ohanian, "How to Create a Generation of Aliterates," *Education Week*, 12 October 1988, pp. 32, 26.

6.   G. Spache and E. Spache, *Reading in the Elementary School* (Boston: Allyn & Bacon, 1973).

7.   R.C. Anderson et al., *Becoming a Nation of Readers: The Report of the Commission on Reading* (Washington, DC: National Institute of Education, 1985).

8.   P. Freire and D. Macedo, *Literacy: Reading the Word and the World* (South Hadley, MA: Bergin and Garvey, 1987).

9.   H. Gardner, *Frames of Mind: The Theory of Multiple Intelligences* (New York: Basic Books, 1983).

10.   S. Ashton-Warner, *Teacher* (New York: Simon & Schuster, 1963).

11.   L.M. Calkins, *The Art of Teaching Writing* (Portsmouth, NH: Heinemann, 1986); D. Graves, *Writing: Teachers and Children at Work* (Portsmouth, NH: Heinemann, 1982); and F. Smith, *Essays into Literacy* (Portsmouth, NH: Heinemann, 1983).

# Reading as a Whole
## Why Basal Reading Series Are Not the Answer

### by Constance Weaver

*Connie Weaver is a Professor of English at Western Michigan University, where she teaches courses in the reading and writing processes and in integrating the language arts in elementary school. A holistic approach to the development of literacy is discussed in her recent book,* **Reading Process and Practice: From Socio-Psycholinguistics to Whole Language** *(Heinemann, 1988). She is currently Director of the Commission on Reading of the National Council of Teachers of English, which sponsored the* **Report Card on Basal Readers** *discussed in this article.*

In the first issue of *Holistic Education Review*, Edward Clark contrasts the pervasive mechanistic, *technological* approach to education with a holistic, *ecological* approach.[1] Perhaps nowhere in education is the pervasiveness of the outmoded technological model so apparent as in the methods and materials typically used in teaching children to read. The fact that the majority of our young people do become at least minimally literate is a tribute not to the reading instruction to which they are subjected, but to the complexity of the human mind and our innate drive to make sense of our world.

This concern about a technological approach to reading is shared by many in the field of English education and reading, and in particular by the members of the Commission on Reading of the National Council of Teachers of English, of which I am currently the Director. What we shall try to do in this and subsequent articles is offer a taste of the kinds of research that support a holistic approach to the teaching of reading, discuss some of the concerns about basal reading series and the technological paradigm that they both reflect and promote, and characterize what has come to be known as a "whole language" approach to the development of literacy, showing how it stimulates far greater growth in understanding and using language than is often the result with a technological approach. The present article will focus particularly on

This selection originally appeared in the Fall 1988 issue of *Holistic Education Review*, Vol. 1, No. 3.

the first two of these aims, indicating how our understanding of the reading process and the acquisition of literacy demonstrates the inappropriateness of a technological approach to teaching children to read.

At the request of the Commission on Reading, Kenneth Goodman, Patrick Shannon, Yvonne Freeman, and Sharon Murphy have prepared a *Report Card on Basal Readers* that documents our concerns about basal reading series and the model of education that they represent.[2] Unfortunately, reading instruction is dominated by a basal reading series in approximately 90 percent of American schools today.[3] A basal reading series is not merely a set of books for children to read from; rather, it is a comprehensive *program* consisting of pupil books with reading selections, teachers' manuals that tell the teacher exactly how to teach the lesson, workbooks and dittos, tests and more tests, plus various other paraphernalia. The fact that a 55-page pupil book for first grade can be accompanied by a teacher's manual of 350 pages, as well as all the other materials, should itself cause us to ask, "What's going on here?"

The *Report Card on Basal Readers* documents in detail how basal reading materials and instruction came over half a century ago to be based upon concepts from classical science, behavioral psychology, business and industry, and how these outmoded concepts are still reflected in most basal reading series today. Such concepts lead to the aforementioned "technological" view of teaching and learning, which is characterized by such assumptions as the following:

1. The learner is passive.
2. Children will learn only what they are directly taught.
3. Knowledge is constructed "bottom up" from elemental building blocks, from the smallest parts to increasingly large wholes.
4. Errors reflect a learner's failure to learn and/or apply what has been taught.
5. What's important is the measurable *product* of instruction, not the process of learning.[4]

To quote from the *Report Card on Basal Readers*, "In this view learning is the result of teaching, piece by piece, item by item. The whole, reading, is the sum of the parts, words and skills. Learners are passive and controlled." In such a view, teachers are not expected to be responsible professionals who make informed decisions; they're "scripted technicians," most of whom do in fact follow the directions, the scripts, in the teachers' manuals. And of course, children are reduced even more, to manipulated parts in the educational machine.

This view might not be detrimental to learning to read if it in fact reflected how people read, or even how children learn to read. But it reflects neither.

Let us consider, first, some examples[5] that should help to demonstrate that proficient readers do not read primarily by going from part to whole: that they do not build meaning by decoding words letter-by-letter, or by determining the meanings of sentences word-by-word, or even by determining the meanings of paragraphs and larger wholes sentence by sentence. Try, first, to read the following paragraph of a version of "Little Red Riding Hood," told from the wolf's point of view:

-nc- -p-n - t-m- th-r- w-s - h-nds-m- y--ng w-lf n-m-d L-b-. L-b- l-v-d w-th h-s m-th-r -nd f-th-r -t th- -dg- -f - d--p, d-rk w--ds. -v-r- d--, L-b- w-nt t- h-nt -t th--dg- -f th- w--ds, n--r th- l-ttl- v-ll-g- -f C-l--s.

Surely it is clear from even this brief example that when we can use semantic and syntactic cues, we do not decode words letter by letter as we read. It should be equally clear that we do not need nearly all the graphic clues normally available to us.

What, then, of building the meaning of sentences word-by-word? A brief example should again suggest the impossibility of such a procedure. Take, for instance, the word "run." How would you define it? See if your definition or definitions are appropriate for the following sentences:

1. Can you run the store for an hour?
2. Can you run the word processor?
3. Can you run the 500-yard dash?
4. Can you run in the next election?
5. Can you run next year's marathon?
6. I helped Samuel with his milk run.
7. They'll print 5,000 copies in the first run.
8. Sherry has a run in her hose.
9. There was a run on snow shovels yesterday morning.
10. It was a long run.

In how many of these sentences did your definition, or definitions, fit? Clearly we cannot take meanings for words out of our mental dictionaries and simply fit them into the sentences we're reading; we have to determine what each word means in combination with the other words.

One last example may begin to illustrate the fact that we do not build the meaning of paragraphs and larger wholes merely sentence by sentence. See if you can get some sense of what a *blonke* is as you read the following paragraphs:

The blonke was maily, like all the others. Unlike the other blonkes, however, it had spiss crinet completely covering its fairney cloots and concealing, just below one of them, a small wam.

This particular blonke, was quite drumly—lennow, in fact, and almost samded. When yerden, it did not quetch like the other blonkes, or even blore. The other blored very readily.

It was probably his bellytimber that had made the one blonke so drumly. The bellytimber was quite kexy, had a strong shawk, and was apparently venenated. There was only one thing to do with the venenated bellytimber: givel it in the flosh. This would be much better than to sparple it in the wong, since the blonkes that were not drumly could icchen in the wond, but not in the flosh.

Obviously we can tell that this blonke is in certain ways not like the others, that it is probably the blonke's "bellytimber" that had made him so drumly, unlike the others, and perhaps that it is advisable to keep the other blonkes away from the venenated bellytimber. We are not simply building meaning word-by-word or sentence-by-sentence, but using everything we know to construct relationships among words and sentences. That is, in order to construct meaning as we read, we must have and use adequate background knowledge, we must continually apply various strategies to make sense of the sentences and words on a page. Meaning is not merely the end of reading, the product, but the beginning and the means as well.

If learning to read were significantly different from mature, proficient reading, there might still be justification for part-to-whole technology in teaching children to read. However, children who learn to read in the home, or in what are nowadays often called "whole language" classrooms, learn to read in much the same way as they learned to talk.[6] Starting with an intention to make meaning, they tend first to read a book holistically, telling the story from the pictures or reciting the memorized story. Then, gradually, they fill in the parts: they learn to recognize the words (at first, only in familiar contexts) and begin to grasp some of the correspondences between letters and sounds. Thus for young children too, meaning is the beginning and the means of reading, not merely the end.

Let us examine, as an analogy, how children learn to speak their native language. Imagine, if you will, the following scenario:

> A young mother greets her husband enthusiastically as they sit down to dinner. "Guess what, dear? I've found this marvelous program for teaching Johnny to talk. It's called "Getting Back to Basics: Teaching Your Child to Talk." It's a great program. It starts with the basic sounds, like /d/ in *dog*. First you teach the child to say these sounds in isolation and then you teach him to blend them together. Why, in a couple of weeks Johnny might be able to say "dada."

Fortunately, in this scenario, the woman's husband is not impressed. He dismisses his wife's suggestion by commenting that he never heard of a child being "taught" to talk that way, one sound at a time, blending sounds to make words.

We do not directly *teach* children to talk. We do not teach them rules for putting sounds together to form words and words together to form sentences—partly because we do not consciously know most of the rules ourselves. For example, unless you have had some training in linguistics, you probably do not know the "rule" for making regular verbs past tense; *love* becomes *loved*, with a /d/ sound; and *hate* becomes *hated*, with a vowel plus a /d/. But why? What is the "rule" that governs these regular patterns? Clearly even if we did know these rules, it would be futile to try to teach the rules directly to infants. Fortunately, however, *children do not need to be taught the rules directly.*

While children to some extent imitate what they hear, they also create the language anew, forming increasingly sophisticated hypotheses about how the language is structured. A simple negative sentence like *No* will give way in time to sentences like *No cookie*, then perhaps *No eat cookie*, then to more sophisticated sentences like *Me no ate cookie*, later *I didn't ate the cookie*, and finally to an adult structure, *I didn't eat the cookie*. All of this occurs without explicit adult instruction. We adults facilitate language growth by modeling adult language for children, by transacting with them verbally in functional and meaningful contexts, by focusing on the meaning of children's utterances rather then the form, and by generally ignoring "errors" of form rather than fact, since we realize that most children's language will gradually come to resemble that of the adults in their environment.[7]

## A new paradigm

In short, the way children learn to talk is characterized not by a mechanistic, reductionistic, technological model of learning, but by a transactional model that reflects not classical science, but the paradigm offered by quantum physics, the "new" paradigm emerging in a variety of disciplines. This paradigm can be contrasted point-by-point with the paradigm that underlies much of today's education, and certainly much of the instruction in today's basal readers. According to this paradigm:

1. The learner is active, gradually formulating increasingly sophisticated hypotheses about the environment in order to learn.
2. Children do not learn merely, or even mainly, what they are directly taught.
3. Knowledge is not simply constructed "bottom up," from smaller parts to increasingly larger wholes. Rather, the whole is achieved by working at least as much "top down," by drawing upon one's entire lifetime of knowledge, experience, and cognitive strategies.
4. Errors often reflect the learner's current stage of development; as such, they are not necessarily to be viewed as "wrong."
5. What's most important is the *process* of learning. Paradoxically, focusing on the process of learning rather than the measurable product of instruction generally produces more sophisticated and more long-lasting products.

This paradigm describes, as I have indicated, the way in which children learn to talk and, later, the way in which they learn to read most naturally. But when these same children begin school, we all too often treat them as if the only way they could or would learn is through the "technology" of the basal reader, a totally opposite approach. According to the NCTE Reading Commission's *Report Card on Basal Readers*, underlying virtually all of the basal reading series available in the United States today is the assumption "that the learning of reading can happen skill by skill and word by word and that learning is the direct result of teaching." Not only are "decoding" and word recognition taught skill-by-skill, but so is comprehension.

The difference between these approaches and the kinds that facilitate learning to read more naturally can be illustrated by an excerpt from a major American basal reading series and an excerpt from a little book in the Ready to Read set of materials that are used in New Zealand. Both would be for approximately first grade level, or perhaps kindergarten.

*Excerpt from Economy Level C Pre-Primer*[8]
The Dog in the Van

Did I see a dog?
I did!
The dog went into the van.
Did I see a red dog?
Is the dog red?
Is the dog in the van?
Is it red?
Is a red dog in the van?
I did not paint the dog.
I did not paint Happy.
Happy went into the paint.
The dog is red.
The paint made it red.
I did not see a red dog.
It went into the van.
A red dog is in the van.

*Excerpt from* Greedy Cat, *by Joy Cowley*[9]

Mum went shopping
and got some sausages.
Along came greedy cat.
He looked in the shopping bag.
Gobble, gobble, gobble
and that was the end of that.

(Subsequent episodes have identical language, except for the new item that Mum buys. Finally, she buys a pot of pepper—and that is the end of *that*!)

In the first selection, we can see concern for repeating words time and again, to ensure mastery; we also see an attempt to use primarily words that reflect regular letter/sound patterns (the short vowel sounds, for example). However, the "story" as a whole is virtual nonsense, and the reader cannot very readily use context or cognitive schemas to predict what will come next. This is in sharp contrast to what readers do normally, as we began to understand from reading the "Red Riding Hood" passage. We use our knowledge of syntax, the developing meaning of a coherent text, and our lifetime of experience to predict as we read. The selection about the dog in the van thwarts such productive reading strategies.

The book *Greedy Cat*, on the other hand, encourages such prediction, because the episodes repeat with only a word or phrase being changed. Furthermore, reading is enhanced by the rhythm, and by the rhyme in the third and sixth lines. Such features in beginning reading materials help make books like *Greedy Cat* as easy to read as possible, whereas the materials found in the early levels of most basal reading series make reading and learning to read as difficult as possible.

In sum, then, both reading and learning to read are in many respects whole-to-part processes that begin with what the learner brings to the task, both in the way of cognitive processing strategies and specific knowledge and experience. The fact that most basal reading materials adopt a part-to-whole approach, and most teachers teach reading that way, does not mean that it is typically *learned* that way. In fact, there is considerable evidence that the poorer readers tend to be the ones who try to read using little more than the skills they have been explicitly taught, while the better readers intuitively use more sophisticated and more productive strategies. Janet Emig's summary of the teaching-learning relationship seems particularly applicable to the direct teaching of reading: "That teachers teach and children learn no one will deny. But to believe that children learn *because* teachers teach and only what teachers explicitly teach is to engage in magical thinking."[10]

To put it bluntly, the mechanistic, reductionistic, technological paradigm is simply not an appropriate model for literacy education. The fact that millions, even billions, of children have learned to read with basal readers is a tribute not to the technology of basals, but to young childrens' drive to make sense of the world, including the world of books and print. But why should we persist in reading instruction that thwarts rather than facilitates children's natural strategies for making sense of the world? Paradoxically, freeing ourselves from a technological concept of reading instruction is vital in order better to facilitate the technological literacy that is increasingly demanded by our post-industrial society.

## Notes

1. Edward T. Clark, Jr., "The Search for a New Educational Paradigm" *Holistic Education Review* 1 (Spring, 1988), pp. 18-30.

2. Kenneth Goodman, Patrick Shannon, Yvonne Freeman, and Sharon Murphy, *Report Card on Basal Readers* (New York: Owen, 1988).

3. Richard C. Anderson, Elfrieda H. Hiebert, Judith A. Scott, and Ian A. G. Wilkinson, *Becoming a Nation of Readers: The Report of the Commission on Reading* (Champaign, IL: Center for the Study of Reading, 1985).

4. Constance Weaver, *Reading Process and Practice: From Socio-Psycholinguistics to Whole Language* (Portsmouth, NH: Heinemann, 1988), pp. 181-183.

5. These exercises are taken from Weaver, *Reading Process and Practice.*

6. See Don Holdaway, *The Foundations of Literacy* (Sydney: Ashton-Scholastic, 1979; Jerome C. Harste, Virginia A. Woodward, and Carolyn L. Burke, *Language Stories and Literacy Lessons* (Portsmouth, NH: Heinemann, 1984); William H. Teale and Elizabeth Sulzby, eds., *Emergent Literacy: Writing and Reading* (Norwood, NJ: Ablex, 1986); and, for an excellent summary, Judith M. Newman, ed., *Whole Language: Theory in Use* (Portsmouth, NH: Heinemann, 1985), pp. 1-36.

7. Judith W. Lindfors, *Children's Language and Learning* (Englewood Cliffs, NJ: Prentice Hall, 1980); Celia Genishi and Anne Dyson, *Language Assessment in the Early Years* (Norwood, NJ: Ablex, 1984).

8. L. Matteoni, F. Sucher, M. Klein, and K. Welch, *Economy Reading Series* (Oklahoma City), 1986.

9. Joy Cowley, *Greedy Cat* (Illus. by Robyn Belton) (Wellington, N.Z.: Department of Education), 1983. (Available from Richard C. Owen, Publishers, New York).

10. Janet Emig, "Non-Magical Thinking: Presenting Writing Developmentally in Schools," in *The Web of Meaning: Essays on Writing, Teaching, Learning and Thinking* (Portsmouth, NH: Boynton/Cook, 1983), pp 135-144.

# Do Grades Cause Learning Disabilities?

## by Charles H. Hargis and Marge Terhaar-Yonkers

*Dr. Charles H. Hargis is a professor of special education in the Department of Special Services Education at the University of Tennessee, Knoxville. He is a classroom teacher who became a teacher educator. His interests include reading, language development, and measurement. His recent books are* **Curriculum-Based Assessment: A Primer** *and* **Teaching Low Achieving and Disadvantaged Students.**

*Marge Terhaar-Yonkers is Clinical Assistant Professor in the Special Education and Literacy Department at the University of North Carolina at Chapel Hill.*

If a spelling test made up of twenty words were given to the students of a typical elementary classroom, it would surprise no one to see a wide range of scores result. It would be expected. This range of scores would provide the basis for assigning grades. The same things could be said for tests or assignments given in most subject areas. A test or assignment is given to a class or group of students, the teacher checks or scores the papers, and grades are assigned. A distribution of grades usually results. The fortunate, able students will get As, and the unfortunates will get the Fs.

It is as if we did not recognize the normal array of individual differences in learning ability that exists in every classroom. We readily accept differences in artistic, athletic, and musical talent. We also expect myriad differences in physical and personality traits. However, we seem to have a rigid, unyielding view of academic aptitudes and abilities, despite the wide variation in the same groups of students as occurs with so many other traits and characteristics. We provide the same curricula to all students at normative levels that are grouped in a classroom. The curricula are designed with no concern for the individual learner's interest but are established for the means of chronological age groups over thirteen academic years. This is done in spite of the fact that the academic performance and readiness levels in any primary grade will range by more than 2½ years.[1] The demands of the curriculum will be too great

This selection originally appeared in the Fall 1989 issue of *Holistic Education Review,* Vol. 2, No. 3.

for some students and very easy for others. It will be pertinent to some and irrelevant to others. As Emmett Betts noted many years ago, the curricular sequence is laid out in lock-step. He claimed that the primary reason for most of the learning problems that students experience is the unyielding nature of the lock-step curriculum. Students are expected to perform up to (or down to) the curricular activities and material levels that are assigned to their grade.[2] This inevitably produces the failure described above.

We must accept the variations in academic readiness levels, learning abilities, interests, and relevance that exist in every classroom. We must, therefore, recognize that providing a level of instruction from one curriculum level to each of these classrooms will produce a distribution of scores and grades that matches the range of levels and abilities. The variation of scores and grades simply confirms the variability of the students.

The most frequently cited reason for dropping out of high school is poor grades. Estimates for dropout rates are frequently in the range of twenty to thirty-five percent.[3] These figures usually refer to the number of students who start high school but fail to finish. They do not include the students who drop out before they actually start high school. These figures seem very high, but they reflect a definite improvement over the dropout rate of the previous generation. Mandatory attendance laws have improved graduation or completion rates, and some attention has been given to meeting individual differences. Grouping or tracking systems made possible the survival of some lower achieving students at the secondary level. Some additional students survived when they were referred to emerging special education programs. In recent years, even more students have qualified for special education after having failed for a length of time sufficient to qualify as being "learning disabled" by a discrepancy formula.

We seem to accept that students will receive failing marks in most classrooms each and every term. Why do we have such expectations? Are there some benefits associated with giving failing grades? The authors' view is that there are no good reasons or benefits to be derived from our grading system. Moreover, we believe that grades are primarily responsible for the veritable hemorrhage of normal students into special classrooms, and that they are responsible for a greatly reduced level of achievement and literacy in a large percentage of lower achieving but nonhandicapped students.

Chronic failure produces or exacerbates learning and behavior problems. Chronic failure produces the discrepancy between achievement and potential that leads to the "learning disabilities" label. Chronic failure produces the injury to self-concept that makes for serious emotional disturbance in many children. Poor grades cause most "learning disabilities" and behavior disorders. Time and time again, we note the dramatic change in the behavior of students so labeled when they receive special education placement, and are given work that they can do and which allows them to feel some success.

To reiterate, chronic failure leads to a discrepancy between achievement and potential. Failure is nonproductive. As W. Glasser pointed out, all you can learn from failing is how to fail.[4] Actually, a student cannot learn adequately unless he or she is performing well. Students who are getting poor grades are not achieving their potential. Students must experience success in order to achieve their potential. Students who experience failure are actually falling farther and farther behind.

K.E. Stanovich discussed "Matthew effects" in learning to read.[5] Basically, Matthew effects, sometimes called the "bootstrapping effect," describe the rich-get-richer and the poor-get-poorer phenomenon. They explain the divergence between good and poor patterns of reading achievement. Students who are not experiencing success in learning to read fall increasingly farther behind their potential for learning to read. Matthew effects occur in "learning-disabled" students, too.[6] They account for the poor pattern of achievement and for the emergence of the discrepancy between achievement and potential. Students must be given reading activities that they can do successfully, if they are to achieve to their potential. The more they read successfully, the more successfully they can read. They should not need to get failing grades for a period so long that the inevitable discrepancy emerges.

Grades cause a double standard to exist in the way we treat students. As E.R. Forell points out so well, the history of higher achieving students has been one of success and of comfort with the instructional materials.[7] On the other hand, low achieving students are frequently challenged with materials above their skill level. In higher achieving students, the evidence of success is commonplace. They read easily and fluently in reading groups, they encounter few unknown words, and their comprehension is high. In math and other subject areas, the same evidence of success appears. It should seem obvious that this level of success is basic to achievement. Low achievers need the same standard as high achievers. Low achievers need a comfortable placement on the curricular path in order to achieve to their potential. Success is fundamental to achievement: lack of success retards achievement. There should be none of the double standard that grades foster. Grades make it acceptable, even desirable for some students to do poorly.

## Grades and "learning disabilities"

Recently, special education has been criticized for not being special at all. Of course the observation is correct, but the criticism is not warranted. The bulk of the students who are currently enrolled in special education programs are not really handicapped at all. They are simply normal but low-achieving students who consistently have received failing grades. There typically will be no other evidence of a "learning disability" and no signs of any organically based difficulty. These students do not need a special method of instruction; they have the potential to learn on the continuum of topics from the regular curriculum. The instruction simply needs to be conducted at a rate or pace that matches the student's ability, not the normative pace dictated by the lock-step curricular sequence that is assigned in rigid structure over the grade levels through which students are required to move in near unison.

How do grades contribute to this problem? Are grades simply evidence of rigidity in the curriculum, or are they a cause? Grades are not really a symptom of curricular lock-step; they are a contributing factor to its continuation. We often think of grades as a tool for maintaining "standards" in school (e.g., "We shouldn't give students a passing grade if they cannot do acceptable grade-level work.") This common notion holds the curriculum in a sacrosanct position, while transferring the blame to the student ("It is the student's fault that he is not working up to grade-level standards.") Also, we seem to hold the grading system in a similarly elevated position. ("We must give grades, and we must give a real distribution of grades. After all, who wants to contribute to grade inflation; grades wouldn't mean anything then.") Having a grading system creates the illusion that each child alone is responsible for his or her accomplishments.

We seem to have institutionalized our commitment to our grading system, in spite of voluminous evidence that grades do little or no good and have tremendous negative impact on lower achieving students. We believe we can use grades to motivate students. However, poor grades do little more than to demoralize students. The only students who are motivated by grades are those who can and already do get good grades.[8]

Grades isolate students from one another and prevent healthy cooperative learning arrangements. Students are admonished to do their own work, not ask for help from other students. Students are discouraged from helping one another. They are placed in competition. This environment is nothing like the learning environment found outside school, where social skill is needed and cooperation is necessary.[9] When students are isolated and placed in competitive environments, they have little opportunity to acquire social and cooperative skills that are necessary and desirable in dealing with persisting life problems.

High grades replace learning as the objective of education. The problems with grade-driven educational systems were dramatically illustrated in the books Wad-ja-get[10] and Teaching Without Grades.[11] Students can expend enormous energy in trying to get a high grade without regard to what they are learning. They try to find what the teachers want on tests and projects. They seek out and exhibit quirks and prejudices in their teachers. The more able students are often more successful in this game, but real learning suffers and curiosity is stifled.

In the isolated and competitive situations created by grades, students often cheat. For the least able students in these classrooms, cheating is perhaps the only hope for getting a passing grade. Cheating is virtually an accepted practice because of the importance of grades. In addition, real substantive assessment is diminished, because real achievement can be measured and reported only by determining what skills and objectives have been learned. But most assessment time in school is devoted to giving grades, grades that provide no substantive information about where a student is on any curricular sequence or what content has been mastered.

Grades alleviate the need for truly individualizing instruction. We have this system that just about demands a distribution of grades in every classroom and a significant portion of those grades to be in the failing range. The system insures that a wide distribution of grades is produced by providing only grade-level instructional activities. This practice perpetuates the kind of classroom condition of which the authors are most adamantly critical. A wide distribution of grades from any classroom is primary evidence that there is little or no attention paid to the individual differences of the students in it. If instructional level activities were matched with each student, each student would demonstrate evidence that such a match had been made by performing at the same high proficiency levels.

## Individualized learning

Why should students be working at uniformly high performance levels? Doesn't this mean that all students would have to get the same grade? If everyone gets the same grade, would grades mean anything? Taking these questions in reverse order, we conclude the following: We don't believe that grades mean anything anyway. They simply show that we don't individualize instruction. They do not tell a thing about the learner's progress, or exactly what level of achievement or proficiency a student has attained. All students should get the same grade; more precisely they should all be getting the same range of scores. These scores would reflect that the student is working at an appropriate instructional level. The answer to the first question, then, is that all students should be working at high performance levels because success is necessary for optimal achievement, for an adequate self-concept, and for maintaining interest and involvement in learning activities.

Grades have given us an erroneous notion of what individualized instruction is. Many think that it is individual attention such as small groups or one-to-one tutoring relationships. Almost always the aim of individualized instruction is to help the student work up to grade-level standards or to get a passing grade in grade-level work. Some feel that individualized instruction is achieved merely if the instructional activity is tailored to the individual learning style or modality preference. Here also the effort or change in method is aimed at getting the student up to grade level or to get a passing grade on work being done at the student's grade placement. The essential feature of individualized instruction is overlooked. Instructional activity should be matched to the ability level of the students. The learning activity must be doable. The individualized match has been made when the student performs at the same level expected of adequately achieving students. High achievement is demonstrated by high performance. If anything in a classroom should be graded, it should be the quality of the instructional activity to student match. Good individualized instruction is evidenced by good performance.

This pervasive view of individualized instruction was illustrated, with considerable irony, by a teacher in a rural school near us. This particular teacher's classroom contained twenty-eight students and comprised the primary grades in her school. She was doing a remarkably efficient job of coordinating the instructional activities of students working at many different levels. All of the students were working—with a great deal of concentration—at an appropriate instructional level. Much work was done as a form of supervised study. There were several learning centers set up. The children were completely free to ask questions of one another or to help one another. When the teacher was asked how she managed so much individualized instruction, she looked astonished and replied, "I don't do any individualized instruction. I don't have time for it!"

One question this teacher raised had to do with the difficulty she had with assigning grades to her students. She couldn't figure out how to give grades, since she always had to give students work they could do so they would continue working. The response that she really didn't need to worry about giving grades, because she was doing such a good job, was even more ridiculous to her than the notion that she was individualizing instruction.

Possibly the most significant feature of this teacher and her instructional "method" was that she had never made a special education referral! She even seemed apologetic for this; she felt that some specialist might have done more for those of her students over the years who seemed somewhat slower or who seemed a little "off."

This teacher's instructional delivery system had many features of the model we advocate. All classrooms have a remarkable range of individual differences, and each teacher should be prepared to deal with students as many rural teachers already must do. Only in this way can we stop producing such staggering numbers of "learning-disabled" students who are in fact curriculum casualties.

It is difficult, if not impossible, to use a conventional grading system in this model. Children who are given instructional activities that are appropriate for their individual instructional needs will perform appropriately well at it. Grading systems cause or encourage curricula to be laid out in lock-step. Grades make it all right to set curricular objectives appropriate for the average students at each grade level. This may be well and good for the students who are average academic performers, but it is devastating for students who fail.

Holistic educational systems are typically structured to operate without grades. An early advocate of holistic methods, Francis W. Parker, indicated adamant opposition to the use of grades in the late nineteenth century.[12] This was about the time grades became a part of common educational practice. Some alternative education programs operate without grades as a matter of policy. The C4R programs are examples.[13]

Holistic systems are invariably structured in ways that discourage the use of grades. Socialization and cooperation are encouraged. Students are supposed to help one another, and students are supposed to be successful. Cheating is not even an issue, if by matter of policy everyone is supposed to do well. Teaching is not curriculum or grade centered, but student centered. Learning is the valued process and product. Learning need not occur on a prescribed date and time for all students; it is individually guided.

Unfortunately, most public schools are not guided by holistic principles. Many districts have set up dropout prevention programs for so-called "at-risk" or "problem" students, but the existence of such safety valve programs encourages regular education programs to continue in the same old way. When such safety valves are available, schools can continue to blame the student rather than the system that produced the problems in the first place.

We believe that our institutionalized system of grading is an important factor in handicapping children. Grades are a major obstacle to providing humane educational opportunities for all children. However, grades are such a fundamental part of our educational system that we fear they will be abandoned only with the greatest reluctance.

## Notes

1.   C.H. Hargis, *Teaching Reading to Handicapped Children* (Denver: Love, 1982); *Curriculum Based Assessment: A Primer* (Springfield: Thomas, 1987).

2.   E.A. Betts, *The Prevention and Correction of Reading Difficulties* (Evanston: Row, Peterson, 1936).

3.   E.E. Gickling, V. Thompson, and C.H. Hargis, *Curriculum Based Assessment: A Task Success Approach* (Newton: Allyn and Bacon, in press); "The Dropout Crisis," *NEA Today* 4, no. 1 (1988), p. 3; Andrew Hahn, "Reaching Out to America's Dropouts: What to Do?" *Phi Delta Kappan* 69, no. 4 (1987), pp. 257–266.

4.   W. Glasser, *The Effect of School Failure on the Life of a Child* (Washington: National Association of Elementary School Principals, 1971).

5.   K.E. Stanovich, "Matthew Effects in Reading: Some Consequences of Individual Differences in the Acquisition of Literacy," *Reading Research Quarterly* 21, no. 4 (1986).

6.   C.H. Hargis, M. Terhaar-Yonkers, P.C. Williams, and M.T. Reed, "Repetition Requirements for Word Recognition," *Journal of Reading* 31, no. 4 (1988).

7.   E.R. Forell, "The Case for Conservative Reader Placement," *The Reading Teacher* 38, no. 9 (1985).

8.   F.B. Evans, "What Research Says about Grading." In *Degrading the Grading Myths: A Primer of Alternatives to Grades and Marks*, edited by S.B. Simon and J.A. Bellanca, pp. 30–50 (Washington: Association for Supervision and Curriculum Development, 1976).

9.   L.B. Resnick, "Learning in School and Out," *Educational Researcher* 16, no. 9 (1987).

10.   H. Kirschenbaum, R. Napier, and S.B. Simon, *Wad-ja-get? The Grading Game in American Education* (New York: Hart, 1971).

11.   M.S. Marshall, *Teaching Without Grades* (Corvallis: Oregon State University Press, 1968).

12.   R. Miller, "Two Hundred Years of Holistic Education," *Holistic Education Review* 1, no. 1, (1988).

13.   D.N. Lombardi and R.J. Corsini, "C4R: A New System of Schooling," *Holistic Education Review* 1, no. 3 (1988).

# School Corporal Punishment:
## Legalized Child Abuse

### by Robert E. Fathman

*Robert E. Fathman, Ph.D., is Chairman of the National Coalition to Abolish Corporal Punishment in Schools. Comprising more than 30 national organizations including the National Committee for the Prevention of Child Abuse, the American Medical and Bar associations, the National PTA, and others, it has helped to spur many state legislatures to prohibit physical punishment. Dr. Fathman has appeared on the "Today Show," the "Sally Jessey Raphael Show," and many local television and radio talk and news programs. He is a clinical psychologist in private practice in Columbus, Ohio. His doctorate is from the University of Texas, in Austin. His wife is a teacher, and they have four children.*

Do you recall the following scene from a Charles Dickens novel, describing education in the England of 150 years ago? A sunny day, children on the playground, when a nine-year-old girl whispers to another that the teacher kissed another student's father? They giggle, but the girl is overheard. For this horrible affront to the teacher's image, she is held upside down by the ankles by one teacher while struck repeatedly with a board on the front of her legs by another, breaking the board and cutting and scarring her thigh. In another school elsewhere in the country, an eight-year-old boy is similarly suspended by the ankles and shaken, and later choked. The same teacher made other seven-year-old students in the class run around the schoolyard for two-hour stretches until exhausted and dehydrated, or threw them to the floor with her knee in their backs, their arms twisted behind them.

This may sound like interesting, poignant material for a historical novel, but this wasn't written by Dickens. Both of these incidents are described in modern-day U.S. court documents from Penasco, New Mexico,[1] and Greenville, South Carolina,[2] respectively!

Corporal punishment, a euphemism for the legal assault and beating of our schoolchildren, is legal in 31 states. Definitions in state laws are so vague (or nonexistent) that children effectively have no rights and

This selection originally appeared in the Spring 1990 issue of *Holistic Education Review*, Vol. 3, No. 1.

no protection under federal or state laws. Children may be punched, paddled, pinched, and pushed into lockers or down stairs, and their parents have little recourse.

Jim and Beverly Logan of Portsmouth, Ohio, were certain that the law would be on their side when their daughter Jamie was paddled so severely by the male vice-principal at her high school that she sustained horrible bruising to her buttocks, and she walks with an occasional limp two years after the incident. An orthopedic surgeon attributes the limp to permanent damage to two discs in her spine caused by the beating in school. Yet the Logans could not convince the police, the child abuse authorities, nor the county prosecuting authority to file charges in the case. And when Jamie filed a civil suit to pay for her medical expenses, she lost in court. "I guess it's open season on kids in Scioto County, Ohio," said her dad. "This verdict sends a message to teachers that they can do whatever they want to and get away with it."

Information from the U.S. Department of Education indeed shows an "open season" mentality among American educators, with schools reporting over a million children struck by teachers annually.[3] When children are injured, only rarely do courts hold teachers to the same standard of child abuse to which they hold parents. What are we doing to our children when we allow teachers, coaches, and principals to hit them? Are we teaching them respect? Is it necessary for maintaining order in the classroom? Does it create a better educational environment?

No! It is a demeaning, dehumanizing blow to self-esteem that is causing physical and emotional harm to children, and it is unnecessary. Every manual on training dogs tells the owner not to hit but to reward good behavior. And it is against the law to hit pets or farm animals with boards. The Humane Society could bring charges of cruelty to animals. Children, however, end up being treated, legally, in ways we do not treat cows or hogs or German shepherds.

In industry and in the military, hitting is no longer allowed, and no one there regrets it. It cannot be used in prisons nor in juvenile detention centers. Hitting children teaches them to fear adults, not respect them. It engenders a climate of fear, and that ruins concentration and attention span. Worse perhaps than the medical injuries hitting can cause, is the damage it inflicts on self-esteem. A fourth grader near Houston was being paddled daily, for months. His parents didn't know at first. They knew their son was becoming more depressed, more easily frustrated, and finally he began expressing suicidal thoughts. He spent a few months in a psychiatric hospital, where he finally revealed the abuse he was receiving in school. He hadn't told his parents because he felt so down on himself, unworthy of a defense. He was later found to have a learning disability that had caused the distractibility for which he was being paddled.

Children do have learning disabilities, or vision problems, or other things that prevent smooth learning. An understanding of child development means accepting that kids will make mistakes, be impulsive, and sometimes act immaturely. Instead of demanding conformity and punishing nonconformity, good educators accept these individual differences and make allowances for different needs. For example, a high school in a western state has gone to a flexible schedule, not the seven periods a day with five minutes to change classes. Periods are 90 minutes, four a day, three times a week for each class. This allows fifteen minutes between classes, and both teachers and kids can use the time for socialization, phone calls, and bathroom visits. The new schedule has cut out most disciplinary infractions because students rarely talk in class or pass notes, and they aren't tardy for class. Many schools are making more use of "cooperative learning," in which children can talk together to solve problems and work in small teams. These approaches allow kids to stand up and move around more, interact with each other more, and establish a more positive, looser atmosphere in school. All of this cuts down on punishments, allows more room for praise, and sets up a better environment for nurturing self-esteem. The kids learn more and work harder for someone they like.

Hitting children may attain immediate compliance with the wishes of the aggressor, but studies show it does not lead to long-term change or internalization of values. Students learn to be more deceptive, and the misbehavior occurs again when the risks of discovery are lessened— as most teachers already know. The National Education Association, the nation's largest teachers union, has been on record since 1972 calling for an immediate end to the use of corporal punishment in any form. A recent national poll shows only 11% of teachers ever hit kids. The others know it isn't a good practice. It is an archaic throwback to the Middle Ages, a form of behavior control out of step with the professionalism of today's teachers.

Hitting perpetuates a cycle of violence. It teaches children that it is okay for big people to hit little people, for the strong to assault the weak, for disapproved behavior. It is a lesson many kids will then use on their own children, or that children will use against each other, with terribly harmful consequences for our society.

Problems with child abuse are a constant concern in society. We spend millions to prevent it and treat its effects. Our jails overflow with violent criminals who report a childhood filled with corporal punishment at home and in school. Yet we model violence in our schools. We sanctimoniously condemn the violence used against student demonstrations in China, South Africa, and Eastern Europe, yet we allow violence of our own in our tax-supported schools.

The victims of this practice are not just those injured in the many flagrant cases of injury I could cite. We victimize even the children who are not themselves struck. My daughter, Michelle, came home from her first day of kindergarten at a Columbus, Ohio, public school in tears. The teacher had toured the school with her charges, and the principal had shown these new students his paddle and described the circumstances in which it would be used. Welcome to school! The children were not charged with enthusiasm, hope, or self-confidence—just intimidation. The tears were repeated Michelle's second day, when the kindergarten teacher slapped the hand of a boy who had accidentally broken his own crayon. Yes, we make victims of all the children, those who are struck and those who witness.

The most frightening of the victims to me are the children who buy into the system of violence, saying the paddling was "deserved," by themselves or others. These children have lost their sensitivity to violence, and have become an unwitting part of it. When they witness the teacher, the person in authority, hit a child, they begin to find acceptable rationalizations to explain this action to themselves. Soon, they have concluded that if the teacher says so, it must be correct to act this way. In one school, the band director had five students become an active part of the violence by having them "discipline" another student by punching, kicking, dragging him down stairs, and pulling his pants down to humiliate him. In a suburb of Detroit a teacher had every other child in the class take a turn hitting a girl who had chewed gum in her sixth grade class—something that had been allowed in the school from which she had just transferred. Only one child refused to take part. Any way you look at it, we do all of our children a grave disservice with physical punishment, not just those who bear the most immediate brunt of it.

Will sparing the rod spoil the child? Will we have chaos in the classroom if we abolish corporal punishment? Of course not. These are worn out defenses of the pro-paddlers. With nineteen states and thousands of other local districts already having abolished paddling, we now have many models of successful, positive school discipline. Districts or states that have abolished it would quickly revert to using it again if problems developed. Instead, they find that teachers have become more creative, that the classroom atmosphere is more positive for both students and teachers, and no one wants to bring back the old way. When physical punishment stops, vandalism rates go down, and more students stay in school to graduate.[4] One young man from Florida told me that for talking in study hall he was given the choice of a three-day suspension, or bending over, grabbing his ankles, and taking three hits. He told the teacher, "I have a third choice: I quit!" He did.

Those who quote the Biblical "spare the rod" passage are off base. It's a quote from King Solomon, not God. Solomon had many children with his multiple wives and concubines. That he was a poor model of parenthood can be seen in the way his son, Prince Rehoboam, turned out—a brute who enslaved and mistreated his people. Can you picture Jesus beating the heck out of a child with a board, saying, "I'm doing this for your own good"? Others use the argument, "I was paddled and I turned out okay." Many of those same people attended schools with outhouses, too, but neither the outhouse nor the paddle is the reason for their current success. We need to send the paddle the way of the outhouse, relegating it to the history books or the pages of a Dickens novel.

What are the alternatives? There are many. When we discuss alternatives, keep in mind that the word discipline comes from the Latin root meaning to teach. It doesn't mean "punish." Good discipline can occur with no punishment system in place. It is important for teachers to keep kids stimulated by having good lesson plans that don't let the day drag. Positive rewards, such as compliments for things we usually take for granted, will work wonders. Continued problems need discussion to find out the cause, not just a quick-fix reaction. Parents or guidance counselors may need to be consulted. Time out, in the hall or in the principal's office (not a cardboard box) for a very brief period can be used, or in-school suspension in very serious cases. The alternatives are not as important as just plain stopping the hitting, now. Nothing fancy or expensive needs to be set up to take the place of hitting. The alternatives are there already, being used by the teachers who don't hit, usually some in every building. Teachers who hit need only to ask how their peers handle similar situations.

The tide has turned in this country. In 1989 eight states abolished corporal punishment in schools, with more expected to follow suit this year. Courts are just starting to give parents a few victories. Editorial condemnation of physical punishment has spread all over the country. Parents aren't willing to accept this outmoded concept passively. Federal legislators are starting to talk about hearings, and the media is taking a keen interest. There is no longer the question of whether corporal punishment will be outlawed in this country; the question is how soon.

In educating our young, we need to consider the whole child—feelings, self-concept, psychological development—not just the acquisition of knowledge, the rote memorization of facts. We can so easily help children to feel good about themselves, through praise and encouragement and an attitude from us that truly conveys a positive regard. We need to abandon the punitive attitude of catching children being bad and adopt a positive attitude of catching them being good. Showing children that we like them, that we expect good things of them, not just mouthing the words, will earn us their respect. And most important, we will teach them by our example.

Most of the world sees hitting as hitting, as assault. Only in the United States and a handful of other countries do we have to invent a new phrase, corporal punishment, to delineate a form of hitting that is acceptable. In all of the industrialized countries of the world, except the United States, South Africa, a part of Australia, and Canada, hitting by teachers is assault. Let's call it what it really is. And let's get rid of it.

## Notes

1. Carl T. Rowan, "High Court Should Settle School Punishment Question," Houston Post, 6 January 1988.

2. "Teacher, Aide, Principal Arrested for Assault, Neglect of Youths," Anderson, SC Independent-Mail, 6 August 1989.

3. 1985-86 Civil Rights Survey, U.S. Department of Education, Office for Civil Rights, January, 1988.

4. A. Maurer and J. Wallerstein, The Influence of Corporal Punishment on Learning: A Statistical Study (Berkeley: Generation Books, 1983); and J. Wallerstein, "Vandalism: A Statistical Study of Fifty-Five Junior High Schools," The Last Resort 11, no. 3 (1983), p. 12.

# The Medicalization
# of the Classroom:
## The Constriction of Difference
## in Our Schools

### by Steve Harlow

*Steve Harlow is the Chair of the Special Education Department, Center for Teaching and Learning at the University of North Dakota. He has in the past held positions with the University's Medical School. He has also taught in the Denver Public Schools, at the University of Nebraska, Kansas State University, and summer sessions at the University of Wyoming. He is host and co-producer of the regional public radio program* Considering Children. *In addition, he works with teachers and parents in developing ways of engaging children who reveal some area of difficulty.*

"Teaching is impossible. All of the great quests of life begin as impossibilities."
—William Ernest Hocking

This essay will explore certain key assumptions that have informed the practice of the special education arm of the schools. My thesis is that these assumptions and their resulting practices have aided in the invalidation of the uniqueness and selfhood of the very youngsters special education purports to serve. I will focus on the use of the medical model and its shortcomings in dealing with children experiencing difficulties. Because the stimulant Ritalin (and its generic counterpart methylphenidate) has become the "drug of choice" among the pharmacological agents that are used with elementary school-aged youngsters diagnosed as having attentional and activity disorders,[1] I will focus on Ritalin as a symbol of the increasing medicalization of our schools. Finally, I will argue that the type of educational experience youngsters with school-related handicaps receive shrinks their sense of self and disempowers them.

To begin with, I wish to offer a distinction between true handicaps and school-related handicaps. A true handicap refers to a permanent

This selection originally appeared in the Summer 1989 issue of *Holistic Education Review*, Vol. 2, No. 2.

physical or intellectual condition that places important limits on the individual's ability to handle certain situations. The definition implies that the condition can be shown to exist by objective and verifiable means. The verification process involves both professionally administered tests as well as collaboration by the individual and/or those who know him/her best. When dealing with physical or sensory conditions (like blindness or orthopedic handicaps), objective verification does not pose any real difficulty. Here the medical model and its tests appropriately identify and verify the nature of the condition. Using the second part of the verification process—obviousness—the individual and those around him/her are also aware of the handicap and its limitations. The verification process can also be used in the identification of intellectual handicaps such as severe mental retardation. Here again, medical and psychological tests would reveal that an individual is functioning at a very low level intellectually. The presence of severe mental retardation may not be obvious to the individual but certainly would be visible to those who know him/her best.

With most real handicaps, then, the presence of the handicap is known to those who are most familiar with the individual, even before the objective diagnosis is conducted. The handicap is obvious in its presence and in its limitations, and is also present in the totality of the person's environment.

Most of the handicaps that the special education arm of the school deals with do not fulfill the criterion of obviousness or visibility. Such presumed handicaps as educable or mild retardation, learning disabilities, and emotional disturbance are often only visible within the school context. This is not to deny that difficulties in functioning exist; it is, rather, to question the way in which we typically deal with such difficulties. The process of "handicapping" begins as the youngster attempts to meet the social and academic expectations of the school. Difference is not a welcome visitor in the conventional classroom. A student whose needs are not being met is often frustrating to the teacher, either because of the child's seeming inability to learn what is to be learned, or because the student exhibits behavior that puzzles the teachers and others. It is often because of the teacher's failure to understand or reach the child that the child is considered different. The onus usually falls on the child.

The alchemical transformation from a youngster with school-related difficulties to a "disabled" or "handicapped" child occurs through a misapplication of the medical model. The medical model has as its emphasis the detection of faulty functioning. It is the primary paradigm in the identification of special education students. The medical model is a disease or disability schema that rests on the assumption of biological or mechanical dysfunction. It is, therefore, intrinsically reductive; a problem is viewed as a pattern of symptoms that have a physiological or anatomical basis. To identify that set of symptoms means to unlock its biological mechanical underpinnings. Once the biological is unearthed (the etiology), an accurate diagnosis can be determined. After the determination of diagnosis of disease, an approach that may deal with its symptoms is prescribed. Increasingly that approach involves medication.

## Biological dysfunction or academic mismatch?

The use of the medical model may be quite appropriate when dealing with real handicaps (such as deafness or spina bifida). But when the schools use such terms as "handicap," "disability," or "disorder" to refer to children who reveal academic, stylistic, or adjustment difficulties, then the medical model is misdirected and its effects limit human potential. This deflects our attention from difficulties that may stem from academic and social mismatches between the child and his/her school settings to the presumption of biological dysfunction. High activity level, impulsivity, organizational difficulties, poor conduct, and reading below grade level may indeed represent genuine problem areas of student functioning; framing them as handicapping conditions, however, is not a necessary precondition to helping children come to terms with them.

Increasingly, school-related handicaps are defined in terms of a presumed underlying organic etiology. For example, the proposed definition of learning disabilities by the National Institute of Health contains this statement: "These disorders are intrinsic to the individual and presumed to be due to central nervous system dysfunction."[2] Yet the author, in endorsing this definition, then goes on to acknowledge, "Certainly, the causes of most learning disabilities remain unknown." It is quite a leap to bound from "unknown causes" to the ascription of central nervous system dysfunction. This is quite typical of the reasoning process when the medical paradigm is applied to difficulties in learning and living.

A disturbing example of the increasing medicalization of the schools is seen in the growth of the number of children diagnosed with Attention Deficit Hyperactivity Disorder (ADHD). As Gottlieb notes, "epidemiological surveys suggest a significant but variable prevalence of hyperactivity ranging from 3 to 15% of school-aged children in the general population." Viadero similarly points to studies of ADHD that "range from 3 to 10 percent of the 45 million school children, mostly boys."[3] The basic characteristics of the "disorder" are problems with inattention, impulsivity, and hyperactivity. Though ADHD is presumed to be neurologic in its etiology, the necessary signs for its diagnosis are behavioral as reported to the clinician by the teacher. As Andrew Morgan, Professor of Pediatrics of the University of Illinois School of Medicine, points out, "Attention deficit disorder is a clinical diagnosis. At present, there are no specific laboratory tests that will conclusively diagnose the disorder."[4] In other words, the functioning associated with ADHD could well be a direct effect of an inappropriate curricular or educational approach. In these situations, relying on the observations of teachers to fortify the diagnosis is to displace pedagogical responsibility from teacher to child.

The primary treatment of ADHD is the prescription of stimulant medication, usually Ritalin. In fact, from 1983 to 1987 orders received for Ritalin, according to a spokesperson for CIBA (the company that produces the medication), increased 23%.[5] But even this fact does not tell the entire story of its growing use, because sales of Ritalin's generic counterpart, methylphenidate, must also be taken into account. Methylphenidate is frequently prescribed because, while identical to Ritalin, it is less expensive. The *combined* sales of Ritalin and methylphenidate may have *doubled* between 1985 and 1987.

Parents are being persuaded by school officials that Ritalin is necessary to their child's education and adjustment. Of course educators cannot prescribe drugs, but there is evidence that too many educators are suggesting to parents that their children's learning problems require medical intervention. In a similar vein, LeShan points out that

> those children who object to poor teaching and poor educational theory are turned over to the medical arm of the establishment for drugging and retraining. The belief is that Ritalin will cure them of their objection to an educational system on the brink of disaster.[6]

In assuming an organic basis for the child's functioning, school personnel then look beyond their own profession to the physician for an intervention. The use of Ritalin serves as an inadequate response to a child's educational difficulties. It diverts teacher and school responsibility from discovering approaches to a child's needs and talents. The use of medication also prompts teachers, parents, and the student himself to view positive efforts as attributable to the medication. Waddell found, for example, that children who were medicated "were less likely to develop internalized controls, relying instead on medication to moderate their moods and behavior."[7]

Two major reviews of research that examined the effects of Ritalin or methylphenidate on school achievement revealed that the drug had no significant effect on academic performance. Barkley and Cunningham found that stimulant medications including Ritalin had "little if any effect on academic performance of hyperkinetic children." The major effect of the medication was to provide short-term manageability of hyperkinetic behavior. They went on to conclude, however, that "any positive behavioral response to the stimulants is not likely to be accompanied by improvement in academic performance." Aman similarly found that educational gains when stimulant medications were used were negligible.[8]

As Gerald Coles has stated in his important book, *The Learning Mystique: A Critical Look at Learning Disabilities*

> The continued failure to find evidence to support the use of Ritalin and other stimulant drugs for LD required drug advocates and drug companies to retrench. Of course they now said—dropping the claim about drug effects on dysfunction neurology underpinning cognition—stimulant drugs could not be expected to improve academic skills because drugs cannot replace instruction.[9]

Coles, in reviewing the few sound studies that dealt with hyperactivity and emotional adjustment, concluded that the benefits of Ritalin were dubious at best.

What is as serious as the abdication of responsibility on the part of the educator in providing the best learning environment for the child on Ritalin is the potential physical and psychological risks to the child. Morgan, even while advocating the use of stimulant medication with children, mentioned the following "minor" side effects: loss of appetite, insomnia, irritability, headache, emotional lability, and transient growth impairment.[10] Morgan states that the minor side effects are frequent and that while they result in symptomatic complaints, these "are never life threatening and almost always resolve spontaneously or when the medication is discontinued." But this optimistic attitude requires a more critical look.

First, I would argue that the side effects listed are not minor but affect the quality of life of the child in quite a major way. Eating and sleeping difficulties, for example, have a direct impact on a child's responsiveness in the learning environment; there are effects on the energy level of the child and in his/her readiness to engage in class and home activities. Moreover, the presence of emotional lability can profoundly influence the way the child interacts with others.

Second, some of the side effects have important long-term consequences. The mood swings that Waddell found associated with the use of Ritalin robbed children of a sense of control of their emotional lives. As adolescents there had been a constriction in their ability to moderate moods and behavior.

Evidence exists that with high doses of Ritalin there is a suppression of growth in height.[11] There is concern that such growth suppression does not reverse itself with the disuse of the drug. Moreover, since individuals differ in their reactions to Ritalin, what constitutes a high dose for one child may be within the bounds of the recommended dosage for the average child.

Controversy surrounds the effects of Ritalin on cardiac arrythmia. In a letter to the *New England Journal of Medicine,* five physicians of the National Institute of Mental Health cited two methylphenidate-induced cardiac arrhythmias among eight physically able adults treated with the drug.[12] The physicians were prompted to write the letter of warning because of recent cocaine-induced cardiac deaths of two prominent athletes. They remarked about the similar actions of cocaine and methylphenidate on the nervous system as it affects heart rhythm. CIBA lists arrhythmia as a possible side effect from its usage.

All of this points to the tragic fact that our schools are operating as *the* conduit for a major drug that can and does produce physical and psychological damage in its students. School personnel have, perhaps unwittingly, embarked in a Faustian pact that exchanges short-term management of student behavior for potentially long-term psychological and health difficulties. It is far from a fair bargain for the students we should be educating.

Fortunately, a few parents are beginning to bring legal challenges to school districts who encourage the promiscuous use of Ritalin. At the present, however, most parents whose children are taking the drug are not well informed about its significant physical and behavioral side effects. Advocates of Ritalin talk of its calming qualities, but—as many teachers who have had students on the drug will attest—there appears to be a thin line between calming and sedation.

It seems that ADHD is a unique phenomenon of American schools. The likelihood of being diagnosed ADHD is 20 times greater in the United States than in Great Britain, for example. Similarly, Koestler warned that American psychologists have a tendency to find disturbance and abnormal functioning where their British counterparts do not. He concluded that Americans and their mental health practitioners are highly conformist in their viewpoints of differences in behavior. What is hyperactive to American authorities would be attributed to a difference in style by their British counterparts.[13]

## The dominance of the medical model

While the WISC (intelligence test) is not a stethoscope and a Wood-cock-Johnson educational diagnostic test is not a CAT scan, they provide the same instrumentation to the medical orientation within the schools. The movement of the medical model into the schools does not rely on the active presence of the medical practitioner. Rather, its movement rests on the need to create a tensionless environment in the classroom, to reduce human functioning to simple components (e.g., activity level, intelligence scores), and to the quarantining of differences. Today's schools operate from a fixed axiom that a narrow homogeneity of the regular classroom is necessary to educate efficiently.

A great multiplier effect seems built into the medical model as it seeks to identify present learning and behavioral difficulties. For example, Smith and Robinson estimate that as many as 20 percent of the school population "has been labeled and served as learning disabled."[14] Yet Bower estimates that ten percent of the school population "could reasonably be considered as emotionally disturbed."[15] There is a strong tendency in the medical orientation to overclassify those who differ from the normal or typical into categories of pathology. Rosenhahn explains it this way:

> physicians are more inclined to call a healthy person sick (a false positive: Type II error) than a sick person healthy (a false negative: Type I error). The reasons are not hard to find; it is clearly more dangerous to misdiagnose illness than health. Better to err on the side of caution, to suspect illness even among the healthy.[16]

This tendency to be on guard for illness and disorder may be appropriate when dealing with possible physical problems. It is, however, quite a different matter when the medical approach focuses on problems that involve social and academic adjustment. Diagnostic classification has social and emotional implications that affect the ways others—students as well as school professionals —will respond to the child.

The question as to why the medical model should become so influential in the determination of how we deal with difference is in part answered by viewing the greater culture. As Zilbergeld has observed, the

> tendency to focus on what is wrong and problematic, rather than on the total situation or on what is good and problem-free, has become a part of modern sensibility . . . . We have accepted a fantasy model of well-being and mental health, and therefore of life, that probably cannot be attained by anyone. So we have plenty of deficits to attend to, meaning both that we stay in a constant state of discontent and in continual need of assistance to make things better.[17]

The absence of well being becomes illness. Departure from the norm becomes disorder. Christopher Lasch has stated that the therapeutic community "would abolish the hospital only to make the whole world a hospital."[18] And the school has become a ward of this great hospital.

In sum, a subtle but thorough transformation has occurred in the schools. When we deal with difference that provokes any type of tension in school settings, we turn to the medical model rather than educational models for a solution. With this transformation have come diagnostic categories that essentially keep labeled children from participating in the same educational experience as their nonlabeled peers. But even more than that, the process of sorting freezes the child at the level of objective description with preset limits drawn from the category of disability, while not freely permitting the process of discovery and growth. It is not long before the label replaces the child. With this an insidious reduction occurs: *difference* becomes equated with *inferiority*.

### *Special* education

If, by sorting out differences according to *educational* needs, a qualitatively better education—something that could by truly deemed "special"—resulted, then the practice would be defensible. In the final analysis it is the type of education the child participates in that becomes the touchstone of our efforts. Let us briefly examine the quality of education the child with a school-related handicap receives.

What should we mean by education? Richard Mitchell has pointed out the importance of framing basic questions with the sense of "should-ness." He points out that in such matters as intelligence, love, or education we are dealing not with questions of fact, but rather with questions of moral consequence.[19] In education we are reminded that our work is with human potential and human struggle. It begins with the meeting of a child with his or her teacher and classmates. Such a meeting should neither be clouded by labels, nor should it deny the presence of the difficulties a child may bring into a setting. Education does not have as its prerequisites an optimum bioanatomy, a difficulty-free learning style, a compliant disposition, or a harmonious home life.

Education should be an elevating process that enables the child to gain increasing knowledge of self and also a deepening sense of the world. In reality, the children designated with handicaps are treated quite differently from their nonhandicapped peers. First they have a specialist (e.g., special education teacher, learning disabilities teacher) who makes the major educational decisions for them. They may also have a special classroom provided. Both of these factors underscore and reinforce their difference. Knowledge of self is thus distorted.

Second, the educational regimen calls for a selection of tasks that the child can readily achieve—a *reduced* rather than deepening sense of the world. IEPs for most children are legal agreements that guarantee the child's attainment of concrete and uninteresting objectives. Exclusive emphasis is placed on what John Passmore has described as closed capacities.[20] Closed capacities are those areas of learning that allow for total mastery. They are by their nature objective and prescriptive. When dealing with closed capacities the personal qualities of the learner are secondary to what is to be learned. In contrast, open capacities are those areas that one can gain a deepening knowledge about, while permitting a sense of self-expression; they cannot be totally mastered (e.g., interpretation, chess, writing, storytelling, or sculpting have no final state of completion). Open capacities involve personal ways of knowing and expression. The emphasis is on the extension of meaning as students immerse themselves in the educational setting. The rhythms of the open are process and form, concept and feeling. Closed capacities, as Passmore notes, are readily converted into routines.

In teaching, staying with closed capacities has the advantage of being able to gauge and manage the progress of an activity. The purported value for the student of staying with the easily achievable is a steady current of success. Yet such success is an imposter. To the student these tasks are unrelated to discovery of self or the world. They are dehydrated of meaning. How can we enable a child who might have attentional difficulties to look and grasp when we pay so little attention to what is alive in him and around him? No, the answer to such a child's difficulties lies elsewhere. In the end the true value of emphasizing closed capacities for the special student is the predictability that the routine brings. However, curiosity, imagination, and self-expression are not well nourished by routine.

A paradox may be discerned. The special education program focuses upon the problem area of a child's being, while at the same time attempting to create a setting where few problems confront him. The child with a school-related handicap is thought by those who plan and care for him to be unable to handle much of the real world. His or her special teacher mediates the demands of school and life by drastically reducing them to fragmented and closed capacities. Few accommodations are made by regular teachers to permit adjustment to the regular classroom. Rather than aiding the child in one's understanding and involvement of the world, school removes him or her from it. In the process the child is subtly convinced that s/he cannot handle much of what is ordinarily to be explored and learned. The authority of the school, after all, has mirrored to him that as a child possessing a handicap he can handle so much and no more.

What is denied the child in all of this is his or her sense of uniqueness and personal experience. As Malcolm Ross contends, "People need to feel whole and must be responsible for their own wholeness. That means they must be helped to make their own sense of the whole of their experience, body and soul, mind and feelings."[21] Such is the type of education that should be available to all youngsters, but particularly to those who are experiencing difficulties in school. A piecemeal education that uproots the child from one's peers is not conducive to the wholeness Ross describes. Inclusion in the community of the classroom is a requisite for the child to come to terms with his or her uniqueness. Short of that, we are imprinting within the child's conception of self that he or she is a member of a special subspecies of students: the handicapped.

Difficulties in functioning can be met with patience, flexibility, and accommodation. It is not the absence of struggle and tension that makes us human, but rather the quality of our engagement. With support and understanding, struggle may prove to be a catalyst to gaining self-knowledge and self-agency. Education in this sense is truly special.

## Notes

1.   G. Coles, *The Learning Mystique: A Critical Look at Learning Disabilities* (New York: Ballantine, 1987); M.I. Gottlieb, "The Hyperactive Child" in M.I. Gottlieb and J. Williams (eds.),*Textbook of Developmental Pediatrics* (New York: Plenum Medical, 1987).

2.   J. Kavanagh, *New Federal Biological Definition of Learning and Attentional Disorders*. Presentation at fifteenth annual conference, Orton Dyslexic Society, New York, March 4, 1988.

3.   Gottlieb, "The Hyperactive Child," p. 308; D. Viadero, "Debate Grows on Classroom's Magic Pill" *Education Week* 7, no. 7 (October 21, 1987), p. 19.

4.   A.M. Morgan, "Use of Stimulant Medications in Children," *American Family Practitioner* 38, no. 4 (October 1988), p. 197.

5.   Personal communication, April 1989.

6.   L. LeShan, *The Mechanic and the Gardener* (New York: Holt, Rinehart, and Winston, 1982), p. 19.

7.   K. Waddell, "The Self Concept and Social Adaptation of Hyperactive Children in Adolescence," *Journal of Clinical Child Psychology* 13, no. 1 (1984), p. 54.

8.   R.A. Barkley and C.E. Cunningham, "Do Stimulant Drugs Improve the Academic Performance of Hyperkinetic Children?" *Clinical Pediatrics* 17, no. 1 (1977), p. 90; M.G. Aman, "Psychotropic Drugs and Learning Problems: A Selective Review," *Journal of Learning Disabilities* 13, no. 2 (1980).

9.   G. Coles, *The Learning Mystique*, p. 94.

10.   Morgan, "Use of Stimulant Medications in Children."

11.   D.J. Safer and R.P. Allen, "Factors Influencing the Suppressant Effects of Two Stimulant Drugs on the Growth of Hyperactive Children" *Pediatrics* 51, no. 4 (April 1973).

12.   P. Lucas, D. Gardner, O. Wolkowitz, E. Tucker, and R. Cowdry, "Methylphenidate-Induced Cardiac Arrhythmia," *New England Journal of Medicine* 315 (1986).

13.   D. McGuinness, *When Children Don't Learn* (New York: Basic Books, 1985); A. Koestler, *The Heel of Achilles* (New York: Random House, 1975).

14.   D.D. Smith and S. Robinson, "Educating the Learning Disabled" in R. Morris and B. Blatt (eds.), *Special Education: Research and Trends* (New York: Pergamon, 1986), p. 236.

15.   Quoted in J. Kauffman, "Educating Children with Behavior Disorders" in Morris and Blatt, *Special Education*, pp. 249-271.

16.   D. Rosenhahn, "On Being Sane in Insane Places," in B. Goleman and D. Heller (eds.), *The Pleasures of Psychology* (New York: New American Library, 1986), p. 348.

17.  B. Zilbergeld, *The Shrinking of America: Myths of Psychological Change* (Boston: Little, Brown, 1983), p. 20.

18.  Quoted in Zilbergeld, *Shrinking of America*, p. 94.

19.  R. Mitchell, *The Gift of Fire* (New York: Simon and Schuster, 1987).

20.  J. Passmore, *The Philosophy of Teaching* (Cambridge: Harvard University Press, 1980).

21.  M. Ross, *The Creative Arts* (London: Heinemann Educational, 1978), p. 62.

# Bilingual Learners:
## How Our Assumptions Limit Their World

### by Yvonne S. Freeman and David Freeman

*Yvonne S. Freeman, PhD, Language and Literacy, University of Arizona; MA, ESL, University of Arizona, is presently Director of Bilingual Education, Fresno Pacific College, Fresno, CA. She is coauthor of* **Report Card on Basal Readers,** *and has written book chapters and journal articles on the topics of basal readers, reading, and whole language approaches for second language students.*

*David Freeman, PhD, Linguistics, University of Arizona; MA, ESL, University of Arizona, is presently Director of the Language Development Program at Fresno Pacific College. He has written book chapters and articles on text cohesion, reading, and whole language approaches for second language students.*

The assumptions we make limit what can be learned. Alter those assumptions and the potential for learning expands.[1]

On the subject of how children learn, educators, parents, and even politicians have often formed their assumptions on common sense rather than on research-based theory. In many cases, these assumptions never have been stated explicitly, but they have served as the basis for important educational decisions. This is particularly true of assumptions about bilingual learners. In a review of the research on bilingualism, Hakuta points out, "There are emotional and political realities underlying the controversy over bilingual education that no amount of scientific investigation will smooth over."[2] Misunderstandings about the nature of bilingualism, how bilinguals learn, and bilingual education have influenced not only classroom methodology and family learning activities in homes but also local, state, and national legislation for bilingual education. Unfortunately, many assumptions about bilingual learners have hindered rather than helped.

Bilingual students are not merely a fringe element in schools. The 1988 California Tomorrow report, *Crossing the Schoolhouse Border*, notes

This selection originally appeared in the Winter 1989 issue of *Holistic Education Review,* Vol. 2, No. 4.

that "5.3 million Californians—20% of the population—are foreign born," and that "soon after the turn of the century there will be no single majority ethnic group in California."[3] California provides a preview of the future in this country—one that cannot be ignored. Already there are California school districts where as much as eighty percent of the school population are limited or non-English speakers. These students come from all over the world, with the largest number of recent immigrants from the Americas and Asia.

These immigrant children have been misunderstood in this country for some time. The dropout rate for these students is increasing, but their lack of success is not surprising in view of the fact that they enter a school system that is foreign, where the language is incomprehensible, where faces of classmates are of many colors, and where parents feel unempowered and frustrated. The authors of *Crossing the Schoolhouse Border* point out, "While we talk about democracy and equal opportunity, in reality many of our students are barely given a chance to get out of the gate. The basic question is not how we can teach these students, but whether we really want to."[4]

Bilingual students who do not achieve certain levels on standardized tests or state-approved English language tests often are labeled as "Limited English Proficient" (LEP) or as "functionally illiterate."[5] Proponents of bilingual education point out that children labeled LEP often are believed to be semilingual or to have no language. In most cases, the child, the child's family, or the child's culture has been blamed for the lack of success in schools.[6] As a result, instructional models for bilingual students in this country have been developed with the assumption that education must overcome some sort of deficiency.

For example, Flores lists several kinds of deficits educators and the general public have used over the years to explain the academic failure of Hispanics in our country's schools:

1920s—Spanish speaking children were considered mentally retarded due to language difficulty.

1930s—Bilingualism and its effects upon the reading aspects of language were considered a problem.

1940s—Because of their "language problem," it was thought that Mexican children should be segregated.

1950s—Schools were called upon to provide for deficiencies by providing "a rich and satisfying program."

1960s—The child's home and language were viewed as the primary cause of school failure.

1970s—It was thought that when bilingual children code switch, mix their languages, it is an indication that they know neither well.[7]

If educators, parents, and politicians view bilingualism as a deficit, they may act on certain assumptions and adopt educational practices that actually limit the potential of bilingual students. In the sections that follow, we examine five common assumptions which we believe limit the potential of bilingual students. After considering the ways in which each of these common-sense assumptions limits the potential of bilingual learners, we describe a program based on recent research that can help bilinguals to develop their full potential.

**1.  Learning is the transfer of knowledge from teachers to students**

The idea that learning results from the transfer of knowledge from teachers to students underlies much current educational practice. Inherent in this thinking is the notion that what is taught explicitly is what is learned directly. Students are perceived as being like plants: passive and in need of nourishment from outside sources in order to develop and bloom.[8] For example, during social studies period, a teacher might lecture on world religions, world geography, or world economics without ever first finding out what students already have experienced or read about in these areas.

Teachers who view students as plants often adopt what Freire calls the "banking" concept of education: "In the banking concept of education, knowledge is a gift bestowed by those who consider themselves knowledgeable upon those whom they consider to know nothing."[9] Students passively receive deposits of knowledge to file and store. Since the assumption is made that teachers know the language and bilingual students do not, "the teacher teaches and the students are taught . . . the teacher talks and the students listen—meekly . . . the teacher chooses and enforces his choice, and the students comply."[10]

This assumption that students learn what teachers teach contains some truth. However, teachers sometimes don't realize what it is they are teaching. As Frank Smith points out, we may look at what students have learned and deduce what they were taught.[11] In math classes, for example, students might have learned that math is boring. In language arts, they might have learned that reading is sounding out words and that good readers are those who pronounce words well in Standard English dialect. Above all, bilingual learners might have learned that they lack the language and the cultural background that teachers and schools consider necessary for success in school and society.

As these examples suggest, it is possible for both teaching and learning to be going on in the same room at the same time, but often what teachers think they are teaching is different from what students are learning. This discrepancy is the result of viewing students as plants. Lindfors suggests that teachers would do better to think of their students as explorers who interact with their environment, their peers, and their teachers as they learn about the world.[12] This idea is supported by Halliday, who, through studying his own child learning language, discovered that children actively "learn how to mean" in meaningful, functional social interaction.[13]

In an explorer classroom the teacher does not simply transmit knowledge about religion, geography, or economics. Instead, the teacher explores the topics with the students, drawing on what they know, and involves them actively in the process of discovering more. A teacher teaching at any level with children of varying cultural and linguistic backgrounds could read Peter Spier's book *People* as a stimulus for study on similarities and differences, world population, individual physical characteristics, religion, recreation, housing, means of making a living, and different world languages.[14] Students then could chose areas of special interest to them to read about further and become "experts" in those areas.

This type of exploration can be done in the children's first or second language, but in either case the children are seen as having something to contribute to the learning, not as passive recipients of someone else's knowledge. Instruction in an explorer classroom develops the potential of bilingual students rather than limiting it.

## 2. Learning oral language precedes learning to read and write

Whatever image they hold of learners, one of the most common assumptions that teachers make is that they must teach oral language before written language. This assumption limits the potential of students. Harste, Woodward, and Burke discovered that preschool and kindergarten teachers working with monolingual English speakers often ignore meaningful reading and writing activities in language arts because they assume their job is to develop oral language. The same attitude is even more prevalent in second language and bilingual classrooms, where teachers delay the use of writing in the second language even though written language is crucial for academic success.[15]

Often, bilingual students can read and write before they can understand and produce conventional English orally. Frequently, bilingual students are limited to learning to pronounce Standard English, while their English speaking peers are developing their literacy skills as they study various content areas. As a result, when bilingual students are mainstreamed into all English classes, their lack of experience with reading and writing puts them at a disadvantage.

In second language teaching, oral language has had supremacy since the formulation of the slogan inspired by structural linguists: "Language is speech, not writing."[16] In two popular approaches to second language teaching, the Natural Approach and Total Physical Response, speaking, reading, and writing are postponed to give students an aural comprehension base first. For example, the general belief among some language educators is that readers must be able to say the words to understand them. However, research is disproving this. Krashen, whose hypotheses form the basis for the Natural Approach, has found that "reading exposure" or "reading for genuine interest with a focus on meaning" provides language learners with reading "comprehensible input" similar to oral "comprehensible input."[17] The reading exposure contributes to second language acquisition, just as oral language does. Krashen also proposes that reading contributes to competence in writing, just as listening helps children to acquire oral language.[18]

Hudelson's research supports Krashen's more recent views; namely, children who speak little or no English can read print in the environment and can write English, using it for various purposes. In fact, Hudelson found that some second language learners can write and read with greater mastery of English than their oral performance might indicate.[19]

Along the same lines, Edelsky's research in bilingual classrooms indicates that written expression in English may precede formal reading instruction, and that bilingual learners use knowledge of their first language and of the world and actively apply their knowledge as they write.[20]

The research suggests, then, that functional reading and writing, as well as speaking and listening activities, should be integral parts of all language classrooms, because all processes interact. Harste, Woodward, and Burke describe individual reading, writing, speaking, and listening encounters as all feeding into a common "pool" from which other encounters draw. Rather than assuming that speaking, listening, reading, and writing are separate and should be kept separate, Burke explains that all expressions of language "support growth and development in literacy."[21] This data pool concept suggests that requiring bilingual students to master oral skills before they write and read actually can limit their learning potential.

In explorer classrooms where both teachers and students are involved in learning and teaching, bilingual students can develop all of their language skills. For example, the teacher or students can read stories that reflect different religious backgrounds. Together they can discuss what interests them, and then students can write reactions to what they have heard, talked about, and read about and report back to their peers. In this way, students can read, listen, speak, and write about topics they choose to explore.

### 3. Learning proceeds from part to whole

A third assumption is that real, whole language is too difficult for bilingual students, and that learning is easier if language is broken down into smaller parts. This assumption has guided instruction for both English-speaking and bilingual students. In language arts classes for English speakers, children are asked to underline parts of speech, put in capital letters and punctuation, and circle pictures of things that begin with the same sound. Bilingual students might also be asked to fill in correct verb forms, substitute plurals for singulars, and practice minimal pair sounds.

In either case, the assumption is made that mastery of these exercises dealing with parts of language in isolation will lead to mastery of real language. The faulty assumption is that if students begin with simplified sentences and isolated grammar points, they will more easily be able to build up to the production of correct, whole language. In other words, some educators believe that learning goes from part to whole and that it is the teacher's job to select and present the parts the students need to learn. This assumption, like the first two, serves to limit student potential.

The idea that learning goes from part to whole is a common-sense idea. In industry, complex tasks are often broken down into simple operations to improve production. However, what works in business does not seem to work in learning. Research indicates that language is learned from whole to part rather than from part to whole. Vygotsky believed that word meanings, for instance, develop in a functional way from whole to part, even though in quantity language seems to develop from part to whole as the child moves from one word, to several words, to full sentences.

> In regard to meaning . . . the first word of the child is a whole sentence. Semantically, the child starts from the whole, from a meaningful complex, and only later begins to master the separate semantic units, the meanings of words, and to divide his formerly undifferentiated thought into those units.[22]

Even though children begin by speaking in single words, the words really represent whole ideas that have broad and often vague meanings. For example, "milk" may mean "I want some milk," "I spilled the milk," or "Where is the milk?" Thus, single words such as "milk" move semantically from whole, generalized meanings, toward more definite, specific meanings close to adult meanings with more complex syntax.

Goodman explains that we are "first able to use whole utterances" and that, "only later can we see the parts in the wholes and begin to experiment with their relationship to each other and to the meaning of the whole."[23] Parts are harder to learn because they are more abstract. Words embedded in meaningful intonation patterns and produced in meaningful and familiar contexts are easier to learn than isolated words.

Many parents have experienced the difficulties imposed by a lack of context when asked by their children to give a definition for an isolated word from a vocabulary list. The parent often will ask the child to use the word in a sentence or explain the situation where the child heard the word. Only in the context of the whole is it possible to explain what most words mean. In the same way, individual facts or dates from a social studies book are harder to learn than facts and dates embedded in historical contexts. When older students in a social studies class first read Hunt's *Across Five Aprils* and then study the details of the Civil War in the United States, they have a picture of the whole situation, the people involved, and the setting.[24] It is only at that point that the isolated facts, dates, and names can take on meaning. The same principle holds for all subjects. For example, it is easier for elementary second-language students studying the vocabulary and concepts of large numbers to read (or have read to them) *How Much Is a Million* by Schwartz than it is for them to do isolated exercises in translating numbers like 1,000,000 into words.[25]

In many bilingual classrooms, the approach to language teaching has been to isolate parts of the language in order to make learning easier. However, many successful teachers in bilingual classes are now beginning to treat language as communication and not as a separate subject made up of skills to be taught in isolation. Wong-Fillmore found that teachers who saw the task of teaching language as "explicit instruction on the language" rather than language "as a medium of communication" provided poor instruction.[26] Enright and McCloskey point out that teachers in communicative bilingual and ESL classrooms "speak of developing 'literacy' and 'communicative competence' rather than of teaching 'reading,' 'writing,' and 'language arts'."[27] When the language is kept whole, the focus is not on the linguistic system, but on content that is functional and meaningful for students. This accomplishes what Goodman calls the "double agenda": students develop concepts through study of the content and, at the same time, teachers are aware that the students are learning language.[28]

Organizing teaching by breaking down subjects into parts and presenting one part at a time may be easier for teachers but more difficult for learners. Teaching part to whole is logical, but it is not psychological.[29] Students often fail to see how the individual pieces go together to form a coherent picture. It is as though they are trying to do a jigsaw puzzle without being able to see the picture on the box. Thus, although teachers sometimes assume that teaching the parts will help their bilingual students, the process limits students' potential. Particularly in bilingual classes, if students are forced to focus on bits and pieces of English, they may fail to learn English and, at the same time, fall further behind their monolingual classmates in knowledge of subject area content.

**4.  Learning to read is different in different languages**

Some bilingual teachers who believe in a communicative approach for the teaching of English as a second language and teach reading and writing in English with a focus on meaning, switch to a phonics approach for the teaching of reading in the first language. These teachers are acting on the assumption that learning to read is different in different languages, and this assumption may limit the potential of their bilingual students.

It may be that teachers teach reading differently because they themselves remember learning their first language through phonics, but it may also be the result of misconceptions about language differences. Barrera points out that in Spanish–English bilingual education there exist the notions that "first-language reading and second-language reading are disparate processes," and that "language-based differences in second-language reading are reading problems to be eradicated."[30]

As Barrera notes, many educators believe that Spanish reading "is different from reading in English—that it is much easier—because of the greater regularity of the Spanish sound-letter system."[31] This view of instruction encourages a phonics approach, which emphasizes the code rather than the meaning. However, Barrera points out that reading in the first and second languages are both meaning-seeking processes. This view of reading is strengthened by miscue analysis research done with other non-English-speaking children reading in their first language. The results of this research show that Hispanic, Polish, Yiddish, and Arabic children are not "bound by letter-by-letter processing of print," but use both "selected visual cues and their knowledge of language and the real world to anticipate, to predict, and to hypothesize about print."[32]

Other teachers avoid teaching reading in the first language because they assume that teaching children two languages at once will confuse them. The belief is that because the two languages are different, they will interfere with each other, and children will learn neither language. In reality, as children in a bilingual environment learn language, they work out the contexts in which to use each language and learn naturally when each language is appropriate to use.[33] Children in bilingual programs in the United States who are learning to speak, read, and write their first language will naturally be learning English at the same time because of their surroundings and the need for English. Children hear English spoken by others at school, in stores, and on television. Much of the print in the environment is in English. Children respond to the English in their environment and, when encouraged, can learn to understand, speak, read, and write in both their first and second languages at the same time.

The assumption that learning to read is different in different languages limits student potential in at least two ways: Most obviously, students who do not develop literacy in their first language lose something of their own culture, and they also lose the advantage of being fully bilingual. At the same time, if literacy instruction is limited to the second language because teachers believe that the reading process is different in different languages, then teachers may delay reading in English until oral language is mastered. Therefore, bilingual students will fall behind their English-speaking peers who are benefiting from reading and writing as well as speaking and listening.

5. **Learning should take place in English to facilitate assimilation**

The first four assumptions, although they impact on bilingual children, can limit the potential of all learners. The final assumption, however, applies directly to bilingual learners. This is the two-part assumption that (a) for bilinguals the purpose of instruction is assimilation and (b) instruction in English is essential to school success. The first part of this assumption is often voiced by politicians and put into practice by educators.

In 1917, Theodore Roosevelt stated:

> [A]ny man who comes here . . . must adopt the institutions of the United States, and therefore he must adopt the language which is now the native tongue of our people. . . . It would be not merely a matter of misfortune but a crime to perpetuate differences of language in this country. . . .[34]

A similar view was expressed more recently by William Bennett, former U.S. Secretary of Education: "In America . . . we can say *E Pluribus Unum:* out of many we have become one."[35] Though he went on to say that we "respect our differences; each of us is justly proud of his own ethnic heritage," the Secretary's basic message was that minority children should be taught English and English only, and schools should not waste time and money teaching the native language. The underlying political philosophy expressed is one of assimilation.

Many proponents of bilingual education have suggested that our country would be better served by taking a pluralistic view of the place of the minority child in our society and rejecting the "melting pot" image. Instead of having to conform to the majority culture and language, bilingual children could be encouraged to maintain their first language and culture, develop their second language, and understand their second culture in order to participate fully in it. Rather than seeing the United States as a "melting pot," these cultural pluralists view the country as a "salad bowl" with children from each culture contributing flavor or spice while maintaining their individuality. In fact, in a truly pluralistic society, bilingualism is promoted for all students, not just minority students.[36] In a pluralistic society, bilingual citizens come to understand not only languages, but other cultures and points of view in order to deal with the modern problems of society. Thus, the assumption that the goal of education is assimilation limits the potential of both bilingual students and the nation as a whole.

Proponents of assimilation, such as former Secretary Bennett, further assume that instruction should be in English for "full participation in this remarkable nation of ours. . . . English only should be taught because . . . a sense of cultural pride cannot come at the price of proficiency in English, our common language."[37] The assumption is that more instruction in English makes students more proficient in English, while instruction in a second language takes away from English proficiency.

Again, this common-sense assumption that more English makes for better English has been challenged by recent research. Cummins found that bilinguals taught in their native language not only developed concepts more rapidly than bilinguals taught the same concepts in a second language, but that they also developed greater English proficiency even though they received less English instruction.[38] Cummins argues that concepts, including knowledge of the forms and functions of language, are most readily developed in the first language, and, once developed, are accessible through the second language. Once a child knows how to read in one language, the child can transfer that knowledge about reading to the second language. The child does not need to learn to read all over again any more than Einstein needed to learn physics all over again when he came to the United States.

Assuming that English-only instruction will benefit bilinguals may, in fact, limit their potential for learning English. This is especially true in situations where English instruction emphasizes oral language over written language and presents oral language in bits and pieces rather than in meaningful wholes.

The five common-sense assumptions about what's best for bilingual learners combine, in many educational programs, to prevent bilinguals from developing their full potential. If these assumptions are rejected, a different sort of instructional program could be considered, one designed to build on the strengths that bilingual learners bring to schools in the United States rather than concentrating on their deficiencies.

## A whole language approach for the bilingual learner

One approach to education that builds on the strengths of bilingual learners is the whole language approach. Whole language teachers base their practice on current research in language and literacy development.

As Goodman, Goodman, and Flores point out, "The basic assumption on which to build the bilingual curriculum, including biliteracy, must be based on sound views about language and language learning."[39] A review of this research leads whole language teachers to reject the five false assumptions discussed above, because those assumptions are based on common sense rather than research.

In the first place, whole language teachers reject the notion that a class should be teacher centered—that teachers have all the knowledge and that students are no more than passive plants. Instead, in making curriculum decisions, they follow Dewey's advice: "The child is the starting point, the center, and the end. . . ."[40] Dewey argued that learners are frequently capable of doing more than adults/teachers think they can. In whole language classes, in order to build on student strengths, educators turn to the child as informant. Goodman proposes that all teachers should be "kid watchers" and carefully observe students in action in the classroom.[41] By watching children, teachers can gain insights into how learning takes place. Consequently, whole language teachers are better able to meet students' needs. They can create lessons that build on what learners bring to the learning situation. Research has shown that children, including bilingual learners, learn when they are active participants in the learning process. In addition, Frank Smith states that children do not learn when (a) they already know it, (b) they don't understand it, and (c) they don't want to risk.[42] In whole language classrooms, teachers create a risk-free environment in which students may explore what they do not already know in a meaningful way, drawing upon what they do know in a way that makes sense to them.

In a whole language classroom, teachers reject the notion that oral language must be mastered before written language is introduced. Instead, they integrate speaking, listening, reading, and writing in every activity. They recognize that oral language can build on written language at the same time that written language expands on the oral language base, and that learners cannot afford to delay the development of literacy skills.

Whole language teachers also reject the idea that learning goes from part to whole. Rather than breaking down language or content area subjects into parts in order to simplify them, whole language teachers work to keep the concepts whole and teach from whole to part. They realize that both language and concepts develop naturally when they are studied in real, functional contexts. Providing additional contexts helps bilingual students to grasp new concepts, while focusing on isolated parts out of context makes learning more difficult.

Whole language teachers also realize that, although languages differ, the process of learning to read is the same for all students. For that reason, teachers use the same method to teach reading in both the first and second languages, emphasizing that reading is a meaning-seeking process, not an exercise in pronouncing words. They know that learning takes place when it is functional and meaningful to the learner. Therefore, a whole language classroom offers students functional reading tasks that are an extension of natural learning outside of the classroom in an atmosphere that encourages their bilingual learners to take risks as they make sense of the world.

Finally, whole language teachers reject the idea that more English leads to better English. Instead, they encourage their bilingual students to draw upon both their languages as they learn. They discover that their students actually develop English proficiency more completely and rapidly as a result. In addition, by emphasizing the importance of the first language, whole language teachers advocate cultural pluralism rather than assimilation. Instead of stifling differences, they celebrate diversity.

Therefore, in a whole language classroom, instead of beginning with the one thing the bilingual students lack—English—teachers build on their students' strengths. They help their students to expand on the background experience they bring to the learning situation. They draw on the rich knowledge bilinguals have in both their first and second languages and cultures, so students can develop both languages and become both bilingual and bicultural. For whole language teachers, the goal of education is not to assimilate bilingual children in a "melting pot," but rather to allow them to add flavor, texture, and spice to society's "salad."

## Notes

1.   J. Harste, V. Woodward, and C. Burke, *Language Stories and Literacy Lessons* (Portsmouth NH: Heinemann Educational Books, 1984), p. 70.

2.   K. Hakuta, *Mirror of Language: The Debate on Bilingualism* (New York: Basic Books, 1986), p. 13.

3.   L. Olsen, project director, *Crossing the Schoolhouse Border* (San Francisco: California Tomorrow, 1988), p. 5.

4.   Ibid., p. 40.

5.   E. Thonis, "Reading Instruction for Language Minority Students," *Schooling and Language Minority Students: A Theoretical Framework* (Los Angeles: California Evaluation, Dissemination, and Assessment Center, 1983).

6.   P. Pelosi, "Imitative Reading with Bilingual Students," in *Ethnoperspectives on Bilingual Education Research,* edited by R. Padilla (Ypsilanti, MI: Dept. of Foreign Languages and Bilingual Studies, 1981); T. Carter and R. Segura, *Mexican Americans in School* (New York: College Entrance Examination Board, 1979); and E. Hernández-Chávez, "The Inadequacy of English Immersion Education as an Educational Approach for Language Minority Students in the United States," in *Studies on Immersion Education* (Sacramento: California State Dept. of Education, 1984), p. 145.

7.   B. Flores, *Language Interference or Influence: Toward a Theory of Hispanic Bilingualism* (unpublished doctoral dissertation, Univ. of Arizona, Tucson, 1982).

8.   J. Lindfors, "Exploring in and through Language," in *On TESOL '82,* edited by M. Clark and J. Handscombe (Washington DC: TESOL, 1982), pp. 143–155.

9.   P. Freire, *Pedagogy of the Oppressed,* translated by Myra Ramos (New York: Continuum, 1987), p. 58.

10.   Ibid., p. 59.

11.   F. Smith, *Insult to Intelligence* (New York: Arbor House, 1986).

12.   J. Lindfors, "Exploring in and through Language," pp. 143–155.

13.   M. Halliday, *Learning How to Mean—Explorations in the Development of Language* (Wheeling, IL: Whitehall Co., 1975).

14. P. Spier, *People* (Garden City, NY: Doubleday, 1980).

15. J. Harste, V. Woodward, and C. Burke, *Language Stories and Literacy Lessons*, pp. 61–62; and S. Hudelson, "Kan Yu Ret and Rayt en Ingles: Children Become Literate in English," *TESOL Quarterly* 18 (1984), pp. 221–239.

16. K. Diller, *The Language Teaching Controversy* (Rowley, MA: Newbury House, 1979), p. 19.

17. S. Krashen, *Inquiries and Insights*, (Hayward, CA: Alemany Press, 1985).

18. S. Krashen, *Writing: Research, Theory and Applications* (New York: Pergammon, 1984).

19. S. Hudelson, "Kan Yu Ret and Rayt en Ingles," pp. 221–239; and S. Hudelson, "ESL Children's Writing: What We've Learned, What We're Learning," in *Children and ESL: Integrating Perspectives*, edited by P. Rigg and D. Enright (Washington, DC: TESOL, 1986), pp. 23–54.

20. C. Edelsky. "Writing in a Bilingual Program: the Relation of L1 and L2 Texts," *TESOL Quarterly* 16 (1982), pp. 211–229.

21. J. Harste, V. Woodward, and C. Burke, *Language Stories and Literacy Lessons*, p. 53.

22. L. Vygotsky, *Language and Thought* (Cambridge, MA: MIT Press, 1962), p. 126.

23. K. Goodman, *What's Whole in Whole Language?* (Portsmouth, NH: Heinemann Educational Books, 1986), pp. 19–20.

24. I. Hunt, *Across Five Aprils* (New York: Berkeley Books, 1964).

25. D. Schwartz, *How Much Is a Million?* (New York: Scholastic, 1985).

26. L. Wong-Fillmore, "The Language Learner as an Individual: Implications of Research on Individual Differences for the ESL Teacher," *On TESOL '82*, edited by M. Clarke and J. Handscombe (Washington, DC: TESOL, 1982), p. 170.

27. D. Scott Enright and M. McCloskey, "Yes, Talking! Organizing the Classroom to Promote Second Language Acquisition," *TESOL Quarterly* 19 (1985), pp. 431–453.

28. K. Goodman, *What's Whole in Whole Language?* p. 29

29. Idem, p. 19.

30. R. Barrera, "Bilingual Reading in the Primary Grades: Some Questions about Questionable Views and Practices," *Early Childhood Bilingual Education: A Hispanic Perspective*, edited by T. Escobedo (New York: Columbia Univ. Press, 1983), p. 165.

31. Ibid., p. 166.

32. S. Hudelson, ed., *Learning to Read in Different Languages* (Washington, DC: Center for Applied Linguistics, 1981), p. v.

33. K. Hakuta, *Mirror of Language*, p. 49.

34. T. Roosevelt, *The Foes of Our Household* (New York: George Doran and Co., 1917).

35. W. Bennett, U.S. Secretary of Education, press release of address to Association for a Better New York, 26 September 1985.

36. H.T. Trueba, "Implications of Culture for Bilingual Education," in *Bilingual Multicultural Education and the Professional*, edited by H.T. Trueba and C. Barnett-Mizrahi (Rowley, MA: Newbury House, 1979), pp. 161–164; and W. Tikunoff, *Significant Features Study in Bilingual Education* (CA: Far West Laboratories for Educational Research and Development, 1980).

37. W. Bennett, press release.

38. J. Cummins, "The Role of Primary Language Development in Promoting Educational Success for Language Minority Students," *Schooling and Language Minority Students: A Theoretical Framework*, (Los Angeles: California Evaluation, Dissemination, and Assessment Center, 1983).

39. K. Goodman, Y. Goodman, and B. Flores, *Reading in the Bilingual Classroom: Literacy and Biliteracy*, (Rosslyn, VA: National Clearinghouse for Bilingual Education, 1979), p. 35.

40. J. Dewey, *My Pedagogic Creed* (Washington, DC: The Progressive Education Assoc., 1929), p. 14.

41. Y. Goodman, "Kid Watching," *National Elementary School Principal* 57 (1978), pp. 41–45.

42.   S. Kagan, "Cooperative Learning and Sociocultural Factors in Schooling," in *Beyond Language: Social and Cultural Factors in Schooling Language Minority Students* (Sacramento: California State Dept. of Education, Evaluation, Dissemination, and Assessment Center, 1986), pp. 231–298; and F. Smith, *Psycholinguistics and Reading* (New York: Holt, Rinehart, and Winston, 1973).

# Race, Knowledge, and Pedagogy:
## A Black–White Teacher Dialogue

### by Donald Murphy and Juliet Ucelli

*Don Murphy is a New York City public school teacher and education activist.
Juliet Ucelli has worked with inner city youth as a teacher and social worker
for the past ten years in high school, GED and community college programs.
Both are members of* **People About Changing Education (PACE),** *a multiracial network of parents and educators working to improve New York City's
public schools from the bottom up.*

This article was conceived when both of us—a black working-class
man and a white working-class woman who have taught inner-city
children and adolescents encountered copies of Lisa Delpit's *Harvard
Educational Review* essay "The Silenced Dialogue: Power and Pedagogy
in Educating Other People's Children," on the same day.[1] Juliet commented, "I just saw this really interesting article by a black teacher
talking about how a lot of standard 'progressive' methods in education
sometimes don't work for inner-city black kids, and about why black
teachers and parents feel disrespected by white progressive teachers."
Don replied, "Oh, I heard about that article; a white acquaintance
thought it was racist because Delpit seemed to be saying white people
couldn't teach black kids, and she wanted me to read it." The extreme
and emotional quality of the responses to Delpit affirmed our sense
that something important was being addressed.

We both had believed for some time that a dialogue between educators
of color and their white counterparts is the key transitional step to a
teacher–community alliance in urban public schools. In other words,
if white teachers could listen to the black colleagues whom they see
every day, they would probably learn more about how the black community feels and try to meet these concerns in their teaching practice. So
we were fascinated by Delpit's attempt to explain why that dialogue
was not occurring.

This selection originally appeared in the Winter 1989 issue of *Holistic Education Review,*
Vol. 2, No. 4.

Both of us had experienced many foreshortened conversations between black and white teachers wherein each felt treated unfairly and
misunderstood, and we believed that Delpit had captured some of the
polarities. The two of us share a common perspective as educators. We
are struggling to make public schools part of a democratic public sphere
and, within that democratic public sphere, to empower and legitimize
the voices and stories of people disenfranchised by race, class, and
gender. This mission in our classrooms, populated primarily by working-
class children of color, is interconnected with struggles in other classrooms and in the wider society—to increase African-American student
recruitment and professor hiring in universities, to acknowledge in curricula the many Afro-Asiatic contributions to "Western" civilization, to
improve living and working conditions in the inner cities, and, in the
long term, to challenge the corporate domination of society.

In the short term, this mission is also interconnected with making
sure that those students know how to read, write, go for job interviews,
and take college admission exams in the "dominant discourse" when
they leave our classrooms. The tricky part is, we must simultaneously
legitimize black vernacular and offer some tools for challenging the
dominant culture. Since we believe that many teachers of all colors share
our goals and struggle with the same questions, we felt that an honest
dialogue about our experiences and dilemmas as teachers, from two
different historical subject positions, African-American and white American, might help to clarify how to forge alliances among progressive
teachers and between them and inner-city communities.

**Juliet:** Delpit asserts that black students need—and their parents want
them to have—access to the "discourse patterns, interactional styles
and spoken and written language codes that will allow them success
in the larger society." She believes that teachers who favor a writing
process approach tend to minimize the importance of Standard English
mastery and ignore the stated desires of black students and parents.
She also explicitly states, "Even while students are assisted in learning
the culture of power, they must also be helped to learn about the arbitrariness of the codes and about the power relationship they represent."
So I was shocked to find that many white teachers interpret her as
conservative, authoritarian, as upholding the dominant culture.

**Don:** I've talked to several white progressives who have a wronghead-
ed notion that students of color will automatically buy into the dominant
culture or fall prey to "false consciousness" if they learn the dominant
discourse. This is not true, because, even if you talk and write well,
you're still hit constantly with the realities of being black or Latino in
the United States: housing discrimination, police violence, and so on.
We want the option of utilizing the dominant discourse in order to
struggle in various situations, and of critiquing the discourse and the
power relations it embodies.

**Juliet:** I think that sometimes white educators, especially those who
come from middle- or upper-class backgrounds and pursue public school
teaching rather than more lucrative or glamorous professions, may proj-

ect their own ambivalence, status anxiety, and uncertainty of allegiance onto black parents and students.

**Don:** I know so many black people who are verbally articulate and incisive political thinkers and activists but can't get their ideas systematically down on paper with standard grammar and spelling. This causes people enormous humiliation and pain, keeps their ideas from being taken seriously, and holds them down occupationally. Standard English fluency is a privilege, and it's easy to minimize its importance if you already have it. You can wind up inadvertently reaffirming your privilege when, out of guilt, you simply don't acknowledge that you have cultural capital that others need, and help them to access it.

**Juliet:** Delpit makes that point also. For me, Delpit's was the first written piece I had seen that resonated with my own teaching experience—which had made me question a lot of my pedagogical assumptions. My students were 16- to 24-year-old "dropouts" testing at 6th or 7th grade reading levels, and had been through hard times and, in some cases, hard time. They became more involved and worked harder when I gave explicit orders in loud tones and directly expressed my anger at their goofing off and their attempts to get out of doing work. Although I never used it in the classroom, one of the Latino teachers offered me a phrase that really expressed my feelings: "I'm not some stupid white girl who comes here so you can mess with my head. I'm here to help you learn." My students asked for structured assignments with tangible goals and criteria, and regular tests. Although we read and wrote about some African and African-American literature; we had discussions that challenged power relations; and we reflected critically on students' experiences—these activities occurred much less frequently than I would have liked. This was due at least partly to my lack of training and familiarity with the students' life world. On the other hand, most students improved their reading scores significantly, many earned their GEDs, and several told me, gratefully and pridefully, "You're the only one who made us really work!"

This is in keeping with Delpit's observation that black young people, and many others from working-class backgrounds, may perceive a teacher who gives indirect or veiled commands as weak and ineffectual. These young people tend to benefit when a teacher pushes them to achieve a clear standard and holds their attention through a direct and engaging interactional style. I was lucky to be part of a multiracial teaching staff where black and Latino teachers were acknowledged as educational leaders—which is rare—and were very generous and compassionate in giving me guidance.

**Don:** But you were able, as Delpit says, to *hear* teachers of color. Due to both race and class-based arrogance, many teachers of color have experienced self-identified white progressives—especially university professors—coming into our schools, assuming that they have educational theory to impart and know the correct way to teach. I've actually been called a separatist more than once when I've criticized this patronizing attitude. This is not the way to begin a collaboration; and besides, some of us actually read Paulo Freire too, along with Malcolm X, Amilcar Cabral, and other pedagogues of African descent whose theories we apply.[2]

At the same time, to *hear* black teachers and parents doesn't mean that you have to agree with everything they say. Many black teachers and parents are coming from a notion of quality education and access that is rooted historically in the experience of segregation. They believe that black kids have to prove that they are more capable than whites, that we have to master Greek and Latin and all the skills that white people have, in order to "function in the white man's world." They look on progressive educational methods as lacking discipline and rigor, and as encouraging laziness.

I always respond in two ways. Yes, I will do my best to help students do well on the standardized tests and to be fluent in the dominant discourse, or bidialectical. But I also point out to parents and colleagues that the so-called "white man's world" is in profound ideological crisis. Now—when more and more scholars are following in the footsteps of W.E.B. DuBois[3] and exposing the Eurocentric view of knowledge and history as a social construct by the ruling class and their intellectuals that serves to justify imperialism and racism—for black educators and parents to uphold the traditional canon makes no sense.

**Juliet:** I think it's important to note that Paulo Freire, whenever I've heard him speak, points out that if the teacher has a concept of education that differs from the concept held by the community, then the teacher has to dialogue and compromise. You can't impose your "liberating pedagogy." What you're advocating is a dialogue, really a "trialogue" with students and their parents, because the students may in fact be coming from a very different place than their parents, right?

**Don:** In my junior high level mini-school, many of my students (who are predominantly the children of working-class Caribbean immigrants) have rejected the notion that they have to prove to white people that they are capable. In an intuitive way, they have a complex sense of the need both to assimilate and to deconstruct official school knowledge; with their Africa medallions and haircuts, they're much more in tune with the Stanford protestors against Eurocentric curricula than their parents. They struggle to define what is legitimate for them and their community.

For those of us who are interested in the education of black students, or any students for that matter, our starting point cannot be blind acceptance of what the dominant social order promotes as legitimate. Both black and white students find schools an alienating fortress. They have to memorize countless facts and figures that have nothing to do with their real lives. What I make clear to students and parents is that my job is to create an environment in which students are free to develop meaning about the day-to-day lives they live, to try to situate themselves in some historical context.

**Juliet:** I think it's important to sort out that we're dealing with three interrelated issues here. First, we're saying that Standard English fluency must be taught, while cultural diversity in general, and black vernacular in particular, are also affirmed. At the same time, the historical experience and power relations that shape and rank discourses must be uncovered. Second is the issue of styles of interaction and learning. This includes the style and affective content of our communications with students as well as pedagogical strategy more narrowly defined—write process methods, drill. And third is what you just raised: challenging and expanding the canon, the body of knowledge we teach as history, literature, art. In particular, we have an incredible flowering of scholarship (with honest white academics now beginning to add to the work of pioneering black researchers) showing that what we think of as "Western civilization" emanating from Greece and Rome, is actually rooted in earlier scientific and cultural achievements of African and Asian societies. This is still a topic of controversy in universities and not integrated into most university curricula, much less elementary and secondary textbooks.

But let's talk about pedagogical strategy. What do you do in the classroom that enables students to situate themselves in a historical context *and* to express themselves in Standard English?

**Don:** I stress an incredible amount of writing, based on their own experience and their family's. They are asked to interview various family members on various questions, and to put down their own experiences and thoughts. This is the basis for group discussion in which students probe one another. My role in particular is to help enlarge their worldview and to challenge their narrowness and their ethnocentrism and objectification of other peoples that always comes out in frank discussion.

Through whole group evaluation, through students' exchange of papers and critique of one another's work, kids get to see the patterns of grammatical, spelling, and syntactical errors, and also to rethink and reorganize their writing. I drill, I make up exercises or use existing ones as needed to teach the grammar rules that come up. My students will have produced 300 to 400 pages of autobiography by the end of the year, some of it rewritten three or four times to improve grammar, style, and clarity. The way our mini-school is structured, I have the same students for a couple of years, which really builds a bonding and consciousness of collective process among the students.

For social studies and science, which I get to teach to the same group because of how we structured ourselves as a teacher-led mini-school, I start with hands-on stuff to get their interest. We've built a model of an African village, then studied its culture, history, economy, and religion; we've kept animals and observed their growth and development.

I don't use many texts or write on the board much. At any given point, some students might be writing, others playing music or chess, others reading or involved in small group discussions. For example, I've had parents tell me that, because their children had low reading levels, "endless book reports and writing" would only frustrate them, and then ask for multiple-choice reading comprehension exercises. I am in a constant dialogue and struggle with parents who freak out because my classroom is not structured in a traditional way. Because my students like the class and, very important, also scored high on the required standardized reading tests, and because I address parents' concerns respectfully, I can keep on doing this.

**Juliet:** Your approach and the way that you employ skills work in the context of meaningful, experience-based communication makes perfect sense. I think it's harder for white teachers to combine this so organically. As a result of racism, most white teachers are not already knowledgeable about black culture and history—unless maybe they've had the experience of a political mass movement, or a close personal friendship with a person of color that involves breaking through stereotypes. While as new teachers we're focused on how to understand our students' experience, which is so different from our own, how to win their trust and draw them out; we're not yet able to integrate it with skills work.

There's another issue here, too. I'm a white person who's made some effort to study black history, follow black culture and media, and work with black-led progressive political campaigns. Still, I wonder why a black child or teen should believe that I could listen to her or him without objectifying or judging, given the racist attitudes which that child probably has experienced from so many whites. Why should that child bother to probe his or her experience for me, the way that your students do for you?

**Don:** I think that students are very discerning about your intentions and feelings toward them, and that whites can be effective teachers of black students, given certain conditions. First, they have to avoid judging and writing people off: "This kid's father is a junkie; his mother is a single mother stuck in the underclass"; stuff like that. Two of my best students are children of single mothers.

Second, as you said, you need to familiarize yourself with the histories of people of color, and be willing to critique texts like those that talk about Christopher Columbus "discovering" America, and so forth. In principle, the onus shouldn't all be on the individual teacher. Texts should be rewritten, and urban school systems should provide staff development to overcome Eurocentric bias; but, due to institutional racism, they won't do it without massive pressure from communities. Teachers' unions should consider offering workshops to members about the histories and contributions of peoples of color, if they want to be more than business unions and build real alliances with the communities they serve.

On an individual level, you can help students use reading and writing to study their own community. You should also feel free to share aspects of your own ethnic, national, or religious culture with your students. You can familiarize yourself with the culture of the community you're working with, through histories and literature written by people of color, and through informal consultations with teachers of color. I don't know a lot about Haitian culture, but I have my students tell Haitian ghost stories. If I were teaching Jewish children, an understanding of the Holocaust would be key, and I would look to the oral histories and writings by Jewish people to get at it. I don't at all mean that you restrict students to studying their own community, but I've found it's often best to help students recover their own history and broaden out from there.

## Notes

1. See Lisa Delpit, "Skills and Other Dilemmas of a Progressive Educator," *Harvard Educational Review* (May 1988); and "The Silenced Dialogue: Power and Pedagogy in Educating Other People's Children," *Harvard Educational Review* (August 1988).

2. Paulo Freire, *The Politics of Education* (Amherst, MA: Bergin & Garvey, 1985); Malcolm X, *Malcom X Speaks* (New York: Grove Press, 1965); and Amilcar Cabral, *Return to the Source: Selected Speeches* (New York: Monthly Review, 1973).

3. W.E.B. DuBois, *The Education of Black People: 10 Critiques, 1906–1960* (New York: Monthly Review, 1973).

# Alternative Education and "Alternative" Schools
## Why Dropout Schools Aren't Alternative

### by Mary Ellen Sweeney

*Mary Ellen Sweeney has been involved in alternative education as a teacher and researcher since 1973. She was co-editor of* Holistic Education Review *in 1988-1989 and is currently editor of both* Changing Schools, *a national journal on alternative education, and* The Catalyst, *a newsletter on educational reform in Colorado. She is a full-time faculty member of the University Without Walls at Regis College, and Adjunct Faculty at the University of Colorado at Denver.*

At the 1987 National Alternative School Conference held in Port Townsend, Washington, a heavily attended workshop was one presented by Dr. Roy Weaver, professor at Ball State in the School of Education and former editor of *Changing Schools,* and myself on the topic, "At-Risk Students: A Place in Alternative Education?" *Alternative* has become a buzz word for the popular culture as well as in the field of education. For example, the outgoing director of a private secondary school for dropouts in Oregon recounted that they dubbed their program as "alternative" because this was an innovative term in education and a word that they could hang their hat on.

There is confusion about true alternative schools, schools of choice, and dropout programs. Too many uninformed parents and educators equate alternative education with a "special education" connotation or with "at risk" youth who are in jeopardy of dropping out or leaving high school before their graduation. This paper will present a more precise definition of alternative schools. The historical roots, philosophical premises, and organizational characteristics of alternative schools will be discussed. Finally, some of the myths surrounding alternative education will be examined to make sense of the confusion and the term *alternative* in the field of education. First, let us discuss the matter of defining *alternative.*

This selection originally appeared in the Summer 1988 issue of *Holistic Education Review,* Vol. 1, No. 2.

## Definitions of alternative

There is little agreement on *definitions* of *alternative* schooling. Some theorists emphasize distinct school features: providing alternative learning experiences from conventional high schools,[1] choice for families in a community at no extra cost,[2] less bureaucratized formal structures,[3] and separateness from traditional school units.[4]

For purposes of this paper, *true alternative* schools will refer to those schools that make different basic assumptions about learners compared with traditional school philosophies. That is, alternative school programs assume in their philosophy that they are dealing with the "whole" of the child, including in their goal setting the *physical, moral, social, emotional, spiritual,* and *aesthetic,* as well as the *intellectual* developmental realms of a student. In true alternative schools, the assumption is made that different learners learn in distinct ways, thus the individual talents and needs of each child are what is valued. In the best interest of the learner, students and parents choose the type of program most tailor-made for individual student needs.

In summary, this discussion advocates a definition of *true alternative schooling* (henceforth to be called alternative schools) to be synonymous with the schooling program that deals with the *whole child*—not with programs that, at best, promise the acquisition of basic skills in reading, writing, and arithmetic. Also, alternative schools are created to offer choice and diversity. True alternative schools differ from "back-to-the-basics" type schools because, while parents and students may choose back-to-basics schools, the needs of individual students are not the guiding philosophy.

## Historical roots

A debate exists over the historical origin of the alternative school movement. Just as agreement has not been reached on a universal definition of alternative schooling, consensus has not been reached on the roots of alternative schools. For example, Deal and Nolan claim that alternative school themes are rooted in the Progressive education movement of the 1920s, associated with John Dewey,[5] while other theorists claim that alternative schools were initiated in public school systems in the early 1960s.[6] Two explanations are given for the later evolution of alternative schools: first, that they are a spin-off of the free schools model (Summerhill-type)[7] established in the private sector in the early 1960s, and second, that the social themes which characterized 1960s thinking (humanism, egalitarianism, participatory decision making) spawned educational alternatives in the public sector.

Ideologically, the growth of alternative schools has followed two lines of thought. First, they were influenced by anti-establishment and countercultural sentiments with the supposition that they would be exemplary models to *replace* traditional schooling. Raywid has stated: "Most viewed their programs as the kind of reform desperately needed by all education."[8]

In the mid-70s alternative school advocates offered a second line of thought, arguing that they were experimenting with different organizational arrangements in an attempt to offer a variety of ways to educate children. Alternative education was a way of moving away from a monolithic system toward more diverse ways of educating an increasingly pluralistic youth population.[9]

In summary, alternative schools can be traced back to the Progressive movement of the 1920s, with a more recent version being the free schools of the 1960s. Some would argue that alternative schools originated to replace the monolithic "one best system"[10] of conventional schools but now exist to offer choice and diversity to a pluralistic student population. How alternative programs rearrange their organizational structures is the topic of discussion for the next section.

## Organizational characteristics

True alternative schools have key characteristics that distinguish them from conventional programs, such as comprehensive goal setting, innovative curricula and teaching strategies, broader student choice and innovative school governance practices, close interpersonal relations between students and teachers, diffuse roles for principals and teachers rather than formal ones, and personal advisory systems. These structural characteristics typically result in greater student satisfaction and the virtual elimination of school vandalism and violence.[11]

Among the ingredients or characteristics of a successful alternative school are distinctly stated *goals* and a clear school philosophy.[12] (The demise of numerous alternative programs has been attributed to the lack of well-defined goals and philosophy.) One study found that alternative schools' goals differed according to curricular emphasis, site location, size, and academic achievement.[13] An important goal of many alternative schools is stressing *learning how to learn;* according to Raywid, an option school for disruptive youth is much more likely to spend time on basic skill development and behavioral modification techniques to reward appropriate behavior, so that students can return to their home schools. But an open alternative school tries to turn students on to the excitement of learning. One way it does this is by involving students themselves in the setting of school goals. Jefferson County Open High School in Evergreen, Colorado (popularly known as Mountain Open High or MOHS), is an exemplary program with comprehensive goals and objectives that are reviewed and renewed annually by all school members.

Then there is the matter of teaching strategies. Numerous reform studies of this decade recommend the use of *multi-teaching technologies* and *methodologies* because of the criticism of the reliance and predominance of the lecture method of teaching in conventional schools.

Alternative schools utilize numerous instructional strategies to affect learning: individualized instruction, discussion, independent study, some lecturing, films, guest speakers, simulation games, frequent field trips, group study, experimental learning, multi-age and multi-grade level learning, peer teaching and tutoring, extended field trips, intervisitations between alternative schools, action learning, heterogeneous grouping, work opportunities, community service experiences, and learning contracts. Innovative instructional methods are a major point of emphasis in alternative programs.[14]

Alternative schools look beyond curricula and instructional methods to encourage learning on the part of individual youth. They make use of a humane school climate, smaller school size, flexible organizational arrangements and the ability to change program components, unconventional grading systems, career explorations and work opportunities, and extended field or school trips. Some alternative programs are organized around one major theme; for example, Mountain Open High School utilizes the Walkabout Program.[15] Schools-without-walls organize their curriculum around a central theme which is the city as classroom. Some alternative programs offer a variety of interdisciplinary courses encompassing perspectives in sociology, psychology, history, art, and philosophy.

A key ingredient or innovative technology of alternative schools is *choice*. Free choice aids students, parents, and teachers in the process of overcoming feelings of powerlessness and alienation. Free choice allows involved parties to feel empowered. Often "schools of choice" like the back-to-basics type involve choice only when selecting the program. Once immersed in a true alternative school, students are involved throughout their programs, making educational plans and decisions

The *formal structures* of alternative schools are unique. All-school governance systems prevail and they depart from the student council systems of conventional high schools.[16] In part, they follow the model rooted at Summerhill and other free schools in the private sector.[17] Governance systems in many alternative schools are called town meetings, all-school meetings, student-staff meetings, and all-school governance meetings. Participation in the governance system is an essential ingredient of schools like Mountain Open High.[18] Typically, the agenda for governance meetings is decided in advance by staff and students in advisory meetings and a democracy class. At governance meetings, discussion in small groups of twelve or less is employed so that students are directly involved in issues, learn to articulate their opinions, and are exposed to all levels of moral development and reasoning.

Students learn democratic practices by being active participants in the democratic process. Communication and decision-making skills are refined. Students become more committed to school and their self-concept is positively enhanced.

## Flexible roles

*Principals* have a diffused and not neatly defined role in alternative schools. One principal recounted that he swept floors at the end of each day. Fantini recommended that alternative school principals be the central planner, bringing together students, parents, teachers, and community people.[19] The traditional role of the administrator is altered, as principals are in closer contact with students, teachers, and the class-room due to smaller school size. In essence, they are closer to the experiences that brought them into education initially.

*Teachers* are the backbone of alternative schools and central to their programs. Going beyond the role of information disseminator, teachers must be willing to interact with students and support them. Three of the four most distinct features of alternative schools in the Raywid survey are teacher related, emphasizing the impact of teachers rather than curriculum.[20] The three departures from conventional schools relating to teachers were teacher roles, teacher-student interaction, and instructional methods.

Similar to alternative school administrators, teachers have a demanding and diffused role. Because of small staffs, teachers share jobs and responsibilities and perform multiple functions. Due to the value that alternative schools place on individual educational plans that are tailor-made for individuals, teachers often work extra hours and weekends aiding students. For example, on extended school trips, teachers are responsible for students on a 24-hour basis.

There are "burnout" problems for teachers at alternative schools because of the degree of involvement and other demands. But teachers seek alternative school experiences as a way to individualize instruction for students and escape the formalities of slowly changing conventional school structures. They report high morale despite the pressing demands on their time.[21] *High morale* is due to teachers experiencing success with students and the programs, feeling *ownership* of alternative programs, and having the ability to change program ingredients when necessary. Staff turnover is minimal and the acquisition of available positions is highly competitive and emotional.

The *advisory system* at alternative schools differs from the once-a-year or crisis visit to the counselor, typical of large conventional high schools. In alternative schools like Mountain Open High, weekly advisory meetings of small groups of students and a teacher or staff member exist to establish personal relationships between students and their advisor, to discuss social and academic problems, to initiate issues for governance meetings, to understand the various functions and components of their school, and to report individual student academic and social progress. Variations of advisory systems allow student responsibility and ownership of the school program to be fostered through the weekly check in and update of problems and progress.

Advisory systems are the heart of alternative programs, establishing a dialogue between students and between students and their advisor about the importance of the individual's affective and academic needs and aspirations. The satisfaction of one student from Mountain Open High School is indicated in the following quote:

> At my old school, I didn't like it because everybody bothered me. It was a downer to go to school. I'd wake up dreading school. I felt like I had more enemies than friends. It is easier to get along with the teachers at MOHS. I like it that everything

revolves around "trust." I do miss some of my old friends but it is less violent at MOHS.[22]

Alternative schools were found to be superior when meeting higher level needs and alternative school students were more satisfied with the climate of their schools.[23]

## Structure and responsibility

Many who are uninformed believe that alternative schools are unstructured. On the contrary, such schools are carefully structured, although the structure is arranged differently from conventional high schools.

Conventional school arrangements imply that students are uniform, and that teachers know how and what to teach students; therefore efficiency, mass production, and end products (translated in graduates and number of students going on to college) are the valued good of conventional schools. On the other hand, alternative educators make significantly different assumptions about youth: students are different from one another, and school personnel often do not know a great deal about the learning process; therefore schools tailor their programs to individuals, utilizing a variety of teaching strategies.[24]

But individualization of programs does not mean that students in alternative schools "do their own thing" and that basic skills are not taught or learned. In a national study, Raywid found that 79 percent of the respondents stated that their schools emphasized basic skills.[25] In part, students at alternative schools *apply* basic skills to higher level in-depth projects, such as the six passages in the Walkabout curricula at Mountain Open High. Learning the importance of *responsibility* or that actions have *consequences* is a goal of alternative schools. Students learn that freedom and choice entail responsibility. Often alternative school students work and interact with their advisor to ensure their individualized progress through a program. Students may be asked to leave, or may choose other programs because of unsatisfactory progress or their apparent unsuitability to the program.

Alternative programs encourage greater responsibility among adults as well; we have seen how teachers and administrators are more involved in the overall operation of the school. Parents and community members are involved as well. Alternative schools initiated and sustained by concerned members of the public are often more viable than schools operated by independent educators; for instance, the demise of the public alternative program of Adams High School in Portland, Oregon, was due, in part, to its creation by seven Harvard graduate students rather than by local community people.

## Alternatives serve all

Alternative schools contain heterogeneous student populations. Some students choose alternative schooling because (1) they have been in the alternative system since preschool days, (2) they are gifted and talented students who want a more individualized and challenging approach to learning, or (3) they are disenfranchised youth because of personal and social problems. On the other hand, "at-risk" programs consist of homogeneous or targeted populations of potential dropouts.

## Summary

At-risk or dropout programs are not true alternative school types because in many cases they act as safety valves for comprehensive high schools. Alternative schools offer a clearer choice. They nurture a way of learning that is different from the traditional approach offered in the monolithic system. Alternative schools represent innovations in educational reform in the areas of: (1) advancing pluralism, diversity, and equal educational opportunity for *all* students through choice; (2) decentralizing the formal structures of schools; (3) localizing aspects of curricula for individualized needs; (4) involving students, parents, teachers, and community members in planning, operating, and evaluating public schools; and (5) reducing school violence, vandalism, and disruption. The whole student is central to the organization of innovative alternative schools. The talents and potential of the individual are crucial in the goal setting and philosophical statements of alternative programs.

At-risk and dropout programs are designed to perpetuate the one best system. These programs act as holding tanks for troubled youth. Youth are repaired and sent back to their home high school, graduate with a GED or the equivalent of a high school diploma, or simply drop out. Some students do find success in "at-risk" type programs. On the other hand, alternative schools are intentionally planned to offer diversity and choice for learners seeking a way of schooling different from the conventional method.

Alternative schools offer a reform model at a time when few exemplary ideals exist in public education. Such school types hold out hope for the development of individuals with a grasp of the problem-solving techniques and higher level interdisciplinary thinking skills necessary to solve the global crises we are destined to face in coming ages.

### Notes

1.   Allan C. Ornstein and Daniel U. Levine, "Strategies for Reforming Metropolitan Schools," *Urban Education* 16, no. 1 (1981), pp. 93-107; Vernon H. Smith, "Alternative Education is Here to Stay," *Phi Delta Kappan* (April 1981).

2.   Robert D. Barr, "Alternatives for the Eighties: A Second Decade of Development," *Phi Delta Kappan* (April 1981).

3.   Terrence E. Deal and Robert R. Nolan, *Alternative Schools: Ideologies Realities Guidelines* (Chicago: Nelson-Hall, 1978).

4.   Mary Anne Raywid, *The Current Status of Schools of Choice in Public Secondary Education* (Hempstead, New York: Hofstra University, 1982).

5.   Terrence E. Deal and Robert R. Nolan, "Alternative Schools: A Conceptual Map," *School Review* (November 1978).

6.   Robert Arnove and Toby Strout, "Alternative Schools and Cultural Pluralism: Promise and Reality," *Educational Research Quarterly* (Winter 1978); George B. Krahl, *Alternative Education: Current State of the Art* (New York: Institute for Urban and Minority Education,

1977); Mary Anne Raywid, "The First Decade of Public School Alternatives," *Phi Delta Kappan* (April 1981).

7.   A.S. Neill, *Summerhill: A Radical Approach to Child Rearing* (New York: Hart, 1960).

8.   Raywid, "The First Decade," p. 551.

9.   Barr, "Alternatives for the Eighties."

10.   David B. Tyack, *The One Best System* (Cambridge, Mass.: Harvard University Press, 1974).

11.   Robert Arnove and Toby Strout, "Alternative Schools for Disruptive Youth," *Educational Forum* (May 1980), pp. 453-471; Daniel Duke and Irene Muzio, "How Effective Are Alternative Schools?" *Teachers College Record* (February 1978), pp. 461-483; Mario Fantini, "Alternatives in the Public School," *Today's Education* (September 1974), pp. 63-66; Raywid, *Current Status;* Mary Ellen Sweeney, "An Exploratory Structural-Functional Analysis of American Urban Traditional and Alternative Secondary Public Schools" (Doctoral dissertation, Portland State University, 1983).

12.   Barbara J. Case, "Lasting Alternatives: A Lesson in Survival," *Phi Delta Kappan* (April 1981).

13.   Thomas B. Gregory and Gerald R. Smith, *High Schools as Communities: The Small School Reconsidered* (Bloomington, IN: Phi Delta Kappa, 1987).

14.   Raywid, *Current Status.*

15.   Bert Horwood, *Experiential Education in High School: Life in the Walkabout Program* (Boulder, CO: Association for Experiential Education, 1987).

16.   Elas R. Wasserman, "Implementing Kohlberg's Just Community Concept in an Alternative High School," *Social Education* (April 1976).

17.   Barr, "Alternatives."

18.   For further discussion, see Wasserman, "Implementing Kohlberg's Just Community Concept."

19.   Fantini, "Alternatives."

20.   Raywid, *Current Status.*

21.   Raywid, *Current Status.*

22.   Sweeney, "Exploratory."

23.   Gregory and Smith, *High Schools as Communities.*

24.   Leo W. Anglin, "Teacher Roles and Alternative School Organizations," *Educational Forum* (May 1979).

25.   Raywid, *Current Status.*

# New Goals for Education

# New Goals for Education

## Introduction

### by Ron Miller

In the last section, we saw that the holistic paradigm offers fresh solutions to longstanding problems in education. For this reason alone, the holistic approach deserves serious consideration in light of the severe crisis in American schools today. Yet holistic education offers still more: in contrast to most of the "restructuring" rhetoric and even to some of the work in critical theory, holistic thinking recognizes that a post-industrial age is presently in the making. This new historical era, which has been termed the "postmodern" or "information" or "solar" age, will place entirely new demands on education.

The contours of this new era are not yet firmly established, but it is quite clear that the rapid exchange of information through expansive global networks will be one defining characteristic. To thrive in this information-rich environment, people will require a high degree of flexibility and adaptability in their thinking, an ability to synthesize, interpret, and evaluate information, and an openness to change and diversity. Such abilities and attitudes are not well developed through traditional educational methods, which place a premium on the student's dutifully absorbing and reciting discrete facts, data, and bits of information.

If we continue to think in terms of industrial-age assumptions, these new abilities will be considered merely as particular "skills" that better enable people to succeed in the world marketplace and the corporate environment. Thus, the schools will attempt to imbue "thinking skills" or "people skills" in the same fragmented, morally neutral way in which they have taught the "basic skills." But the coming age demands an education which is integrative, ecological and global—that is, holistic—in outlook. A truly holistic approach asserts that *human consciousness itself is subject to growth*, and that this emerging cultural era is a renewed opportunity to advance the evolution of our species. As we start to develop the "right brain" abilities of synthesis, creativity, and contextual understanding, we will be exploring what the psychologist Abraham Maslow called "the farther reaches of human nature"—the latent, largely untapped potentials of human consciousness.

This unavoidably brings us into the realm of the transpersonal, the archetypal, the spiritual—a realm largely unexplored and misunderstood by the reductionistic culture of the modern age. The standard criticism lodged against this aspect of holistic education is that the schools cannot become involved with religion. But the holistic paradigm is not riddled with the dogmas and schisms that characterize "religion"; rather, holistic thinking seeks to recognize the inherent, intricate interconnections between human consciousness and the processes of life in the universe. Our present culture can only label this concern as "supernatural" and the private domain of religious institutions; the postmodern culture, however, may return to the ancient understanding of the "perennial philosophy" that *our interconnectedness is the very essence of our humanity* and must no longer be ignored. Unfortunately, for the time being this focus on spirituality remains a major stumbling block for many in our culture. Liberal humanists tend to dismiss it as superstition or even as a new theocracy, while more conservative, more conventional religious groups denounce holistic spirituality as "New Age" godlessness. Both of these caricatures miss the mark, but they are likely to impede the full-scale development of the holistic approach for the foreseeable future.

Even so, today's holistic educators are pioneering teaching methods that aim to develop the inherent creativity and latent abilities of the whole person. The articles that follow provide an overview of this new educational territory. Lynn Stoddard opens this section with a call for developing the "three dimensions of human greatness"; he observes that this orientation is a major break from conventional education's obsession with the curriculum. Following Stoddard's essay, Gary Render and his colleagues discuss the importance of creativity in education and describe a possible approach for developing it in every child. Then David W. Anderson writes about the role of imagination; in holistic education it is a very large role indeed.[1]

Next, W. Nikola-Lisa focuses on wonder and ecstasy—and here we are moving subtly (because there is no firm dividing line) from a psychological to a more explicitly spiritual emphasis. An attitude of wonder—that is, reverence in the face of the great mystery of the universe—is the beginning of a spiritual perspective. Richard Graves and Karen Carlton state it explicitly: education must nurture the spiritual depths of the human being. The human soul, they argue, is the source of our identity and, in addition, links the individual with the larger human community and with the cosmos. A fragmented, specialized education, they claim, denies the wholeness of experience which the soul requires for its nourishment.

One holistic spiritual movement that is inspiring a growing number of educators (among many others) is the Creation Spirituality of Matthew

Fox. Fox is a Dominican priest who is attempting to synthesize the insights of Christian mysticism with the cutting-edge thinking of modern physics, feminism, and liberation theology. In this section, Andy LePage gives a brief summary of Fox's thinking and explores its implications for education. In place of fragmentation, a Creation-centered education would offer connection, compassion, and a deep sense of caring for the planet.

Finally, the ancient rite of passage known as the Vision Quest is described by Steven Foster and Meredith Little, two of the leading modern interpreters of the ritual. They argue here that human development proceeds through important transitions that need to be honored and celebrated through meaningful ritual.[2] Indigenous cultures have retained these rituals which support the individual's growth while binding the entire community together. Modern education, like our entire culture, has lost these meaningful rituals; holistic education seeks to restore them. Indeed, the common theme underlying all these selections is their insistence that *education is most fundamentally a quest for meaning, connection, and wholeness.*[3] If we would nurture healthy, fulfilled human beings, we must transform our fragmented methods of teaching into a spiritual, holistic sense of reverence for the deeper, more subtle qualities of the human spirit.

### Notes

1.   For a comprehensive and sophisticated treatment of imagination in the educational endeavor, see Douglas Sloan, *Insight-Imagination: The Emancipation of Thought and the Modern World* (Westport, CT: Greenwood, 1983).

2.   Foster and Little, along with Louise Carus Mahdi, have edited a superb anthology on the subject of rites of passage, *Betwixt and Between: Patterns of Masculine and Feminine Initiation* (LaSalle, IL: Open Court, 1987).

3.   This critique of the fragmented, meaning-impoverished condition of modern education has been well developed in three recent scholarly works: *The Moral and Spiritual Crisis in Education: A Curriculum for Justice and Compassion in Education* by David E. Purpel (Granby, MA: Bergin & Garvey, 1989); *Education, Modernity and Fractured Meaning: Toward a Process Theory of Teaching and Learning* by Donald W. Oliver and Kathleen Gershman (Albany: SUNY Press, 1989); and *Elements of a Post-Liberal Theory of Education* by C. A. Bowers (New York: Teachers College Press, 1987).

# The Three Dimensions of Human Greatness
## A Framework for Redesigning Education

### by Lynn Stoddard

*Lynn Stoddard is a retired elementary school principal. He retired "early" after thirty-six years to promote full time an idea for redesigning education from the bottom up. He has published several articles in educational and religious journals and is a co-author of a handbook for redesigning education,* Designing Education for Human Greatness, *soon to be reissued by Zephyr Press, from which comes much of the material for this article. During his tenure as President of the Utah Association for Supervision and Curriculum Development, he wrote a controversial position paper, "Learning to Read Should Not Be the Primary Purpose of Elementary Education," which resulted in a state debate on reading.*

It is now possible to design a system of education that will help individuals develop their full potential and realize their great worth to society, while at the same time drastically reduce crime, teenage pregnancy, drug abuse, and suicide. My colleagues and I have developed, over a twenty-year period, a framework or pattern to follow in designing such a system. It is the result of teachers and parents of several different schools working together using a nontraditional approach.

This article will accomplish three things: First, it will show why traditional education has been so resistant to change—so reform-proof—an understanding we must have before we can move ahead. Second, it will introduce a mental frame of reference that frees teachers and parents from the slavery of obsolete traditions so that education can be redesigned. And third, it will give examples of strategies that can be used immediately with students to begin the process of building a totally new system of education.

### Curriculum worship: The impenetrable barrier

The decade of the 1980s was one of much talk about educational reform. In the name of reform, a few surface changes were made, but

This selection originally appeared in the Spring 1990 issue of *Holistic Education Review*, Vol. 3, No. 1.

nothing really significant has occurred to affect, deep down, the things that have been happening in schools for hundreds of years. Great teachers are still fighting the system in order to touch hearts and change lives, but more and more are "burning out" in the process. They find that there is a limit to the energy they can give to overriding bureaucratic requirements, rules, and regulations in order to reach their students.

After studying and being involved in education for a combined total of nearly a hundred years, my colleagues and I believe that we have discovered the great barrier that prevents needed reform from taking place. It is a stubborn obstacle that will not move until we realize it is there.

The enormous dam that prevents progress in education is an attitude that is held by many educators—a belief that curriculum is king. Our society has an obsession with curriculum. Every few years another reform tide sweeps across the land and with it comes an irresistible urge to write a new curriculum in hope that this will cure our ailing system of education.

My associates and I have found that it is impossible to reform education within the prevailing frame of reference, which is characterized by a mental fixation on curriculum development instead of human development. Because of our nation's preoccupation with curricula, education has evolved into a purposeless organization that emphasizes standardized achievement and "minimum competence" over maximum achievement and the full development of individual potential. We have found in numerous surveys with groups of teachers and parents that they cannot name their state, district, or school goals of education. The people responsible for helping students learn do not know what the curriculum is supposed to accomplish. Thus, instead of being guided by goals, our teachers are slaves to curriculum, which has become an end in and of itself. All students are fed the same bland curriculum diet regardless of vast differences in gifts, talents, interests, and experiences. Teachers are required to do the impossible: standardize students.

An emphasis on standardization may be a major contributor to the alarming increase in suicide, teenage pregnancy, drug abuse, and crime. Students who do not fit the common mold into which they are being forced are dropping out of school in record numbers. Standardized achievement testing has become the trademark of the "effectiveness movement," through which a school's effectiveness is revealed to the bureaucrats who show their lack of trust by trying to control, through tests, everything teachers do. Neill and Medina, in an article in the *Kappan*, show how standardized testing is "harmful to educational health":

> When they are used as promotional gates, standardized tests can act as powerful devices to exclude groups.... Minority students and those from low-income families are disproportionately affected. Research has shown that, when a student repeats a grade, the probability of that student dropping out prior to graduation increases by 20% to 40%. In other words, students who are not promoted because they have failed to reach arbitrary cutoff scores on often unreliable, invalid, and biased standardized tests are more likely to drop out of high school.[1]

Perhaps the most serious consequence of trying to standardize and control everything teachers do is the resultant huge deficit in human development. There are millions of brilliant, talented youths who have failed to develop their talents and gifts fully because our system of education is not organized to foster the personal development of individuals. When we aim for standardized achievement and minimum competence, we unknowingly and unintentionally rob each student of the full development of his or her unique potential, and we make nearly everyone feel cheated. The resultant loss of self-esteem often alienates students and causes them to withdraw from the mainstream to engage in drugs, early sex, and crime. Those who leave the school system feeling devoid of personal development—those who feel of least value—often choose to end their misery with suicide. All of this adds up to a colossal, dangerous national deficit in human development.

### Breaking the barrier: Education for greatness

A plan that has proved effective in helping parents and teachers change their mental frame of reference about education is called *Education for Human Greatness*. It hinges on a mental attitude best described by Marilyn King:

> To accomplish any lofty goal, you must have a crystal clear image of that goal and keep it uppermost in your mind. We know that by maintaining that image, the "how-to" steps necessary for the realization of the goal will begin to emerge spontaneously. If you cannot imagine the goal, the "how-to" steps will never emerge, and you'll never do it. Clearly the first step to any achievement is to dare to imagine that you can do it.[2]

King provides the key for breaking out of the curriculum trap. Education for Human Greatness consists of eight design "frames" into which individuals can paint their own mental images of a new system of education.

The first design frame is a mission statement designed to evoke a clear mental image that can be kept constantly in mind:

| **The Mission of Education** |
| :---: |
| Develop great human beings who are valuable contributors to society. |

This mission represents a new definition for education: the process of becoming a valuable contributor to society. If we put our minds to it, we can help every student develop a mental image of personal greatness. We have found, in our work with teachers and students, that even very young children can experience the joy of being contributors to their family and school. The design frames that follow show that it is not difficult to help each child develop an identity of greatness—a mental picture of oneself helping the world become a better place, and realizing that this is what it means to become educated.

The second design frame consists of three specific master goals that further clarify the mission:

---

**2**

### Master Goals:
### The Three Dimensions of Human Greatness
**Identity**
Individual talents and gifts, confidence, self-esteem, honesty, responsibility, spirituality, character, and physical fitness.

**Interaction**
Love, respect, empathy, communication, and responsible citizenship.

**Inquiry**
Zest for learning; the powers of acquiring, processing, and using information to create knowledge and solve problems.

---

These master goals are the result of years of effort to identify the qualities and characteristics that make people inclined to be contributors to society. As my colleagues and I studied the lives of outstanding people down through history, we found three qualities that stand out in those who have made significant contributions: a strong sense of self-worth, deep feelings of love and respect for all people, and an insatiable hunger for truth and knowledge.

These qualities, represented by the terms, *identity, interaction*, and *inquiry*, are intended to be kept constantly in mind as a "crystal clear" image to guide teaching and parenting. While teachers and parents may not be able to keep all of the elements comprised by each dimension firmly in mind, they will be able to concentrate on the three dimensions of human greatness.

The three dimensions of human greatness offer a different frame of reference for education. As master goals they are people oriented rather than curriculum oriented. They help us to concentrate on human development—maximum individual achievement—instead of curriculum development with its twin brothers: minimum competence and standardized achievement. The three dimensions provide a framework for redesigning education and allow us to escape from the curriculum trap and its confining, limited view of human potential.

The first dimension of human greatness, *identity*, probes the question, Who am I? It describes the most intense need of every person: the need to be an important "somebody." Identity comprises all of the elements of a person's self-image.

For a good many years in education we have been aware of the central role that self-image plays in our lives as the governor of all behavior. Each of us is always true to our self-image and behaves according to the kind of person we perceive ourselves to be.

Whenever we help a person elevate his or her self-image, we ourselves become contributors to society. In our work with students, parents, and teachers, we found that an effective way to raise self-image is to focus on a person's assets, which is in contrast to the traditional system that focuses on correcting inadequacies. Confidence and self-esteem result when students discover what they can do well and strive to develop their unique talents and gifts. When we accept identity as the first dimension of human greatness and primary goal of education, we tap into a force that offers the greatest potential for growth: a person's self-image.

The second dimension of human greatness, *interaction*, answers the second most pressing need of all people: the need to have warm relationships with others. It includes the elements of love, respect, empathy, communication, and responsible citizenship. People who are lacking in this dimension often have difficulty keeping a job even though their other skills and knowledge may be high. It is through positive interaction that many people make valuable contributions to society.

The third dimension of human greatness, *inquiry*, describes the third major drive of the human race: a built-in hunger for truth and knowledge. The term *inquiry* in this context represents all that the human brain does to acquire, process, store, and use information to build personal meaning and create new knowledge. This term best describes how the human brain works. Recent research on the nature of the brain indicates major changes are in order from the logical-sequential, imposed, test-based kind of instruction that is the trademark of traditional education. It appears that learning accelerates immensely when it is based on personal inquiry.

The third design frame envisions parents and teachers working together in a new kind of relationship:

---

**3**

### E.T. Partnerships
Parents and teachers work *equally* and *together*
to help students grow in the three dimensions of
human greatness.

---

Traditionally we have viewed parents as subordinates to teachers. They are people who go into the school to help the teacher as "volunteers." With a change of mission for education, we see parents and teachers working together as equals to help students grow in identity, interaction, and inquiry, each performing his or her own special function.

The fourth frame returns control of education to students, parents, and teachers:

---

**A Take-Charge Philosophy**
Teachers, parents, and students use curriculum
as "means" rather than "ends,"
as "servant" rather than "master."

---

There is no need to develop more curricula. We literally are drowning in workbooks, duplicated worksheets, and irrelevant textbooks—the stuff that turns students off. The take-charge philosophy allows us to turn to other sources for information: the real, here-and-now world of people, events, and interesting things. It also solves another curriculum fixation problem that has plagued education for many years: the tendency to view each subject or course of study as a separate, isolated body of knowledge that is unrelated to anything else. Viewing curriculum as *means* "puts Humpty Dumpty back together again" and integrates various disciplines of knowledge into a unified whole. Money now wasted on workbooks, textbooks, and worksheets will buy many microscopes, magnifying lenses, binoculars, scales, newspapers, library books, and other materials that invite personal, self-initiated inquiry.

We now know that it is not curriculum that touches hearts and changes lives, but teachers and parents who are in tune with the three central drives of students: the drive to be an important "somebody" (identity), the drive for warm human relationships (interaction), and the drive for truth and knowledge (inquiry). These primary human drives coincide with the three dimensions of human greatness. Students want the same things as we want for them. When we shift our focus from curriculum to students, we find that teachers and students are no longer the adversaries that they have been in traditional schools, but now work together for the students' full development.

The fifth design frame matches assessment procedures with what we are trying to accomplish:

---

**Evaluation of Greatness**
Evaluation is used to assess student growth
in greatness, and for feedback and guidance.

---

New assessment procedures will evaluate what we are trying to accomplish: student growth in identity, interaction, and inquiry. Since in general these goals are not measurable with paper-and-pencil tests, we will need to turn to other evaluation techniques for feedback and guidance. We will look for manifestations of student growth in individual talents and gifts; self-initiated personal inquiry; and love, respect, and concern for others.

The sixth design frame helps us to form a mental image of each student as a unique creation:

## 6

### Multiple Intelligences
Each person in the world is born with a unique set of intelligences to be developed, not a single IQ.

Howard Gardner and Joseph M. Walters have proposed a "theory of multiple intelligences" and have identified *seven intelligences* that are common to all human beings, but which vary in degree with each person. These are musical, bodily-kinesthetic, logical-mathematical, linguistic, spatial, interpersonal, and intrapersonal.[3]

Others have verified what we have known all along, that each person is a unique creation. Calvin W. Taylor has identified nine creative talents that are scattered unevenly across individuals, with each person possessing a unique profile of the nine talents.[4] Over 20 years ago, J.P. Guilford identified 120 different mental functions, of which IQ tests claim to measure no more than eight.[5]

Because of our traditional obsession with curricula, we have tended to ignore the work of those who reveal the individuality of human nature. A focus on people, instead of curricula, allows us to incorporate these valuable findings. To help each student acquire an identity of greatness, we must emphasize the discovery and development of each student's unique gifts and talents. The most important facet of a child's identity is his or her unique set of intelligences, and it is this human attribute that deserves our greatest attention. It appears that this part of human development is the most critical in determining whether a person will achieve the self-esteem and confidence necessary to become a contributor to society.

The seventh design frame give us an updated view of how the brain works:

## 7

### How the Brain Works
Humans learn through personal, self-initiated inquiry—the way they learned to talk and walk.

Brain research is telling us that logical-sequential, test-based instruction actually may interfere with learning. The workbooks, worksheets, and textbooks that are an integral part of the drill-test syndrome cause anxieties or boredom, which in turn causes human brains to shut down or to learn that schooling is irrelevant to life. We have found that a child will learn more through personal inquiry than through traditional methods that employ these dreary materials.

The work of Leslie A. Hart and Frank Smith have helped us to understand that it is an "insult to intelligence" to "teach" the brain how to think.[6] The brain thinks automatically just as the heart beats and the lungs breathe. There is evidence that the brain files information according to the purpose for which it is to be used. This is the reason for the difficulty that so many people have remembering information they learn in order to pass tests. After the information has served its purpose, it is usually tossed into the brain's "dead" file. We are beginning to understand why test-oriented instruction seems to work for the short term but fails to produce long-lasting results. Brain research is helping us better understand Plato's wise adage, "Knowledge acquired under compulsion obtains no hold on the mind."

On the other hand, it appears that the brain handles information derived from self-initiated, personal inquiry much differently. This information goes to the brain's "smelter," where it interacts with all previous and future inputs and is refined into the nuggets of personal meaning that are imbedded therein. We are beginning to grasp how grossly we have underestimated the power of the human mind, and how we can release this great power through an inquiry-centered approach.

The eighth design frame gives us a place to invent and collect strategies that help students grow in the three dimensions of human greatness:

| **8** |
| --- |
| **Strategies for Greatness** |
| Strategies are the how-to steps that emerge when we hold a clear vision of our mission and goals constantly in mind. |

Over the years, many strategies have been created to help students grow in individual greatness. Many of these strategies are not welcomed within the traditional system of human standardization. Others are embraced for a short period but are soon abandoned because teachers can't find enough time to fit them into the rigid, lock-step schedule, which points out the need for education to be redesigned completely from the bottom up.

### The results of maintaining a clear mission

In our work with several schools, we watched students, teachers, and parents blossom with a burst of enthusiasm and creativity as they shed their preoccupation with curricula to focus on helping students develop the three dimensions of human greatness. When everyone concentrated on building identity, interaction, and inquiry, the school and indeed the entire community radiated a climate for creative inquiry. Many people became enthusiastic about inventing strategies for accomplishing the mission.

The following strategies are just a few examples to illustrate what can happen when students, parents, and teachers keep a clear vision of their mission constantly in their minds:[7]

*The Great Brain Project*. The first strategy that emerged from a different focus was called the Great Brain Project. In this strategy, students are invited to choose a topic of interest to them and study that topic in depth over a period of several weeks or months, trying to become a Great Brain—a "specialist," "expert," "mastermind," or "genius," until each student knows more about a topic than anyone else in the school, including teachers. When the student feels ready, he or she is encouraged to share this new knowledge with friends, relatives, and classmates in the form of a carefully prepared Great Brain presentation that includes one's drawings, posters, charts, collections, demonstrations, and other visual aids.

As each student and his or her parents fill out an official Great Brain entry blank, they are furnished with suggested guidelines, which include recommendations to (a) develop a list of questions to guide the search, (b) interview authorities, (c) visit locations, and (d) keep a journal or scrapbook for collecting pictures, writing down thoughts, and keeping track of sources of information. During the research phase, parents and teachers serve as mentors to help the student find information and suggest promising paths to follow. Each student is encouraged to strive for the "genius" level of knowledge and to produce an original product of his or her own thinking about the chosen topic.

It is gratifying to see what happens to students when they are given freedom and assistance to learn, as Leslie Hart would say, "with the brakes off." We do not need achievement tests to find out what is being accomplished, nor would they serve any useful purpose, since students learn things that benefit their own interests, abilities, and personal needs. Achievement is clearly evident in the results of self-initiated, personal inquiry.

Of hundreds of projects, I shall relate only a few typical examples: Allison, a fourth-grade student, decided to study the workings of the state legislature. She and her mother contacted a state senator and asked for his cooperation in helping the child learn all she could about her chosen topic. This very busy man was so impressed with Allison's enthusiasm and eagerness to learn that he arranged for her to visit the floor of the state senate while it was in session, took her on a tour of the capitol building, and explained how bills become law. As part of her report, Allison showed a video she had made of herself interviewing the senator and of her tour of the capitol.

After studying dinosaurs for several weeks, Kimberly, a fifth grader, composed lyrics and music for a delightful song, which she expertly played on the piano and sang as part of her outstanding presentation.

Justin, an energetic six-year-old, demonstrated an amazing knowledge of trucks as he explained the many uses of a great variety of them, including tow trucks, dump trucks, cement trucks, delivery vans, tankers, and eighteen-wheel transports. Justin's original, childlike drawing of a large diesel truck and trailer with all of the parts labeled was magnificent, as was his collection of toy trucks.

Justin's nine-year-old brother, Jason, did an intensive study of the moon with a telescope he had purchased with money earned by selling Christmas cards door to door. In his presentation, Jason demonstrated his telescope and showed many original drawings of different phases of the moon.

Mary, a first grader whose father had died the previous year in an airplane crash, wanted to find out how airplanes work. During her research, she went for a ride in a small plane similar to the one in which her father had died, and the pilot let her take the controls to help her understand the effects of changing the position of the ailerons, rudder, and elevators. Mary's classmates were fascinated as Mary showed her drawings and models to explain how airplanes fly.

During these presentations, the students were observed to be more attentive while listening to their peers than they normally were in listening to their teachers. They also seemed to ask more and better questions of their fellow presenters than they did of their teachers.

These two phenomena give us evidence that learning increases when adults change their focus and philosophy of education. By the time a student prepares dozens of Great Brain presentations and listens attentatively to hundreds more during the elementary school years, he or she will have assimilated much more knowledge and developed more skills than the same student would in the traditional system.

The Great Brain Project incorporates all of the principles explained earlier in the design frames. Parents and teachers use it to help each child develop an identity of greatness—a realization that one can become brilliant in nearly any endeavor one chooses, and thus become a special contributor to society. Each year a Great Brain fair is held to allow students to display their accomplishments and thus add to their feelings of self-worth. They may also receive Great Brain badges to wear, certificates of achievement, recognition over the school public address system, and coverage in the school newspaper.

As we worked with several schools to implement the project, we observed large numbers of students changing their behavior and attitudes toward school and learning. Teachers were delighted to witness several unmotivated, alienated students become eager, cooperative learners as they studied self-selected topics and received recognition and praise from their peers for outstanding accomplishments. This was the first clue that schools can play a vital role in preventing people from becoming burdens to society.

We found that the Great Brain Project is an excellent strategy for placing responsibility for learning where it rightfully belongs: first with the student, second with the student's parents, and finally with teachers. In our traditional lock-step system with its rigid requirements, tests, report cards, grades, and behavior-modification, assertive-discipline style of management, students get the message that they are not responsible for themselves.

As we concentrated on helping students to develop an identity of greatness—to learn who they are as human beings and as individuals— we became conscious of a primary human attribute: *Every person is born with freedom of thought.* This freedom makes every one of us responsible for our own thoughts, learning, and behavior. When responsibility for learning and behavior is left where it belongs, students learn that they can handle the trust that is placed in them and they respond enthusiastically.

*Challenge Education.* Another strategy that leaves responsibility for learning with the student is a big brother to the Great Brain Project. It is a strategy for high school students called Challenge Education. This strategy, developed by Maurice Gibbons,[8] is patterned after the Australian aborigine walkabout in which the young adolescent native must prove that he is ready to accept the responsibilities of adulthood in a very harsh environment. He must pass a severe test of stamina, endurance, bravery, and skill while venturing into the wilds alone on an extended walkabout. In the tribe, most of adolescence is spent preparing for the walkabout challenge.

In Gibbons' American equivalent of the walkabout, a high school student spends most of the high school years preparing to make an elaborate presentation to friends, relatives, and classmates to prove that he or she is ready to enter the adult world and be a valuable contributor to society. Gibbons suggests that schools should help students prepare to meet five basic challenges:

(1) *Adventure*: a challenge to the student's daring, endurance, and skill in an unfamiliar environment.

(2) *Creativity*: a challenge to explore, cultivate, and express his own imagination in some aesthetically pleasing form.

(3) *Service*: a challenge to identify a human need for assistance and provide it; to express caring without expectation of reward.

(4) *Practical Skill*: a challenge to explore a utilitarian activity, to learn the knowledge and skills necessary to work in that field, and to produce something of use.

(5) *Logical Inquiry*: a challenge to explore curiosity, to formulate a question or problem of personal importance, and to pursue an answer or solution systematically and, wherever appropriate, by investigation.[9]

Challenge Education is another strategy that helps students to develop the three dimensions of human greatness. Gibbons shared this exciting vision of a new kind of high school fifteen years ago. At that time it was embraced intellectually and emotionally by many people, but alas, Challenge Education has not been able to make a dent in the thick armor of tradition because of our obsession with curriculum development and standardized achievement. Education for Human Greatness, with its focus on individual students, now makes it possible for such promising ideas to be welcomed, to be developed, and to bear fruit.

*The School Post Office.* As teachers at Whitesides Elementary School made a commitment to help children grow in positive interaction, they stumbled onto an amazing strategy almost by accident. A group of students and their teacher decided to organize a postal system to encourage written communication within the school. They built a large, official-looking mailbox and placed it in the center of the school near the office. They then announced to the school that they would make daily pick-up and delivery of mail within the school. It was deliberately planned that the School Post Office would make next-day delivery so that students could concentrate on "sending" one day and "receiving" the next.

The School Post Office made an immediate, dramatic impact on the life of the school. The flood of mail was so great that the students who started the project had to reorganize their room into a mail-processing center and eventually had to share the responsibility with other classes. Parents reported that students were eager to go to school each day to read their mail. Teachers found that this was one writing activity that involved students without coaxing or assignments. Many students were often caught writing letters instead of doing teacher-assigned work.

Perhaps the most gratifying outcome of the School Post Office was the finding that students learned to read and write without being taught in the traditional sense. They learned without tedious drills on word analysis, phonics, spelling, punctuation, and decoding. Teaching came in the form of teachers' responses to individual student needs—How do you spell _____? How do you address a letter?—and children helping one another.

In addition to helping us understand how people learn to communicate through writing, the School Post Office provides impressive evidence that human minds learn through personal inquiry. Frank Smith cites a study in which students who had invented their own punctuation and collaborated in their writing did better on standardized achievement tests than those who had been taught punctuation in traditional ways.[10] Our work with School Post Offices confirms this finding. We have seen first-grade students leap, in six-months' time, to the skill level of an average ten-year-old—not by being taught in the traditional sense, but by being engaged in the process of writing and reading. This verifies Smith's finding that people learn to read and write by "joining the club" of people who read and write, and by doing what people in the club do. People learn to read by reading, to write by writing, and to solve numerical problems through "hands-on" manipulation of real objects (counting, weighing, measuring, comparing, and investigation).

*Shining Stars Talent Development.* The Shining Stars Talent Development strategy was created to help students discover and develop their unique sets of gifts and talents. Students are invited to "try on" various talents as they prepare for regularly scheduled talent shows, art exhibits, and physical fitness challenges. Parents again become full partners with the school to help students prepare recitations, patriotic speeches, editorials, debates, solo singing, barbershop quartets, homemade bands, gymnastics, juggling, sculpting, whistling, impersonations, role-playing, mime, painting, modeling, and other presentations. Over a period of time, students begin to identify their unique set of intelligences and catch a vision of their own great potential to be a special contributor to society.

The scope of this article does not permit description of all of the strategies that emerge when parents, teachers, and students keep the clear goals of identity, inquiry, and interaction at the front of their minds. In addition to those already mentioned, the following strategies were created:

1.    A community priorities survey to verify and validate the goals.

2.    Parent/teacher/student planning meetings.

3.    An assessment device for evaluating student growth in identity, inquiry, and interaction.

4.    An intelligence profile sheet for mapping a child's unique set of "intelligences."

5.    A school zoo/aviary.

6.    An industrial arts and crafts shop.

7.    A media center containing a large variety of objects, inquiry kits, and science equipment, as well as books and other printed materials.

8.    A special system of field excursions into the community for first-hand investigations.

9.    Many presentations by parents and other members of the community to share hobbies, talents, and areas of expertise.

10.    Part-time, family-type grouping of students to allow older and younger students to learn from each other.

To be fair, I need to explain that the strategies described in this article were not all developed in one place. The total philosophy of Education for Human Greatness came from a piece here and a piece there, from several elementary schools where my colleagues and I worked. We are pleased that one of the strategies, the Great Brain Project, is being used in many schools nationwide. In addition to those mentioned, we are confident that a great many strategies will roll forth as parents and teachers "maintain a crystal clear image of their mission uppermost in their minds."

In education, as in anything else, we get what we aim for. If we aim for nothing, that is what we get. If we continue to aim for curriculum as an end in itself, we will get a copious amount of curriculum development. Human development bankruptcy will increase, along with crime, teenage pregnancy, drug abuse, and suicide. On the other hand, if we aim for individual human development, our efforts will be rewarded with a large increase in the number of valuable contributors to society. We have watched students grow in greatness as parents and teachers maintained a clear vision of their mission and united to help students grow in identity, inquiry, and interaction. We have seen enough change in the lives of children and youths to be confident that Education for Human Greatness works to help individuals develop their full potential and thus lose any desire to ingest harmful drugs, commit crime, hurt others, or kill themselves. Our experience has proved to us that we can help people become valuable contributors to society, if we just put our minds to it.

## Notes

1. D. Monty Neill and Noe J. Medina, "Standardized Testing: Harmful to Educational Health," *Kappan*, May 1989, p. 688.

2. Marilyn King, "Ordinary Olympians," *In Context*, no. 18 (Winter 1988; Sequim, WA: North Olympic Living Lightly Association).

3. Howard Gardner, *Frames of Mind* (New York: Basic Books, 1976); and Joseph M. Walters and Howard Gardner, "The Development and Education of Intelligences," in *Essays on the Intellect* (Alexandria, VA: Association for Supervision and Curriculum Development, 1985).

4. Calvin W. Taylor, "Cultivating Simultaneous Student Growth in Both Multiple Creative Talents and Knowledge," in *Systems and Models for Developing Programs for the Gifted and Talented*, edited by Joseph F. Renzulli (CT: Creative Learning Press, 1987).

5. J.P. Guilford, "Intellectual Factors in Productive Thinking," and Robert Wilson, "The Structure of the Intellect," in *Productive Thinking in Education* (Washington, DC: National Education Association, 1968).

6. Leslie A. Hart, *Human Brain and Human Learning* (New York: Longman, 1983); and Frank Smith, *Insult to Intelligence* (New York: Arbor House, 1986).

7. For more complete information about ways to build student greatness, see Lynn F. Stoddard, Max Berryessa, and Charleen Cook, *Designing Education for Human Greatness* (Available from Great Brain Associates, Box 582, Farmington, UT 84025).

8. Maurice Gibbons, "Walkabout," *Kappan*, May 1974, p. 596.

9. Ibid.

10. Frank Smith, *Insult to Intelligence*.

# Toward a Holistic Definition of Creativity

## by Gary F. Render, Je Nell M. Padilla, and Charles E. Moon

*Je Nell Padilla is counseling coordinator for the Upward Bound program at Millersville University in Pennsylvania.*

*Dr. Gary Render is a professor of Educational Psychology at the University of Wyoming, Laramie.*

*Dr. Charles Moon is head of the Department of Education at Heidelberg College, Tiffin, Ohio.*

There is a great deal of investigation going on in the field of educational psychology that promises to have far-reaching implications for human growth and development. We would like to focus on some of these topics of investigation, and their ability to increase creative potential and other aspects of human potential.

We are on the threshold of new ways of perceiving humanness. The transpersonal approach to psychology and education is a field coming to be known as the fourth force in psychology, going beyond, and in some ways blending, the elements of psychoanalytic, behavioral, and humanistic psychology.[1] One of the early models of this approach was Maslow's hierarchy of needs.[2] Maslow postulated that the most basic human needs are the physiological—air, water, food, and warmth. Then as one works up the hierarchy, there are safety needs, love and belonging needs, esteem needs, and the need for self-actualization.

As needs are satisfied, new higher level needs come into play; as low level needs are satisfied, higher level needs come to the forefront. Prior to his death, Maslow expanded the hierarchy. He proposed a level above that of self-actualization. He said,

> I should say also that I consider Humanistic, Third Force Psychology to be transitional, a preparation for a still "higher" Fourth Psychology, transpersonal, transhuman, centered in the cosmos rather than in human needs and interests, going beyond humanness, identity, self-actualization and the like.[3]

This selection originally appeared in the Winter 1988 issue of *Holistic Education Review*, Vol. 1, No. 4.

Maslow went on to suggest that the need for transcendence is a healthy, normal, rational quest for human beings. From this hypothesis of transcendence have come several areas of investigation that have relevance to educational practice and the creative process. The following discussion focuses on some of these areas.

## States of consciousness

Consciousness is a variable that is receiving increasing attention from psychologists. As the field continues to grow, we will find the term consciousness appearing with greater frequency. There is even a field of "consciousness education" being explored and expanded.[4]

Our traditional way of viewing consciousness generally limits us to three states: waking, sleeping, and dreaming. It is possible that there may be hundreds and even thousands of states of consciousness at our disposal. Consciousness does not simply mean to be awake, as in "he regained consciousness after being in a coma." It does not mean the aggregate of thoughts or feelings of a group, as in "she is raising her woman's consciousness," and it doesn't mean awareness of one's self, as in "he became conscious of his ability to make decisions." It means a pattern, an organizational style of one's overall mental functioning at any given time.[5] The predominant research paradigm in use (the scientific method) has been developed from the state of consciousness in which we are limited by the variables of time, space, and identity. Because of this, we should not expect science, at present, to be able to confirm or contradict the mystical view of consciousness.[6] It is possible that this paradigm has reached a point of limiting an interaction with, and understanding of, the world. This is not to say that it is time that we abandon the paradigm. Not at all. It is important that we expand the paradigm, modify it, and, in places where it is limiting, develop new paradigms or new ways of looking at the world.

We are finding more and more evidence that there is much to be learned from all states of consciousness. In fact, recent investigations are indicating new ways of looking at the workings of the mind and we seem to be on the way to developing drastically new definitions of "humanness." We see humans as living simultaneously on more levels than earlier life forms.[7]

The problem has been, up to this time, that if experiences do not readily lend themselves to investigation with the tools of the scientific method, we tend to reject the experiences—they just don't fit into the way we perceive reality in the world. The result is that all too often we tend not to pay attention to experiences that have not been labeled as being "scientifically valid." Not only do we then *not* attend to the phenomena we experience, but we insulate ourselves *from* the experiences.

Many of us would feel foolish to say to someone that the solution to a problem was facilitated by a dream, a vision, a psychic event, or a meditative experience. Are these experiences not real? Certainly they are, and certainly it is important for us to understand, explore, and use these experiences. But first we do have to believe that these experiences are part of reality.

Transpersonal psychology is attending to these kinds of concerns. According to Grof, transpersonal psychology is the study of experiences which expand or extend consciousness beyond the usual ego boundaries and the limitations placed upon us by time and/or space.[8] According to Capra, transpersonal psychology is "concerned with the recognition, understanding, and realization of non-ordinary states of consciousness, and with the psychological conditions that represent barriers to such transpersonal realizations."[9] This is certainly an area worthy of our attention.

## Brain hemispheres

Another area of interest related to transpersonal psychology is the notion of brain hemisphere specialization. For some time, psychologists have been aware of two types of mental organization, or two types of brain function in human beings. Neisser stated:

> Historically, psychology has long recognized the existence of two different forms of mental organization. The distinction has been given many names: "rational" vs. "intuitive," "constrained" vs. "creative," "logical" vs. "prelogical," "realistic" vs. "artistic," "secondary process" vs. "primary process." To list them together casually may be misleading . . . nevertheless, a common thread runs through all the dichotomies.[10]

A great amount of research has been generated regarding hemispheric specialization. Basically, it appears that the left hemisphere of the brain deals with the world in a rational, logical, sequential way. The right hemisphere deals with information in an intuitive, metaphoric way, often with analogies.[11]

Most of the work in hemispheric specialization indicates that the two hemispheres work together. They complement each other. They are not opposing forces. Attending to one hemisphere only is done at the expense of the other. Schools and our society generally have emphasized "left-brain knowing." That is, the focus has been on dealing with information in an orderly, logical, and sequential manner. All too often the right-brain capacities have been ignored and, in some cases, challenged and attacked. This has often been done in subtle ways.[12]

For example, when we, as teachers, demand that students support their statements in logical, rational ways, we negate some "right-brain knowing" of a more intuitive nature. Students very clearly get the message that what they know does not really count unless there is a logical argument for their position. Hart described the brain as multimodal, capable of using a variety of stimuli simultaneously to process information.[13] If children are forced to learn in "logical order," they may be denied the opportunity to learn in a very natural random style. The result of this is clear to those of us who teach. Students tend to be reluctant to talk and to explore their ideas in an open forum.

We must encourage the less rational, more intuitive ways of knowing. That means we must learn to become tolerant of ambiguity and "gut-level" intuitive forms of knowing. We need to develop strategies that incorporate more of the total capacity of the brain in the learning process. Samples, Charles and Barnhart wrote that:

> the right hemisphere has tremendous inventive capacities. The right hemisphere sees things in pictures, senses them fully, and frequently manages to slip past the censoring voice of the rational left hemisphere to make its "knowing" known. But let us not forget that without verbal ability, the right hemisphere could not describe the resulting analogic arrangements and complete the magic of discovery.

These authors went on to discuss how we are often able to solve problems using insight or intuition. This mode is one that is probably familiar to most of us, but hard for us to explain.

> How can humans effectively explain skills like these? We frequently have turned to words like "intuition." We say things like, "I can't explain it . . . it just popped into my head." Now we're finding that these intuitive leaps, inexplicable feelings of insight, creative but unpredictable solutions to problems, need not be apologized for—but rather are the legitimate functions of one half of each of our brains.[14]

## Creativity

Studies involving creative people are indicating that relative equilibrium exists between the hemispheres of their brains. In creative people the right and left hemispheres seem to be integrated and achieve high levels of activity together.[15]

Creativity is hindered in people all too often because of left-brain thinking on the part of a culture. This hindrance often takes the form of cultural rules that no one seems to take credit for formulating, but that so many of us seem to follow. Parents, teachers, and adults in general must learn not to punish or threaten children if they show special abilities. They need to learn to be at ease with children who are telepathic or clairvoyant, or have other parapsychological abilities. Children who see auras and are therefore able to interpret the physical status of people should be encouraged. The diagnosticians of the future may come from their ranks.[16] We, as educators, have to help our students develop awareness of the fact that they can manipulate and control themselves. They can create their own worlds and realities; they are in control of their joys, ecstasies, hurts, pains, moods, and feelings. Only from that awareness does the ego strength required to create emanate.

This awareness combined with attention and respect for both brain functions will help unlock so much of the creative potential locked up inside so many of our students. As Samples states:

> Students cannot be fully educated unless a legitimacy is attached to the functioning of their metaphoric and intuitive maturity as well as their rational brain capacities. The high degree of credence attached to rationality is a manifestation of our Western cultural posture. Because of this, it will not be easy to diminish the forceful and dominant role of cognitive psychological premises. Yet we have not lost sight of the realization that only the whole mind is a healthy mind. The self-actualizing persons described by Maslow were, without exception, those humans with high maturity in both cerebral hemispheres.[17]

Roberts and Clark have combined the traditional four-stage model of creativity in education with the split brain and consciousness ideas and have formulated the model in Table 1.

Table 1
*A Model of Creativity*

| (1)<br>preparation | (2)<br>incubation | (3)<br>illumination | (4)<br>verification |
|---|---|---|---|
| left side | right side | left becoming aware of right | left side |
| learning facts, cognitive knowledge, verbal, memory | relaxation and letting mind wander, holistic, preverbal association | insight, tuning the left side into the right side, intuitive, transition from preverbal to verbal | testing, hypotheses, experimentation cognitive reasoning, verbal analysis, critical thinking |
| conscious | unconscious | preconscious | conscious |

From: T. Roberts & F. Clark. *Transpersonal Psychology in Education* (Bloomington, IN: Phi Delta Kappa Education Foundation, 1975).

They suggested that in teaching we concentrate on only half of the process (steps 1 and 4) and tend to ignore the other half (steps 2 and 3). Most creative scientists describe their work as starting with intuitive visualization (right brain) and then following that with reasoning (left brain). To further explore this combination of consciousness and cerebral hemispheric specialization, we strongly recommend a fascinating paper by Krippner, Dreistadt, and Hubbard, which explores the sources tapped by creative people for their original ideas.[18] It is hypothesized at the outset that one source may be the time creative people spend at different levels of reality, or in other terms, time spent in various states of consciousness. It has been theorized and generally supported that the creative person's originality is at least partially related to:

1. One's ability to see the world differently than do other persons;
2. Being less bound by cultural conditioning than others;
3. Retaining a childlike capacity to open-mindedly experience the world in a personalized, innovative manner;
4. A childlike ability to fantasize, to imagine, to express curiosity;
5. One's emotional stability and self-confidence (Creative persons tend to be more emotionally stable and self-confident than their peers.).

Krippner and his colleagues looked at hypnosis and found that hypnosis can facilitate creative thinking and problem solving because it tends to allow the subject to regain some of the childlike sense that appears to be characteristic of creative persons.

Second, it was found that creative persons often report solving problems by using imagery without resorting to verbal behavior. It is possible to solve problems very rapidly if verbalizing processes are removed. Krippner et al. also reported that creative persons were found to use the right-brain faculties and more mental imagery in approaching tasks than their less creative peers.

Third, these writers reported many fascinating stories regarding the role of dreams in the creative process. For example:

• Richard Wagner's opera, *Tristan und Isolde,* came to him through a dream: "I dreamed all this; never could my poor head have invented such a thing purposely."

• Robert Louis Stevenson wrote that he could dream complete stories and could return to his dreams and give them different endings. He trained himself to remember his dreams and to dream plots for his books.

• Jean Cocteau dreamed of watching a play about King Arthur and from that obtained the information to write *The Knights of the Round Table.*

• Mendeleev attempted to categorize the elements based on their atomic weights. He reported that he went to bed exhausted after attempting this chore. He went on to say: "I saw in a dream a table where all the elements fell into places as required. Awakening, I immediately wrote it down on a piece of paper. Only in one place did a correction later seem necessary." The result was the Periodic Table of the Elements.

• Elias Howe worked for years to invent a lock-stitch sewing machine without success. He then had a dream. In the dream he had been captured by a tribe of warriors. The leader commanded that he finish his machine or be killed. He could not solve his problem. In the dream the warriors surrounded him and he noticed the spear they carried. All the spears had holes near the points. From this he was able to complete his invention. He had experimented with needles with holes in the middle of the shank, not near the point. He awoke and built a model of a needle with a hole near the point and the sewing machine was completed.

Dreams apparently find and give expression to non-ordinary reality by providing insight into people and events, and they do so by consolidating or integrating past material.

Krippner et al. also explored the role of psychedelic drugs and ESP in the creative process and found, generally, that many creative endeavors were related to altered states of consciousness.

Additional support for expanding views on creativity comes from Shear, who examined the relationship between transcendental meditation and creativity. He described seven characteristics of creativity:

> The full creative process (1) takes place in a state of consciousness different from and deeper than the ordinarily experienced waking state; it is associated with (2) innocence, (3) restfulness and (4) joy; it has (5) preverbal contents, (6) unfolds automatically and (7) when most complete involves experience of an interaction with pure unboundedness (pure consciousness, self.)[19]

## Conclusion

The evidence does suggest some direction for those of us interested in the creative process and does provide us with some information regarding educational practice. We would summarize as follows:

1. Human beings have at their command many states of consciousness and all of these should be respected and encouraged. They should be explored. All of them provide us with alternative means of perceiving reality. They can provide insights into self that can lead to integration and healthier functioning. Various states can also provide new ways of viewing reality which can result in productive, creative thought.

2. It is becoming clear that our brains have at least two different ways of handling information. These two ways are complementary, and a "holistic" approach to education is required for total human development. That does not mean that we should abandon left-brain activities and focus on the right brain. We need to provide experiences for students that will involve the total intellect. Remember, reason is important, but it is only half the process. There may be many ways of perceiving reality and some of those may appear to us as foreign, but we must develop tolerance for modes that are different from ours.

3. It is important to impart to students that the pictures in their heads (dreams, fantasies, images, psychic phenomena) are valuable. There are ways to strengthen our abilities in these areas. There are ways of creating greater self-awareness and understanding. They also can be sources for creative thought and problem solving. "While we cannot expect a creative genius in every school child, we may be able to develop creative abilities by showing people how to tap the unused potential of their minds."[20]

4. Research is needed to develop strategies that are not only fun (as many creative programs tend to be), but that result in personal growth. Greater depth of exploration is required to increase our understanding of states of consciousness and hemispheric specialization. Other areas of the transpersonal realm that have not been treated extensively in this paper require investigation in relation to learning and creativity. These include biofeedback, suggestology (suggestopedia), relaxation, parapsychology, death and dying, and spiritual growth and development. Basically, we need to reassess our views of human capacities. Can we say with any certainty that there are really dumb kids and smart kids, creative kids and noncreative kids? Perhaps not. We are finding indications of the possibilities of the potential of the human mind. We are at the threshold of discovering new meaning to being human. Let's use some right-brain thinking regarding our students (the right brain tends not to be able to know that something is impossible). Quite certainly we have imposed artificial constraints on our students' potential. Let's not have reason to feel guilty. Some guidelines to follow: (a) Allow humans to be themselves and celebrate that selfness; (b) Love the metaphoric mind and respect the rational; (c) Nurture motivation; (d)

Consider any attempt at communication appropriate; (e) Celebrate the whole person.[21]

To quote Carl Rogers:

> Man is wiser than his intellect . . . . His whole organism has a wisdom and purposiveness which goes well beyond his conscious thought . . . . I think men and women, individually and collectively, are inwardly and organismically rejecting the view of one single culture-approved reality. I believe they are moving inevitably toward the acceptance of millions of separate, challenging, existing informative *individual* perceptions of reality. I regard it as possible that this view—like the simultaneous and separate discovery of quantum mechanics by scientists in different countries—may begin to come into effective existence in many parts of the world at once. If so, we would be living in a totally new universe, different from any in history.[22]

At this point, it is necessary to return to the focus of this discussion, which is creativity. We do not purport to have defined creativity as a separate component of human functioning that can be viewed apart and distinct from other aspects of the human experience. We believe that all students have creative potential as well as cognitive, affective, psychomotor, and spiritual potential. We do not believe that the best way to facilitate the realization of human potential is to provide creativity programs, emotional development programs, spiritual growth programs, and psychomotor skill improvement classes. We must develop "holistic" programs. Programs that approach the teaching-learning process in a "total human" way. A school curriculum should include all forms of the human experience.

We need to provide experiences that facilitate greater self-awareness and understanding. This requires attention to interpersonal and intrapersonal relations. We need to provide experiences that assist students in exploring various states of consciousness. Through these experiences we can learn about our individual learning styles, develop a greater understanding of who we are and what our potentials may be. We need to provide experiences that use all of our self to learn—including our bodies (our bodies facilitate the learning of cognitive material). But we must go beyond the traditional physical education approach regarding the psychomotor domain. We can incorporate movement, centering, dance, and relaxation into our curricula. We need to facilitate and encourage students' attention to learning from fantasy and through dreams. Basically, we must deal with the *total* person and release some of the restraints we may have unknowingly placed on the human potential. We must be willing to entertain and celebrate the possibilities.

As an example of how our conceptions about humans are expanding, consider that it is now being hypothesized that:

- There may be as many as fifteen to twenty different senses that human beings have at their disposal,[23] rather than the five we commonly consider;
- In some approaches to learning, students have been able to learn foreign language vocabulary at the rate of up to 1,000 words a day with high rates of retention;[24]

- It is theorized that there may be twelve or more domains of learning rather than the three we are accustomed to;[25]
- There may be hundreds or even thousands of states of consciousness available to us to explore and expand our worlds.[26]

These are just a few ways that our conceptions of humans are changing. The possibilities are definitely exciting. We should be reminded of the words of William Blake (1927): "If the doors of perception were cleansed, everything would appear to man as it is, infinite. For man has closed himself up, till he sees all things through narrow chinks of his cavern."[27]

Let's break out of the caves. Let's understand that creativity, along with other facets of the human being, cannot be approached without attention to the whole organism. Classroom teachers need to modify their perceptions and move into new space. It will pay off in helping more and more students realize greater and greater potential.

## Notes

1.  T.B. Roberts, *Four Psychologies Applied to Education: Freudian, Behavioral, Humanistic, Transpersonal* (New York: Schenkman, 1975).

2.  A.H. Maslow, *Motivation and Personality* (New York: Harper & Row, 1970).

3.  A.H. Maslow, *Toward a Psychology of Being* (New York: Van Nostrand, 1968), pp. iii-iv.

4.  T.B. Roberts, "Education and Transpersonal Relations: A Research Agenda," *Simulation & Games* 8, (1977), pp. 7-23; "Consciousness Counseling: New Roles and New Goals," *Elementary School Guidance and Counseling* 14 (1979), pp. 103-107; "Expanding Thinking Through Consciousness Education," *Educational Leadership* 39, no. 1 (1981), pp. 52-54; "States of Consciousness: A New Intellectual Direction, a New Teacher Education Direction," *Journal of Teacher Education* 36, no. 2 (1985), pp. 55-59.

5.  Roberts, "Education and Transpersonal Relations"; also see C.T. Tart, *States of Consciousness* (New York: Dutton, 1975).

6.  F. Capra, "The New Vision of Reality: Toward a Synthesis of Eastern Wisdom and Modern Science," in S. Grof, ed., *Ancient Wisdom and Modern Science* (Albany: SUNY Press, 1984), pp. 135-148.

7.  S. Grof, "East and West: Ancient Wisdom and Modern Science," in Grof, *Ancient Wisdom*, pp. 3-23.

8.  S. Grof, *Realms of the Human Unconscious: Observations from LSD Research* (New York: Dutton, 1976).

9.  Capra, "The New Vision of Reality," p. 145.

10.  V. Neisser, *Cognitive Psychology* (New York: Appleton-Century-Crofts, 1967), p. 297.

11.  R.E. Samples, "Educating for Both Sides of the Human Mind," *The Science Teacher* 42 (1975), pp. 21-23ff; "Learning With the Whole Brain," Human Behavior 4 (1975), pp. 16-23; "The Intuitive Mode: Completing the Educational Process," *Media and Methods* (1975), pp. 24-27.

12.  R.E. Samples, C. Charles, and D. Barnhart, *The Wholeschool Book: Teaching and Learning in the 20th Century* (Reading, MA: Addison-Wesley, 1977).

13.  L.A. Hart, "The Incredible Brain: How Does it Solve Problems? Is Logic a Natural Process?," *National Association of Secondary School Principals* 67, 459 (1983), pp. 36-41.

14.  Samples, Charles, and Barnhart, *The Wholeschool Book*, p. 49.

15.  R.E. Samples, *The Metaphoric Mind: A Celebration of Creative Consciousness* (Reading, MA: Addison-Wesley, 1976).

16.  Roberts, "Expanding Thinking Through Consciousness Education."

17.   Samples, "Educating for Both Sides of the Human Mind," p. 27.

18.   S. Krippner, R. Dreistadt, and C.C. Hubbard, "The Creative Person and Non-Ordinary Reality," *The Gifted Child Quarterly* 16 (1972), pp. 203-228, 234.

19.   J. Shear, "The Universal Structures and Dynamics of Creativity: Maharishi, Plato, Jung and Various Creative Geniuses on the Creative Process," *Journal of Creative Behavior* 16 (1982).

20.   T.B. Roberts and F. Clark, *Transpersonal Psychology in Education* (Bloomington, IN: Phi Delta Kappa Educational Foundation, 1975), pp. 15-16.

21.   Samples, *The Metaphoric Mind*, p. 144.

22.   Quoted in Samples, *The Metaphoric Mind*, p. 204.

23.   Samples, Charles, and Barnhard, *The Wholeschool Book.*

24.   J. Canfield and P. Klimek, "Education in the New Age," *New Age* (February, 1978), pp. 27-39.

25.   T.B. Roberts, "Some Educational Implications of the Psychology of Consciousness," (no date; available from the author, Dept. of Learning and Development, Northern Illinois University, DeKalb, IL 60115).

26.   Tart, *States of Consciousness.*

27.   W. Blake, *The Marriage of Heaven and Hell* (New York: Dutton, 1927).

# Imagination Running Wild

## by David W. Anderson, Ed.D.

*David W. Anderson holds an earned doctorate in Special Education and Early Childhood Education from the University of North Dakota. He is currently Professor and Coordinator of the Special Education Program at Lock Haven University of Pennsylvania. His professional experience includes teaching handicapped and nonhandicapped preschool and elementary school children and teacher-consultation.*

In the Dickens novel *Hard Times*, schoolmaster character Thomas Gradgrind makes the following assertion:

> Now what I want is Facts. Teach the boys and girls nothing but Facts. Facts alone are wanted in life. Plant nothing else, and root out everything else. You can only form the minds of reasoning animals upon Facts; nothing else will ever be of any service to them. . . . In this life, we want nothing but Facts, sir; nothing but Facts![1]

This views children as empty vessels waiting to be filled with facts known only to the schoolmaster. We know, however, that learning results when children physically and mentally manipulate, combine, recombine, and relate information and concepts gathered through their active exploration of the environment, rather than when they receive facts passively from the outside. Nevertheless, although most teachers acknowledge children's need for active learning, there remains an overemphasis on the teaching and learning of facts. And too often these facts are presented in isolation without clarifying the relationship of the individual elements to the whole, or underscoring their significance to everyday life. For example, educators use task-analytic procedures to break a complex task into its constituent parts; move the student through the individual steps; and assume, often incorrectly, that the student is able to integrate the steps, in his or her mind or performance, so as to "see" how those several steps form a whole.

Approaches that stress only facts fail to capitalize on a very basic characteristic of children (really, of all human beings)—their natural inclination to imagine.[2] An emphasis solely on the facts of *what has been* and *what is* ignores the element of imagination, often fails truly to engage the child's mind, and neglects to ask the child to consider *what could be*.

---

This selection originally appeared in the Fall 1989 issue of *Holistic Education Review*, Vol. 2, No. 3.

Imagination has been described as "the core of our humanity," while fantasy has been called "a process quite central to human functioning."[3] Lewis observed:

> We must assume that all human beings, from birth on, have the ability to imagine. . . . All children need to have an environment where the act of imagining and its expressions are not only respected but given visible outlets. Children's *playing* should be seen as a profound manifestation of this process. *Dreaming*, so alive in all children, is another capacity of the imagination to mingle and stir the images of our memories of the past and a sense of the future. Out of playing and dreaming comes the child's love of creating and doing—of bringing together what the child is thinking and feeling, of finding a means of expressing the inward world outwardly.[4]

Gardner's theory of multiple intelligences[5] specified two essential components of an intelligence: (a) a set of problem-solving skills that enable the individual to resolve difficulties encountered and to create an effective product; and (b) the potential for discovering or creating problems that will lead to the acquisition of new knowledge. Imagination can be regarded as basic to these prerequisites of an intelligence, thus establishing its importance in the intellectual life of every individual. In this essay, I hope to underscore the ways in which imagination contributes to the development of a child and to draw implications for educators on the basis of that knowledge. Once the significance of imagination to the development of young children is appreciated, teachers will need to become aware of methods for its support, encouragement, and use in educational settings.

## The concept of imagination

Imagination, "the creative faculty of the mind,"[6] enables children to use images retained in memory from prior visual, auditory, and haptic experiences. Both noncreative and creative forms of imagination have been described.[7] Noncreative forms include less controllable types, such as hallucinations and nightmares, and more controllable types in which visualization and imagery are used to recall past events, to "see" how parts blend together to form a whole, and to place oneself in another's position. The truly creative forms of imagination involve anticipatory imagination (as in foresight) and creative expectancy ("looking forward to"), and serve two functions: *to hunt* (e.g., search, analyze, explore, discover), and *to change* (e.g., invent something new, produce novel ideas, mix or combine elements). These aspects of the creative forms of imagination correspond to Gardner's prerequisites for an intelligence. Thus understood, imagination can be seen as "the leap of mind"[8] that enables us to envision the real or potential relationship between and among elements; to consider the "what if" and "what could be" in the present world and the world of tomorrow. It is, as Allen so eloquently put it, "the discipline of wonder."[9]

Imagination may be conceived as an *action* of the mind and body, involving cognitive processes that contribute to the child's developing understanding of the world. Cognitive processes involved in imagining are likely to be those usually associated with the forms of mental organization characteristic of the right hemisphere of the human brain, most often described with terms such as intuitive, creative, artistic, analogic, and holistic.[10] Imagination is an integral part of the psychological makeup of every human being, although some are able to access and use imagination more freely than others. Imagining continues to be active in all humans, throughout life—only the content and focus of imagining change over time, as overt make-believing goes underground and assumes the form of private fantasies and daydreaming. Fantasy and daydreaming, as tools of the imagination, are believed to form a continuous stream of mental activity to which we return when not directly engaged in either scanning or acting upon our environment. The overt pretend play of childhood appears to decrease as more realistic symbolic play and games with rules become more prominent. These changes in imagining activity coincide with and reflect changes in cognition and social awareness.[11] Perhaps those regarded as the more creative or inventive—such as Thomas Edison, Albert Einstein, C.S. Lewis, and Madelyn L'Engel—were able to draw from their imagination more freely throughout their lives.

Teachers need to develop sensitivity to the "forms" assumed by these cognitive processes, and to the benefits derived from the existence and use of imagination throughout a person's lifetime. With a clear discernment of their educational value and advantage, imaginative and fantasy activities can be incorporated into classroom planning and may lead to more effective teaching and learning.

## Manifestations of imagination

Realizing that imagination is a cognitive activity places a child's imaginative processes in a more positive light and permits proper respect to be ascribed to such creative enterprise. As research into learning styles and the various states of consciousness continues, particularly in relating to our understanding of creativity,[12] intuition and imagination may gain the credibility they deserve. In fact, imaginative activity can be recognized in a variety of childhood endeavors, including symbolic and make-believe play and curiosity.

*Symbolic and pretend play.*   Children's play has been the subject of much investigation and theorizing. Through imaginative pretense, the child manipulates, recombines, and extends associations between and among things, actions, people, and words. Accordingly, the elaborate imaginative play of a child may be linked with creativity, and it reflects both increasing cognitive development and the child's social experience. Playfulness may be viewed as consisting of several traits—manifest joy; humor; and physical, social, and cognitive spontaneity (the principle components of which are imagination, creativity, and flexibility of thought).[13]

*Curiosity.*   Kamii and DeVries suggested that one objective in early childhood programs was for the children "to be alert, curious, critical, and confident in their ability to figure things out and say what they honestly think. . . . to have initiative; [to] come up with interesting ideas, problems, and questions; and [to] put things into relationships."[14] This view is based on Piagetian theory, which asserts that interactions with people and objects enable the child to place things into relationships with one another, resulting in a continuous process of differentiation and integration of cognitive concepts and structures (i.e., knowledge) previously developed by the child. Kamii and DeVries hold that the qualities of alertness, curiosity, and critical thinking are essential to this constructive activity: "Constructivism implies the importance not only of the child's figuring out the answer in his own way but also of his coming up with his own questions."[15] Consequently, curiosity is viewed as an important prerequisite to learning, reasoning, and problem solving. Bradbard and Endsley observed that, although children with a high degree of curiosity will not necessarily score higher on standardized tests of intelligence, "they are more creative, flexible, and secure about and interested in their environment, and have a better self-image."[16] The curious child was portrayed as one who showed a positive reaction to novel or incongruous stimuli, and persistence in exploration of those stimuli in order to gain information about them. Perhaps the most vivid description of the curious mind is that provided by Jacobs, Biber, and Raths:

> The mind that is *wonderful*—full of wonder, piqued by the marvels of what has been and what might be; the mind that is *playful*—that expects the stuff of experience in thought and feeling to change, to be full of "what-ifness": these are indicators of a curious mind.
>
> The mind that is *responsible*—able to respond to ideas and feelings; able to reorder, discriminate and refine what is known and felt; able to engage with others of different persuasions than one's own: this too characterizes the curious mind.
>
> The *constructive* mind that builds and interprets and composes and, on the basis of new insights, imaginings, or findings, reconstructs; the *future-oriented* mind that not only looks ahead but also uses the past for looking ahead: these connote the curious mind.[17]

There is a direct connection between the child's natural curiosity and his or her world of imagination and fantasy. Both stem from the human desire to understand the world, to see the relationship between objects and events in order to understand how things fit together. It is through the exercise of one's curiosity and imagination that new ideas or insights are born, later to be tested out against reality. Said Gerard, "Imagination, not reason, creates the novel. . . . Imagination supplies the premises and asks the questions from which reason grinds out the conclusions as a calculating machine supplies the answers."[18]

## Benefits of imagination

> Human beings spend nearly all of their time on some kind of mental activity, and much of the time their activity consists not of ordered thought but of bits and snatches of inner experience: daydreams, reveries, wandering interior monologues, vivid imagery, and dreams. These desultory concoctions, sometimes unobtrusive but often moving, contribute a great deal to the style and flavor of being human. Their very humanness lends them great intrinsic interest; but beyond that, surely so prominent a set of activities cannot be functionless.[19]

With this reminder of the great amount of time each of us spends in imaginative activity, and with the assertion of the "naturalness" of such mental activity, Klinger asks us to consider the benefits of imagination. In fact, a number of purposes of imaginative activity can be identified.

*Understanding the world.*  The use of objects, words, and images in fantasy and play are idiosyncratic and reflect each person's understanding of the nature of those objects and of the words and images symbolized. As new or novel objects and experiences are encountered by the child, they are related to prior experience and knowledge of the world. Observation of the young child at play, whether solitary or in a group, can yield insight into the child's current conceptualization of the world—how the child views things as fitting together and how the child has organized or structured (constructed) reality.

Imaginative play activity can also lead the child to entirely new discoveries full of wonder and promise—"the reward of his own active imagination."[20] To describe this aspect of imagination, Jones coined the term *outsight,* which he defined as "grasping, enlivening, discovering, making one's own this-or-that datum in the real world—by virtue of gracing it with this-or-that private image."[21] Thus, through the exercise of their imaginative capacity, children are able to discover relationships and explore the possibilities of the objects, words, or ideas that their environment comprises, so as to solidify their understanding of the relationships that exist and to expand their knowledge of the world.

*Problem solving.*  Simply stated, imagination allows an individual to use and recall images. Mental manipulation of those images allows the child to create unique patterns, forecast future events, or discover solutions to problems. Osborn suggested three elements of creative problem solving: (a) *fact finding*—problem definition and the gathering and analysis of pertinent information; (b) *idea finding*—production and development of ideas through brainstorming; and (c) *solution finding*—evaluation and verification of the proposed solutions, followed by implementation of that approach predicted to be the most likely to lead to a successful resolution of the problem. That these stages of problem solving involve imagination is clear: The more imaginative the individual, the more "problems" may be defined and the more ideas and solutions may be proposed. Imagining promotes the development of problem-solving skills by permitting and encouraging playing with possibilities, exploring alternatives, and anticipating consequences.[22]

*Goal setting and planning.*  The ability to exercise forethought and planning is also associated with ability to imagine the possible outcomes of an action or event. The conscious use of visual and verbal images retained within the child's mind (imagining) requires the recollection of past experience, the application of those recollections to present situations, and the prediction or anticipation of likely outcomes.[23] This can be observed in something as mundane as the planning and decision making required of day-to-day activities, in planning a school project or a weekend outing, and in long-range planning (dreaming) (e.g., the child's thinking about a future career as an astronaut or a lion tamer).

*Creativity.* Children considered to be high fantasizers have been found to possess many cognitive skills believed to contribute to creativity: originality, spontaneity, verbal fluency, free-flowing ideas, and flexibility in adjusting to new situations.[24] Bruner introduced the concept of *effective surprise,* "the hallmark of creative enterprise," which he explained as consisting of three elements: (a) *predictive effectiveness,* such as the theoretical statements and predictions made in the sciences; (b) *formal effectiveness,* described as "an ordering of elements in such a way that one sees relationships that were not evident before, groupings that were not before present, ways of putting things together not before within reach"; and (c) *metaphoric effectiveness,* which allows the individual to see relationships between and among hitherto unconnected domains of experience.[25] In each case, combinatorial activity—the placing of things in new perspectives—gives rise to effective surprise, which Bruner described as taking us beyond common ways of experiencing the world. Thus, the creative act (effective surprise) is a product of novelty. Discovery, said Bruner, "is in its essence a matter of rearranging or transforming evidence in such a way that one is enabled to go beyond the evidence so assembled to new ideas."[26] The more fluid one's ability to fantasize and to imagine, the greater the ability to "rearrange and transform evidence" and, so, to produce novelty.

*Conflict resolution.* The usefulness of imagination in the resolution of conflicts and frustrations common to young children in their dealings with objects and people has been stressed by many. Imagination may provide the means for children to cope with their inability to succeed in every situation or to please every authority figure at all times, to tolerate having to delay gratification, or otherwise to accede to the demands of the "real" world. Fraiberg suggested that excursions into fantasy at such times strengthen the child's ability to deal effectively with the environment. She proposed that, "the child who employs his imagination to solve his problems is a child who is working for his own mental health." Similar ideas were held by Bettelheim, who felt that the child's ability to imagine future successes in the face of present failure may preclude feelings of helplessness and hopelessness.[27]

*Handling stress.* After describing pockets of abject poverty in Kowloon, China, Buscaglia proposed that each of us has an unconscious dream of beauty toward which we strive, and for the realization of which we will endure hunger, pain, suffering, and degradation. For those caught in such situations, Buscaglia suggested that this dream and the hope that it may someday be realized allows the individual to continue on in spite of circumstances, led by the idea that "from dreams, changes can be made."[28] The suggestion that dreams (imagination) are related to change in the life of the individual and society is consistent with what has already been stated about the link between imagination and problem solving, planning, creative endeavor, and conflict resolution. Wood suggested that the richer and more varied a person's fantasy life, the greater the resources from which to draw strength and to devise effective solutions by which to reduce stress and anxiety. Put simply, "fantasy is an *active* mental process in which a child seeks to cope with discomfort by changing its form or by substituting a more desired form"; the child who has not learned how to play and how to use fantasy lacks "a significant tool for coping constructively with the environment."[29]

A child's ability to engage in fantasy play or imagining is related to the child's sense of control and self-concept. Through play, children can create a world they are able to control, one in which objects or events take their direction from the children's imagination, unbounded by natural laws. Make-believe, or imaginative play, enables the child to work through real-life conflicts and to resolve them so that the child comes out "on top" rather than as a loser, as often may occur in reality because of the child's lack of competence or understanding. Thus, children may experience a feeling of power or mastery over their environment. This suggested cathartic purpose to symbolic play can be extended to all forms of imagination, and it may be viewed as essential for emotional stability and adjustment to the real world.[30]

*Social development.* Increases in fantasy play have been associated with social and cognitive gains, suggesting that imaginative play can enhance the social development of children. Furthermore, Singer argued that an increasingly differentiated concept or awareness of self results from the make-believe play in which the child experiments with various roles and learns "who he is."[31] Children with well-developed fantasy-making abilities have been found to display "higher levels of imaginativeness, positive affect, concentration, social interaction, and cooperation during free play than children with low fantasy-making tendencies."[32] Her work with emotionally disturbed children led Wood to assert that fantasy can be a powerful tool for promoting adjustment and social-emotional growth of troubled children.[33]

## Implications for teachers

A primary goal of the educator is to help children develop cognitively and affectively by providing a safe and nurturing environment in which to interact with animate and inanimate objects that will both challenge and excite the learner. Unfortunately, many teachers fail to build upon the imaginings of a child. Many even attempt to root out any flights of fantasy without giving thought to how these may enhance children's emotional and cognitive development, and without considering what children's imaginings might reveal about their understanding of the world and of themselves. In 1952, Gerard made the following observation:

> Formal education is directed to our conscious reason, which can at least be supplied with content and practice; if the more intuitive and unconscious imagination can be cultivated, we have yet to learn the secret. *There is the danger of reasoning stifling the imagination. . . .* To teach rigor while preserving imagination is an unsolved challenge to education.[34] (emphasis added)

Gerard's warning seems still to be appropriate. Iverson wondered (with some sarcasm, no doubt) how often teachers post signs urging their students to daydream, play, imagine, or reflect, and observed that "the playful daydreaming stage of creative thought is actively discouraged in most classrooms."[35] Perhaps the most telling criticism of the schools is that of Samples, who asserted that "by ignoring [the realms of fantasy, dreaming, and feeling] and emphasizing rationality and logic, our culture has chosen to define learning and intelligence in amazingly limited ways."[36] The words of the character Thomas Gradgrind in Dickens' *Hard Times*, encouraging teachers to "Teach only Facts," again come to mind. Gradgrind's declaration that teachers should deal with "nothing but Facts" may be especially inappropriate in today's world, considering the information explosion and the speed with which new data are obtained and "old" ideas (facts) are corrected or discarded in our technological society. Said Iverson:

> Schooling today needs to address the rapid obsolescence of facts and promote the adaptive strategies needed to deal productively with change. If one of the long term purposes of education is to prepare children to take their places in our fast-changing society, they will need open, flexible minds and the ability to combine information in new ways.[37]

Samples posited that "school institutionalizes the world of 'outside senses,' the sense of culture, rather than the inside sense of the child."[38] In so doing, schools may fail to engage the child in truly meaningful learning. According to Yardley, "an active imagination leads to creative learning, to learning which is full of meaning because it is linked with personal experience and therefore makes sense to the child."[39] Teachers need to remember that a child does not simply absorb knowledge (facts) as dispensed by the teacher, like so many pills to be taken each day. Rather, knowledge is constructed by each child as she or he puts things into relationships on the basis of actual experiences (interactions with objects and people) and understanding. As Plutarch observed centuries ago, "The mind cannot be seen as a pitcher that needs to be filled, but as a flame that needs to be kindled and fueled." Again, the words of Samples: "Students cannot be fully educated unless a legitimacy is attached to the functioning of their metaphoric and intuitive maturity as well as their rational brain capacities."[40]

Proper application of Piaget's insights into young children's cognitive development demands of teachers more than simple acknowledgment that young children are at a different level of cognitive development than adults. The teacher must cultivate an awareness and understanding of the child's thought processes as they are revealed in all teacher–learner interactions. This requires that the teacher become a student of children, that is, a keen observer of children's thinking as demonstrated in their behavior and speech.[41] Not only must the teacher observe the child as objects are manipulated and ideas expressed, but the teacher must also probe the child's thinking through questioning. The teacher's attention must be focused on how the child attempts to solve problems, how the child uses fantasy or imagination to approach and attempt to assimilate reality. Children learn as they try to work out their own way of doing things (constructing relationships); thus, their errors can be as constructive as their successes. Simply correcting the learner's error, therefore, is insufficient; teachers must seek to understand the reasoning processes that led the child to an incorrect understanding or response, and they must suggest another approach for the child to try. Samples' comment is to the point:

> Children never give you a wrong answer, they just answer a different question. And the answer they give you is the correct answer to that different question. . . . [I]t is our responsibility to find out what the child answered correctly—we have to honor what the child *knows* as well as what we *want* the child to know.[42]

The interests of the child should provide the teacher with clues to appropriate curriculum content. Teachers need to capitalize on the natural curiosity and wide range of interests of children. They need to convey to the child a healthy respect for the child's interests, curiosity, and imagination, and accept rather than criticize or discourage fantasy play.[43] In this way, students will feel free to pursue their own imaginative directions in learning and exploration. Duckworth believed that "the having of wonderful ideas . . . [is] the essence of intellectual development."[44] Hence, occasions must be provided within the classroom for the child to engage in creative thinking (imagining) and exploration in the pursuit and exercise of these "wonderful ideas." Duckworth suggested that a child's curiosity and resourcefulness diminish in later years because the child's intellectual discoveries are less valued, dismissed as trivial, or otherwise discouraged as unacceptable by significant adults in his or her life. To avoid this, teachers must accept and encourage children's ideas and imaginings, and they must provide settings in the classroom that suggest to the children avenues of "research" to pursue their interests and curiosities leading to further discoveries.[45]

Involvement and excitement in learning would seem to follow logically from the child's own imaginings and wonderment about the world. Focusing on that "wonder" would promote more personalized learning, greater understanding, increased motivation, and higher commitment to learning and the learning process. As the child's interests and curiosity become a central concern, the teacher's planning must remain somewhat flexible and open to change. The teacher, out of respect for the child and recognition of the benefits derived from the outworking of the child's imaginings, will select and provide materials to stimulate and challenge the child's interests, but will also accept and encourage the pursuit of the unexpected, following the child's lead.

A crucial first step to freeing the children's imaginations appears to be a change in teacher attitude toward imagination, so that students perceive the classroom atmosphere as open to such activity. Such an environment will recognize the need and provide the time for imaginative or fantasy activity, provide fantasy models, and communicate that imagination is valued. The teacher serves as the most important "fantasy model" by being full of wonder and questioning, by revealing curiosity and divergence of thought and action, by allowing the occasional "crazy idea" to be expressed, and by bringing novelty into the classroom.[46]

Teaching that respects and encourages a child's imagination will present the child with more open-ended assignments rather than focus on a single correct response. Such convergent exercises "develop linear and logical thinking at the expense of more expansive and intuitive thinking."[47] Rather than presuming to be the source of all wisdom, teachers should question, challenge, suggest different approaches, and otherwise stimulate each child's creative and divergent imaginings, encouraging children to continue exploring, evaluating, and building on their imaginative wonderings. As Kamii expressed, "it is far better for children to seriously wonder and remain curious about the environment than to be told the answers and learn incidentally that the answer always comes from the teacher's head."[48]

Jones generalized that all forms of instruction begin by appealing to students' imaginations.[49] Rather than viewing imagination as a distraction or obstruction to real learning, teachers need to recognize that to engage their students more actively in learning, an appeal to their imaginations may be necessary. Something novel may challenge the student's sense of competence and thereby incite his or her imagination. Children need to be assured by their teachers that it is permissible to hold and express highly subjective ideas. Both teachers and students need to understand the legitimacy of *inventing* a solution to a problem rather than simply finding an answer in a book.

Sadly, it may be possible for students to complete twelve years of schooling without ever being made aware of their own creative abilities, and with only a "minimal sense of how their expressiveness and imaginative knowledge can be pivotal in communicating and understanding the very ideas and concepts the school wishes to teach them."[50] To counteract this, teachers need to facilitate and encourage the curiosity of their students by recognizing and supporting their need to explore, by honestly answering their questions, and by "displaying the positive characteristics of curious people."[51]

The active imagination of childhood can fade or become stunted or twisted if it is not properly nurtured. Yardley explained:

> The adult who understands is willing to share the child's wonder and delight, to treat his discoveries with all the respect due to the one who makes them. . . . In this way the child's imagination is nourished and encouraged to develop so that he retains and uses his imaginative powers instead of losing them.[52]

This is consistent with Torrence's conviction that imagination is a cognitive skill that requires guided practice for its development, just as do logical reasoning and judgment. Environmental manipulation and specific training procedures have proven effective in developing imaginative play.[53] Wood explained: "Healthy fantasy in children at all stages of development can be fostered by high levels of adult–child and child–child interaction involving imaginative play, creative activities, reading, creative writing, games, puppets, storytelling, and other forms of dramatic play."[54] Many of these forms of imaginative activity are also methods used for developing specific academic skills (e.g., reading, writing, measurement) and involve the child in social interaction by allowing the development and practice of social amenities. Of added value is that such creative activities move the teacher and student away from the constant and usually routine use of ditto papers and workbooks! The more creative and imaginative the teacher is in working with students, the more the students will become free to experiment with their own ideas and imaginings. Fantasy and imagining can be used in conjunction with the written modality to promote self-expression, self-exploration, and problem solving. Magic has been used to increase children's attention span and motivation, to create new avenues for communication, and to stimulate the senses, while at the same time improving various psychomotor skills, self-concept, and interpersonal skills.[55] The many ways by which a child's imagination can be engaged and put to profitable use in the classroom are limited only by the teacher's imagination! Yardley's admonition provides a fitting summation:

> If we do not find a place for the inventor, the unorthodox thinker, the investigator of a fresh line of inquiry, or the contemplative as opposed to the traditional doer, then the educational system will perpetuate only what already exists and society will stand still. . . . [A]s teachers we have a great responsibility for the survival of imagination. It can so easily get lost in childhood, and once imagination has been allowed to die, it is very difficult to restore.[56]

## Notes

1.  C. Dickens, *Hard Times* (New York: Norton, 1966), p. 1.

2.  M.M. Wood, ed., *Developmental Therapy Sourcebook* (Baltimore: University Park Press, 1981), vol. 2, *Fantasy and Make-believe*.

3.  P. Dickinson, "Fantasy: The Need for Realism," *Children's Literature in Education* 17 (1986), p. 43; and E. Klinger, *Structure and Functions of Fantasy* (New York. Wiley, 1971), p. 5.

4.  R. Lewis, "A Child's Right to Imagine," *Young Children* 39 (1984), p. 62.

5.  H. Gardner, *Frames of Mind. The Theory of Multiple Intelligences* (New York. Basic Books, 1985).

6.  A. Yardley, *Young Children's Thinking* (New York: Citation, 1973), p. 110.

7.  A.F. Osborn, *Applied Imagination*, 3rd ed. (New York: Scribner's, 1963).

8.  Dickinson, "Fantasy," p. 43.

9.  R.B. Allen, *Imagination* (Portland, OR: Multnomah Press, 1985).

10.  E.J. Dehouske, *Listen to the Story: Using Spontaneous Story-writing with Students* (Monograph of the Arts in Special Education Project, Pennsylvania Department of Education, 1982); "Story-writing as a Problem Solving Vehicle," *Teaching Exceptional Children* 15 (1982), pp. 11–17; and B.M. Vitale, *Unicorns Are Real: A Right-brained Approach to Learning* (New York: Warner Books, 1982).

11.  R.M. Jones, *Fantasy and Feeling in Education* (New York: New York University, 1968), p. 58; C. Garvey, *Play* (Cambridge, MA: Harvard, 1977); Klinger, *Fantasy;* and J. Singer, ed., *The Child's World of Make-believe* (New York: Academic Press, 1973).

12.  Cf., G.F. Render, J.M. Padilla, and C.E. Moon, "Toward a Holistic Definition of Creativity," *Holistic Education Review* 1, no. 4 (Winter 1988), pp. 4–9.

13.  J.S. Bruner, A. Jolly, and K. Sylva, *Play: Its Role in Development and Education* (New York: Basic Books, 1976); Garvey, *Play,* 1977; J.E. Johnson, J.F. Christie, and T.D. Yawkey, *Play and Early Childhood Development* (Glenview, IL: Scott, Foresman, & Co., 1987); J. Levy, *Play Behavior* (New York: Wiley, 1978); J. Piaget, *Play, Dreams, and Imitation in Childhood* (New York: Norton, 1962); M. Piers, ed., *Play and Development* (New York: Norton, 1972); and B. Sutton-Smith and S. Sutton-Smith, *How to Play with Your Children (and When Not to)* (New York: Hawthorne, 1974).

14.  C. Kamii and R. DeVries, *Group Games in Early Education* (Washington, DC: National Association for the Education of Young Children, 1980), p. 12.

15. *Ibid*, p. 20.

16. M.R. Bradbard and R.C. Endsley, "How Can Teachers Develop Young Children's Curiosity?" *Young Children* 35 (1980), p. 26.

17. L.B. Jacobs, B. Biber, and L.E. Raths, "A Symposium: Value-outcomes of the Curious Mind," *Childhood Education* 51 (1975), p. 245.

18. R.W. Gerard, "The Biological Basis of the Imagination," in *The Creative Process: A Symposium*, edited by B. Ghiselin (New York: Mentor, 1952), pp. 226–251.

19. Klinger, *Fantasy*, p. 347.

20. Yardley, *Children's Thinking*, p. 115.

21. Jones, *Fantasy and Feeling*, p. 60.

22. Yardley, *Children's Thinking;* and Osborn, *Applied Imagination*. Cf., Dehouske, *Listen to the Story;* and Gardener, *Frames of Mind*.

23. J.L. Singer and J.S. Antrobus, "A Factor-analytic Study of Daydreaming and Conceptually-related Cognitive and Personality Variables," *Perceptual and Motor Skills* 17 (1963), pp. 187–209; and Yardley, *Children's Thinking*.

24. M.A. Pulaski, "Toys and Imaginative Play," in *The Child's World of Make-believe*, edited by J.L. Singer (New York: Academic Press, 1973), pp. 74–103.

25. J.S. Bruner, *On Knowing: Essays for the Left Hand* (Cambridge, MA: Harvard, 1964), pp. 18–19.

26. *Ibid.*, pp. 82–83.

27. B. Bettelheim, *The Uses of Enchantment: The Meaning and Importance of Fairy Tales* (New York, Vintage, 1977); Dehouske, *Listen to the Story;* S.M. Fraiberg, *The Magic Years* (New York: Scribner's, 1959), p. 23; Klinger, *Fantasy;* and Wood, *Developmental Therapy*.

28. L. Buscaglia, *The Way of the Bull* (New York: Fawcett Crest, 1973).

29. Wood, *Developmental Therapy*, pp. 4, 11.

30. I. Athey, "Piaget, Play, and Problem-solving," in *Play as a Learning Medium*, edited by D. Sponseller (Washington, DC: National Association for the Education of Young Children, 1974); and H. Ginsburg and S. Opper, *Piaget's Theory of Intellectual Development* (Englewood Cliffs, NJ: Prentice-Hall, 1969); cf., Bettelheim, *Uses of Enchantment*.

31. L. Nahme-Huang, D.G. Singer, J.L. Singer, and A.B. Wheaton, "Imaginative Play Training and Perceptual-motor Interventions with Emotionally Disturbed Hospitalized Children," *American Journal of Orthopsychiatry*, 47 (1977), pp. 238–249; and Singer, *Child's World*.

32. Johnson, Christie, and Yawkey, *Play*, p. 76.

33. Wood, *Developmental Therapy*.

34. Gerard, "Biological Basis," p. 249.

35. B.K. Iverson, "Play, Creativity, and Schools Today," *Phi Delta Kappan* 63 (1982), p. 693.

36. B. Samples, *Openmind/Wholemind* (Rolling Hills Estates, CA: Jalmar, Press, 1987), p. 4; cf., Gardner, *Frames of Mind*.

37. Iverson, *Play, Creativity*, p. 694.

38. Samples, *Openmind/Wholemind*, p. 14.

39. Yardley, *Children's Thinking*, p. 111.

40. R.E. Samples, "Educating for Both Sides of the Human Mind," *The Science Teacher* 42 (1975), p. 27.

41. D.W. Anderson, "Implications of Piaget for the Elementary Classroom," *Christian Educator's Journal* 14 (1975), pp. 12–15, 29–31.

42. Samples, *Openmind/Wholemind*, p. 93.

43. Anderson, "Implications of Piaget"; and M.R. Jalongo, "Imaginary Companions in Children's Lives and Literature," *Childhood Education* 60 (1984), pp. 166–171.

44. E. Duckworth, "The Having of Wonderful Ideas," *Harvard Education Review* 42 (1972), p. 217.

45. Anderson, "Implications of Piaget."

46. Dehouske, *Listen to the Story;* cf., J.M. Brunswick, "My Ten Commandments to Creative Teaching," *Journal of Creative Behavior* 5 (1971), pp. 199–200.

47. Iverson, *Play, Creativity,* p. 694.

48. C. Kamii, "Piaget's Interactionism and the Process of Teaching Young Children," in *Piaget in the Classroom,* edited by M. Schweble and S. Raph (New York: Basic Books, 1973), p. 225.

49. Jones, *Fantasy and Feeling.*

50. R. Lewis, "The Magic Fish and the Yellow Print," *Childhood Education* 52 (1976), p. 254.

51. Bradbard and Endsley, *Young Children's Curiosity,* p. 29.

52. Yardley, *Children's Thinking,* p. 115.

53. E.P. Torrence, *Encouraging Creativity in the Classroom* (Dubuque, IA: Brown, 1970); and Nahme-Huang, et al., "Imaginative Play Training."

54. Wood, *Developmental Therapy,* p. 11.

55. Dehouske, *Listen to the Story;* and G.H. Frith and J.C. Walker, "Magic as Motivation for Handicapped Students," *Teaching Exceptional Children* 15 (1983), pp. 108–110.

56. Yardley, *Children's Thinking,* pp. 118–119.

# On the Education
# of Wonder and Ecstasy

## by W. Nikola-Lisa

*W. Nikola-Lisa's first two years of teaching were at the World Family School, an alternative pre- and lower-elementary grade school in Bozeman, Montana. As head teacher he drew on Waldorf and British integrated curriculum approaches. After another five years teaching primary grades in the Bozeman Public Schools, Dr. Nikola-Lisa attended Montana State University where he received his Ed.D. in Elementary School Curriculum and Instruction.*

*Currently, Dr. Nikola-Lisa teaches in a student-centered graduate field-based M.Ed. program in Curriculum and Instruction at National-Louis University in Evanston, Illinois. He teaches courses in group processes, human development and learning theories, developmental play theory, and children's literature.*

*Recently he has worked as a storyteller and writing consultant for the Children's Literacy Project, a collective of artists, writers, and educators working with Hispanic school populations on Chicago's southside.*

We are now in the midst of a reawakening, a reshaping of our ways of being in the world. *Holistic Education Review,* and a growing number of trade and professional journals like it, is evidence of this conscious resighting of the human experience. One facet of this reawakening is that we are beginning to look at hitherto neglected realms of human experience that have stood outside the common boundary of acceptable societal behavior. Ecstasy is one of these experiences which, though ever-present through time, has stood outside our common cultural consciousness. Historically, ecstasy has had limited appeal to Western psychologists, being dismissed as either a bracketed "religious" experience or an aberrant state of consciousness associated with the hallucinations of the schizophrenic.

It has only been within the last twenty years, with the rise of the human potential movement, that ecstasy has been able to steer a course into more traditional psychological circles. It was the psychologist Abraham Maslow who first opened up the field with discussions of the "peak experience," a palatable surrogate term for ecstasy. Although most of the excitement over Maslow's fertile work generated a series of

This selection originally appeared in the Summer 1988 issue of *Holistic Education Review,* Vol. 1, No. 2.

discussions aimed at placing altered or higher states of consciousness within the mainstream of general psychological theory, a number of other voices arose in a variety of related fields calling for a general reestimation of the accepted boundaries of possible human experience.

In education, particularly, excitement over the possibility of including the ecstatic experience in curriculum discussions exploded in the field with the arrival of award-winning journalist George Leonard's *Education and Ecstasy*.[1] This polemic against existing practice called for a redefinition of the entire educational enterprise that would effectively put at its heart the transcendent experience of ecstasy.

Although Leonard's voice was loud and articulate, it did not last long. Like many of his humanistic colleagues writing during the late 1960s, Leonard's response to an entrenched educational system was to propose the substitution of a set of *affective* outcomes for an already existing and somewhat suffocating *cognitive* set. Not only have educators since seen the futility in such a neat exchange of educational outcomes, they have as well become aware of the inherent fallacy which keeps these two domains separate in the first place.

The ecstatic experience, in particular, has forced educational psychologists and learning theorists to look again at the relationship between cognitive and affective states. And, in so doing, it has created a climate within which the "whole person"—or child—movement has come of age. Holistic educators, naturally, seek to define the child within the broad framework of varied states of consciousness. It is an ecological approach sensitive to a multitude of impinging factors, i.e., environmental impact, developmental influences, transcendent states of consciousness, the natural states of play and wonder, etc. Indeed, it is from this more liberal viewpoint that an understanding of the role and importance of ecstatic states is even possible. To understand this, however, it might be helpful to recap briefly some of the explanations given historically to this intensely unique human experience.

## Attempt at an explanation

As I have already mentioned, looked at from the perspective of religion, ecstasy is typically defined or explained as a mystical—and as such *mysterious*—union of the individual self with the Absolute, God. Religious history is replete with allusions to such explanations, explanations which appeal to the supernatural, and thus to the inexplicable. Ecstasy, seen through this lens, is that rare experience which crashes unexpectedly through the devout's intense religious belief structure to produce an unexplainably intoxicating—though not necessarily institutionally sanctioned—experience.

Looking from a broader angle, on the other hand, cultural anthropologists and mythologists explain ecstasy quite differently. They see the ecstatic experience from a phenomenological point of view, i.e., a perspective that seeks the more understandable and explainable "good fit" between cultural expectations and individual response patterns. Typically, such explanations deal with cosmogenic phenomena in which an individual or group of individuals strive to return to some ancestral or primitive time in order to relive an important aspect or event in their cultural past.

Psychologists, moreover, can be grouped into two or three different camps depending upon their specific emphasis. Early psychoanalytic assessments, as I have already mentioned, have associated ecstasy with the schizophrenic mind, seeing it as a loss of ego control. Another related psychodynamic interpretation, similar to the cultural anthropologist, views ecstasy as a type of regression on the part of the individual back to a primitive or undifferentiated state of childhood.

More recent explanations have focused on the psychological mechanisms involved in either producing or sustaining the ecstatic experience. In particular, Arthur Deikman[2] has used the concept of deautomatization to explain the mystical or ecstatic experience. Recognizing that most of our ability to perceive the world is bound up in automatic perceptual responses which limit to a certain extent our ability to "see" the world as it is, Deikman suggests that ecstasy is merely the undoing of those automatic ways of seeing, an undoing which enables us to pay closer attention to certain perceptual phenomena.

A last category of responses to the ecstatic experience, falling still within the parameters of a psychological framework, involves those psychologists who seek to place the ecstatic experience naturally along a broad continuum of humanly possible states of consciousness. Such psychologists are less interested in the actual psychological mechanisms involved in the ecstatic experience (recognizing that it is extremely difficult to actually enumerate them); they are more interested in expanding our ways of seeing that elusive concept, *human potential*. Their treatment of the subject is usually epistemic, i.e., focused on the knowledge-bound context of the experience. Andrew Greeley,[3] though not himself a psychologist, represents this point of view clearly in his discussion of knowledge domains—four in all—that lead ultimately to "ecstasy knowledge."

## Ecstasy as knowledge

The first domain of knowledge that Greeley outlines, one that is familiar to us all, is that of rational or discursive knowledge. This type of knowledge provides a foundation for all of Western thought; it is the linear, left-brained sequencing of analytical knowledge. Typically, we associate the roots of this type of knowledge with the ancient Greeks who first awakened in human consciousness the desire to know the world objectively.

A second domain of knowledge identified by Greeley involves metaphysical knowledge. This type of knowledge is also rational—observing "the conventions of discursive language, the language of prose, the laws of logic, the methods of rational discourse"—but instead of being interested in the proximate, it is more interested in an elaboration of the Ultimate.

Of a qualitatively different nature is mythopoetic knowledge. Although also concerned with the Ultimate, mythopoetic knowledge appeals to the whole person, a being of subtly emotional, sensual, and cognitive faculties. Mythopoetic knowledge differs in both style and language in its use of symbols (presentational language), rather than the more rigid expressions of discursive language. And, rather than trying to *explain* particular settings or situations or phenomena, mythopoetic knowledge seeks merely to *illuminate* the ambiguities, to highlight the inconsistencies.

Greeley's fourth level of knowledge involves, of course, mystical or ecstasy knowledge. It, too, involves the whole person—but this time without requiring either the exigencies of logical understanding or the felicitations of symbolic representation. It is better termed an *apprehension* than a firm, clear understanding. And, most importantly, ecstasy knowledge intimates a special relationship between the perceiving individual knower and the object to be known. In this relationship, there is a marked redefinition of the line that separates self from not-self: the process of self-definition begun at infancy is temporarily circumvented allowing the individual to experience a renewed intimacy with the cosmos.

## The child in wonder

If ecstasy knowledge is rooted in the disturbance of the boundary that separates self from not-self, then it seems that there can be no better place to view this realignment than in the young child. In fact, it was that venerable Western philosopher Plato who urged us centuries ago to look for the genesis of knowledge in the child's emerging sense of wonder.

Picking up on this notion, cultural historian Edith Cobb, in her highly visionary book, *The Ecology of Imagination in Childhood*,[4] stresses repeatedly that it is through wonder that we come to know the world-at-large at all. For Cobb, however, wonder is not an abstract term, a lofty ideal, but is concretely rooted in the child's developing perceptual capabilities. Each individual—from birth on—possesses an overwhelming desire to organize the environment. Such an organizational drive for order occurs through the interplay of perceptual activity and natural form. Wonder, in particular—as 'true metaphor'—derives

> from the overlapping of the energies of the perceiving nervous system and energy systems in nature at the level of unity which is the specific interest of ecology, where temporal and spatial relations are of supreme importance in the drive toward organization or form and meaning.[5]

Cobb, in short, advises us that children learn "by becoming," by vibrating sympathetically with the surrounding natural form of the immediate environment. This type of learning is not bound by either discursive or presentational language. And, although rooted in the concrete or proximate, it resounds in the Ultimate. In this way, then, it resembles uncannily Greeley's fourth category of ecstasy knowledge,

and perhaps finds its most ecological and poetic statement in the words
of that great American poet Walt Whitman.[6]

> There was a child went forth every day,
> And the first object he look'd upon, that object he became,
> And that object became a part of this child,
> And the grass and white and red morning-glories, and white and
>      red clover, and the song of the phoebe-bird,
> And the third-month lambs and the sow's pink-faint litter, and
>      the mare's foal and cow's calf,
> And the noisy brood of the barnyard or by the mire of pond-side,
> And the fish suspending themselves so curiously below there,
>      and the beautiful curious liquid,
> And the water-plants, with their graceful flat heads, all became
>      part of him.

If it was not obvious, it should be from the above account—and the
basic thread of this entire discussion—that the precursor to mystical or
ecstasy knowledge as outlined by Greeley previously is the child's experience of wonder in early childhood. This experience, generated naturally
by the plasticity of the developing perceptual system, enables the young
child to "know" the universe by direct immediate apprehension. Although this peculiar "knowing by becoming" is mediated by the manipulation of concrete objects, objects in-and-of-themselves serve only as
a catalyst inciting the mind to organize novelty of experience into a
palpable whole.

## The universe-at-large

This underlying holism of which we are all a part is the natural state
of apprehension in the young child. Evidence of this fact emerges early
as those peculiarly cosmic questions begin to issue from the astutely
perceptive child. Questions about the nature of time, space, dreaming
and waking, the mind, etc., all fall within the purview of the young
child's native intelligence and curiosity.

Philosopher Gareth Matthews[7] calls this particularly childlike quality
"naivete," and reminds us that every society, at one point or another,
has needed "a barefoot Socrates to ask childishly simple (and childishly
difficult) questions, to force its members to reexamine what they have
been thoughtlessly taking for granted." Citing philosopher Robert
Spaemann, Matthews encourages us as a society even to cultivate a
type of "institutionalized naivete."

In a similar stance—though in much stronger terms—poet, architect,
philosopher, and inventor Buckminster Fuller addresses this same
phenomenon—those "embarrassingly important cosmological questions" of the young child. In his book-length essay, *Intuition*,[8] Fuller
reprimands parents and educators alike for their ofttimes short-sighted
view of the world of the young child. Playing social critic in that peculiarly Fullerian poetic voice, he admonishes us to concentrate less on
the A, B, Cs, and 1, 2, 3s—that is, only the parts—of our child's "Elemen-

tary Education," and to stress more the essential beginning of the entire learning process: the underlying holism that holds the universe together. It is a holism, again, that is directly intuited or apprehended by the young child—displayed through a profound and resilient sense of wonder.

In the end, Fuller calls for a reestimation of the effect that industrial "specialization"—seeing only the parts—has had on contemporary society. He emphasizes the need for a holistic point of view—a synergistic point of view—a point of view that is naturally operative in the ecological response system of the young child. Education, in particular, according to Fuller, should play an important role in this reestimation process. In a world of behavioral objectives, anticipatory sets, criterion-referenced outcomes, and microanalysis, the refreshedness of natural wonder and curiosity—forming a chain of embryonic growth toward ecstasy—should not only be acknowledged, but encouraged wholeheartedly.

If wonder and ecstasy do indeed form the basis for learning, for apprehending the "true metaphors" of the universe as mind interacts with nature, then it seems that the charge to us—parents and educators alike—for this new dawning era is to encourage our children to make those connections. We can do this by providing a richly stimulating and natural environment, developing an attitudinal mindset that recognizes the importance of natural forms of play, wonder, and ecstasy, and, finally, by taking the time ourselves to venture out into the universe-at-large to explore, to dream, to ponder, and perhaps even to wonder ourselves into ecstasy.

## Notes

1. George B. Leonard, *Education and Ecstasy* (New York: Dell, 1968).

2. Deikman's account can be found in Andrew Greeley's *Ecstasy: A Way of Knowing* (Englewood Cliffs, NJ: Prentice-Hall, 1974), pp. 43-44.

3. Greeley, *Ecstasy*, pp. 56-72.

4. Edith Cobb, *The Ecology of Imagination in Childhood* (New York: Columbia University Press, 1977).

5. Cobb, *Ecology of Imagination*, pp. 34-35.

6. F. Matthiessen, (ed.), *Oxford Book of American Verse* (New York: Oxford University Press, 1950), pp. 276-278.

7. Gareth B. Matthews, *Philosophy and the Young Child* (Cambridge, MA: Harvard University Press, 1980), pp. 90-95.

8. R. Buckminster Fuller, *Intuition* (New York: Doubleday, 1972), p. 46.

# Education for the Soul
## Spiritual Values and the English Curriculum

## by Karen A. Carlton and Richard L. Graves

*Karen A. Carlton is Associate Professor of English at Humboldt State University in Arcata, CA, where she directs the Composition Program and teaches literature and writing courses. She received her Ph.D. from New York University.*

*Dick Graves, professor of English Education at Auburn, holds the B.A. from Baylor, the M.Ed. from the University of Florida, and the Ph.D. from Florida State. He is director of the Sun Belt Writing Project at Auburn and co-sponsor of the Gulf Coast Conference on the Teaching of Writing.*

The soul is constantly about to starve; it cannot live on fun alone. If the soul gets no other food, it will first tear apart other creatures . . . then itself.
— Selma Lagerlof

We believe that of all the components of the English curriculum—the study of literature, the development of skill in writing, the understanding of grammar and usage, the refinement of taste and aesthetic sensibility—the most fundamental and important aspect of our subject is the cultivation of spiritual values.

Our conception of spiritual values is broad and generic, not limited to a narrow theistic or sectarian framework. Spiritual values as we conceive them are those ideas and ideals which are basic to all religions. They encourage us to know, love, and perfect ourselves as personal beings. They promote the growth and welfare of our communal lives, leading toward order and justice, fostering peace and tranquility. They seek harmony between humankind and the natural world.

Because spiritual values exist at the deep center of being, where, as Quaker John Woolman said, "the heart stands in perfect sincerity," they cannot be approached or evoked by methodologies which succeed in exercising only the more surface levels of knowing. They are not developed through the acquisition of factual knowledge or critical thinking skills having only to do with reason and argument. Similarly, strong

This selection originally appeared in the Summer 1989 issue of *Holistic Education Review*, Vol. 2, No. 2.

spiritual values are not always present in students and teachers who are successful in the traditional dimensions of the English curriculum— reading, writing, grammar and usage, and aesthetics. Indeed, some learners who lack English language skills—vocational students, ESL students, remedial students, learning disabled students—may have highly developed spiritual values, and therefore come to this dimension of an English curriculum as authorities on that which is best within the human heart. For spiritual values are often experienced in the realm of the nonverbal, in the fullness of life itself.

What can we do to open our classrooms, our schools, our selves to the cultivation of spiritual values? First of all, we can acknowledge that education exists to develop not only the mind and the body, but the soul. Poets speak often of the soul, referring to that which is related and connected to all other souls, regardless of more superficial differences, and is capable of union with all life. Having no boundaries, the soul seeks to understand and embrace whomever or whatever the superficial self might regard as separate or alien. It is the soul which forgives, which feels the pain of the lonely, the homeless, the hungry, and which knows, as the Tewa Indian prayer says, that "all life is one life." It is the soul which feels the flight of the egret or the deep strength of a redwood, which experiences union with the cosmos.

The soul is the source of those values we call spiritual. It is that deep center which holds together our experiences and gives us a unique identity. The soul is a story, a process, a whirlwind of energy, with a history either long or short. Embracing all our various inner dimensions, it is an inclusive force containing masculine, feminine, and shadow elements. The soul has vision without which a person loses one's sense of relationship and harmony with the world around him or her. Without a developed and active soul, a person is caught in the limiting darkness of the ego.

## Fragmented thinking

In this age of fragmentation and specialization, the soul is denied the experience of wholeness which is so fundamental to its health. Rational formulations are valued over poetic ones, with jargon and doublespeak threatening to silence all expressions of the heart. In many English classrooms, students are asked more often to write voiceless critical essays than to write stories or poems. In discussions they are pressured to "think critically," to dissect, argue, doubt, and analyze more often than to attend, empathize, believe, and connect. It is standard practice to use literary criticism in the presentation of the literary text instead of offering the work as an opportunity for pleasure or celebration, or as a source for inspiration and imitation.

However, in an English classroom where spiritual values are actively nurtured, the critical voice does not silence the creative voice. Students are encouraged to respond to literature with their own art, since art (poetry, fiction, nonfiction, music, image) is the expression and therefore the exercise of the soul's voice. Allowed to dream as well as to control, to contemplate as well as to memorize, students in such English class-rooms learn to express their own visions and truths in response to the writers and works they study. They are given opportunities to achieve a state of heightened awareness similar to that which many artists describe as preceding the creative act—a state in which they are whole persons, completely present to what is in the moment. In this state the reasoning mind with its powers is absorbed by the larger response of the total being. Ralph Waldo Emerson wrote in his *Journal:*

> Keep your eye & ear open to all impressions, but deepen no impression by effort, but take the opinion of the Genius within, what ought to be retained by you & what rejected by you. Keep, that is, the upright position.[1]

To "take the opinion of the Genius within" is to listen to the soul's voice. And it is the soul's voice, our most inward voice, to which we listen when we write our best work; it is the soul's ears and eyes we use to read the stories and poems we most love or to discern that which is sacred in the world. Denise Levertov describes the process of listening to the soul, of reading and writing from the soul, as dialogue with the God in oneself.[2] Donald Hall speaks of the "vatic voice" within us—a prophetic voice which comes through dreams and reveries, which is original and inspired, as if from the gods. We do not initiate such a voice. We receive it, letting it speak, not only to make poems and stories, but "because it feels good, because it helps us to understand ourselves and be able to love other people."[3] Inasmuch as this soul's voice, this sacred place, lies within each one of us, it can be used to make meaning of what otherwise might appear as a dark and profane world.

In her book, *The Mind of the Maker*, Dorothy Sayers describes the human mind while engaged in an act of creative imagination and arrives at the conclusion that "creative mind is in fact the very grain of the spiritual universe." Her words challenge all educators, but particularly those of us who teach English:

> if we conclude that creative mind is in fact the very grain of the spiritual universe, we shall have to ask ourselves whether the same pattern is not also exhibited in the spiritual structure of every man and woman. And, if it is, whether, by confining the average man and woman to uncreative activities and an uncreative outlook, we are not doing violence to the very structure of our being. If so, it is a serious matter, since we have seen already the unhappy results of handling any material in a way that runs counter to the natural law of its structure.[4]

## Opening to the soul

In reading stories and poems aloud, in journal writing, poetic writing, meditation, recording dreams, listening to music, and contemplating art, we are able to listen to the soul, to create, and thus see through differences to discover the unity that is always beneath oppositions. We are able to hear where words come from and to heal the divisions within ourselves that cause us to project our own weaknesses on the world. For listening to the soul leads us to listen to the world. It enables us to feel reverence for all things, to know our interrelatedness with all of nature. Thus we experience wonder and humility before we master intellectual concepts, allowing material knowledge to stand on the solid foundation of spiritual understandings. We love the world best when we realize the presence of a transcendent reality that is, nonetheless, that which is nearest of all, immanent in the world and in human life itself. Through reading and writing from the soul's center we can love and praise the things and peoples of this world; we can enter into the cosmos of the word in its most creative capacity.

An English curriculum centered in spiritual values stresses the intersections of inside and outside worlds. It attempts to relate literature and its dilemmas and worldviews to the students' lives. It enables students to write from inside out, to follow the delicate yearnings of feeling, image, dream, and body. For as Goethe reminds us, "every healthy effort is directed from the inward to the outward world." We do not simply reflect what we encounter; we meet and internalize it according to our passions and our conceptual structures. In observing the intersections of inside and outside worlds, we learn to shift our ways of seeing in order to affirm the complexities of positions that are different from our own.

Such an English curriculum helps our students wear "world-colored" lenses by having them write freely from multiple points of view, read widely among a magnitude of authors, and examine their own ethnocentric assumptions, which can lead to racism, sexism, and exploitation of the earth. It relates English to math, to science, to history and other disciplines because it sees in wholes and thinks not only globally but cosmically. "Indifference to the cosmic," says Marshall McLuhan, "fosters intense concentration on minute segments and specialist tasks, which is the unique strength of western man. For the specialist is the one who never makes small mistakes while moving toward the grand fallacy."[5] Thus, an English classroom emphasizing spiritual values encourages students to quest for a vision of human life that will make room for humans' sense and taste for the infinite.

Because we are, in many ways, "the company we keep," we need to surround ourselves and our students with persons and matters of worth, so that the intersections of outside and inside worlds will be fruitful and enriching. We need to furnish our environments with the best of art and life—paintings on the walls, music, readings, and creative silence. In thinking about which literary texts best serve the cultivation of spiritual values, it is clear that English teachers cannot rely on the traditional canon for direction. For the values and ideas which young people derive from a work of literature are more important than the work itself. Some works which were appropriate yesterday are now out of style, and some of today's favorites will be gone tomorrow. It is therefore not the literature which is timeless but the values embodied in the literature. It is not the story itself but the *unarticulated essence* of the story which is eternal. And what is true with literature is also true with the other aspects of the English curriculum: always below the surface of the study of grammar or usage or correctness are larger issues, the issue of purpose and intention of the reader or writer, revealed and disguised truth, the issue of voice, and ultimately the issue of spiritual values.

If our aim is to encourage spiritual growth according to a vision of what is of ultimate eternal value, then we must not leave the education of our children to chance. We must deliberately build an environment which promotes the ideals of wholeness, wisdom, and love. We should have for all persons what Plato wished for his ruling class:

> We would not have our Guardians grow up among representations of moral deformity, as in some foul pasture where, day after day, feeding on every poisonous weed they would, little by little, gather insensibly a mass of corruption in their very souls. Rather we must seek out those craftsmen whose instinct guides them to whatsoever is lovely and gracious; so that our young people, dwelling in a wholesome climate, may drink in good from every quarter, whence, like a breeze bearing health from happy regions, some influence from noble works constantly falls upon eye and ear from childhood upward, and imperceptibly draws them into sympathy and harmony with the beauty of reason, whose impress they take.[6]

As teachers who recognize and value the soul, the source of those values we call spiritual, we should cultivate in ourselves and our students the will to know what is true; to create what is beautiful; to endure pain and fear; to resist the allurements of pleasure; to be brave and temperate—in the interests of oneself and one's community; to take for oneself, to give to others, not what one is inclined to but what is due.

## Notes

1.   Merton M. Sealts, (ed.) *The Journals and Miscellaneous Notebooks of Ralph Waldo Emerson*, Vol. V (Cambridge: Harvard University Press, 1965), p. 6.

2.   Denise Levertov, *The Poet in the World* (New York: New Directions, 1973).

3.   Donald Hall, *Goatfoot Milktongue Twinbird: Interviews, Essays and Notes on Poetry, 1970-76* (Ann Arbor, 1978), p. 5.

4.   Dorothy Sayers, *The Mind of the Maker* (San Francisco: Harper & Row, 1941), p. 185.

5.   Marshall McLuhan, *Understanding Media: The Extensions of Man* (New York: New American Library, 1964).

6.   Plato, *The Republic*, trans by G.M.A. Grube (Indianapolis: Hackett, 1974), p. 401.

# Creation Spirituality
# and the
# Reinventing of Education

## by Andy LePage

*Andy LePage holds a B.A. in philosophy, an M.A. in counseling, and a Ph.D. in religious studies. He was a therapist for twelve years and since 1980 has been an educational consultant and inservice provider to public schools. Dr. LePage is the author of* Transforming Education: The New 3 R's *(1987, Oakmore House) and a contributing author of* Cooperative Discipline *(in press). He lives in Tampa where he directs the Florida Center for Self-Esteem. He is host of WTKN's weekly radio call-in show "Parents and Kids."*

As an institution, American public education is no longer providing energy, awareness, power, and direction to society. It is dysfunctional. "It lives in the space age," says George Leonard, "but teaches the horse and buggy."[1] Rarely does it engage, give power, or give meaningful direction. Its students, teachers, and graduates know little about life and life's interactions—the planet and its support system, personal power which serves to empower the common good, the fragile and wonderful ecosystem that we need but are choosing to kill. Most difficult of all, the educational institution has numbed so many of us that we do not know that we do not know.

We do not know that humans are capable of getting along consistently with each other and with other species. We do not know that we pay lip service to our children but fail to offer them responsible education. We seem to not want to know that we have separated science from religion and thereby lost a living cosmology. We have no way of telling the story of the Earth and our part in a magnificent evolving creation. We seem to not want to care that many of our human systems are rooted in cynicism, authoritarianism, and elitism. Many educators see no need to know that an elitist power structure robs the Third World blind while it enhances the few who forcibly control in the First World. We seem to not want to know that education is shortchanging everyone

This selection originally appeared in the Summer 1989 issue of *Holistic Education Review*, Vol. 2, No. 2. © Copyright 1989, Andy LePage because we insist on perceiving it as industry rather than as art. We seem to not want to know that we have substituted pathology for wellness, and with this substitution, believe we are "doing" education.

Why are so many students unable to perform creative works? Why do they feel so bored? Schools, and the adults who run them, are giving students unchallenged specified content, but are not opening them to a worldview, not offering guidance and opportunities to express creativity. Students do not know where they came from, their place in the universe, their cosmic relatives. Little or nothing is offered to help students develop self-confidence, become responsible, instruct them in caring for property, or help them in their character development. Because education has lost its ability to be alive, to engage, to give direction, it robs students and keeps them from developing meaning in their own lives and in the world.

## The loss and rebirth of a spiritual connection

American schools are beset by many problems, but the fundamental problem is a spiritual one. American civilization began with a frontiersman mentality in which European settlers took the land, moved the natives wherever they pleased, made slaves of African people and brought them here, and used both the land and the people as they saw fit. From this difficult beginning flowed a school system which became as flawed as the culture it served. It took away beauty, truth, goodness, and the idea of an undivided land and replaced these with a fragmented, piecemeal, divvied up, and partial vision. In this vision, truth is filtered and incomplete, and creativity is sapped by authoritarianism. The link to the land is lost because it is presided over by people who sense no interrelationship among themselves and their universe.

The loss of the spiritual connection keeps humankind from understanding education within the intrinsic dynamics of the Earth. We do not know what we are about as a species because we are alienated from the cosmos and imprisoned in our narrow frames of reference. Brian Swimme says, "We will discover our larger role only by reinventing the human as a dimension of the emergent universe."[2]

This larger role of the human and the rebirth of the spiritual connection is at the heart of Creation Spirituality—a tradition being revived in the West by theologian Matthew Fox. His work is effectively tearing down the prison walls of one-dimensional thinking, revealing a panorama in which creation itself emanates from the center. He shows how the fall/redemption tradition of St. Augustine—characterized by struggle—shuns creativity and interaction. That tradition urges adherents to escape the evil of "this" world for the joy of the "next." But Creation Spirituality—which Fox traces back to the ninth century B.C.—is rooted in the goodness of all created life, in love for the Earth and care for the cosmos, and in passion for living. It is characterized by celebration of the human and the divine, flowing creativity, and interdependence.

In researching its roots, Fox has uncovered the work of thirteenth century Creation-centered mystic, theologian, feminist, and prophet,

Meister Eckhart. Fox calls Eckhart "a spiritual genius and a declared heretic"[3] and notes that he was silenced by the Roman Catholic Church because his spirituality was rooted in experiencing the creation, rather than in following authoritarian pronouncements which the fall/redemption dichotomy dictates.

True to his Creation-centered roots, Eckhart's profound spiritual maturation did not come from academia and seminary, but from his mixing with the lay feminist movement of his day. As Fox notes, "Perhaps that is why Eckhart could declare, contrary to those who find a comfortable refuge in academia, that 'the most noble kind of knowledge is learned by living.'"[4] (Fox, who has recently published a penetrating essay titled, "The Church as Dysfunctional Family," is himself presently being told not to teach and preach. His theology, centered in his view of creation as original blessing rather than original sin, is said to be leading the faithful astray.)

Creation Spirituality opens the frame of reference for a more excellent way to see. Essentially, it offers Eckhart's four ways of looking at the world. From the viewpoint of befriending creation, it helps us to savor the diverse and fragrant perfume of life. From the viewpoint of nothingness, a true letting go and letting be, it offers a rationale for emptying to perceive the depth of fullness. From the viewpoint of befriending creativity, it urges us to trust inner voices and images. From the viewpoint of transformation, it shows us the development of new institutions which breathe life rather than rigidity into structures of compassion, justice, celebration, and trust.

The central gift Creation Spirituality gives to society is a worldview that is centered in the very workings of the universe itself. It offers both a structure and answers to the age-old questions of humankind: Where did the universe begin? How did it evolve? Who or what was responsible for it? What about a creator? What about a meaningful story that bespeaks this marvelous creation?

Creation Spirituality is about wholeness, about interconnectedness, about the fragile and wonderful web of dynamic energy that self-organizes and pervades all life. Erich Jantsch speaks about a self-organizing universe; he says that evolution itself is an emerging paradigm.[5] Former spiritualities saw life as adaptation and survival, but we know today—especially from quantum physics—that life is more than adaptation and survival, that all life, from the infinitely large to the infinitely small—from atoms to quarks—"hangs together." It self-organizes—the heavens, Earth, the entire solar system. Jung offers a crucial insight on this self-organization and its processes when he says that "there are things in the psyche which I do not produce, but which produce themselves and have their own life."[6]

All levels of life are evolving, changing, interconnected, and still making new connections. Those of us tied to former spiritualities have had a ready answer to the questions of life, but the answer neither helps us understand or make necessary connections. That answer calls for a type of faith that is both blind trust and an acquiescence to further questioning, and thereby further answers. In *Dune*, Frank Herbert says that "Deep in the human unconscious is a pervasive need for a logical universe that makes sense. But the real universe is always one step beyond logic."[7] Deep inside each of us is the gnawing certainty that our certitude is uncertain. And so we stay on the journey, we search for meaning and a new sense of understanding.

## What Creation Spirituality offers education

Creation Spirituality, precisely because it is not a rigid theology but a process spirituality open to the novelty and confirmation of self-organization, can present an educational framework for understanding this new sense of meaning. Truly, in the last half of the millennium we have not thought about things in this way; we did not even realize this could be. Social and political structures of the last four hundred years were only questioned for the first time in the decade between the 1960s and 1970s. Most leaders and cultures followed the traditional roles of rigidity, seeing reality through dualistic eyes, seeing men over women, seeing science and religion *apart* from each other and therefore alienated from social reality, each claiming its own eminence. What Creation Spirituality allows education to perceive is the process-oriented aspect of the creation combined with the power of individual imagination, producing visions capable of changing the very structures of reality. Simply put, it is not that the old does not work any more, it is that the former ways of seeing and perceiving structures are so fundamentally changed, that we need to find new categories with which to speak. Cold war, gross national product, presidential politics, and arms for strength are totally meaningless. Traditional spiritualities were incapable of seeing all life married to itself, incapable of seeing that life is self-organizing in its core. Education suffered from the same incapacity. Its categories were as life-suppressing as Newton's mechanistic approaches to the universe.

Today, humankind is operating on a different plane; the former age has passed away. Put in terms of Creation-centered Spirituality, we are a resurrected people living in a self-organizing universe and we ourselves are part and parcel of the self-organizing process. This is a totally different viewpoint than was offered to humankind even just twenty years ago. We are people of Spacebridge, linking the people of Moscow and the people of New York City and San Francisco, speaking a new language, motivated by an utmost desire to find out about our brothers and sisters. When Marlo Thomas brought children of the U.S.S.R. and the U.S.A. together by satellite link, they did not talk about ideology. They spoke about family life, sports, rock bands, and the world of emotions. "Do you fall in love?" one little Soviet girl asked her new friends.[8] "We are the World" is not only a popular song, but a statement of who the human is. Arms are being reduced not only because our world is going bankrupt, but because in our hearts we truly believe that arming ourselves is a dumb idea.

History is life, all of life, twenty billion years of it that we know about now. This is the vision that Creation-centered Spirituality births in us and demands our educational system elucidate. As we scratch our collective heads and realize that we have *always* been part of this great creation, and that we get our animation, vivification—our very life—from it, we begin both to be open to its processes and to be a lot less self-righteous. It was only in 1965 that the discovery of background radiation created an opportunity for the direct study of an effect originating in the hot early beginning of the universe.[9] Perhaps it was to this phenomenon that Meister Eckhart spoke so eloquently when he said, "God is creating this entire universe fully and totally in this present now."[10] He also said, "I am younger today than I was yesterday, and if I were not younger tomorrow than I am today, I would be ashamed of myself."[11] Creation Spirituality is helping to bring about perestroika in our thinking which will bring about perestroika in society, in our homes, in our schools, and in our houses of worship, in our work, in ourselves, and in our institutions. When we "hang together" with all of life, rejoicing in our self-organizing dynamics, truly thankful for the creation of this universe, we will unfold in a paradigm of celebration and acceptance, never to be the same again.

## Components of a Creation-centered education

A Creation-centered education rests on a reinvented curriculum; one that is inclusive, life-relevant, practical, and Earth-related. A Creation-centered curriculum teaches that the tiniest organisms present in the schoolyard share a cooperative life-system with all of us. It fosters stewardship of and cooperation with the Earth. It helps prepare students to live responsibly so they will not be wasting resources. It teaches about sharing scientific knowledge and joint ventures with other cultures and other countries. A Creation-centered curriculum teaches reverence for the interconnectedness of all of life.

Teachers using a Creation-centered curriculum will plant a garden with students, they will show them how to make a shirt, knit socks, make a book, tell a story, set up a lab experiment. They will know that the garden is part of the Earth, related to sun and moon, to weather and seasons, to nourishment of body and soul, to insects, birds, cows, and worms, to the mystery and cycle of sprouting, harvesting, and seed growing, to spring and winter, to death and resurrection, to myth, poem, play, and worship, to history, to science, and to the present community.[12] Students need to know the world and know how to fit into it. They need to learn to care enough to prevent problems and be compassionate enough to solve the problems we already have.

A Creation-centered curriculum addresses the total web of life and enables us to understand and have compassion for people of all cultures, and creatures of space and of the deep. It engages students to study the infinitely large and the infinitely small.[13] Students using a living curriculum will delve into the stars, outer space, the sun, the Earth's physics including climate, atmosphere, and biosphere. A Creation-centered curriculum teaches about the mysterious ways of the seas and oceans, lands, deserts, mountains, and water. It urges students to have an intimate knowledge of plant life, animal life, and human life; energy, minerals, microbiology, genetics, chemistry, and nuclear physics.

A Creation-centered curriculum means that students would know the intricacies, power, and politics of the human family spread around the globe. They would know about world population and its changes, human geography and migrations, human longevity, basic races, cultures, and the gifts of people to the planet; sexes, children, youth, adults, the elderly; and they would see the disabled not as handicapped but as "differently-abled." Students exposed to a Creation-centered curriculum would know about nutrition, health, wealth and poverty, skills and employment, education, morality, spirituality, human lifestyles, professions, corporations, institutions, multinational business, transnational networks, and world organizations.

Making the educational curriculum Creation-centered means that students would become familiar with time. They would investigate their cultural heritage, the landmarks of evolution and history, and look into the future to decide how we can hand over to succeeding generations a well-preserved and better-managed planet. They would understand that institutions, factories, systems, states, ideologies, and theories exist only as servants and instruments for bettering human and planetary harmony. They would investigate creating ways for making each child feel like a royal person, in kinship and membership with the rest of the created universe. They would help to ban the military conscription of children throughout the world.

Creation-centered education means dealing with human development, behavior, leadership, individual and group processes; it means educating for critical and corporate consciousness, and knowing world trends. It includes policy making, compassion, justice, healing, leisure, communication, and it sees self-esteem as the key to all well-being.

Finally, in Creation-centered education, art as meditation would take its rightful place at the inner core of students' being, waking up their depths so that creativity can flow and dance. When students write poetry, photograph a sunset, or create beauty in the flower garden, says Thomas Merton, their minds respond to the intellectual and spiritual values that lie hidden within, waiting to be uncovered.[14] Art as meditation teaches students about the sacredness of work and keeps their world from going flat. It teaches that there need be neither reason nor profit, but only a sense of the sacred in working the loom, in painting, in making pottery, furniture, or jewelry.

There are many expressions of art as meditation. Painting focuses on students' perception of the universe, photography shows a fuller process of seeing, musical instruments teach musical heritage, joy, and delight. Chorus, singing, and song writing, befriend both individuals and the Earth. Creating rituals calls forth energy for bonding and social transformation; hatha yoga help students learn to accept their bodies and cherish their breath. Acupressure teaches the art of regulating the flow of blood and energy; movement, dance, improvisation, mime, clowning, and storytelling help students experience creativity.

## Living compassionately and making justice

Creation-centered education sees compassion as justice making. A practicum for justice enables students to learn firsthand how other human beings function, live, hope, interact, and die. It awakens students to the interdependencies of creation, the threats to our global village, the violence of nature and of people, and the power found deep within the human race to create alternatives to the problems faced by our world and planet. A practicum for justice helps them focus not on whether our economy is growing yearly in gross national product, but whether worldwide economics are providing housing for the homeless, feeding the hungry, educating the ignorant, caring for the sick, humanizing the prisons, creating good work for the unemployed, encouraging technology with a human face, and celebrating with the forgotten.[15] An internship in compassion gives students hands-on experience in social change. Students in elementary grades need to be apprentice workers, while older students take on leadership and larger work roles. There are many areas in which schools can help to bring compassion through education. Some suggestions follow.[16]

● Residential health and eldercare for senior citizens. Students would experience working with senior citizens in health care, nutrition education, self-esteem, and identity among the aged. They could help to organize get-togethers for the homebound and have daily interchange with senior citizens.

● Weekends in the neighborhood program. Student groups would celebrate with the people in mime, storytelling, music, dance, juggling, poetry, dramatic reading, art, folkdancing, pottery, and creative movement. Students would help organize such neighborhood events as family massage, rituals, clowning, games, neighborhood cookouts, movies in the streets, and street dances.

● Rehabilitation of housing. Students would perform work in all phases and processes of home rehabilitation; planning, carpentry, plumbing, electrical, plastering, painting and decorating, cement repair, and landscaping. Through their caring, blighted neighborhoods would be renewed.

● Cooperative gardening and farm stand. Applying their learning from school gardens, students would aid residents—especially senior citizens—in preparing land, seeding, and harvesting. They would help organize the program with families and help sell produce at the farm stand.

● Community chorus. Students would aid in developing a chorus and band to compose, sing, and play all styles of music; travel from community to community, and aid members in beginning other choruses where invited.

● Performing arts group. Students would help develop drama groups whose members would perform original and professional plays sponsored by businesses in neighborhoods.

● Handyperson program. Students would lend their talents to work for the poor, the elderly, and those who simply could not do a job that needs to be done. Students would learn the art of negotiating, setting prices, and bartering. Their work would include electric wiring, painting, plumbing, cleanup, washing windows, masonry, carpentry, and helping with income taxes.

- Day care and parenting center. Students would help operate day care centers for infants and children, and help organize parenting sessions.
- University of the streets. Students would survey neighborhoods to determine needs for educational outreach in communities. Working with educational institutions, interested businesses, merchants, and residents, they would help organize classes and degree courses for a personal growth academy. This academy would include courses in any area people wished to learn.

## Conclusion

If we want our children to have an honest view of the world, education must give students a correct view of reality. A Creation-centered education would help educators, students, and parents find and develop meaning in their lives; it would help them to feel connected to the Earth, effectively eliminate boredom, and help them to design and create jobs that make sense and have purpose.

Institutions are made up of dedicated people who come together for the good of the whole. Hence, they should provide a workable structure in government, education, religion, medicine, law, etc., to ensure full living and interaction with all life on the planet. When the institution forgets its vision and its mission, when it no longer provides energy, awareness, power, and direction needed by the members, it ceases to be alive. If, however, the institution *reflects* on itself, learns from itself, and allows itself to evolve and become self-organized, it will always be a catalyst for transformation in the society it serves.

### Notes

1.   George Leonard, cited in Linwood Laughy, *The Interactive Parent* (Kooskia, ID: Mountain Meadow Press, 1988), p. 125.

2.   Brian Swimme, *The Universe is a Green Dragon* (Santa Fe: Bear & Co., 1985), p. 18.

3.   Matthew Fox, *Meditations with Meister Eckhart* (Sante Fe: Bear & Co., 1982), p. 3.

4.   Fox, *Meditations*, p. 4

5.   Erich Jantsch, *The Self-Organizing Universe* (New York: Pergamon, 1980), p. 1.

6.   Carl Jung, cited in Erich Jantsch, *Self-Organizing Universe*, p. 286.

7.   Frank Herbert, cited in Jantsch, *Self-Organizing Universe*, p. 307.

8.   Marlo Thomas, "Free to be . . . a Family," *Parade*, Dec. 11, 1988, p. 5.

9.   Erich Jantsch, *Self-Organizing Universe*, p. 4.

10.   Matthew Fox, *Meditations*, p. 24.

11.   Matthew Fox, *Meditations*, p. 32.

12.   Mary Caroline Richards, *Towards Wholeness: Rudolf Steiner Education in America* (Middletown, CT: Wesleyan University Press, 1980), pp. 63-64.

13.   I am indebted to Robert Muller, *New Genesis* (New York: Image Books, 1984) for many of these ideas.

14. Thomas Merton, cited in Matthew Fox, "The Case for Extrovert Meditation," *Spirituality Today*, June 1978, p. 165.

15. Matthew Fox, *A Spirituality Named Compassion* (Minneapolis: Winston, 1979), p. 220.

16. Originally published in Andy LePage, *Transforming Education: The New 3Rs*, (Oakland, CA: Oakmore House, 1987), pp. 119-121.

# The Fasting Quest as a Modern Rite of Passage

## by Steven Foster and Meredith Little

*Formerly Assistant Professor of Humanities at San Francisco State University, Steven Foster, Ph.D. retired from college teaching in 1971 to devote his time to the reintroduction of ancient passage rites into the mainstream of modern culture. In 1974, he met and married Meredith Little, a trainer of hotline volunteers at Marin Suicide Prevention and Crisis Intervention Center. They founded and for seven years co-directed Rites of Passage, Inc., the first school of wilderness transition rites in recent history. The fruits of their research, teaching, apprenticeship to a variety of medicine teachers, and explorations of natural solitude are set forth in several books:* The Book of the Vision Quest: Personal Transformation in the Wilderness *(Prentice-Hall, 1980, 1987, 1988);* The Trail Ahead: A Course Book for Graduating Seniors *(1983),* The Sacred Mountain: A Vision Quest Handbook for Adults *(1984),* The Roaring of the Sacred River: The Wilderness Quest for Vision and Healing *(Prentice-Hall, 1989), and* Betwixt and Between: Patterns of Masculine and Feminine Initiation, *edited with Louise Mahdi (Open Court, 1987). They continue to lead wilderness passage rites through the School of Lost Borders, P.O. Box 55, Big Pine, CA 93513.*

> I suspect it was . . . the old story of the implacable necessity of a man having honour within his own natural spirit. A man cannot live and temper his metal without such honour. There is deep in him a sense of heroic quest; and our modern way of life, with its emphasis on security, its distrust of the unknown and its elevation of abstract collective values has repressed the heroic impulse to a degree that may produce the most dangerous consequences.
> —Laurens van der Post, *Heart of the Hunter*[1]

Human growth is characterized by social change. We must pass from one life stage to the next. The mother-womb of infancy dies when we are weaned. Weaning brings us into the world of childhood. We pass from childhood to adolescence. Adulthood looms ahead, a seeming impassable barrier. One way or another we become "adult," in society's

---

This selection originally appeared in the Fall 1988 issue of *Holistic Education Review,* Vol. 1, No. 3.

eyes or in our own. We leave the single state when we marry or enter a committed relationship. Sometimes we divorce, re-entering the single state at a later stage of growth. We make our way through the various passages of our middle and later years, facing predictable crises brought about by parenthood, aging, and retirement. Finally, we cross the last threshold and begin our sacred journey through the underworld of death.

In traditional cultures, changes in life station were celebrated by rites or ceremonies of passage. Everyone participated in these ceremonies. If they did not, they were denied entrance to the next stage of their lives. Without rites of passage, they could not have understood their life experiences, nor could they have been capable of assuming the social responsibilities and privileges required by their change in life station. Without orderly rites of passage, tribal units would have become unstable and ceased to survive.[2]

In modern times, the rise of technological science, the emergence of large nations and cities, the influence and omnipotence of the media, the thickening of the wall between humans and their natural environment, the dawn of the computer age, the threat of thermonuclear annihilation, the breakdown of the basic family social unit, the dehumanizing pressure of modern life, and many other factors, have contributed to the weakening of traditional values, including the various ceremonies of life passage. The careful, ritual footprints left by our ancestors have been paved over by the traffic of modern civilization. Because these changes have tended to drain contemporary life of its meaningful spiritual or mythical content, the "old ways" are glaringly apparent by their absence.

Consider, for example, the modern rite of passage from childhood to adulthood. On the long anticipated day, while their loved ones look on, graduating high school seniors march to solemn music. They find their place in rows and hear speeches made by school, civic, and student leaders. A religious official gives an interdenominational prayer. The moment finally comes to graduate from the childhood world of high school. As the music sounds triumphantly, the graduates switch their tassels to the other side of their mortar boards. Where is the experiential "ordeal of passage" in this modern rite? The fast on the sacred mountain has devolved into the switching of a tassel. What modern high school student would insist that commencement from high school is adequate, meaningful, "experienced proof" that he or she is ready to live as an adult?

Apparently, our culture only dimly recognizes the value of traditional rites of passage. Dismissing native, indigenous, or traditional ways as mere superstition, or of little relevance to our automated lives, large numbers of us suffer changes in life status like victims—burdens to ourselves and others. Lacking inner resources developed from living a meaningful life, we too often nurture negative pictures of ourselves as helpless pawns unable to escape the blows of fate or the manipulations of others. We think someone else must heal us because we cannot heal ourselves. Someone else must lead us because we cannot lead ourselves. Someone else must be the hero or the heroine for us because there is nothing we can do, we are but the helpless victims of meaningless life stories.

The sanest, healthiest models of human growth regard crises, accidents, changes, and life transitions as challenges and opportunities of the highest order. If we can "pass through" our personal difficulties, we find ourselves enlarged and renewed, with direction and purpose, on the other side. The *I Ching* proverb says: "A hundred times you lost your treasure—and must climb the nine hills" (Hexagram 51). If we refuse to climb, we do not grow. Indeed, the truest of human teaching tells us how necessary it is to climb the nine hills if we expect to fulfill the promise of our lives. How many times in our span of years will we be called upon to uproot and transplant, to let go of the old and embrace the new, to end it and go on, to plow under and plant the new seed, to cease being ignorant and find out?

It is difficult to assess the extent to which the loss of meaningful rites of passage has crippled the growth of modern people through the impasses of their lives. The symptoms of crisis are seen everywhere. Panic, hysteria, shock, anxiety, uncertainty, anger, boredom, drug abuse, vague apprehension, guilt, self-hatred, twistedness, helplessness, and "psychosomatic" illnesses of all kinds attend the experience of a life crisis. How often are we able to resolve the crisis with our own inner strength and determination? How often do we resort to the medical and social service professionals for help? How often do we consult our minister, medium, medicine man, psychiatrist, healer, guru, astrologer, or psychic? How often do we need help and support? And how often do we "go it alone," finding within our own life and value system a way of surviving, and finding meaning in, our crisis experience?

What of those who do not have an adequate myth or value system? They fish in troubled waters, unable to turn away from the past and look to the healing future. They move from one locale to another, but something of them gets stuck in-between. They change their occupation but cannot make a go of the new job. They cannot get over the loss of a friend or the death of a loved one. They conceive, give birth to, miscarry, or abort a child, but are not prepared to live with the changes brought about by the event. Devastated by natural disaster or accident, they never quite seem to get back on their feet. Suicidally depressed, they finally succumb to the hopelessness rather than to.the dangerous opportunity their situation represents. They do violence or have violence done to them and cannot learn from the consequences. They become parents or stepparents but are unable to accept the demands of their new life station. They become enslaved to the thralls of drugs or alcohol but cannot find medicine in themselves to shrug the demons from their back. They burn out on the job but cannot find adequate ways to renew themselves.

Those without a life story all too easily trap themselves in nets fashioned by others to ensnare them—or they swallow themselves in their own ignorant thrashings. Either way, they are "at risk" to themselves, others, and the earth they live on. They need to be helped to see that they are not victims, that they possess the inner gumption to make meaning of the quandary they got themselves into, that they *do* have a life story. *Would it not be more beneficial if they were helped to see that they did not need help?*

> If you do not get it from yourself,
> Where will you go for it?
> —The Zenrin[3]

## Modern prototypes of the wilderness fasting or vision quest

A wilderness rite of passage such as the "vision quest" takes life, concentrates it into a brief/eternal span of literal/allegorical time, composes a story with a real/symbolic meaning whose mortal/immortal protagonist undergoes an ordeal/epiphany in a bounded/limitless environment where ordinary/nonordinary realities exist simultaneously. The story is both the stuff of action (rite) and the stuff of contemplation (myth). As the protagonist moves through the plot of the story (which he/she creates), he/she finds the self in a double-meaninged universe. An animal is both animal and spirit. A mountain is a mountain and a quest. A star is a star and an angel. A direction walked is a trail and a Way. A dream is a dream and divine visitation. A mosquito is a pest and a messenger.

The story is always different, depending on the life that is telling it. But no matter how stories differ, there is always a basic, underlying similarity, a kind of archetypal plot or dynamic. This dynamic energizes countless heroic myths, ancient and modern, and stands at the head of Christianity, Buddhism, Islam, and many other religions. Joseph Campbell identifies it as the "mono-myth."[4]

The mono-myth is often phrased as a dragon battle, a dismemberment, a crucifixion, an abduction, a night-sea journey, ingestion by a monster, a herculean task, an entombment, a dream or spirit journey, a territorial passage, an ascent of a mountain, or a descent into the underworld. The hero(ine) undertakes the trial in a sacred, threshold world in order to be transformed for the benefit of the people. A king or savior elects to die so that the kingdom may be saved. A goddess is dismembered in the netherland so that she may ascend again in the spring corn. Prometheus journeys to the lair of the gods to bring back fire to his people. The Sacred Twins challenge the Lords of Death to a contest on the great ballcourt and outplay them. The Ugly Duckling endures a hard, lonely winter before he inherits his beautiful adulthood. For the sake of love, the fairy tale princess leaves the protected zone of her childhood castle and enters the dark forest where dwarf-tricksters live and witches come prowling with poisoned apples for sale. Such allegories comprise the archetypal underpinnings of rites of passage and provide a physical/mythical landscape or process within which the candidate marks (confirms, celebrates, formalizes) his/her change in life station.

As in ancient times, modern candidates leave everything behind and go alone to the sacred river of nature. There they are tried by monsters, often of their own making, and visited by their own versions of spectres, spirit guides, helping inner voices, guardian angels, animal totems, goddesses, or universal forces/spirits. Through a long, dark night of the soul, they are rewarded with wisdom, strength, insight, understanding, acceptance. They are revived; their inner eyes are opened; vision, in its many forms, is granted. But the main condition of the gift received is that they must return to their world, their people, with this healing vision.

A wilderness passage quest such as the vision quest is "enacted mono-myth," or "experienced allegory." The story must be reduced to a prac-tical, functional form/process. The plot must be choreographed into a "script," scenario, or drama, and adapted to fit an environment (the "wilderness theater") that suits and enhances the role that the pro-tagonist will play. Every act and scene must glue ordinary (physical) and nonordinary (spiritual) together into a coherent synthesis. The Sufis describe an "interworld," an immediate kingdom between spirit and body that combines the two into one state of being. The threshold phase of the vision fast is such an interworld.

Mono-myth variations of the vision quest are endless and relative to cultures. Plot and setting are rendered into a myriad of different vari-ations on the same theme. Among American Indians, there are countless different wilderness rites, or fasting quests, depending on who is con-ducting them. Though the Paiute version might differ from the Crow, or the Cheyenne from the Ojibway (or one medicine man's version from another of the same tribe), each model is but a variation of the mono-myth.

Perhaps the best and most effective vision fast guides are those who are most loyal to the mono-myth itself, who seek to sew fine stitches at the fold of bounded and limitless. They build models they can trust that will faithfully contain and nurture the student's body and spirit. The most trustworthy prototypes are those which have traditionally (and safely) served others. Hence, the effective guide masters a tradi-tional prototype of the mono-myth before he ever begins to experiment with versions of his own creation. The last thing he wants to do is manipulate his charges with a script that contains his own hidden agen-das. He knows full well that his charges must find their own agenda, and that his task is to offer a reliable ritual framework within which they will do the finding.

Because the mono-myth always presents an ordeal, the vision quest prototype must contain an element of risk or trial. Without an ordeal, the activity cannot be properly called a rite of passage. Therefore, the guide must tread a fine line between severity and safety. The ordeal must be attuned to the capabilities of the candidate in such a way as to tax him/her to the breaking point, but not to destroy or harm him/her. There are many ways to try the candidate without overdoing it.

The prototypes we are familiar with are ordeals primarily involving fasting (without food or sometimes water), solitude (strict isolation), and exposure to the ways of nature (with only minimal protection—knife, rope, water, tarp, sleeping bag, matches, bandanna, jacket, change of clothes, and a journal). Alone in the solitude and silence of a wilderness place, the candidate endures hunger, privation, loneliness, and the onslaught of the elements, in order to earn a gift of insight for the people. While the candidate is in the wilderness phase of the rite, the guide watches over him/her to insure bodily safety. In case of emergencies, the guide is available and equipped with appropriate emergency supplies and procedures.[5]

When the period of fasting is complete (usually three or four days and nights), the candidate returns to the secular world with a story to tell. This story is his/her own variant of the mono-myth and is treated as such by the guide, who hears this story clearly and points out its salient features to the candidate. The return of the "hero/ine" from the sacred mountain requires an integration of the candidate with the deepest meanings of the story, i.e., the candidate "owns" the story.

## Why do modern people vision quest?

In the year since we began, candidates came to us for diverse reasons. Some of these reasons may help identify those who genuinely benefit from the experience of fasting alone in a wilderness place. In the beginning, the first who expressed interest were high school students. Unschooled in theories of social anthropology, they instinctively recognized the relevance of a traditional fasting quest to their life situation. They saw it as a means of confirming their passage to adulthood in a meaningful way. Because they wrestled with ideas of what it meant to be an "adult," they felt the vision quest in their gut. They experienced the same feeling when they contemplated living on their own in the wilderness of modern civilization. To them, the ceremony was an acceptable and meaningful alternative "graduation." Not surprisingly, a large number of adults have also participated because they had never meaningfully confirmed their passage from childhood to adulthood.

Separation, divorce, loss of fortune, death of a child or spouse, an "empty nest," visible aging, loss of potency, a serious illness, suicidal depression, and a change of vocation were reasons why many middle-aged adults participated. They sought to put crises behind them and to initiate a new phase of growth in their lives. The ceremony spun them out of their habit-tracks and confirmed their own ability to initiate or accept growth-change. Sheltered by the absence of civilization, surrounded by the almost forgotten mirror-face of nature, they drew apart from their lives and pondered the plot and purpose of their life story. When they returned, they often found open doors leading out of old rooms.

Some fasted because they faced the prospect of separation or divorce. The need was insistent to be alone and to make important decisions regarding their future life path. The ceremony provided them with a chance to take a meaningful step toward incorporation into the body of singlehood. Others wished to confirm a decision to marry. By participating, they marked the end of singlehood and the beginning of togetherness. Likewise, expecting parents formalized their attainment of parenthood.

The loss of an unborn child, through miscarriage, abortion, or complications at birth has moved women to utilize the ceremony as a means of healing their grief and deepening their understanding of the meaning of such events. Victims of violence, rape, and child abuse—and those dealing with their own tendencies to be violent—have also found the ceremony to be a means of symbolically putting an end to extended periods of grief, fear, self-pity, resentment, guilt, or self-loathing. Solitary fasting while living close to Mother Earth is an effective way to bind up old wounds or to open eyes closed to the promise of dawn.

The time of "retirement" often precipitates a crisis manifested by severe illness or death. A number of persons over 60 years old participated as a means of coming to grips with their own aging. These "elders" had an opportunity to "practice their dying," to regard the long sweep of their lives from a distance, and to see how they could best utilize and enjoy their remaining years. Individuals facing life-threatening illness returned with a better understanding of their bodies, their illness, and the ways in which they could fight or accommodate the disease.

Individuals mourning the death or loss of someone close to them found the ceremony to be an effective way of signifying an end to the time of grieving. With the aid of self-initiated ceremony, the mourner incorporated the deceased into his/her life as a companion or guide. In the deepest misery of self-loathing, addicts also have been known to hear the call of a wilderness passage rite. If they can leave their habit behind, they stand a good chance of having a bracing conversation with themselves. Individuals undergoing sexual identity crises find that Mother Nature and her creatures do not make judgments regarding sexual preference.

## The three phases of the wilderness passage quest

The basic dynamics of the wilderness fast are described by a formula that underlies all such passage ceremonies. First identified by the German anthropologist, Arnold van Gennep, this formula states that all rites and ceremonies have three phases: an end, a middle, and a beginning—in that order. In other words, a rite of passage begins with an ending and ends with a beginning:

> To make an end is to make a beginning.
> The end is where we start from.
> —T. S. Eliot, "Little Gidding"

Van Gennep describes these three phases as Severance (*séparation*), Threshold (*marge*), and Incorporation (*agrégation*). We use his classic formula because it aptly characterizes the adventures of the candidate.

He/she began with an ending. What came before was over. In order to do this he/she had to prepare to leave it all behind, to prepare to make the end—so that there could be a beginning. Next, the candidate encounters the middle stage of the ceremony. This stage we call "the threshold," the actual experience of the trial or ordeal of passage, the time spent alone in nature. When his threshold time was over, he/she "incorporated," i.e., ended the adventure with a beginning. He/she blended with the physical setting of a new life story by returning to civilization.

Note that van Gennep's ceremonial formula is quite the opposite of the flow of life as we tend to perceive it. Usually, we think of our birth as the beginning, our life as the middle, and our death as the end. But the rite of passage merely takes up where life ends—and death begins. We begin with death, we pass through the middle stage of death, and we end with birth. This "death journey" is the irreducible, adamantine, symbolic kernel of the wilderness passage quest. It is the formula for human transformation.

Although all three stages of a rite of passage are of equal import, the middle term, "threshold," invites further scrutiny. Social anthropologists often use the French word, *marge* ("margin") or the Latin word, *liminal* ("limit"), instead of "threshold." Nevertheless, "threshold," with its diversity of connotations, is the most useful word. It suggests a boundary, margin, border, limit, door, crossing, gate, or opening. In our way of seeing the ceremony, the threshold phase has two doors: an inlet and an outlet. These doors symbolically define the border or limit itself. Their existence establishes finiteness to the sacred time/space they lead into and out from. Without these two doors (one death, the other birth), the threshold would not exist. Which door is which? Are they not the same, yet totally opposite?

With very little effort, one may discern the end—middle—beginning formula in almost all that we do, whether or not it is an intentional ceremonial act. Driving off to work, for instance, involves a severance (ending the life at home), a threshold trial (the passage through traffic), and an incorporation (beginning with the world of work). Leaving work and driving home involves the same formula. So does making love. We sever from the old world of separateness and cross the threshold into the sacred passage world of union. When our love making is complete, we incorporate again into the world of separateness, but at a new stage of awareness. Going on a vacation, we sever from home, enter the threshold of the vacation, and return to incorporation at home. Climbing a mountain, we leave everything behind and go to the mountain, then enter the threshold door, the climb itself. We emerge from the sacred passage at the summit. Then we return, the mountain now within us. If we get very ill, we confirm our desire to end sickness by entering the threshold passage called "hospital." When our journey through the "underworld" passage is complete, we make a new beginning as healed individuals—or we incorporate within the body of death.

Once a candidate is able to recognize this tri-partite formula in the events of his life, he/she can initiate and perform ceremonial actions that are useful. To this basic framework of action he/she can add the flesh and bones of a creed or value system. The formula will aid him/her to better understand his/her role within the larger ceremonial perspective of the vision quest. He/she will come to view life from a transformational point of view. He/she will see that there is never a beginning without first an ending, and then a passing through.

Candidates often raise the question: "How can I leave it all behind if I'm just coming back to it? How can I make a new beginning if I simply return to the old?" Such thoughts invariably occur to them before they go on the fasting quest—rarely after they return. For the answer lies in the return. One does not come back "to the same old thing." What we return to has changed—because we ourselves have changed. Our perspective has been altered; the wheel of perceptions has been spun. We will not incorporate into the same body, status, or world that we left behind. As the Greek sage Heraclitus put it, "Into the same river we step and do not step" (Fragment 110). Yes, we return to the same river, but while we were gone, the river kept flowing. Now, from an altered perspective, we can see that it is not the same river.

## Modern benefits of the wilderness vision quest

A civilized person's ability to transform him/herself through the modern fasting quest is directly proportionate to the intensity of the motivation to leave the past behind. In other words, you get out of it exactly what you put in. If we jump as high as we are able, we will reach more than if we decide not to sweat too much. Truly, we have to *want* to change. No amount of fancy talk will bring about desired alterations. The fasting quest is not a "magical cure." The quester does not get something for nothing.

We have always insisted that the decision to fast alone in the wilderness should not be made lightly, or in the heat of romantic passion. The candidates should examine their motives. They should ask themselves: "Why do I want to do this?" They should look very carefully at their expectations. If, like Prometheus, they want to steal the fire from the sacred altar of vision, what they steal will die in their hearts. Do they hope to take a recreational dance through a phantasmagoria of altered states? If so, they will be unable to find a comfortable place to sit. Do they expect a "quickie" transformation, hoping not to have to work too hard? If so, they will return from the threshold feeling cheated, puzzled, no more prepared to serve their people than they were before. The ceremony is nothing but a circle drawn in the dust, an empty form that is filled with the values and perceptions of the candidates. It is a mirror in which they see themselves reflected.

The experience of the ceremony is heightened and focused, given meaning and direction by each quester. The experience will rarely be continually uplifting, mystical, or transcendental. Highs/lows, excitement/boredom, hope/despair, sacred/profane will mingle to compose a flow of experienced events that also include times when the gears are in neutral or the engine has fallen asleep. The vision fast is no more a "prescriptive" answer than is life itself—and all the same laws of karma apply. If a prescription is to be written that will positively affect the candidate's health and well-being, then it must be written by him/herself, in collusion with Mother Nature, the teacher.

The mystery and the beauty of the quest is that it calls out the best in us and reflects back precisely how high or far we have jumped and what we saw when we were airborne. No one else does the jumping for us. No one else sees how far we jump or sees what we see. Of course, we are not always alert enough to catch what is going on. Sometimes we will goof ourselves up with expectations of one kind or another. Sometimes we will return disappointed that we didn't have a "vision." We wanted angels and all we got was a violent thunderstorm. Sometimes we return so high you would swear we had taken kite medicine. But then we fall flat when we try to sail through the first crisis at home. Sometimes we crawl back to base camp, feebly protesting that we are not ready to return—only to become towers of strength the moment we hit home. We marvel at the diversity of the stories we hear about how high or far this person jumped, what he saw, and what he landed in. Through each story runs the priceless threads of the mono-myth.

In every story there is the one constant—Grandmother Nature. She bestows her favors, her teachings, her moods on everyone, regardless of how they perceive her. Some candidates are blinder than others. Some hear better than others. Some learn quicker than others  but to all she imparts the same information. She covers them all with the same dirt and showers them all with the same rain. What the candidates chose to see or hear is their business. If they care to, they can drink the dew of heaven, for nature sends that too. Then again, they can try to drink tea, as the following woman wrote in her threshold journal:

> I had a hard time with the fire and was somewhat discour-
> aged at the fact that all I wanted was one cup of hot tea. I
> couldn't find the spoon. While looking for it the fire went
> out. The water was kind of warm. I was going to settle for
> warm tea when the pot fell into the smoldering fire. I tried
> again, resorting to toilet paper (as tinder). The T.P. smol-
> dered . . . .
>
> I am sitting up on this rock, drinking slightly warm instant
> tea, which is full of dirt, and there is a bug floating around
> in it. My hands will have to do in fishing it out. My spoon
> is still gone.

Needless to say, every person returns from the wilderness with a greater tolerance for dirt and sweat and a deeper appreciation for the animal functions of the body. No matter how bad the weather has been, they will wax poetic about the beauty of their place. They will speak of having an odd feeling at certain moments that Mother Earth was aware of them. They will begin speaking of "her" with a genuine affec-tion. They might have spent the entire threshold time swatting mosquitoes, nursing blisters, or shivering in their sleeping bags, but their words are filled with gratitude and wonder at her "personalized" care for them. They may even shed tears when they have to leave. A young man, age 22, recorded such feelings during his threshold fast:

> As I sat on the rocks looking west toward the Sierra, my cry came to me. It went like this: "Mother Earth, please be patient with infant man. We are young and have much to learn. Teach us." That is not exactly what I said, word for word, but [it] is close enough. All the while I got all choked up and began sobbing. Afterwards, I felt a mixture of feelings. The picture of this very old woman, who is very wise, patient, forgiving, sad, and lonely came to me. I think that is what made me cry.

A young Anglo-European woman, age 17, put it another way:

> I feel as if I really do belong out here. How can people who have never experienced nature see her as "Mother?" I must have Indian spirit in me. I have a deep, passionate feeling for the Indians. The land was their mother—as I feel it is for me. Sometimes I wish to God I was an Indian.

"There is only one mother for all people everywhere!" chant the Northern Australian aborigines in Rainbow Serpent ceremonies celebrating the magnanimous fertility of the earth. This same gift of love for the Great Mother was given to each candidate at birth. But he may need to go to her, to fast, and be alone with her, before he fully recognizes her gifts:

> In our bones is the rock itself; in our blood is the river;
> our skin contains the shadow of every living thing we ever
> came across. This is what we brought with us long ago . . .
> —Nancy Wood, "Ute Song"[6]

We prefer to think that modern individuals who participate in the vision quest ceremony are essentially no different than their ancestors. Though the cultural circumstances surrounding the modern wilderness fast have vastly changed, the experiential, human element has remained constant. We are still capable of hearing the roaring of the Sacred River. We are still capable of communicating with the Great Mother. One would be mistaken to assume that we live in a world too far removed from nature to fully benefit from jumping as high as we are able. From the beginning, the union of human and nature in passage quest ceremonies has brought forth a healing mythos for the collective woes of the people. We would be foolish to deny ourselves its legacy of self-healing power. We would be helpless indeed if we lost the ability to hear the roaring of the Sacred River—or if, in childish vexation with our brothers and sisters, we destroyed her—for we have no other Mother to "give us, each day, our daily bread."

## Notes

1.   Laurens van der Post, *The Heart of the Hunter* (London: Penguin, 1961).

2.   Arnold van Gennep, *The Rites of Passage* (Chicago: University of Chicago Press, 1972).

3.   Sohl and Carr (eds.), *Gospel According to Zen* (New York: New American Library, 1970).

4.   Joseph Campbell, *Hero With a Thousand Faces* (New York: World, 1970).

5.   Steven Foster and Meredith Little, *The Roaring of the Sacred River* (Big Pine, CA: Rites of Passage Press, 1987).

6.   Nancy Wood, *War Cry on a Prayer Feather* (Garden City, NY: Doubleday, 1979).

# Holistic Education
# in Practice

# Holistic Education in Practice

## Introduction

### by Ron Miller

For the most part, the writings published in *Holistic Education Review* are concerned with theory rather than practice; they aim for a fundamental rethinking of the aims of education rather than prescribe particular techniques or methods. In an important sense, "holistic education" is not a methodology at all but a comprehensive worldview. It is an attitude toward teaching and learning, as well as toward culture and human development. It is a set of guiding values, which, to be implemented with integrity, call for much reflection and self-awareness on the part of the educator. "Holistic education" is not a curriculum—it does not offer complete answers; rather, it is a persistent question: What does it mean to be a human being and how can we make the most of our possibilities?

Still, all educators face a very practical question every day of their professional lives: "What am I going to do today? I am responsible for a roomful of young people for six hours today, so what am I going to do with them?" Holistic theory may not give the complete answer, but it most certainly leads educators in particular directions. After visiting many holistically oriented schools around the United States, I have found that the educational and professional environments in these places are significantly different from most other schools. The four characteristics described in the general introduction to this volume are immediately apparent in almost all of these schools: Teaching styles address multiple learning styles and abilities; a sense of community, even family, is strongly developed among students, staff, and often parents; experiential, self-guided learning—consisting of projects, cooperative work, field trips, independent study—is central; and students are encouraged and supported in their questioning, their critical awareness of the world they will inherit. These characteristics reflect holistic education in practice.

In the following selections, seven contributors to *HER* describe various aspects of holistic practice. John Wolfe gives a moving account of a truly human encounter between student and educator; he observes that a genuine relationship involves recognition of the other person's *presence*— "that part of him or her that is immutable and mysterious." Wolfe's essay shows beautifully that the "spiritual" element of holistic thinking has nothing to do with religious indoctrination, but involves a reverence for the inner world of the person. Mara Sapon-Shevin continues in a similar vein, asserting that teachers need to allow the expression of heartfelt concerns and emotions within the educational setting. By excluding genuine relationship from the educational process, modern schooling prevents children from being "fully human." This is an impoverishment of life which holistic education seeks to remedy.

Next, Clement Mehlman describes an integrated, holistic literature course. For him, the study of English is a spiritual endeavor, a quest for meaning, and it is best carried out in relation to the vast world of nature which is our ultimate source of meaning. His work supports Ed Clark's argument that all good education is environmental. At Fair Oaks School, as Lois Bridges Bird tells us, a whole language approach is similarly transforming the curriculum into a *meaningful* learning experience. Literacy is seen as a "human dialogue" rather than a "skill"—and this difference is crucial, for it transforms learning into a joyful process of discovery.

These essays are followed by two descriptions of alternative public schools. Jefferson County Open School in Colorado and the Alternative Community School in upstate New York are among the best known innovative schools in the country, and in these selections, their principals, Ruth Steele and Dave Lehman, describe what they do differently. Both of these educators believe that keys to their schools' success include close personal relationships and a democratic sense of community, respect for students' divergent interests and ways of learning, and a strong reliance on direct learning experience rather than traditional curricula and evaluation. As we have seen by now, these are central themes in holistic education. As Steele and Lehman tell us, they work.[1]

Finally, we close this section (and this volume) with an introduction to Waldorf education. Roberto Trostli, an experienced Waldorf teacher in New York City, gives the most succinct and accessible overview of this complex method that I have seen.[2] Rudolf Steiner, the originator of Waldorf education, was a genius and mystic who, in the early years of the twentieth century, produced an extraordinary and comprehensive critique of the materialism of the modern age. Waldorf education, in my view, is the most radically holistic approach yet conceived, based upon an incredibly complex and insightful understanding of human development.

Unfortunately, the Waldorf movement has remained significantly detached from other educational approaches, even from its potential holistic allies. It has been one aim of *Holistic Education Review* to encourage a greater degree of cooperation between Waldorf educators, Montessorians, and progressive, humanistic and other person-centered approaches—but this has been a slow and difficult task. Thus, while the principles of Waldorf education are widely applicable and highly relevant, they have largely remained embedded within the fairly strict methodology of the Waldorf schools, guarded with care by a small community of Waldorf educators. It is my hope that this article, and others to follow in *HER*, will generate a productive dialogue among all educators concerned with healthy human development.

## Notes

1.   This past year, Dorothy Fadiman's film *Why Do These Kids Love School?* was shown on PBS as well as to educators around the country. It highlighted a number of other schools where these democratic, humanistic principles are applied with great success to many kinds of student populations. The film is available from Concentric Media, 1070 Colby Ave., Menlo Park, CA 94025.

2.   For a longer, more detailed description, see M. C. Richards, *Toward Wholeness: Rudolf Steiner Education in America* (Middletown, CT: Wesleyan University Press, 1980).

# The Presence of the Child

## by John Wolfe

*John Wolfe has taught in New York City elementary and preschools since 1967. He currently teaches fifth/sixth grade at Central Park East 2. He has published pieces in* **The Nation, Instructor Magazine, Pathways in Progressive Education,** *and other publications.*

It was the morning after spring vacation. The kids had half an hour to mingle and greet each other. We were, for the moment, free of the schedule's tyranny. My tyranny, actually: the kids would gladly socialize all day, working only enough to feel comfortable.

The early morning sun streaked through the windows facing Second Avenue; the kids clustered in knots around the room. These were their affinity groups; this was how they patterned their relationships. In this class of 31 fifth and sixth graders these patterns mirrored sexual and racial lines but there were subtle permutations at play as well—one shouldn't describe these groupings too glibly.

Generalizations about this class and this school are always tricky. The school is Central Park East 2, located in New York City's East Harlem. An alternative public elementary school, its 200 students come from East Harlem, Central Harlem, the West Side, upper Manhattan, and parts of the Bronx and Brooklyn. They form a diverse group—racially, ethnically, and economically.

Central Park East 2 is an "inner city" school. The quotation marks are purposeful; "inner city" is not a particularly illuminating designation, suggesting to some a number of immediate images (you know: crack vials in the playground, decrepit buildings, lost lives).

But a walk through Central Park East 2 belies the myths about "inner city" children and the "economically deprived." The classrooms are rich with vital and self-disciplined children working meaningfully and happily.

I have taught at C.P.E. for seven years and my classes have always been an interesting combination of differences and similarities.

No classroom is an easy place in which to work, however; there are always troubled kids, kids who have in varied ways "failed"; who've

This selection originally appeared in the Spring 1989 issue of *Holistic Education Review,* Vol. 2, No. 1.

been kicked out of other schools; who've not learned; who've been left back; the kids about whom teachers say: "It was a good day. _____ was absent, you see."

Those kids interest me; I've been drawn to them. Now this is in part hubris: *I can reach that kid!* But there's also the sense that if teaching is a calling—and I think it is—then working with such kids is at its center.

For adults failure is hard; for children it is absolutely devastating. Children who experience failure year upon year vibrate with pain that colors their every moment, their every gesture. In a very literal sense, they cease being kids.

One such troubled kid was R. who, amid the welter of returning, chattering kids, sat alone. No one had rushed to greet him when he walked in late. There were no big smiles for him, no happily fluttering hands waving in his face. He had no special group of friends—no single kid to whom to cleave.

He'd complained about being very tired when he came to school that morning and I'd given him a cushion and told him to rest. He sat at his desk, head on pillow, and closed his eyes. In a few minutes he seemed to be asleep.

### "You are a failure"

In a fundamental sense R. did not belong. He had a role in the class, true, but it was not a handsome one. His part: he was the "bad" boy. Taller than most of his classmates, and older by a year or more, he was feared and disliked. At one time or another he had succeeded in alienating nearly every classmate. And though he'd earned a measure of respect for his occasional cool and bravado, he was someone to be avoided or shunned.

During his tenure at three different elementary schools, R. fought, intimidated, or cruelly teased a legion of kids. By sixth grade the fighting had stopped, only the threat of violence remaining—veiled always: "After school, just you wait!"

But the acid-etched tongue still struck—targeted, inevitably, at the vulnerable or defenseless. He'd poke tellingly at someone's ragged sneakers, poorly dressed parents, physical weakness, or "welfare cheese breath." A word here, a phrase whispered in passing, nothing a teacher would ever hear—only the result was apparent: a kid yelling at him or a kid in tears. And R., masquerading in a look of innocence that grew into a glare of distrust, lips curled up in a sneer: "Oh man, I didn't say nothing!"

Socially peripheral, R. was also plagued by profound academic problems—he had difficulty learning to read, write, and think mathematically. Tested early in his school life, he was placed in a Resource Room program in third grade. His parents, however, demanded that he be de-certified. They said they wanted no part of a "special education" program whose students were in the main Black and Hispanic. Politically active in the community, they felt that the Resource Room program smacked of institutional racism. They would not, they said, countenance such an arrangement for their son.

No, they said, they would instead provide outside tutoring. But they never did. Their explanation? Private tutoring proved too expensive and the less expensive public programs had no openings. Arrangements they finally made, they said, had fallen through.

It was late November during my first year as his teacher and we were at the initial family conference. R. fish-eyed his mother curiously as she explained all of this to me.

"Is that really true?" he asked, "Or is it just a story?" It was clear to him that she was lying. For reasons of their own, his parents would not cooperate; they could not accede to the school's suggestions.

For them, as for R., school was a source of deep discomfort—a constant admonition of sorts, the place whose message they heard: "You, R., are a failure, and you, his parents, are failures as well." Whether or not that was the message matters not; that is what they heard. They were angry at everyone who worked in the school, everyone who worked with their son.

They interpreted R.'s school problems in racial terms. Here were White people once again failing to address the needs of Black people. They began to temper this response during the two years I was R.'s teacher, acknowledging that, politics aside, R. had concrete learning difficulties. But they never acted on this realization; they never did anything to help R.

They and their son had, over the years, attended numerous family conferences. They'd sat with teachers, administrators, social workers, and psychologists trying to create workable plans for R. No progress: the wall between R. and the adult world thickened. Bad behavior became a given; so too the continued lack of academic success.

When I became his teacher he was a boy tightly wound into a web of the predictable; like a needle stuck in a record's groove, skipping repeatedly over the same notes.

## Beyond case history

I have tried to be precise in describing him. Case history isn't poetry, though, and descriptions of symptoms skirt the essence of a child. Teachers (as well as others in the "helping" professions) tend to see "bad" children exclusively in terms of symptoms (pathology) and causes (etiology).

But what causes one kid to fail (while another succeeds) is a mystery. Yes, there are codified bodies of thought, ready contexts purporting to explain what is happening to a child. Theories abound and one can talk about R. in terms of family dynamics, the politics of race and class, psychology, traumatic history, and so on. And, with the best of intentions, we can arrive at some nice theoretical construct.

Whatever one's predisposition, though, one is unlikely to get any closer to the child that way. R. existed outside convenient contexts—

seeing him began at the point where preconceived notions stopped. A context was useful, yes, but only as a window through which the child, vital and singular, might appear.

Trying to understand a child too quickly is a hopeless task; at best one engages only an image.

For one thing, kids like R. depend on an ability to keep adults at bay. There is a studied unpredictability to even their most conditioned responses. Skilled at manipulating adults, they keep them off balance. This tends to unnerve adults—especially teachers who are, by nature, tied into the "scope and sequence" of things, a logical world order such kids regularly violate.

But R. was not really bad; no, though the conditioning ran deep, R. was a scared, sometimes sweet, 12-year-old acting like a tough and sophisticated teenager. He wanted to do well in school, wanted to be respected, wanted to have friends. The potential sweetness was well-hidden, but it surfaced fleetingly when he was relatively relaxed and able to be with a few kids, his eyes wide and clear, voice soft and engaged.

That child, R.'s truest self, was mostly secreted away—a presence denied us by circumstance, conditioning, and fear.

There is no easy way to help a child shed these layers of unhappiness. It certainly can't happen in a year or two—especially when that child is already wrestling the demons of adolescence.

I knew R. was mine for two years. I knew his history; I'd heard the stories about him and his parents and I had seen him in action around the school. I decided that there were specific things I would not do: I would not kick him out of the room, no matter the provocation. At most he'd suffer internal exile, being asked to leave one part of the room for another. He'd been kicked out of rooms often enough in the past; being sent to the office was no punishment. This was his room now and he would not leave it. And I would not contact his parents with complaints; nor would I schedule more than the two annual family conferences. There was nothing to be gained by more meetings; family and school needed to function independently for a while.

I also established something important by talking about R.'s behavior in two ways. When there were complaints about his teasing or threatening, I'd publicly say something like, "Look, everyone knows R. teases kids. He's always teased kids. He'll probably always tease kids. You'll have to get used to it."

This was calculated to make public what everyone already knew. It also validated the other kids' anger while simultaneously embarrassing R. By letting him know that, in a way, I expected "the worst," he might react by proving me wrong. In a funny way, then, "good" behavior could be an act of defiance.

In private I'd describe his behavior for him. I tried to voice his frustration and anger about not reading or writing well. I'd point out patterns: "See, when you're embarrassed about not reading, you take it out on L." Such conversations were brief and I tried to cut to the point right away. R. was very practiced at ignoring the wisdom of the adult world.

One had maybe 30 seconds of open air time, then the channel shut down. Economy of expression was vital.

## A human encounter

In all this I was trying to acknowledge his presence—a presence rooted in the encounter between us, an on-going encounter as unrelated to old grievances as possible. Success depended on creating common ground uncontaminated by judgment, harking on past "sins" or rehashing old disappointments. I tried to let him know that he was who he was. He might choose to change, he might not. Much was within his power. There'd be no promises, no guarantees. My role was to attempt to give voice to his other self, that part of R. uninvolved in the negative, that aspect unwedded to failure.

Common ground in the classroom cannot exist when the teacher's vision is cluttered by too much data, when the child is seen largely in terms of past history, or when the child, for example, is seen as "economically disadvantaged," or "culturally deprived," or as an inevitable expression of a "dysfunctional family."

Such thinking always creates a barrier between teacher and child; the child, no longer a presence, is reduced in scope. The attempt to paint the larger picture results in less detail and less specificity. Sloppy thinking replaces real observation; fancy catch-phrases replace real communication.

R. might well be called a "learning disabled" child; he might be called an "angry Black child"; he might be seen as the result of a profoundly unhappy and pained marriage.

But having established that, what has one really said? One has not actually seen him because such constructs are essentially external. They are reportorial truths and in no way assist a teacher in the day-to-day, hour-to-hour, relationship with the child.

There is an unnameable inner landscape to each child; the teacher, if quiet and attentive, can perceive it. Then, and only then, is a relationship possible.

It was essential to acknowledge that R. had problems, essential to acknowledge that he felt pain. But it was as important to believe, and help him believe, that failure was not inevitable, that the present needn't be the past endlessly recycled.

He wanted no more lectures, no more punishments. He wanted success.

I provided R. with an individual study plan—daily assignments on a clipboard. He needed work structured in a way that made progress demonstrable for him. And while this individualized program set him apart, it merely formalized what was happening anyway. He was behind and he was not yet able to do the work others did. To pretend otherwise would be profoundly disrespectful.

He sat alone, at a single desk, close to but still separate from other kids. He worked with me occasionally during lunch periods and we worked together during prep periods as well.

I sometimes chastised him at length for things; other times I simply gave him a look and said: "Come on." I fooled around with him a great deal, teased him affectionately, and praised him loudly and publicly when his work or behavior warranted. I liked R., and he knew it. But my affection was not enough; I also knew what would work for him academically and I provided it.

I made sure he had a set and structured pattern of activities and I was consistent in working personally with him. I learned when to be strict and when to let things go. And most important I learned what he liked: basketball, woodworking, music. There was an enormous richness of curriculum possibilities in these areas and I exploited them.

He was a skilled woodworker; with the help of the school's assistant director he crafted a precisely rendered go-cart. It took months but he finished it. He then began helping other kids with their projects. He was the best woodworker in the class: I began referring to him in passing as "the master of the shop." When a kid would ask for help, I'd say, "Go to R. He's the expert."

And as his reading improved he began reading with kids with whom he would not otherwise relate—they, after all, were the "smart" kids, kids whose company he'd disdained.

It would be wonderful to report that a transformation ensued—flowers sprouting through the concrete playground on 99th Street—but that was not the case. And it would be splendid to report that I was able to maintain a calm and studied demeanor around him at all times. That, too, was not the case.

But by the end of the second year there had been real progress; he was able, for example, to read *The Catcher in the Rye* in a group. True, he read slowly and laboriously—but he persevered and enjoyed the book. Progress was not as dramatic in other areas. Still a very, very weak writer and math student, R. continued to tease others and move through school as if burdened by the weight of ten thousand things.

So, in the end, there was nothing magical in our encounter. Teaching rarely lends itself to neat and concise endings. R. went on to junior high school in certain ways readier to succeed than before. Glorious progress had not been made; great problems remained. Yet something powerful had occurred; he had, silently and impressively, made certain choices. He had, in a thousand small and subtle ways, and a number of larger, public ones, declared himself ready and willing to work.

There is something very moving in the human concourse possible between teacher and troubled child, in real relationship on common ground—a relationship born of the understanding that "I am here, you are here."

This was something new and unexpected for R., who'd been hearing "I am here; wish you weren't" all his life. His years in school had worked to severely limit his options; years of failure eviscerated his potential. He had entered my classroom with very set and well-rehearsed expectations. He was "bad" and was going to act "bad." That was something he did very well.

I refused to accept the pattern. I expected R. to work hard from day one. Not because I wanted to prevail and not because I wanted to show who was the boss, but because it was what he wanted and needed. My role was to find out how best to help him get it.

R. could not have broken with the past if I hadn't broken with it as well. And that depended on my seeing him afresh—with vision uncontaminated. And once he realized that I had not prejudged him, that I was not interested in "understanding" him, he began responding.

There is a geometry to relationship and it's axiomatic that the teacher must see the child as a "self." R. was an individual, not a conglomeration of influences, not a repository of conditions.

When "I am here, you are here," replaces "I am good, you are bad," and only then, is progress and growth for kids like R. possible. As long as kids like R. are seen merely as walking constellations of symptoms, they are diminished and dehumanized.

Sensing a kid's true presence, that part of him or her that is immutable and mysterious, commits the teacher to look beyond the fashionable prejudices of the moment into the heart of relationship where teacher and child meet.

This meeting is the essence of teaching, its very breath and soul.

# Schools as Communities of Love and Caring

## by Mara Sapon-Shevin

*Mara Sapon-Shevin is Associate Professor of Elementary and Special Education in the Center for Teaching and Learning at the University of North Dakota. She is most interested in how teachers and society respond to diversity in children and in how teachers and others can create "inclusive schools." Mara is active in the field of cooperative learning and often leads cooperative games workshops for teachers, counselors, parents, and day care providers. She is a board member of the International Association for the Study of Cooperation in Education. Mara is also active in community peace work and is a member of her institution's Peace Studies faculty. She takes great delight in being the mother of two activist, feminist daughters, Dalia, 12, and Leora, 9.*

When my oldest daughter was in elementary school, we attended the first parent-teacher conference in early October. After telling us about Dalia's excellent academic progress, the teacher said, "We are having one problem with Dalia; she cares too much about other children." As we sat there trying to figure out what the problem was, the teacher went on to explain, "For example, if another child breaks his pencil and starts to cry, she goes into *her* desk and gives him one of *her* pencils. And I tell her, 'Dalia, it's not your problem, it's his problem.'"

The conference ended on a positive note, but my husband and I returned home saddened, for the very values that we treasured most in our child, her tremendous empathy and caring (which we had nourished and encouraged), were seen as problems within the school setting.

I hope to share here a different vision, a vision of what schools could be like if they allowed children to be fully human. What would classrooms be like, and how would children interact in settings in which love and caring were considered not just acceptable behavior, but central organizing values? And I would like to discuss how schools interfere with children's natural ability and willingness to offer love and support

This selection originally appeared in the Summer 1990 issue of *Holistic Education Review*, Vol. 3, No. 2.

to one another. What would schools be like if teachers, rather than blocking this potential, unleashed and fostered the best of what children can be for one another?

Consider the following story which exemplifies the often difficult choices teachers make that can inadvertently block the very values they wish to foster. When my daughter was in kindergarten, she attended a progressive private school. Her kindergarten was team-taught by two wonderful teachers: Bonnie, an older, experienced teacher, was a model of everything a kindergarten teacher should be—loving, warm, unflappable, patient, and calm. Michelle, the younger teacher, was a perfect complement—energetic, lively, and full of excitement—she clearly loved the children in her class. One day Dalia came home all excited. "Good news," she announced, "Michelle is going to have a baby!" Michelle had shared the news of her pregnancy with the class, and they were all delighted. Intending to teach for as long as possible during her pregnancy, Michelle was happy to include the children in her joy and to share her progress with them.

Several weeks later, on a weekend, I received a call from Bonnie. She told me that there was bad news. Michelle had a miscarriage and lost the baby. I offered my condolences, and Bonnie went on: "We consulted a school psychologist. . . . He told us to tell the children that sometimes when a doctor tells a woman she is pregnant, he makes a mistake, and that Michelle was never pregnant." I listened in stunned silence. She was calling parents to, bluntly speaking, ask them to share in this falsehood, to lie to our children. I protested. First, I told her, I am uncomfortable lying to my child. Might not other mothers in the class have experienced (or go on to experience) miscarriage? Wouldn't such an explanation make children suspicious of doctors, or pregnancy, and of what they are told by adults? But, on an even deeper level, if we didn't acknowledge Michelle's loss and her sadness, how could she be allowed to grieve? How would the children make sense of their teacher's subdued behavior? What role would they be able to play in comforting her if there was no reason for her to be sad? Isn't dealing with sadness and loss part of growing into a full and healthy person?

Several hours later, another phone call. Another "expert" had been consulted and had offered different advice. The children were to be told that Michelle had been pregnant, that the baby hadn't lived long enough to be born healthy, and that she wasn't pregnant anymore. I thanked Bonnie for her reconsideration and was satisfied. The new explanation was the truth simplified to what seemed an appropriate level for kindergartners. Free to share the truth with Dalia, I then called her over. "Bad news, Dalia," I told her, "Michelle's baby didn't live long enough to be born, and she's not going to have a baby anymore." Dalia was stunned. "Oh, Mama," she said, "That's so sad!" "Yes," I agreed, "so sad." "Mama," she asked, "wouldn't you have been sad if that had happened to me?" "Yes," I agreed again, "so sad." We then discussed what Dalia might do to help make Michelle happy. Dalia suggested that a hug might help, or maybe a picture and a note that told Michelle that she loved her. I told her those seemed liked good ideas, and she ran off to draw a picture for Michelle.

On Monday, when Dalia returned from school, she shared with me how she (and many of the other children) had given Michelle "a lot of love" and how Michelle had seemed pleased to receive their hugs. Together the children and the teachers had grieved a little, cried a little, and healed a little. It was a powerful lesson in caring, and an exercise in carelessness had been averted.

Of course, there are other commentaries on this story. For example, why did Bonnie, the experienced teacher who knew her class of children so well, feel that she had to defer to an "outside expert" with a doctorate rather than trusting her own judgment (which she told me, would have led her to tell the children the truth)? But the most important point of my story is that the children in that class were nearly denied the opportunity to be fully human, to share another person's pain, and to figure out their roles in easing grief. What a loss that would have been. As it turned out, both the children and the teachers were allowed to be human. The children understood why Michelle was sad, and they felt empowered to help ease her sadness. In the name of "protecting" children from sad truths, however, they were nearly "protected" also from a lesson about love and caring.

Such lessons are not always easy, but they are always important. The first year I taught, I had a class of five- to seven-year-olds in what was called "mixed primary." Upstairs at the same school was another class of the same age, and, in that class, five-year-old Kevin was dying of cancer. Death is never easy to understand, and the death of a child seems utterly incomprehensible to both children and adults. But Kevin was part of that class, and the teachers were intent on making Kevin's life as rich as it could be, and his death as humane as possible for everyone.

Kevin was in and out of school that year; chemotherapy and radiation made him lose his hair, and he wore a little cap. The children asked many questions, and the teachers answered all of them. The class read books about death, and they wanted to know what happened to the bodies of people who died. The teachers tried to be honest. Parents were kept informed of what was happening and formed a web of support around Kevin's parents. When Kevin was in class, the other children rallied around him with love and support. They were not afraid of what was happening. They felt like participants in the drama; they were not excluded. When Kevin died, many of the children attended his funeral. It was a very sad day for the whole school. It was not a usual day, because five-year-olds are not supposed to die, and the children needed to be reassured and to understand that death—any death—was not to be taken lightly, and certainly not to be ignored.

A week after the funeral, the art teacher reported that one of the children in Kevin's class approached her and said, "I've been thinking. You know, Kevin's smock is still hanging on his hook in the art room.

I don't know if it's better if we leave it there, or if we should take it down." Although on one level it is grievous to think of a five-year-old having to weigh the tension between holding Kevin's memory and getting on with life, it is wonderful as well. The teachers in that school created an atmosphere in which the children were free to be sad, free to grieve, and free to be human beings in all of the best senses.

When I shared this story with a group of pre-service teachers, several told of their own childhood experiences with death and loss. One student reported that when a classmate was killed over the weekend, the child's desk was simply removed, and no formal mention was ever made of what had happened. When I asked the class why they thought teachers might be uncomfortable talking about death with their students, they offered various explanations. "Because they don't know what to say," said one. "Because they're afraid they'll make kids feel worse," proposed another. Then, one student suggested an answer that I found provocative and insightful: "I think that teachers don't talk about a child's death because they're afraid that, if they do, they might cry in front of the class themselves." This seems to me to be at the heart of the issue. In order for us to allow children to be fully human with one another, we must, as teachers, be fully human with our students. "What," I challenged my class, "could be better than the teacher and the students all crying together?"

Probably all teachers can offer stories about what has happened when they have trusted their students enough to be honest and human with them. Once, when I was teaching a class of special education students, many of whom had what are now called "challenging behaviors," I came to school quite ill. I confided to my class that I wasn't feeling well, that my head hurt, and I felt dizzy. My class that day was the sweetest they had ever been. They talked in quiet voices, they brought me drinks of water, and they inquired regularly whether I was feeling better. Many of them offered little hugs and tentative pats on the back as well. By the end of the day, my head still hurt, but my heart was full.

What can classrooms be like when children are encouraged to be caring and loving? One particularly dramatic example is provided by a kindergarten teacher who has integrated several children with severe disabilities into her room. She reports that at first the children were wary of Darren, who had multiple disabilities, used a wheelchair, and had seizures. When he had a seizure they were afraid, she said, that he was getting hurt. She reassured them that, as a class, they wouldn't let anything bad happen to Darren, and they began to relax. She reported that, a month after Darren's entry into the class, all of the children had learned how to hold him, how to play with him gently, and how to communicate with him. One day, one of the children approached her and said, "Darren's in a seizure; it's about a minute so far. Should I get his blanket because Darren is having a bad day? Should I put him in the bean bag and give him a cuddle?"[1] This, to me, is the image of how schools can be: children unafraid of one another's differences and able to offer love and caring to one another.

How do we make this happen? In many ways, I think the answers are obvious. Perhaps the most basic answer is that we, as teachers, need to allow ourselves to be loving and caring without embarrassment, without apology. And then, as Rabbi Hillel said when asked to state the principles of right conduct while standing on one foot, "Love one another; all the rest is commentary." Part of that commentary, I believe, is that we try not to stand in the way of children's natural empathy and caring. We can try to create environments in which that caring is easy and natural to display. One teacher I know places her students in little clusters of desks pushed together. She calls these groups "families," and she has a basic rule in her classroom: If anyone in a family group has a problem (of any kind), it is up to the group to try to solve it before coming to her for advice or help. The nature of the problems that these families solve goes beyond not knowing what math page to do, or how to figure out the key on the map, although these have all been addressed. She has also seen these families of children rally around a child who was sad, upset, or worried about something—little heads buzzed together as they figured out what to do to help.

One often hears adults lament how cruel children are to one another. I am not denying that I have seen these behaviors too: children excluded, taunted, and teased. But I have also seen children be amazingly loving, supportive, understanding, and helpful to one another. I have seen big, "tough" sixth-graders helping little first graders with their math; I have seen "typical" children gently wiping the mouth of a child with cerebral palsy who drools; and I have seen children brainstorming to help a child who was having trouble with schoolwork. We must look at schools and teachers who create these environments of love and caring, and study what they do. We must ask these teachers what they do. And then we must listen.

Once while observing a classroom, I was struck within ten minutes by the fact that the children were so nice to one another. They sat on the rug at story time and they didn't push. I watched them sharing scarce materials with ease and grace. I saw children hugging each other and laughing together. I approached the teacher and told her what I had seen. I asked her what she had done to create this environment. Truly, I would have been disappointed if she had said that she had done nothing. But I was not disappointed. "Well," she said, "I tell them that this is their family and that, while we're in this room together, we have to figure out how to get along. It's a real priority in my room." The results were obvious. I saw another teacher, this one a teacher of preschoolers, discuss with three-year-olds which words were "exclusive" (words that pushed other children away), and which were "inclusive" (ones that brought people together). Figuring out how to make an inclusive community out of the classroom was a specific agenda; it was not considered secondary to some academic goal.

I don't think that creating classrooms of love and caring is a difficult task. Complex, yes, and challenging, but not difficult, because I believe that all human beings want to be loving and caring. Many things stand in their way, and many children (and adults) get hurt in such a way that it is difficult for them to be loving and caring; but I believe that the true nature of human beings is to be closely and warmly connected with others. As teachers, we are simply facilitating what can be a natural and organic process, a process of love.

## Note

1. Marsha Forest, "Just One of the Kids," in *More Education/Integration* (Downsview, Ontario: Roeher Institute, 1987), pp. 121-124.

# Walden Within

## by Clement Mehlman

*Clement Mehlman has been teaching in rural Nova Scotia for twenty-seven years, most recently at Park View Education Centre. His teaching has been shaped by interests in humanistic education, the acclimatization work of Steve Van Matre, the intensive journal work of Progoff, and religious and literary studies. He has served on provincial English curriculum task forces, as a church camp director, and, most recently, has done graduate work at OISE in holistic education and masculinity. He wrote this paper while studying with John Miller, author of* **The Holistic Curriculum.**

I have come to believe that students experience as curriculum what the teacher is doing inwardly and spiritually. My childhood in rural Lunenburg County, Nova Scotia, was close to the land and filled with images that parallel the New England of Robert Frost: newborn calves, the bleak and stubbled fields of winter, fenced pasture land, and natural springs in springtime. My flirtation with academics for several decades called me from the land, but a decade ago I began stopping by Ripton, Vermont, and Concord, Massachusetts, during summer holidays. Two moments are etched in my memory. One is a late morning walk on the top of Breadloaf Mountain in Ripton, past the Nobel farm, up the grassy path "that wanted wear," along a stone fence as in "Mending Wall" to the cottage where Frost frequently went to be alone and to write. Its screened-in verandah, its unpainted and weather-beaten boards, its deserted and decaying appearance, its view of "five mountain ranges deep into Vermont" helped me to enter more deeply into the life and work of Frost. The second memory is of an early morning walk at Walden Pond in a people-less woods, a deliberate effort to get but a glimpse of what Henry might have seen and heard. Such experiences, reading, my growing appreciation of my own piece of land and its isolated and beautiful brook, and workshops with outdoor educators such as Steve Van Matre influenced me to adopt several new metaphors in my teaching: the teacher as retreat leader, as nature guide, and as spiritual sojourner.

For the past ten years I have been experimenting with learning and writing holistically in natural settings. The experiments began with "Lit-

This selection originally appeared in the Fall 1989 issue of *Holistic Education Review,* Vol. 2, No. 3.

erature of the Out-of-Doors," a semester-length course for students in the last two years of secondary school. More recently the experiments have been with the teaching of literature, particularly poetry, in month-long units in outdoor settings. "Walden Within" incorporates teaching from the whole language perspective in the context of an experience-centered curriculum, with aspects of environmental education. The holistic intention seeks to emphasize the physical, moral, and spiritual dimensions in addition to the usual public school emphasis on the emotional and intellectual. Primarily, the study of English in natural settings taps the deep roots of the spiritual. Though the course and units represent an English credit, the focus is less on curriculum and more on students in the process of being, of discovering, of expressing. A trust in nature as healer and as restorer underscores our outward and inward journeys.

## The holistic approach

Our lives possess a wholeness, as does the universe. Central to holistic thought is the law of ecology, which states that everything is connected to everything else. Much has been written of the dangers in fragmenting a unified universe. Renée Weber observes: "In fragmenting nature, science loses a sense of the whole. An even greater price is the loss of meaning—of the whole and sometimes even of the details."[1] The whole and the details belong together. As John Muir wrote in *Gentle Wilderness*, "when we try to pick out anything by itself, we find it hitched to everything else in the universe."[2] The notions of holism and ecology are related. *Umwelt*, a German word loosely translated as "surround," attempts to convey the totality of the world in which we and other living and nonliving things coexist. To teach holistically in the natural environment is to bring students into deeper communication with the "lifeworld," to enable them to see the complexity of living as well as the interconnectedness of our selves, humanity, and nature.

David Suzuki argues passionately that we have to reclaim this holism and sense of the "umwelt" and "lifeworld." "What science has done," he says, "is to cut us adrift from any kind of sense of continuity as a part of the stream of life. . . . We have been cut loose from any cosmological significance."[3] In the reductionist approaches that dominate science, Suzuki regrets the loss of concern with emotions, values, ethics, morality, beauty, and love. These are encouraging words for holistic education from a reputed scientist and educator:

> I started with the proposition that humans are very different and special, because we are able to look at whales and whooping cranes and to appreciate their beauty and, in so doing, create something that did not exist before: human appreciation. . . . When we destroy other species, we show such self-contempt for ourselves that it means to reduce some of that dignity and specialness about humans.[4]

In "Walden Within" we open communication between the fields of science and literature; we overcome in some way the classical split of the world into facts and values, into knower and known, into observer and observed. In the context of the whole, we enable students to discover how "order arises from randomness, spirit from matter, personal from impersonal stuff."[5] A holistic emphasis on curriculum strives to offer complete and integrated learning experiences that involve both sensory and spiritual dimensions. There is much to be gained in a blending of the study of literature and writing in a natural environment with a holistic emphasis; shared values of these dimensions are growth in self-realization, development of awareness and respect, increased facility in communication and creativity, nurture of an aesthetic sense, and spiritual growth. In students' emotional responses, in their writing and talking, and in their rediscovery of nature as companion, I see the effects in them of nature's gifts of healing, restoring, and spiritual insight.

## Place, people, and process

> I stood, still, beside the two tall hemlock, looking down on the LaHave. The slate rock bed of the river parallel to the north along this section of the bend in its journey, its edges worn and smooth through the eons of erosion, light green moss covering the submerged cliffs, high boulders washed up along the shoreline of the river that is deep down from this cliff. And today I feel like singing Lauds to the LaHave: its clear waters, its endless journeying, its pristine strength in a land so tamed and civilized.
>
> A bluejay swiftly skims near the river's surface as it travels towards the Source. In the cool woods the morning Sun finds my cheek and warms me; on the solid and supporting Earth the song of the slate-coloured junco from deep in the woods invites me. (Clem, 13 September)

Imagine a warm day in autumn, a group of students, and a teacher in the park, with its pathways amid maple, hemlock, and ancient pine trees; its smaller footpath along the cliff's edge, from which you can see the river twenty-five feet below; and the opposite shore and hill, also covered with pine. A series of rock ledges in the river upstream create small waterfalls, a clearly marked border for fishermen who gather the river's rich harvest. The park, a stand of virgin pine adjacent to the LaHave River in Lunenburg County, Nova Scotia, is within two minutes' walking distance of our classroom. To that place my classes and I retreat to find ourselves, one another, and nature, and to discover some deeper insights into the experience of authors.

Initially we aim at a ten-minute "Seton Watch" and eventually work toward a twenty-minute stillness. Named after the Canadian naturalist, Ernst Thompson Seton, the Seton Watch is a stilling exercise for both mind and body. Seton observed that, after fifteen to twenty minutes of perfect stillness, nature resumed its activity as if people were not present. During the Seton Watch, after the relaxation, students are ready to observe.

Kevin, a twelfth-grader, wrote the following after his first Seton Watch in the park:

> When we were walking through the woods as a group, all seemed to be in confusion. As we broke off, one by one, the confusion (in a sense) seemed to lessen.
>
> I sat down onto the moist spongy moss and leaned against a tree. I took a deep breath and began to feel rather relaxed.

All was quiet as I sat under my tree, except for the odd caw of a passing crow and the constant rushing of the river, over that way, over the cliff, below. Then as I sat longer the area around me seemed to come alive. I could hear birds chirping in the trees above, and the odd chatter of a chipmunk or squirrel. I began to feel alone, just me and my own surroundings. It felt good, comfortable.

Then I saw a rather large flying insect. This was my creature. Not much but a lot better than the minute mosquitoes constantly buzzing in my ears, taking the odd supply of blood from my system. Thieves! I don't know what my creature was but it flew into a little hole in the tree adjacent to where I sat. I stared at the hole in the crevice, until my vision became obscured. . . . Here I was sitting expecting the stupid bug to come back out, and satisfy my curiosity, but it didn't!

The chirping was louder and clearer. I looked through the leaves, of the cluster of hardwood that grew beyond the tree with the hole in it. Fluttering, weaving in and out of branches which provide no obstacle to these little feathered creatures. I only wish I could tell their breed, but that is insignificant, for today they exist for me, as birds, and that is fine. (Kevin, 20 September)

In early November the same class was again in the park. By now they were accustomed to the stilling activity of the Seton Watch for twenty minutes, and on this day we were located in our own Magic Spots. (Magic Spots are those private places in the environment, as Steve Van Matre has named them, to which we go to enjoy and to observe nature.)

Today, I've a new place! It's small, private, very private yet crowded by nature, and this is good. Here three *is* company not a crowd, never a crowd. It is a ledge on the cliff that overlooks the peacefully flowing LaHave. It is solitude. Nature, here, literally surrounds me, except for the open window to the passing, floating fumes below me.

With the rough, jagged cliff side to my right and the long drop into strength (water, essential to the earth) to my left, and pine or perhaps spruce blotting out the sun's warm rays above me, I feel totally enclosed by nature. It's like being in a box and never wanting to come out. I become part of it, or rather it becomes a part of me. Engulfed in its presence, I sit there in silence, just absorbing it through all five of my senses and possibly a sixth.

I hear the constant rushing of the river's waters, way behind me, around the corner upon the awkwardly curved tree, upon which I lean, and way in front of me down the river towards "town." Civilization seems nonexistent here, I hope to God I shall continue this way. Yet the waters below my sitting place are silent, quietly flowing its thousand-year-old path.

Patterns of foam cruise by, spinning and tumbling to the river's currents. The opposite shoreline created with rocks, pebbles, boulders, all smooth and round from years of passing water. This shoreline is only to be perfected by the sun's brightening rays, flowing in perfect line with the horizon between land and river.

To think thousands of years ago this spot on which I sit was probably under this once-gigantic, rushing river, flowing to eternity. Who knows? The evolution of man and the evolution of the earth. Man has much to learn. The earth supplies answers. Man stares at the sun, becoming blinded. (Kevin, 1 November)

Between Kevin's two entries he had encountered several authors, including some transcendentalists: Ralph Waldo Emerson and his essay *Nature,* Henry David Thoreau and *Walden,* and the drama *The Night Thoreau Spent in Jail* by Lawrence and Lee. Kevin is finding his "Walden Within" and has bonded with Thoreau's appreciation of solitude, and his ability to be engaged with nature, and, therefore, with his deeper self. Thoreau wrote of his solitude on the shores of Walden Pond:

> Sometimes, I sat in my sunny doorway from sunrise till noon, rapt in a revery, amidst the pines and hickories and sumacs, in undisturbed solitude and stillness, while the birds sang around or flitted noiseless through the house. . . . I grew in those sessions like corn in the night.[6]

Like Thoreau, Kevin reveals his distaste for the "town" and his concern for preservation of the wilderness.

Symbolic activities highlight and create magic. One spring, on the anniversary of Thoreau's death, we decided to prepare the soil in the woods for a small garden of beans; one of Henry's famous activities of mindfulness was hoeing beans. John brought the tools, Jackie the fertilizer, another student the soil, and another the seed. Together we prepared the soil and planted the seeds, and read from Thoreau's journals of that date. The following fall, I led the puzzled, new class to the site, where we surprisingly found the beans, dry and spiralled, hanging on the plants, awaiting harvest. All of the students were given beans from the spring planting, and they were encouraged to plant some of the beans themselves. A year later, Roberta sent me a bean from her "crop" from an Ontario university, where one of her few delights was browsing among the Thoreau books in the library. On another occasion, using a postcard I picked up at the Lyceum in Concord, I sent the class a note, signed "Henry," which said that he was planning a canoeing expedition to Nova Scotia and that he would be canoeing down the LaHave on a projected date and time. The class gathered at noon that fall day on the LaHave shore above the falls to meet "Henry" and interview him.

Classroom activities include small group, cooperative learning tasks on *The Starship and the Canoe* by Kenneth Brower; discussion groups on the poetry of Gary Snyder, Robert Frost, and William Wordsworth; and total-class consensus exercises on outdoors themes. Kevin wrote of a wilderness survival exercise:

> I would sort of like getting lost. Just to see how and if I could survive. I would really like to "Let's say for a weekend" be confined solely to nature. No outside comforts or burdens to weigh me down. I would like to test myself, truly and wholly, maybe even learn to live like that, as did Thoreau. It would be a good test of myself. Similar to that of the test you gave us today. (Kevin, 5 January)

On very wet and cold days we occasionally "went outdoors" in our imaginings through the use of visualizations, using many of the scripts in Steven's *Awareness*. Kevin recounted his visit to the "Wise Person in the Mountains":

> Walking down the desolate path, the cool, unknown jungle surrounds me in the moonlight. As I walk, I brush the odd batch of oversized ferns or a bough of some kind of tree. The path is narrow and rough, winding slowly up the sloping mountain. The damp overgrowth is thick and the odd protruding rock on the path is hard to see in the dim light. I stumble further.

I come upon a small, more desolate path branching to the left of my climb. It is so thick with growth, used maybe once or twice. I take it gradually plowing through the undergrowth, sloping upwards slowly.

The growth becomes thinner. I see a dim, dancing light up ahead. I break out of the jungle, stumbling into a clearing and then a rock wall. A camp fire, objects lying around (boxes, bear skin, tools, homemade handy things), wood. Then a man, crouching by the fire, arms resting on legs. His glowing eyes staring at the fire. Wise and old. A wide-open cave behind him and a vine-covered rock wall.

I walk up to the fire, crouch down adjacent to him across the fire. I stare at the fire as does the old man. Not a word is spoken. I look up at the scrawny, small, old man, his wrinkled face and big white eyes. He dresses in rags of a hundred years in age. Thin, grey hair on top of his skeleton frame.

I ask him, "What will my future hold?" He stared at me with those big, white eyes and said in a cracking, harsh voice, "You, my son, are the only one who can tell that." (Kevin, 22 November)

On a cognitive level the course provides independent time without the demands to produce and be directed by another person. There is time for students to make the connections between the present experiences and what they already know. With time to do the inner connecting, it is hoped that students will develop higher level concepts, which form the basis of integrative thinking. In the self-discoveries and other discoveries that students make, they become more integrated and whole persons and are thus able to reach out to others more compassionately. The literature and the land enable or lead students to discoveries of that vital, however forgotten, dimension of humanity, the natural dimension.

## Transpersonal dimensions

If we are receptive to nature's lessons, if we learn to read from nature's book, the spiritual quality of our own lives will be enhanced with the gifts of wonder, of scope, and of purpose. As the poet Nancy Newhall aptly remarks: "The wilderness holds answers to more questions than we yet know how to ask."[7]

Rudolf Steiner speaks of the inner work necessary to "unlock the divine within us" before we can find it outside in the environment.[8] Students discover that an intimate interplay exists between nature and self, and that a mood of receptivity and quiescence opens them to an awareness of the earth's presence. Each outdoor class begins with the class and teacher gathering in a perfect circle, standing shoulder to shoulder. A brief time of silence is followed by an opening meditation: Steve Van Matre's anthology of readings, *The Earth Speaks*, provides a rich source of quotations from ancient and contemporary, Eastern and Western writers. One of the readings, the following extract from Wendell Berry, reminds us of the spiritual in nature:

And the world cannot be discovered by a journey of miles, no matter how long, but only by a spiritual journey of one inch, very arduous and humbling and joyful by which we arrive at the ground at our feet, and learn to be at home.[9]

Frequent readings are from Lao Tzu, especially the familiar Taoist images of the emptiness of a wheel's hub and a clay vessel as symbols of stillness and strength. Students are encouraged to focus on these images to attain the emptiness and freedom from current concern with a past problem or a future task. As Shynryu Suzuki says:

> If your mind is empty, it is always ready for anything; it is open to everything. In the beginner's mind there are many possibilities; in the expert's mind there are few.[10]

Students then disperse to separate areas of the field in the early weeks and, as trust develops, to their selected Magic Spots in the park. At first students want to stick together, but after a class or two, they begin to discover the joy of being alone. In school, where the reflective and introspective person is often shunned, students discover the joys of solitude:

> What chance have we, in all this cacophony, of all this prying, to be quietly alone, to contemplate our condition and to take stock of ourselves? . . . One who has never known the autonomy and solitude may make little effort to secure and keep them. One who has savored and enjoyed them for a few precious moments, will likely cherish them and struggle to protect them.[11]

The state of quiescence and readiness is central to developing a vivid inner life. With that readiness, the observer is open to have nature enter the empty vessel. Surya Singer's words for this fresh reopening of spirit to nature are powerful:

> Look at the world around you as if you just arrived on Planet Earth. Observe the rocks in their natural formations, the trees rooted in the ground, their branches reaching the sky, the plants, the animals and the interrelationships of each to the other. . . . When the mind allows its objects to remain unmolested, there may be no mind and no object—just breathless unity.[12]

Students are led to closer perceptiveness of nature by the occasional use of objects from the natural world as meditation points, or for what Kurt Vonnegut calls "grokking." Embracing a mighty oak, smelling its bark, holding an insect or a flower and peering closely into its life and intricacy become meditational. Out of the stillness and engagement with nature, deep dialogue within the student occurs. A student handed me these haiku, after a class in the park, each haiku written on a dry leaf:

> Lines writ on a leaf
> Last long as Nature permits
> Nature governs all.

> River flowing slow
> Moulds earth like moss on old rocks
> Earth and time are old friends.
>                         (John, 28 November)

John and others discover what Renée Weber calls "spiritual aspiration" and find wonder and awe in the simplicity of nature. As I have observed students engaged with nature and in solitude, I have sensed that they are connecting with those years when nature was their playfellow. As six-foot Travis lies with his belly on a slate rock that projects into the river, staring contentedly for a period of time at a small trout at play,

I know that he has rediscovered a bit of the inner child. Weber speaks of this intimacy:

> All my life I have felt close to nature. Her presence was real to me long before I knew anything of the laws by which she works—a child's prereflective though definite awareness of nature's being. Looking back, I realize that since my earliest childhood I have sensed "something" in nature's background and even in the foreground. The beautiful and lavish variety of her form has been a source of real meaning in my life, and from the beginning I felt a kinship with nature's offspring—animals, plants, rocks, forests, water, earth, the sky, and even with the remote stars and galaxies. No one taught me this; I simply awoke to the world with the conviction of my relatedness to these things. This feeling, common in childhood and often lost as we grow up, has remained with me.[13]

Alan Drengson, a philosophy professor at the University of Victoria, writes of the potential for spiritual growth through the outdoors. Modern life brings us doubt, alienation, nihilism. By the river or on a field we get back in touch with self and nature. For him, what I have been describing would be a form of *Rasa Yoga*, the "Yoga which leads to unity of Self via an appreciation of the aesthetic qualities of the natural world and of the natural human self."[14]

> As one travels through the rich silence of the wilderness with its diverse forms of life, one reflects more and more deeply on the source of life and its creative capacities. . . . The sound of falling water and the rush of streams . . . bring us once more into the presence of our immediate experience with the world. . . . One comes to realize . . . the symmetries between human consciousness and the laws of ecology that pervade the natural world.[15]

This spiritual relationship between humans and the earth, or the one "presence" (to use Wordsworth's term) that is at the center of that relationship, may be found not only in the Eastern tradition but also in the thought of native North Americans. Part of the course also includes Ruth Beebe Hill's *Hanta Yo*, John Neihardt's *Black Elk Speaks*, and other native readings. Central to *Hanta Yo* is the "Vision Quest," a ritual in which a young person goes into the wilds to listen to nature and spiritual forces and to be empowered by the gifts that nature grants.[16] Being fully alive, in the native tradition, means being at one with nature.

> When a man has lost his closeness with the earth,
> When he no longer smells the pine trees and the wild flowers,
> When he no longer hears the song of the cricket,
> Then his heart becomes cold, and he begins to die.[17]

Zen and Taoist meditators, native American Indians, modern human ecologists, and students in classes as I have been describing find the outdoors a place conducive to the inward journey. For the students, just as it was for Thoreau, it is a place where can be found "some grand, serene, immortal, infinitely encouraging, though invisible companion, and walk with him."[18] Lawrence Durrell said it so well: "All landscapes ask the same question in the same whisper. 'I am watching you—are you watching yourself in me?' "[19] The land about us is a mirror reflecting back to us the images that we have impressed upon it. As part of this deepening of self-knowledge through landscape, Ralpy Lutts recommends inclusion of narrative work among students as they reflect more on the unique places in their lives. In addition to reflecting and writing on their present environments and celebrating and valuing their positive features, he encourages reflecting and storying on the past and future as well: How did the "historical process through which they and their natural environment . . . evolve into this special place," and how do they see the future alternatives that will create environments of value?[20] Writers such as Carson, Miles, Drengson, and Tanner speak of the contributions to growth of holistic approaches in wilderness environments. Students become more in touch with themselves in solitude and discover anew the delight in being at one with self.

## Communal dimensions

Interpersonal discoveries are also heightened by outward journeys.

What a journey we had today down the river. The spectacular pillars of ice hanging on the cliffs amazed both of us.

You know what felt good? To share a truly natural experience with a close friend of your own age. It was neat to share similar attitudes and beliefs. . . . (Kevin, 25 January)

As Kevin discovered, nature enables us to appreciate the other living beings with whom we share the earth. Out of the silence within ourselves and of the park without, we discover that we share the same source of being. Weber notes:

The awareness of the unity and interconnectedness of all being leads—if it is consistent—to an empathy with others. It expressed itself as reverence for life, compassion, a sense of the unity of suffering humanity, and the commitment to heal our wounded earth and its peoples. All the mystics (and virtually all the scientists) . . . draw this connection between their vision of the whole and their sense of responsibility for it.[21]

Holistic thought reminds us, just as John Donne did, that "No [one] is an island"; we are always in relationship with other human beings and our world, always part of the web of life. Being outdoors, one notes a decrease in conflicts, a lessening in psychological gaming, and a decrease in competitive behavior. Drengson attributes this to the fact that "the principles of community, friendship, and human flowering" are alive and readable in the environment and that the reading of these enables our return to fullness and harmony.[22] After time outdoors with students, I have noted how their sense of humor is restored and their spirits cheered, a return of the enthusiasm and joy of childhood. Rachel Carson writes:

Those who dwell, as scientists or laymen, among the beauties and mysteries of the earth are never alone or weary of life. Whatever the vexations or concerns of their personal lives, their thoughts can find paths that lead to inner contentment and to renewed excitement in living. Those who contemplate the beauty of the earth find reserves of strength that will endure as long as life lasts. . . . There is something infinitely healing in the repeated rhythms of nature.[23]

## Global dimensions

A moonlight flower
solitarily perches
on the forest floor
in the dead of the night
to comfort lonely creatures.
                    (Amy, 20 May)

Amy images an almost spiritual act of the flower for the earth's creatures. Just as the urge for dialogue exists between people and nature's
forms, Amy invites us to consider the relationships of caring within
nature. Compassion for other human beings evolves into a compassion
for other species as well. Living closer to nature shows us that both
aesthetic and ethical reasons prompt more ecologically wise behavior.
All organisms have a beauty of intricacy and design. Claude Levi-Strauss
notes: "Any species of bug that people spray with insecticides is an
irreplaceable marvel, equal to the works of art which we religiously
preserve in museums."[24] At the base of ecological concern and awareness is a discovery within ourselves of affection and compasion for all
of life. The global dimension of "Walden Within" moves learners beyond
the intrapersonal and the interpersonal to the relationship of people to
the planet. Any form of environmental learning provides the opportunity, one might say the obligation, to instill a commitment to end the
spoilage and destruction of our world and to make of it, once more, a
garden to cherish. We need to learn a preference for compassionate
impulses over egotistical ones. I noted earlier that Thoreau's life was
lived congruently and with integrity in accord with the principles he
held inwardly. He wrote: "To be a philosopher is not merely to have
subtle thoughts . . . but so to love wisdom as to live according to its
dictates."[25] At the root of many of our ecological problems is the separation of the spiritual and the moral from nature.

To produce the changes our world requires means informed citizens,
and it is pleasing to see students become actively involved in local action
for social change such as Ducks Unlimited and Operation Ploughshares.
Our world is shifting its focus from competitiveness and technology to
the new person–planetary paradigm, a paradigm shift to intuition and
deeper ecological consciousness. The holistic approach of "Walden
Within," rooted in the literary and environmental interdisciplinary base,
acknowledges that people and their environment are profoundly interdependent. Such an approach must encompass the various ecological,
personal, cultural, literary, and other aspects of the environment. We
turn now to consider how these holistic approaches in the environment
integrate with literary studies in the public classroom.

## Literary and creativity concerns

The course that I have been describing falls in an experience-centered
English curriculum, an approach in which the concern is not simply
with language, literature, and thought but also with the experiences
that lie behind them. The experience-centered mode engages learners

with real feelings, real concerns, and real experiences and explores with them the issues that affect them. Far too often classroom learning omits the "felt experience" out of which learning flows. It is not of much use to have students read and evaluate Wordsworth's *The Prelude*, Byron's "Apostrophe to the Ocean," or Arnold's "Dover Beach" if they are not also invited to explore their own involvement with nature. To read with engagement and creativity as well as to live more vibrantly, the student must be led, as Bruno Bettleheim argues, to "develop one's inner resources, so that one's emotions, imagination, and intellect mutually support and enrich one another."[26] I agree with what Benjamin DeMott calls bringing literature to life in *Close Imaginings:*

> Adeptness at bringing experience to life, shrewdness at speculating about what is taking place from moment to moment in other creatures, responsiveness to imagined feelings, thoughts, reactions—these are qualities without which most days of most lives would be extremely thin. The state of development of our gifts in these areas affects our tastes, our ambitions, and our capacity to realize our own ambitions. It affects our ability to care about the spectrum of human life. . . . The very act of perception itself—taking in the reality around us—depends on our power to animate, to bring the world fully to life.[27]

In another defense of this "felt experience" approach to literature, I suggest that the river or a frog or a fantasy is "text" just as significant as what we normally see as text. The river and its environs are as rich as any book in possibilities for making meaning. What is this experience of nature? For the artist's answers, look at the landscapes of Turner or Thompson. For music, listen to Beethoven's Pastoral Symphony or Debussy's La Mer. For the essayist? Share the reflections of Thoreau, collected upon the shores of Walden Pond, or of Annie Dillard from Tinker Creek. For poets, read Hopkins, Blake (particularly "The Auguries of Innocence"), Wordsworth ("Intimations of Immortality"). But, remember the Eastern poets as well, such as Li P'O:

> You ask me why should I stay in this blue mountain.
> I smile but do not answer. O, my mind is at ease!
> Peach blossoms and flowing streams pass away without trace,
> How different from the mundane world![28]

To the Chinese poets, directness makes images in the poem be themselves. Existence itself becomes poetry. Poetry is simply the expression of such existence. The directness and the poet's inner joy come from the poet's self, which affects the self of the reader. This dissolving and merging of the self of the poet into the selves of others is the secret of poetic creativity. Jacques Maritain observes:

> The creative self of the artist is his person as person . . . not his person as material individual or as self-centered ego. And the first obligation imposed on the poet is to consent to be brought back to the hidden place near the center of the soul, where this totality exists in the state of a creative source.[29]

The Chinese poets, trained in the art of meditation, know that quiet contemplation leads to creative power, and from this seed springs forth beauty. Poetry is a reflection of the degree of enlightenment of the poet, since creativity and interiority are linked.

## The compassionate teacher

Just as I am a guide in the students' literary studies, I become also a model of being "at one" with nature, that world of the LaHave River and "flowing streams" and "peach blossoms." Carson speaks of the powerful role of the guiding adult who invites the young to meet the world:

> If a child is to keep alive his inborn sense of wonder without any such gift from the fairies, he needs the companionship of at least one adult who can share it, rediscovering with him the joy, excitement and mystery of the world we live in.[30]

With students for a decade, I have been present as they discovered that joy, but present in a way of quietness, stillness, and, I hope, humility. We stand equally in the circle as classes begin. We sit equally in the circle at the end of class as we read and talk or simply listen in stillness. I know that for Kevin and John, and for Roberta and Amy, I acquired some of the features of a guide or "master" in the oriental sense. Like Lao Tzu, I strive to "teach without words." The teacher or guide needs to be in tune with the order and beauty of the earth before students can be brought in tune. I need to strive toward the spiritual and that deeper contact with the self in order to guide the sojourners in my care.

The invitation to me and to my students is simple.

And hark! how blithe the throstle sings!
He, too, is no mean preacher;
Come forth into the light of things,
Let Nature be your teacher.

She has a world of ready wealth,
Our minds and hearts to bless—
Spontaneous wisdom breathed by health,
Truth breathed by cheerfulness.

One impulse from a vernal wood
May teach you more of man,
Of moral evil and of good
Than all the sages can.

Sweet is the lore which Nature brings;
Our meddling intellect
Mis-shapes the beauteous forms of things;
We murder to dissect.

Enough of Science and of Art;
Close up those barren leaves;
Come forth, and bring with you a heart
That watches and receives.[31]

## Notes

1. Renée Weber, *Dialogues with Scientists and Sages: The Search for Unity* (New York: Routledge and Kegan Paul, 1986), p. 8.

2. John Muir, *Gentle Wilderness* (San Francisco: Sierra Club, 1964), p. ii.

3.   David Suzuki, "Coping with Science and Technology in the Eighties," in Paul Wilkinson and Mirim Wyman, *Environmental Challenges: Learning for Tomorrow's World* (London, Ontario: Althouse Press, 1986), p. 83.

4.   Ibid., p. 95.

5.   Richard Borden, "Technology, Education, and the Human Ecological Perspective," *Journal of Environmental Education* (Spring 1985), p. 4.

6.   Henry David Thoreau, *Walden and Other Writings of Henry David Thoreau* (New York: Random House, 1950), p. 101.

7.   Ernest Partridge, "Nature and the Personality," *Journal of Outdoor Education* (Fall 1980), p. 6.

8.   Mary C. Richards, *Toward Wholeness: Rudolf Steiner Education in America* (Middletown, CT: Wesleyan University Press, 1980), p. 15.

9.   Steve Van Matre, *Earth Speaks* (Warrenville, IL: Acclimatization Experiences Institute, 1983), p. 181.

10.   Shynryu Suzuki, *Zen Mind, Beginner's Mind*, cited in Ram Dass, *Journey to Awakening: A Meditator's Guide* (New York: Bantam Books, 1978), p. 11.

11.   Ernest Partridge, "Nature and Personality," *Journal of Outdoor Education* (Spring 1972), pp. 20–21.

12.   Surya Singer cited in Ram Dass, *Journey to Awakening: A Meditator's Guide* (New York: Bantam Books, 1978), p. 63.

13.   Weber, p. 2.

14.   Alan Drengson, "Wilderness Travel as an Art and as a Paradigm for Outdoor Education," *Quest 32, no. 1* (1980), p. 115.

15.   Ibid., pp. 115–116.

16.   See *Holistic Education Review 1* (Fall 1988).

17.   Author unknown, *Children of the Earth* (Ottawa, Ontario: Novalis, undated), p. 8.

18.   Thoreau, p. 81.

19.   Lawrence Durrell, "Landscape and Character," *Spirit of Place: Letters and Essays on Travel* (New York: E.P. Dutton, 1971), p. 158.

20.   Ralpy Lutts, "Place, Home, and Story in Environmental Education," *Journal of Environmental Education* (Fall 1985), p. 40.

21.   Weber, p. 17.

22.   Drengson, p. 118.

23.   Rachel Carson, *The Sense of Wonder* (New York: Harper and Row, 1956), p. 89.

24.   Wilkinson and Wyman, p. 4.

25.   Thoreau, p. 13.

26.   Bruno Bettleheim, *The Uses of Enchantment* (New York: Penguin Books 1978), p. 4.

27.   Benjamin DeMott, "Learning How to Imagine a Poem: A Proposal for the Teaching of Literature," *English Education* (January 1988), p. 87.

28.   Chang Chung-yuan, *Creativity and Taoism: A Study of Chinese Philosophy, Art, and Poetry* (New York: Harper and Row, 1963), p. 173.

29.   Cited in Chung-yuan, p. 182.

30.   Carson, p. 45.

31.   William Wordsworth, *William Wordsworth: The Poems, Vol. 1* (New York: Penguin Books, 1977), p. 325.

# Joyful Literacy
# at Fair Oaks School

## by Lois Bridges Bird

*Lois Bridges Bird taught first and second grades in California and Arizona before receiving her doctorate in Language and Literacy at the University of Arizona. Since settling in the Bay Area with her husband and three young children, she has taught graduate courses in Language and Literacy at the University of California, Berkeley, and San Francisco State University; served on the Council of Teachers for the Center for the Study of Writing; and worked as a whole language consultant at Fair Oaks School. With Fair Oaks teachers, she wrote and edited* **Becoming a Whole Language School: The Fair Oaks Story.** *Dr. Bird was also co-editor, with Professors Ken and Yetta Goodman, of* **The Whole Language Catalog,** *published by Macmillan-McGraw Hill.*

At the south end of a barrio, between dilapidated apartment buildings whose balconies are draped with laundry hung out to dry, and Raychem, a huge industrial complex, sprawls a salmon-colored stucco school building, enclosed in an asphalt yard. This is Fair Oaks, a whole language, bilingual school in Redwood City, California, a working class community fifteen miles south of San Francisco. The student population is 85 percent Hispanic and 10 percent other minorities such as Tongan, Asian, and black. The majority of the children arrive speaking only their native tongue, Spanish; by fourth grade, most have made the transition into English instruction. It is the poorest school in the district. Many of the students are recent arrivals in the United States who have fled the war in Central America or economic problems in Mexico. The school's principal has estimated that 10 percent of the students live in garages without facilities most of us take for granted. They do not have a head start in anything related to school, but they, like children everywhere, do have a propensity to learn.[1]

This propensity was not evident when Fair Oaks followed the traditional skills regimen of basals and workbooks. According to test scores, students were three and four years below grade level, well below the test band set for similar schools. In 1975, alarmed by the low scores, the California State Department of Education sent a team to Fair Oaks to investigate, thus initiating several years of soul searching on the part

This selection originally appeared in the Winter 1989 issue of *Holistic Education Review*, Vol. 2, No. 4.

of the Fair Oaks faculty. Spurred on by this visit, the faculty began to take a long, hard look at their educational program. Gloria Norton, the resource teacher, tells what happened:

> I had always known that the way we taught reading made little sense. It was boring, it was deadly and, as a person who loved reading, it hurt that my kids hated it and never read books on their own. I hated the way I taught it, too, but I thought it was necessary so that kids could learn the needed skills, and then they could read the good stuff on their own, just like I had.

Gloria and other Fair Oaks teachers visited a "psycholinguistic reading lab" that Ann Bayer had developed in Abbot Middle School in nearby San Mateo, and they loved what they saw. In Gloria's words:

> As we walked into the classrooms there were seventh and eighth graders reading, and that's all there was to see; a room filled with books and a lovely quiet as students sat and read.

Fair Oaks teachers read professional literature on what was currently known about reading; they participated in in-service sessions with Ann Bayer; and, in 1980, Fair Oaks opened its own reading lab stocked with children's literature. Initially, the lab was open just to fourth, fifth, and sixth graders. Gloria recalls those days:

> We read to the kids daily, and daily assured them that they really could pick the books they wanted to read. They didn't trust that, and seemed to view it as a trick. They believed that teachers are supposed to assign books, and kids are supposed to hate it. Within two or three weeks we noticed significant attitudinal changes. Kids loved coming to the reading room. They came at PE time, during recess and even during classroom parties and school dances. They came after school and wanted to borrow books to take home. The first year and a half we lost hundreds of books and we were delighted. No one had ever taken a basal reader home to keep.

While we believe that there are more humane and effective ways to evaluate children's progress in schools than standardized tests, which violate the integrity of both language and learning, we still must respond to a society that uses such tests as the primary measure of a program's success. In 1981–1982, the first full school year that the reading room was open, we charted this growth for all of the fourth, fifth, and sixth graders on the California Test of Basic Skills:

**Average growth for 1981–1982**

| Grade | Total reading | Comprehension |
|-------|---------------|---------------|
| Four  | 1.8 years     | 1.8 years     |
| Five  | 1.6 years     | 1.6 years     |
| Six   | 1.1 years     | 1.4 years     |

Buoyed by these positive results, and helped by outside consultants, Fair Oaks teachers moved beyond a self-contained school reading lab into schoolwide whole language. A grant from the neighborhood corporation, Raychem, helped to pay for intense in-service and summer courses for the teachers, and helped to fill classroom libraries with fine children's literature. In 1984, Redwood City School District made it official: Fair Oaks was designated a bilingual, whole language school.[2]

The Fair Oaks teachers have written a book about our experiences entitled, *Becoming a Whole Language School: The Fair Oaks Story*. We chose the word *becoming* in order to emphasize the process of learning and change. Since continual learning lies at the heart of whole language—for both students and teachers—the only constant is change. We have not arrived, nor can we ever completely arrive. A sequel to the book written five years from now would still necessarily include the word *becoming*.

Through whole language, our students are gaining access to the full power, beauty, and joy of language and literacy. The benefits are many, but perhaps are best understood as four broad themes: experimentation, authenticity, self-reflection, and empowerment.

## Experimentation

The basis of whole language is a model of oral language learning. Learning how to talk may well be the most awesome human undertaking. Every child, by the age of five, except for a small percentage with severe biological handicaps, learns between ten thousand and twenty thousand words, and one thousand rules of grammar, many of which are so filled with contradictions that no contemporary linguist can explain them adequately. Yet the child learns seemingly with little effort and virtually without direct instruction. How does it happen?

The child is an active, creative constructor of language. The infant's incessant babbling, "bah bah," is neither happenstance nor haphazard. The child systematically experiments with new sounds and new forms, gradually learning to differentiate them and to use them to express ever-increasingly sophisticated meanings. Language learning is an intricate orchestration of multiple systems—muscular, linguistic, perceptual, cognitive, and emotional. The child controls the process moment by moment: self-monitoring, self-regulating, and self-correcting.[3]

The parents respond. They accept "bah bah" as "bottle." They extend and elaborate: "Oh Billy. You want your bottle, don't you? A nice warm bottle of milk, because you're hungry. Here it is." Thus, as Billy fills his belly with milk, he is also filled with the rich possibilities of language.

In this way, the parent is a perfect language-learning partner. There is no fear that the child won't learn to talk, no fear that the child is mentally impaired because he says "bah bah" instead of "bottle," no fear that without immediate correction the child will fixate on "bah bah" and go to his grave unable to enunciate "bottle." Perhaps the most important aspect of the parent–child interaction is the parent's absolute faith in the child's ability to learn. Accordingly, children are allowed to experiment with and approximate the adult model in everything they are attempting to learn. We applaud our children's wobbly first steps, their erratic first attempts at eating with a spoon (which often miss the intended mark!), and the lopsided circle with waving tentacles proudly presented as, "A picture of you, Daddy!"

From time immemorial, sensitive parents the world over have known intuitively that this sort of trial and error is fundamental to learning. What a shame that schools abandoned the parental model and turned instead to the theoretically unsound learning theories of behavioral psychologists. Instead of respecting children's natural learning strategies, which invariably begin with the whole and the global, we followed the dictum of the behaviorists and reversed the process.[4]

We succumbed to the seductive idea that in order to learn how to put something together, first you have to take it apart. But a growing body of research across disciplines shows that children learn language, oral and written, by moving from whole to parts: "They focus on meaning before mastering the fine points of form."[5] The complex, integrated processes involved in human language and learning suffer greatly when reduced to a piecemeal presentation. Indeed, language that is broken down into isolated sounds, letters, syllables, and words loses its communicative function and no longer operates like real language. It becomes little more than bite-sized abstractions. The smaller the unit of language, the more abstract it becomes; in fact, there may be nothing more abstract than the alphabet.

Education's alignment with behavioral psychology has led to programmed instruction and to a component model of learning, in which everything, including language, is broken down into its component parts. These parts comprise the skills that children are drilled on endlessly, in keeping with the behaviorists' formula for learning: stimulus–response–reinforcement. Reading becomes little more than breaking down words into discrete units: initial and final consonants, vowels, blends, and the like. Reading in real books is often postponed indefinitely until children have mastered the manipulation of these abstract bits of language, which leads to what Donald Holdaway terms "criminal print starvation."[6]

Writing is equally fragmented. Children begin with handwriting, practicing first the formation of individual letters before graduating to words. All succeeding drills continue in a similar piecemeal fashion: Children memorize lists of isolated spelling words, punctuate rows of sentences copied from textbooks, and diagram pages of paragraphs in their grammar books.

At Fair Oaks, we reject the behaviorists' theories. Instead, we follow children's natural and powerful learning strategies. We embrace Shirley Brice Heath's advice and provide students with models of "joyful literacy." We immerse them in rich, functional print.[7] (The walls in whole language classrooms are said to "drip with print!") We read to them—two, three, four times a day—beautiful literature, poetry, and song. We give them control and ownership of their reading and writing. With our guidance, they experiment and approximate, and they play with literacy in the same way that they play with all that they are attempting to learn. We understand that literacy, like oral language learning, is a developmental process.

For example, five-year-old Marissa uses only initial and final consonants to represent words:

I have a loose tooth.

At age six, having had many opportunities to explore writing, she spells more completely and uses conventional spacing and punctuation:

"Do you Want To PLay?"
saD the uodKh To The
Prisis. The Prisis saD To The
uoaKn 'yes' saD The Prisis
To The 'uoaKn.

Do you want to play?" said the unicorn to the princess. The princess said to the unicorn, "Yes," said the princess to the unicorn.

## Authenticity

Fair Oaks teachers try to avoid lessons that involve "inauthentic language"—language stripped of pragmatic purpose that occurs only in compliance with teacher-directed assignments. The focus is always on meaning. Just as parents help their children to make sense of conversation, whole language teachers help students to make sense of print wherever they encounter it, whether on grocery shelves, along city streets, in fine children's literature, in the local newspaper, or in reference books. We also help our students use written language to communicate and to express their own meanings. Students write across the curriculum for a wide range of authentic purposes: to protest governmental policies in Central America, to explain to friends how to construct a backyard tent, to note information gathered from an afternoon in the library researching the life of manatees.[8]

The following is an example of language use for a very pragmatic purpose:

Mr. smiTh,
we have a brocen
TebR. 1T nios scus.
can samebaf FixeT
Puis?

Thank you
Chris #14

Dear Mr. Smith, We have a broken table. It needs screws. Can somebody fix it, please? Thank you. (signed by the teacher with room number)

This was written by a Spanish-speaking five year old who was self-trans-itioning into English. It is typical of the notes we receive daily in the school office. Students use reading and writing constantly for a wide range of purposes—to get tables fixed, or, in Peggy Smullin's first grade, to mend hurt feelings. As a new teacher last year, Peggy was over-whelmed by the constant skirt tugging and cries for help from the children: "Teacher, Marisol hit me!" or "Teacher, Pablo stole my pencil!" So she developed problem sheets. "I have a problem" is written on one side, and "Yo tengo una problema" is written on the other. Now, when two kids bump heads, they grab a problem sheet, write about their problem, and suggest a possible solution[9]:

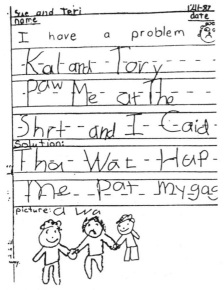

I have a problem:
Kai and Tory pulled me at the shirt, and I cried.
Solution:
They will help me put my jacket away.

One of the most exciting and productive ways in which children are using literacy at Fair Oaks is in the interactive reading and writing program initiated by Shirley Brice Heath in Leslie Mangiola's fifth grade class in 1985 (it's now schoolwide).[10] Twice weekly, Leslie's students team up with Kathleen Short's kindergarten class. Each upper grade student is paired with a kindergartner for half an hour of shared reading and writing. At the end of this period, the fifth graders return to their classroom, take out their stenographer's notepads, and record their ex-periences with their tutees.

These records serve the same purpose that the anecdotal records of a whole language teacher serve: They inform the tutor of their young friend's progress and suggest ways that the tutor might respond next. Once Leslie's students have finished recording their experiences, they all gather on the rug for a fifteen-minute group share. This time provides the tutors with the opportunity to talk about their frustrations and concerns, as well as their breakthroughs and triumphs with their young tutees. When possible, the kindergarten teacher attends these sessions, and, as one colleague talking with another, lends her knowledge and perceptions about the kindergartners as the fifth graders share theirs.[11]

## Self-reflection

Although there is some debate as to the actual value of metacognition and metalinguistic awareness—the ability to reflect upon one's own cognitive and linguistic processing— there are those, such as education researcher Courtney Cazden, who consider it the very essence of education. Debate over its significance notwithstanding, students in whole language classrooms frequently and spontaneously examine their own thinking, reading, and writing. Ray Dawley's fourth-grade students participated recently in a literature study of Robert Smith's *Chocolate Fever*, a clever story about a little boy who drenches everything—hamburgers, pizza, breakfast cereal—with thick, gooey chocolate syrup.[12] The result is a chocolate lover's nightmare: The boy comes down with chocolate fever and breaks out, from his head to his toes, in brown spots the size of chocolate chips. The children agreed that the book was good fun from start to happy ending, but wondered how Robert Smith did it. What tricks of the writing trade did he employ to craft the book's humor and excitement? Nine-year-old Karla thought she knew:

> He saw first on his mind . . . what the author did is first, he saw . . . what he was going to write down. Because what I do is as soon as I'm writing, ideas come to my head like this when I'm writing, writing, writing, writing. Soon, I think he did the same thing! He saw the picture on his mind before he writes it down.

Karla is a writer. She understands her own writing process, and she senses what Robert Smith must do as he puts pen to paper, or sits in front of his keyboard.

What about the content of the story? How did Robert Smith know what to write? Where did he get his ideas? As writers themselves, the children have a ready answer. Rebecca explains:

> He gets . . . he gets . . . like if he was reading a long book and he gets ideas from books or from somebody else; like I was writing a story at my friend's and they were playing a guitar, and everything and that, and that gave me an idea . . . like, "She was walking down the street and she saw a man playing a guitar." and that's, and that's what I wrote down. It gives me ideas when I see something or hear something.

The teacher responds with support, refining Rebecca's insights as a writer:

> You know, Rebecca, what you are doing? You are talking like a writer. You know, that's exactly what writers do. Once you become a writer, every little thing that happens to you becomes a potential story. You're always taking little notes in your head. "Hey, that's something I could write about!"

Karla and Rebecca are readers, and they are also writers. But most important, they are thinkers. Able to "turn thought and language in on themselves," able, as Margaret Donaldson says, "to direct their own thought processes in a thoughtful manner."[13]

How did Karla and Rebecca develop their insights as readers and writers? Through memorizing phonics rules? Through identifying context clues? Through practicing writing topic sentences? No. Their insights have evolved through reading, writing, and much discussion about books, authors, language, ideas, and understanding. At their teacher's invitation, they have entered the human dialogue of literacy.

## Empowerment

Addressing a Center for Expansion of Language and Thinking (CELT) rejuvenation conference held in June of this year, Mike Torbe said, "If students were really empowered, they'd walk out of the classroom." Fair Oaks students haven't abandoned their classrooms, nor do we think that they want to; in fact, Fair Oaks now boasts the highest daily student enrollment district-wide. Through the freedom and support and respect for the language learner that whole language provides, our students have come to believe in themselves as capable, creative learners who know what they need and how to get it.

Two years ago, a young woman, only weeks out of her credential program, was hired to teach sixth grade at Fair Oaks. It soon became apparent that she was overwhelmed and needed help. Thinking it might ease her burden, Gloria suggested that she use a basal for a few weeks while she got herself established. She accepted that advice; her students, however, did not. Many of them had been at Fair Oaks since kindergarten and had never seen a basal, much less used one, and their first reaction was, "Hey! What happened to our *real* books?!" Their second reaction was to go on strike and refuse to read until the literature books were returned. Now that's empowerment, and that was the end of the basal!

Sucar discovered empowerment in another way. In March 1986, when he was eight years old, he transferred from a traditional skills school to Fair Oaks. At first, Sucar found our program somewhat overwhelming. It seemed that he had so much freedom and so many choices. But it didn't take long for him to settle in, and soon he was relishing his experiences in his new whole language classroom, particularly during writer's workshop, when he was free to write about anything of his own choosing, just like a professional writer. Two weeks after transferring, Sucar published his first book by pressing his neatly written text between two cardboard covers and binding them together with colored electrician's tape. Then he wrote the following letter to his teacher:

April 7, 1986
Thank you for leting me grow my own stary I had fun riting my stary becuase It made me happy. The end.

Thank you for letting me grow my own stories. I had fun writing my story because it made me happy. The end.
Teacher's Note: I enjoyed reading your story, Sucar. You can write one anytime you'd like!

Perhaps nine-year-old Karla explained empowerment best. When I asked her what she liked the most about Fair Oaks, she thought long and hard before answering: but, when she finally found the words she wanted, I felt my pulse quicken and goose bumps creep up the back of my neck. It was the kind of response whole language teachers live to hear. She said, "At other schools, they teach you about other people's ideas; at Fair Oaks, they help you discover your own ideas."

At Fair Oaks, we will continue to help our students "grow their own stories," and "discover their own ideas," and, in the process, the students will expand and refine our understanding of what it means to be joyfully literate.

## Notes

1. Lois Bridges Bird, ed., *Becoming a Whole Language School: The Fair Oaks Story* (New York: Richard C. Owen Publications, 1989).

2. Gloria Norton, "What Does It Take to Ride a Bike?" in *Becoming a Whole Language School: The Fair Oaks Story*, edited by Lois Bridges Bird.

3. Don Holdaway, *The Foundations of Literacy* (New York: Ashton Scholastic, 1979).

4. Frank Smith, *Insult to Intelligence* (New York: Arbor House, 1986).

5. Donald Graves and Virgina Stuart, *Write from the Start: Tapping Your Child's Natural Writing Ability* (New York: Dutton, 1985).

6. Donald Holdaway, *The Foundations of Literacy*.

7. Shirley Brice Heath, *Inside Learners* (Stanford, CA: Stanford Univ. Press, 1986).

8. Carole Edelsky, *Writing in a Bilingual Classroom: Habia Una Vez* (Norwood, NJ: Ablex, 1986).

9. Margaret Smullin, "Working and Playing with Literacy," in *Becoming a Whole Language School: The Fair Oaks Story*, edited by Lois Bridges Bird.

10. Heath, *Inside Learners*.

11. Leslie Mangiola, "Interactive Reading and Writing" in *Becoming a Whole Language School: The Fair Oaks Story*, edited by Lois Bridges Bird.

12. Robert Smith, *Chocolate Fever* (Coward, McCann & Geoghegan, 1972).

13. Margaret Donaldson, *Children's Minds* (New York: Norton, 1978).

# Jefferson County Open High School
## Philosophy and Purpose

### by Ruth Steele

*Ruth Steele is principal of Jefferson County Open High and has served on its faculty since 1977. She has led numerous student trips to Mexico and various parts of the United States, and has been a Fulbright exchange teacher in London. She has worked in Jefferson County schools for 24 years as an art teacher, media specialist, and innovator of alternative programs.*

Jefferson County Open High School is a public alternative secondary school of choice located in Evergreen, Colorado. The open schools in Jefferson County began with an elementary program, Open Living School, created in 1970 in response to requests from parents. Then in 1975 the high school program, Mountain Open High School, was added. Although the name was changed by the Board of Education to reflect the county-wide constituency, the school is best known as Mountain Open.

The purpose of the Open High School is to provide an environment that will foster the development of the potential in each student through an emphasis on individualization and self-directed learning to prepare students for the transition from childhood to adulthood. A program has been developed to facilitate this transition through a series of passages which demonstrate a student's readiness to be an adult. While built on the mission and goals of the school district, the approach differs significantly from that of the conventional high school.

The Open High School is a small school of choice. Since the school began, its community (staff, students, and parents with the support of the school district) have shared the belief that these two characteristics, smallness and choice, are necessary for a program that emphasizes individualization and self-direction. The Open High School is small for the sake of having a community where everyone is known, where no

This selection originally appeared in the Summer 1988 issue of *Holistic Education Review*, Vol. 1, No. 2.

one is anonymous. The enrollment has been limited to a maximum of 235. Students are at the Open High School by choice, as are staff members. Whether they hear about the school through friends and acquaintances, counselors and teachers in conventional schools, or news coverage, they share a desire to be a part of an alternative learning community.

These two factors alone could be responsible for the positive climate at the school, but structures have been created which facilitate the continuous development of a sense of community where the individual is valued. One of the most important of these structures is the advisory system.

## Close personal relationships

There is a belief that each student in the school needs at least one adult who knows, cares for, and will listen to him/her. Within the advisory relationship, a student and his or her advisor will develop an individualized educational program based on that student's unique strengths and needs. Advisor responsibilities include helping students set goals and determining how to reach them; monitoring accomplishments and progress in the personal, social, and intellectual domains; communicating with the home; and helping the student determine when the expectations for graduation have been met. In choosing an advisor, a student chooses an advisory group which meets weekly to discuss mutual concerns and plan activities to build group identity.

The governance of the school is a shared responsibility. Staff and students convene in a weekly all school meeting to discuss common concerns, organize groups for action, make decisions, solve problems, reach agreements, and share in celebrations of accomplishment. This meeting, called Governance, is democracy in action.

As students move through the transition to adulthood, their rates of progress and development vary greatly. Students are encouraged to challenge themselves and to learn from their mistakes. In the process of learning, a student makes comparisons between how he or she was relative to how he or she is, or would like to become, rather than comparing self with others.

Grades do not exist at JCOHS. Students are not separated into sophomores, juniors, and seniors, nor are letters or numbers used as a measure of the quality of a student's performance. There is no credit system. Students are expected to demonstrate competence as they work toward personal goals. The issue of quality of performance is highly personal, so the emphasis is on helping students become capable of realistic self-evaluation.

This self-evaluation is an ongoing process for each student at the school. At the completion of each class or other learning experience, students write evaluations of their own performance and seek responses from their teachers or mentors. These responses validate the students' self-evaluations. Evaluations and responses are shared with advisors who help students become aware of the continuing cycle of experience and reflection which gives personal meaning to those experiences. Evaluation is a part of an ongoing process for the student, rather than an end in itself.

The students are encouraged to consider the world their school, and to become aware of the learning that occurs in all of their experiences. For this reason students are able to evaluate or document how such experiences contribute to their growth and development.

## Walkabout

In addition to the advisory system, there are other structures which provide a framework for students so that they can set goals and organize their learning experiences to work toward graduation. There are three phases to this program, known as the Walkabout, a version of the Australian Aborigines' rite of passage, based on the work of Maurice Gibbons.

Phase 1 is a nine-week introduction to the culture of the school with an emphasis on experiential learning in and out of the school. About half of the student's time is structured by required attendance in Governance, a week-long backpacking trip, group and individual advising, triads which are small support groups made up of old and new students, and one full day in an interest group of choice. In one typical semester, interest groups were Spaces and Places, an introduction to design and construction; Challenge Adventure, including outdoor activities such as rock climbing, kayaking, and cycling; Production, organizing and producing for the theater; and Service and the City, emphasizing using the city as a resource and providing service. In the interest groups students share experiences, learn to set individual and group goals, and reflect on learning through discussions and written evaluations. During this phase, the student, working with the advisor, begins an extensive self-assessment in the personal, social, and intellectual domains. The other half of a student's time is spent in classes, activities, and learning experiences agreed upon with the advisor. All of these experiences, both required and selected, provide an introduction to self-directed learning, an orientation, or disorientation as it is sometimes called, which has proven to be an essential step in moving a student into the school so that he or she can experience success, providing a necessary base for the next two phases.

Phase 2 is the stage for building a foundation of knowledge, skills, attitudes, and behaviors necessary to take on an adult role in society. The IEP (Individualized Educational Program) provides a focus for this phase. Each student develops, with his or her advisor, an IEP based on the self-assessment begun in Phase 1. The IEP is the basis for the selection of learning experiences for the MAP (Mutually Agreeable Program), a schedule negotiated by the advisor and advisee. There are countless possibilities for learning; some are listed below.

—Classes at JCOHS, other high schools, community college, or adult education.

—Warren Occupational-Technical Center
—School trips
—Participation in running the school—Munchie, Leadership, Hiring, Features, office help, Preschool
—Community learning—mentorships
—Community Service
—Athletics at other schools or recreation centers
—Music at other schools
—Theater and dance—Denver Center, Arvada Center, and community groups
—Skills lab
—Independent study
—Teaching or assisting with a class at JCOHS or other schools
—Computer software for self-help
—Job
—Passages

Students are encouraged, in fact they are expected to be creative in the discovery of learning opportunities wherever they are, in or out of the school. It is by monitoring the MAP that the advisor keeps track of the attendance of each student, for attendance is based on meeting commitments to the MAP rather than physical presence in front of a teacher.

Extended trips, from one to three weeks in length, provide unique and valuable opportunities for individual growth and group development. Learning goes on 24 hours a day and becomes relevant as students become involved in the real world beyond the confines of the school building. Personal, social, and intellectual development are obvious to students and staff alike as the result of the intensity of trip experiences. A few of the places students and teachers have traveled to recently include Mazatlan to live with Mexican families and learn Spanish; Yellowstone to study history and ecology; the Navajo Reservation in Arizona to plant fruit trees; Tallahassee, Florida, to work on a red wolf habitat for the Junior Museum; Cortez, Colorado, to reconstruct an Anasazi kiva; the Bahamas to learn about sailing and oceanography; and the mountains of Colorado to develop skills in winter survival.

In phase 3, students develop and pursue personally challenging projects that demonstrate their ability to use, in real-life situations, the skills and abilities they have developed. There are six areas, known as Passages, that must be addressed through these projects. The Passage areas are Adventure, Career Exploration, Creativity, Global Awareness and Volunteer Service, Logical Inquiry, and Practical Skills. Each passage must be student-initiated, experiential, preplanned, intense, and in many cases outside the school. These Passages are the actual Walkabout, the transition to adulthood.

There is some overlap of phase 2 and phase 3, and the use of the IEP continues until a student is ready to graduate. The length of time to complete those phases varies with each individual, but generally students take from two to four years to complete the Walkabout process. They begin with a highly structured phase with a great deal of teacher attention, move to a less structured phase in which they work closely with advisors to set up individual programs that include classes and a variety of other learning options, then complete their work in a largely independent manner. They are expected to take increasing responsibility for their own education and, therefore, for their own lives.

## Educational philosophy

There are many philosophical assumptions implied by the very existence of JCOHS. Some of them are listed below. These shared beliefs, held in common by the staff, and eventually embraced by the students, are the basis for a vision of an ideal school or learning environment. This vision provides a focus of understanding that allows for autonomy and creativity as the staff, students, and parents are active participants in the evolution of that ideal school.

- All students already have within them all that they need to become self-actualized adults. To educate them means to help draw out these inner resources so that they may recognize their own gifts, in order to develop, use, and cherish them. The task of the staff is to help students discover their unique talents and then to help them build the skills and confidence to develop these gifts to their fullest.
- Individual rates and levels of development are recognized and respected and students are allowed and guided to make appropriate choices of learning experiences.
- Different learning styles are acknowledged and students are encouraged to work from their strengths to develop those areas that are weaker.
- Physical, safety, and security needs must be met before a student can develop a sense of belonging and self-esteem necessary to accept or seek intellectual or academic challenge.
- Experience can be the best teacher if one reflects on the experience and learns from it. A function of the school is to help students be aware of what they are learning, how they learn, and to discover the personal meanings in what they learn.
- Learning can take place in any environment and continues throughout life. One of the most important tasks of the school is to help students learn how to be self-directed learners.
- Learning is a personal responsibility, but one that can be shared. Students become partners with both staff and other students in the process of learning. Competition is minimized and cooperation emphasized.
- Skill without motivation is empty. Motivation without skill is frustrating. JCOHS is not just for the self-motivated few, but should be an environment that stimulates both self-motivation and skill development. One way this is done is to remove as many extrinsic sources of motivation as possible. Thus students are forced to confront themselves, and with help from supportive staff, students, and parents, to create, for themselves, purpose and meaning in their lives.

• Freedom can be painful. It involves learning from one's mistakes, asking for help, and understanding interdependence. To become an effective citizen in a democracy, one must have the chance to make choices, try out various options and possibilities, to fail, and to be given another chance.

• To develop morally, students need real situations that allow them to understand the consequences of their behavior and they need a variety of role models, both peer and adult.

• Curriculum is the process whereby the school helps each student integrate his or her experiences, both in and out of school, planned and unplanned, into a coherent framework that has personal meaning for that student.

• Personal and institutional growth and change are to be encouraged. The creation of the ideal school is an individual and group responsibility and is an ongoing process.

These assumptions have come from many sources: personal belief systems of the school community concerning human nature and the process of learning, trial and error, readings from a variety of authors, past and present assessment and evaluation of the program as an ongoing process, and perhaps most significantly, the expertise, commitment, knowledge, experience, and intuition of a highly qualified dedicated staff.

The Open High School has grown and developed during its brief history from a shared vision based on commonly held beliefs about the importance of providing a climate that allows and encourages the actualization of individual potential within a community of learners. The process will go on as the members of that community—staff, students, and parents—continue to be creative participants in the process of the evolution of an ideal school based on that vision.

# What Makes Alternative Schools Alternative? The "Blue Ox" Speaks!

## by Dave Lehman

*Dave Lehman has been involved with the Alternative Community School for a number of years, and has been active in alternative school organizations.*

We get asked the question, "What Makes Alternative Schools Alternative?" more times than I would like to remember here at the Alternative Community School in Ithaca, New York. (ACS was pronounced "Ox" by our students early in our history, thus our mascot, the blue ox.) It's hard to answer in words, sort of like the Taoist response to the query about the Tao—it's something you really come to know only through experiencing/living it. But that's not satisfactory for most folks and so we go on to try to describe our school and what makes it different.

In some ways ACS is no different from other schools in Ithaca—our kids ride the school bus, we have certified teachers, and we still teach things like English, social studies, and math. Oh yes, we're different in that we are a combined middle school and high school, but such schools exist elsewhere in New York. And yes, we are smaller—only 215 students in grades six through twelve—but there are still plenty of small schools throughout the country (although not enough!—and too many are still being closed and consolidated into huge schools or factories!).

What makes ACS different has more to do with the way we put our program together, and how we relate to each other. We have *options* for ways of studying everything. Specifically, we offer five different general ways in which students may freely choose to pursue their secondary school education (and even a sixth for our older students). One option is our *classes* or courses. In some ways these are similar to more conventional schools for they meet regularly for 45-minute periods—but only four days a week rather than the typical five, and they typically range in size from 10 to 20 students. Most importantly, they are generated by

This selection originally appeared in the Summer 1988 issue of *Holistic Education Review*, Vol. 1, No. 2.

the staff and students, not by some central office far removed from the specific persons involved in the teaching and learning. Thus, you will find such titles in our English offerings as "Crunch English," "I in writing," "Kings and Things," "Black Voices," "Women in Literature," "Revolution and Romanticism," "Humorous Presentations," "Star-Crossed Lovers," and "Photographic Communication" along with "Shakespeare," "Modern American Literature," and "Creative Writing."

## Beyond the classroom

A second option is our *extended projects*. These projects are offered on Tuesday afternoons and Thursday mornings for longer blocks of time, are often interdisciplinary in nature, and often involve doing things out of the school building as well. These have recently included: "Stories for Children," creating original stories with and for the preschoolers also located in our building; "Cross Country Bicycle Touring," physical education with a first aid/CPR component; "Koffee Klatch," creative writing based on the stimuli of trips to different places in Ithaca; "Video Project," meeting after school hours to have the use of a local community-access television studio to produce youth-oriented programs once a month on such topics as "teenage sexuality" and "violence in America"; as well as other projects. We often utilize other adults from the community, including parents, to come in and offer projects such as "Tie-dying and Batiking," "Tolkien: the Man and the Work," "Watercolor Painting," "Ethnography," and "Fencing." Also, our staff can teach things outside their typical subject areas—e.g., an English teacher who teaches karate (being a third degree black belt), a social studies teacher working with a math teacher to run our cottage industry, "The Silkscreen Workshop," or a special ed teacher who led the Spring canoe group.

A third option at ACS is *independent study*. Here students select the topic they want to study and/or the skills they want to learn and contract with a teacher to work on it independently. Even our middle schoolers have demonstrated their capabilities to do this, particularly when it's their own internal motivation that interests them. Here the teacher is a resource, a guide, a consultant, a critic offering support and ideas to the student who is really doing the work.

Our fourth option is *community studies*. Here we actually have three different programs under the coordination of a half-time teacher. There is the familiar "work study" program for our high school students who have paying jobs out in the community, but can also earn elective credit for this "learning from working." Then there are our "community place-ments," sort of like mini-apprenticeships where middle school or high school students are involved in "learning by doing" at everything from a local veterinarian or a retail sales store to a genetics research laboratory or the local fire station. Here the intent also is career exploration—students having the opportunity to try on various kinds of occupations to see where their own interests may lie. The third community studies program is CAPS—Community Academic Placements—where students can earn credit in various subject areas through "learning by doing" at a local business, industry, or social agency. Patterned after New York City's alternative high school program "City as School," our community studies coordinator works with the student, a teacher from the relevant subject area, and someone from the work site in the community to develop a learning plan for that particular location.

Our fifth curricular option at ACS is *learning at other educational organizations in the community.* This can include taking a German course at our conventional high school, or a calculus course at one of the nearby universities, or a criminology course at our local community college, or music lessons at the Community School of Art and Music, or physical education through a local ballet studio. Any of these can be integrated into a student's weekly schedule and be part of his or her total educational program.

The sixth option at ACS is for high school students only and is *credit by examination.* The student may earn up to six and a half credits by successfully passing a standardized New York State Regents exam in a given subject. This is done in conjunction with a teacher of that subject and includes either an oral exam or a special project as well.

Thus, a significant part of what makes ACS different as an alternative school is the choice of ways of learning things.

## A democratic community

Another key aspect of our program which makes us different is our *democratic self-governance.* We believe strongly in students participating fully with the staff in running the school (and parents as well, particularly in major policy decisions, including hiring of staff). Here we have several structures, from our overall "Advisory Board" (composed of student, staff, parent, other school district, and community representatives), Parent Steering Committee and "Open Parents Nights" to our student-run (staff-facilitated) committees, small Family Groups, and weekly All School Town Meetings.

Yet as important as all the above features of our alternative school are, the underlying thing which makes us different from most schools is the *relationship of students and staff.* Rather than the all-too-common adversarial relationship found in our large conventional secondary schools where teachers are primarily concerned with control and students are primarily concerned with "getting over on the teacher," our students and staff relate to each other on a first name basis out of a mutual respect in which they try to work cooperatively rather than constantly being in conflict. There is more of a relaxed, informal, friendly, family atmosphere about the school in which people really come to care about each other, and can even genuinely enjoy teaching and learning together. It is not uncommon at ACS to see a student give a teacher a hug of thanks!

But lastly, I would hasten to add that *none of these features of our "alternativeness" are things that can only happen here at ACS.* We believe they can happen in any secondary school in the country and we are involved in various state, regional, and national educational organizations to help others see such possibilities within themselves and their schools. We see our work as liberating, helping staff find the freedom to teach, students the freedom to learn, and all of us to find the freedom to be a caring community. In this regard, education is political, for we are all either revolutionaries, striving for this freedom for all, or we are oppressors, denying this freedom to some (and, therefore to all).

So, perhaps in the end, deep down inside there is really nothing different or "alternative" about us at the "Blue Ox"; for isn't this what we all want?—the freedom to be fully our own selves in a community in which everyone else can fully be themselves, and in which we can all fully develop our unique potential?

# Educating as an Art: The Waldorf Approach

## by Roberto Trostli

*Roberto Trostli received his B.A. from Columbia College and his M.A. from the University of Cambridge. Since 1981 he has been a class teacher at the Rudolf Steiner School in New York, which he attended as a child.*

In the early decades of this century a seed was planted which has born fruit manyfold. It was planted in faith and in hope: faith in man's capacity to transform himself and his society; hope for the future of mankind and of the earth. Out of an impulse towards social renewal the first Waldorf School was founded.

Waldorf education has now spread throughout the world. During the last decade so many new Waldorf schools have been founded that is difficult to keep track of how many there are. Together they form one of the largest independent school systems in the world—with more than 100 schools in North America, over 400 worldwide, and an estimated enrollment of 50,000 students. Every Waldorf school is truly independent; no central organization determines that a Waldorf school should be established in a particular town or city. Rather, a group of parents who desire a Waldorf education for their children work together for a period of years to establish a social and financial base that will support a school. Waldorf schools usually begin as a nursery or kindergarten; when conditions are right, new classes are added year by year until the school reaches its full complement of grades. Given that every Waldorf school has been founded independently and has had to overcome both internal difficulties and external challenges, the rapid growth of Waldorf schools reveals the eagerness with which this form of education is being sought by parents throughout the world.

### History

The first Waldorf School was founded in 1919 in Stuttgart, Germany by Emil Molt, the director of the Waldorf Astoria Company. Molt's deci-

This selection originally appeared in the Spring 1988 issue of *Holistic Education Review*, Vol. 1, No. 1.

sion to found a school grew out of his concern for the future of Germany and the other central European countries that had been devastated by the First World War. He recognized that central Europe's hope lay not with those who had experienced the destruction and upheaval, but with the new generation of school children. If they could leave behind the old modes of thought that had proved inadequate for the modern world and could develop new capacities, perhaps they would be able to forge a brighter future.

If these children were to develop capacities that would allow them to transform society, they would need to be taught in a new way—in a way that addressed their essential humanity, that enhanced their concern for other people, and that fostered a sense of responsibility for the earth. They would need an education that went beyond the dry, intellectual schooling of the past, an education that would cultivate their artistic abilities and develop their practical skills; above all they would need an education that nurtured the capacities that would allow them to adapt to a rapidly changing world. Emil Molt knew the man who could develop a form of education that would meet these needs; this man was Rudolf Steiner.

Born in 1861 in Austria, Rudolf Steiner studied sciences at Technische Hochschule in Vienna. As a young man he edited the Weimar edition of Goethe's scientific writings, studied philosophy, and received his doctorate in that field. Rudolf Steiner's first major work, *The Philosophy of Freedom*, appeared in 1894 and established the foundation for the worldview known as anthroposophy. In the early decades of the twentieth century, Rudolf Steiner became increasingly well known throughout Europe as an author and lecturer; he published over 50 books and gave approximately 6,000 lectures on subjects that included philosophy, history, the sciences, the arts, and education. In 1919, at Emil Molt's behest, Rudolf Steiner trained the teachers for the first Waldorf School. He developed the curriculum, gave practical courses in teaching methods, and worked with the faculty of the school until his death in 1925. Because of its philosophical base and its innovative teaching methods, the original Waldorf School quickly grew, gaining international recognition and inspiring the establishment of new Waldorf schools in Germany and many other countries.

## Waldorf education: A total approach

What characterizes the Waldorf approach to education? In my view, three salient features may be distinguished: Waldorf education is based on a developmental approach that addresses the needs of the growing child and maturing adolescent. Waldorf teachers strive to transform education into an art that educates the whole child—the heart and the hands, as well as the head. Waldorf schools are committed to developing capacities as well as skills; their highest endeavor is "to develop free human beings who are able of themselves to impart purpose and direction to their lives."

## Child development

In Rudolf Steiner's view, the process of human development unfolds in cycles of approximately seven years each. Waldorf schools base their curriculum and methods on the recognition that during each of these stages children need forms of instruction and specific subjects and activities that will encourage the healthy process of development.

In his first seven years, a child undergoes a tremendous process of physical development. At no other stage of life is the actual physical development of the body so striking, so profound. During these years, when the young child establishes his relationship to the physical world he is deeply affected by everything and everyone around him. Because it is in his nature to imitate all that he encounters, the words, gestures, activities, and objects in a young child's life make an impression that may remain for the rest of his life.

In the second seven years of life, the child's physical growth continues, but this process is overshadowed by his inner development. During these years, the elementary school age child develops his inner life, his life of imagination and fantasy. Between the ages of seven and fourteen the child is deeply influenced by the people around him. Those people whom a child encounters at this age make a strong impression on him and leave an indelible imprint on his life of feeling.

In the third stage, from about age fourteen to twenty-one, the adolescent again goes through a dramatic process of physical and emotional development, but this process is overshadowed by the development of the thought life. During this stage of development, the adolescent is particularly receptive to the ideas and ideals he encounters. By considering and contemplating the thoughts of others, the adolescent is helped in developing the ability to form his own thoughts.

The sections below are an attempt to illustrate how the curriculum of the Waldorf school addresses the needs of each stage in the life of the growing child.

## The Waldorf preschool

Young children soak up impressions of all that surrounds them. Waldorf teachers thus strive to provide their students with examples that are worthy of imitation in a setting that is full of beauty. Because the physical environment of the preschool age child affects him so strongly, great care is taken in the choice of materials which surround the child and with which he works and plays.

Anyone who has watched young children at play knows that they become totally engaged in whatever they do; to them play is work and work is play. The young child lives in a world of deeds, and Waldorf preschool programs strive to imbue these deeds with an imaginative and practical element. In the preschool, children are encouraged to engage in creative play which strengthens their power of imagination. As a complement to creative play, children also participate in a variety of household tasks. They learn to cook and to bake, to sweep and to wash, to hammer and to build. These activities are a great educative force, for at a time when the child is becoming aware of his body and of his movements, these practical tasks develop both large and small muscle coordination and a sense of spatial relationships. By participating in meaningful tasks children's love of work is strengthened, and they learn to apply themselves with devotion and joy.

Young children respond strongly to rhythm, and they thrive when there is rhythm and regularity in their lives. Waldorf preschools therefore organize their schedule of activities so that they will have a strong rhythmic element. In all Waldorf preschools each day has a rhythm. The morning might begin with a period of play and work followed by circle time, consisting of verses, nursery rhymes, songs, and circle games. A local park or play area allows for a session of outdoor play, and the morning session ends with a nature story or a folk tale. Each week has its rhythm as well, with one day for baking, another for painting, a third for crafts, and so on. Seasonal activities such as harvesting grain, planting bulbs, tapping maple trees, or gathering nuts serve to deepen the children's awareness of the natural world around them, and colorful seasonal festivals, which celebrate the bounty of the autumn or the advent of spring foster a connection to the cycle of the year. Through such activities, which are imbued with a rhythmic element, a child's feeling for the cycles of life and of nature is strengthened. In later years this feeling may translate into a sense of well-being in the world and a sense of connection to the natural world.

Waldorf teachers recognize that the first seven years are a time when the child must be free to grow and develop without the intellectual demands of formal academic instruction. In our experience, academic learning at too early an age is achieved at the expense of the healthful unfolding of the best qualities and capacities inherent in this stage of childhood. Although children in the Waldorf preschool are not taught to read or write, the daily, weekly, and seasonal activities in which they participate prepare and strengthen them for their elementary school years. Called by different names, learning readiness activities have been a part of the Waldorf preschool curriculum for the past seven decades. Songs and nursery rhymes cultivate a sense for language and the world of words. Listening to stories, watching marionette shows, and participating in dramatic play strengthen the power of memory and the imagination. Similarly, counting games and rhythmic activities build a solid foundation for arithmetic and number skills, while the various practical tasks help children develop coordination and the ability to concentrate.

Through such activities, Waldorf preschools prepare students for intellectual learning in the years ahead. By strengthening the imagination, cultivating a sense of wonder, and developing their students' enthusiasm for work, Waldorf preschool teachers work to prepare children not only for their years in school, but for the rest of their lives.

## The elementary school

During the first seven years children establish the foundation of their relationship to the world around them. From the age of six or seven to fourteen, they undergo a tremendous process of inner growth and begin to discover the world within themselves. Whereas the young child learns primarily from his environment and by imitating the words, gestures, and actions of those around him, the child of elementary school age learns through his feelings for those who teach him. Rudolf Steiner emphasized the importance of cultivating this element of feeling for the teachers in a child's life, so children in the elementary grades have a class teacher for a number of years, ideally from first through eighth grades. Although each class is also taught by teachers who specialize in foreign languages, or in music, crafts, woodwork, physical education, etc., the class teacher is in the unique position of working with a class over a long span of time and of introducing and developing the various subjects of the curriculum.

When they first encounter the idea of a class teacher, people typically ask, "What if a child doesn't get along with his teacher?" or "How can one person teach all the academic subjects from first through eighth grades?" These are legitimate questions which deserve consideration, although it should be mentioned that most parents who have been connected with a Waldorf school for a number of years find that their initial concerns proved unfounded.

In our experience, children enter elementary school with tremendous eagerness and with boundless faith in the individuals who stand before them. The young child usually feels a natural and deep connection with his teacher because the teacher stands as a representative of mankind who, day by day, will lead the class into ever wider explorations of the world. By his sincere interest in each child and his genuine enthusiasm for each subject, the teacher tries to prove himself worthy of the children's confidence and love.

Unfortunately, teachers are not always blessed with the gifts of love and trust that children display in such abundance. If a teacher finds that he does not naturally relate well to certain children, he has the duty to understand what lies behind his feelings. More than understanding is needed, however; the class teacher must work on such difficulties within himself until he has transformed them. The fact that he will face these children every day for many years provides both a context and an incentive to pursue such inner work with vigor.

Children are remarkably perceptive beings, and they respond to the special efforts a teacher makes to work on himself and to rise above his shortcomings. Thus the children themselves help teachers in their inner tasks; through their response, our feelings for them are transformed and our relationship with them enriched. Many teachers experience an extraordinary bond to those children with whom they have had difficulties and for whom they have had to struggle within themselves. This bond grows out of the teacher's striving, out of his work to transform himself, and out of a child's response to these efforts. In an age where relationships so easily dissolve for lack of commitment, a child is strengthened by the knowledge that his class teacher loves him, will stand by him, and will accompany him through this part of his journey through life. Such knowledge gives children faith in the power of human relationships to endure.

Throughout the years, the class teacher uses every opportunity to develop in the children a sense of the unity and interconnectedness of the world of knowledge. He teaches each subject with reference to other ones, developing and establishing connections between them. Although he must work to attain a basic foundation of knowledge in all subjects, the class teacher need not be a specialist in every field. More than expertise, it is the teacher's interest in, and enthusiasm for the subject which inspires his students. Many teachers find that those subjects in which they have had the least prior experience are those which they most successfully teach, because through the teacher's own learning process, a magical ingredient enters his teaching.

Class teaching thus demands the continuing education of the teacher. He must become a mathematician, as well as a musician, a poet as well as a painter, a sculptor as well as a scientist. Few teachers have a natural aptitude for all of these areas, and as he works to refine his skills in the various subjects, the teacher demonstrates to the children that much can be achieved through application and effort. In a time of increasing specialization and narrowness, the class teacher stands as an example before the child, confirming the child's belief that the possibility for understanding the world is within his grasp.

## The Waldorf curriculum

Developed by Rudolf Steiner and refined over the past seven decades, the Waldorf curriculum is designed to introduce students to all the important branches of knowledge. It is conceived as a unity, and its subjects are introduced and developed in a sequence that mirrors the inner development of the growing child.

Since mathematics occupies a central position in a Waldorf school's academic program, a sketch of the mathematics curriculum might indicate how topics introduced at a particular time meet the child's interest and needs at each stage of development.

In the first grade, mathematics work grows out of the child's inherent love for numbers and for the process of counting. Every morning classes participate in an arithmetic routine that includes arithmetic poems and games, songs and drills, which are performed in a variety of rhythms. Whereas many schools shy away from drill, we have found that rhythmic drill actively engages the child and helps him master the arithmetic facts and tables.

First graders live in a world of imaginative pictures; they have a natural feeling for the archetypes implicit in the world of numbers. Through stories and descriptions that speak to the child's imagination, the teacher tries to engender in the children a sense for the inner qualities of the various numbers. The number one, for instance, represents more than a digit; it embodies the principle of unity. It can be thought of as the largest number, for it contains all other numbers within it. The number two, in contrast, denotes duality, contrast, opposites. The children in first grade might encounter some of these dualities in stories which contrast a bright sunny day and dark, gloomy night, or a mighty king and the queen who rules with him. With the number three comes a dynamic quality, with four a quality of stability and form. There are four seasons, four directions, four elements. Through his stories and descriptions, the teacher strives to bring the numbers to life in the hearts and minds of his students. A student who has gone through this process will never again consider a number simply as an abstraction or merely as a mark upon a page.

By third grade students have begun to venture out into the world. The pictorial consciousness of the first and second grade has begun to fade, and children want to know more about the world around them. At this time the Waldorf curriculum suggests that teachers begin to teach their classes about the practical activities in life: how houses are built, how food is prepared, how clothes are made, etc. The arithmetic work therefore also enters the practical sphere, and the third grade learns the many forms of measurement which are used in daily life. Since third graders are so active, it is important to allow the children to work with measurement in different ways. A class will measure their desks, their classrooms, themselves. They might pace out the length of the school building, the school yard, or a city block. Third grade students might learn how to make change by having a class store, and they might learn dry and liquid measurement by making muffins and hot chocolate. The specific examples may change, but in Waldorf schools teachers try to bring the material into direct experience, into life.

In the sixth grade, as children become able to think in more abstract terms, they begin to study geometry. Students will already have done a great deal of free hand geometric drawing in the early grades; now they are ready to learn how to use a compass and straightedge and to perform all the basic constructions possible with these tools. Just as arithmetic grew out of stories which revealed something of the inner nature of the numbers, geometry grows out of the beauty inherent in geometric designs. As the sixth grader learns how to subdivide a circle into six, a flower form is revealed, and an element of magic enters into his work. As all the permutations of the six-division of the circle are worked out and understood, this magical element is transformed into the beauty of logic. Drawing beautiful geometric forms speaks to the child's love of beauty and precision, but these forms are not constructed for their own sake; they are also studied because of the laws they reveal about ratios and geometric progressions, spirals, and the geometry of natural forms.

Much more is done in the elementary school mathematics lessons than can be indicated by these few examples, and by high school, students who have gone through the grades have a firm foundation and a deep appreciation for the worlds of arithmetic, algebra, and geometry. When they now pursue studies in the various fields of higher mathematics, they do so with mobility of thought, with an eye for beauty, and an understanding for the practical applications of mathematics in our life and work.

Let us now look at the science curriculum as another example of the way in which a child's studies mirror his development. In the early grades, children hear simple nature stories about the seasons, the elements, and the natural processes which we encounter in daily life. These stories contain pictures of some of the topics they will study in the years ahead. A story about the sun, moon, and stars might prepare—in picture form—the basis for the study of astronomy in the seventh grade. A description of a sandy beach, a rocky coast, or a dismal swamp might contain pictures which will ultimately elucidate the processes of soil formation and erosion which will be studied in sixth grade. Although the concepts are not specifically articulated to the children, the imaginative basis for an intellectual understanding is prepared in these early grades, and in later years the class teacher will refer to and build upon what has been taught before.

By the time they enter fourth grade, most students have developed an active interest in the natural world. At the same time, they are becoming more aware of themselves as individuals and more interested in other people. The Waldorf curriculum of the middle grades meets these new interests through a lively study of man, and of the animal, plant, and mineral kingdoms. The nature study sequence begins with the study of man, and students are led to a deeper understanding of man and of his special tasks upon the earth.

Seventh grade can be a tumultuous year for most students. As they approach this age, many of them start experiencing that sense of profound loneliness that will increase with adolescence; sometimes they begin to feel that their world no longer makes sense. The upper elementary school grades are therefore an ideal time to study the physical sciences with children, for the beauty, order, and consistency of physical phenomena speak strongly to their need for inner logic and for order in their lives. The science curriculum of the upper grades meets the students' needs by drawing them out of their own personal concerns and engaging their interest in the phenomena before them. In the high school, students continue these science studies in the realms of physics, chemistry, earth sciences, zoology, botany, and human anatomy and physiology. Through their work in the elementary school they have gained a foundation for these more advanced studies; at the same time they have had experiences of the natural world vivid enough to last for a lifetime.

## The high school

The third seven-year stage of child development begins at about the age of fourteen. Whereas the child before the age of seven relates to the world primarily in physical terms and the child from seven to fourteen relates to the world much more through his feelings, the adolescent begins to establish a relationship to the world based on the power of thought. The early stage of adolescence is still largely colored by intense feelings; but in their sixteenth year, students begin an intellectual awakening that allows them to recognize, appreciate, and identify with the great ideas, ideals, and achievements of mankind.

High school students need an entirely different kind of relationship with their teachers. Unlike the elementary student who learns largely through his emotional connection to the class teacher, the high school student learns because he respects his teachers' knowledge and expertise. Consequently, it is to individual subject teachers, each an expert in his field, that the education of the high school student is entrusted. The Waldorf high schools offer a rich and diverse academic curriculum in the sciences, mathematics, and the humanities, including literature, history, and history of the arts. The courses address the most basic questions about the nature of the human being, society, and the natural world and they help students in their attempt to establish a sense of meaning and definition in their lives.

A description of the content of a literature main lesson course in the high school might illustrate how the curriculum speaks to the student of a particular age. In Waldorf high schools throughout the world, students in the eleventh grade study the classic Medieval romance, *Parzival*, by Wolfram von Eschenbach. The reader first meets the noble child Parzival in the forest refuge to which he has been taken after the death of his father. Removed from the world of chivalry and from his own kingdom by a mother fearful for his well-being, Parzival grows up ignorant of his identity, his heritage, his nobility. His first encounter with the world outside his cloistered home is a brief meeting with four bright and shining knights. This encounter arouses such an intense longing to be like those knights that Parzival unfeelingly abandons his mother, leaving her to her sorrow and death. In ignorance and dullness of soul, he begins his long quest. It is a quest for glory, a quest for the highest, a quest for his true being.

What better metaphor can be found for modern man than Parzival, born to achieve the highest honor, yet cut off from his rightful heritage, forced to find his way alone through suffering, humiliation, and doubt? Students identify with the bumbling, awkward, simple fool of the early books, who, in his childish unawareness, fails to ask the question which would heal the wounded king. They have compassion for the young man of the central scenes, cursed and condemned for a failing which he does not understand, bereft of hope and faith. And they glory in the triumph of the noble king Parzival, who has achieved the soul's peace and been named the Lord of the Grail.

Through his steadfast striving, even in the face of the abyss of darkness and loneliness, Parzival achieves the goal of his quest—and of his questioning. And eleventh graders, facing the crises of adolescence which lead to so many empty answers—drug abuse, sexual promiscuity, and even suicide—may draw comfort and strength from this ageless tale.

Through this brief overview we have tried to show how the organization of the three parts of the Waldorf school—preschool, elementary school, and high school—is structured to meet the needs of the growing child and maturing adolescent. In each section of the school, a student's relationship to his teachers is determined by the kind of relationship most suitable to the student's age, and for every age our teachers strive to provide the type of instruction which most directly speaks to the forces and capacities which need to be developed at that time.

## The Waldorf method: Education as an art

In his work with the teachers of the Waldorf School, Rudolf Steiner challenged his colleagues to transform education into an art. To this day Waldorf teachers strive to meet this challenge and continue to work to become artists in education who can educate the whole human being, addressing the spirit, soul, and body of the child.

What does it mean to be an artist in education? Is it different from being an artist in another field? One salient feature of artistry is that the artist achieves such a mastery over his medium that he is left free to create and to serve as the vehicle for that which seeks to express itself through him. How does this apply to the teacher? What is his medium? Just as the musician works with melody, harmony, and rhythm, and the painter with light, color, and form, the teacher works with the curriculum, with his pedagogical methods, and most of all, with the children whom he strives to educate. Especially in the elementary school his method derives directly from art; he uses the arts—verbal, pictorial, musical, dynamic, and plastic—to achieve that which only art allows: a connection between the subject and object, a sense of communion engendered by the feeling life of the child.

The "main lesson" in a Waldorf school is the canvas upon which the process of education as a work of art can be rendered. Every day, students in the elementary school and high school begin their studies in a main lesson—a double academic period in which the same subject is studied for a block of three to six weeks. The main lesson allows a class to become thoroughly involved in a subject, for these lessons include a lively presentation, a review and discussion of the previous day's study, and work on academic and artistic projects. Subjects such as history, geography, and the sciences are usually taught in one or two main lesson blocks per year, while subjects needing regular practice, such as English and mathematics, are supplemented by weekly classes as well.

The main lesson contains, in a kernel, many aspects of the Waldorf approach to education. Consider how a person becomes involved in a new activity or field. Do we not first become involved in something because of our feelings—feelings of curiosity, attraction, interest, or awe? Everyone who has ever experienced a vocation, a calling to do something, will recognize that this call came not from the realms of thought or deliberation but from the life of the soul. Only after the stage when the feelings are aroused does a person stop and think about what he has experienced. A second stage then begins, and we further develop our interest by thinking. When we decide to pursue an interest and to find out more about it, we may plan a line of inquiry or follow a course of study. This second stage thus leads us into a third stage of involvement—action. As soon as we begin to be active in a new interest, we begin truly to reap the fruits of our involvement. This sequence of activities—the stimulation of feeling, the development of thoughts, the spur to activity—is a natural process in the human being. Teaching according to this sequence insures that the child will thoroughly learn what is taught, and that his love for the process of learning is strengthened.

How does this sequence apply to a main lesson block in the elementary school? Let us present a block in the sixth grade as an example. A new main lesson block—let us say early Roman history, which is taught in the sixth grade—is introduced. The students who have been in the school for a number of years have anticipated this course of study, for they have seen the work that previous sixth graders have done in this field. Beginning with the story of Aeneas, students are taken back to ancient times. As the teacher tells the story of the Aeneid, the students' imaginations are stirred and they form living pictures of Aeneas as he carries his old father, Anchises, out of the burning town. They wait in suspense as the Trojans' ships are driven across the oceans by violent storms; they mourn as Dido sacrifices herself for this most perfect of men; and they rejoice as Aeneas founds the settlement of New Troy.

Now that their curiosity and interest are awakened, students are eager to hear of what became of that settlement. As the weeks progress, the students still become caught up in the mighty dramas of the stories, but the element of thought now figures more prominently in their studies. It is not enough to hear about the lives and adventures of great men and women, they want to know more about the Roman civilization: how people lived, what they thought, and what their great culture achieved. Throughout the main lesson block, students work actively on various types of projects. They may learn to recite poems in Latin or to draw perfect Roman capitals. They might write their own accounts of the stories of the kings and heroes in the form of narratives, letters, poems, or plays. Pictures are drawn to illustrate their written work, elephants sculpted to bring Hannibal's invasion to life, a meeting of the Roman Senate might be held to try a case, and with lofty gestures and high rhetoric the sixth grader tries to appeal to his classmates' faculty of reason and their love of justice. By the end of a four-week main lesson block, the sixth graders have probably learned more about the essence of early Roman history than many a college student in a semester course. Because the main lesson block allows a student to become totally involved in a subject, because learning is based on experience as well as thought and feeling, whatever is studied will live in the students' memory for many years to come.

Every day the main lesson begins with a morning verse, followed by singing, recitation, and concentration exercises to focus the children on the tasks ahead. Now the teacher makes a presentation. Having familiarized himself thoroughly with his subject, the teacher brings a myth, a biography, or a historical event to life; he awakens interest and amazement for different geographic regions of the earth, or he inspires awe and wonder by his descriptions and demonstrations of the natural world and the physical processes of the universe. Bringing a subject to life is akin to performing a concerto. Every note, every phrase and nuance must be studied in order not to be forgotten when the performance actually takes place. During the actual presentation, the teacher must be free to create; his words must take wing so that the images he invokes in the students' minds will be vivid and true. This part of the lesson stirs the students' feelings, engages them directly in the material by speaking to their hearts.

If making a presentation is akin to performing a concerto, conducting a review and discussion on the following day demands even more artistry and insight, for now one has to be free enough to improvise. In the review the teacher works with what the students learned from the presentation of the previous day, and he brings what was experienced through his feelings into the light of thinking. The students may have been touched by a particular element in a story, or by a specific facet of a science experiment. During the review the teacher listens to what the students are really asking and steers the discussion into realms which he may not have planned, but which are obviously right. Here the teacher's knowledge of his class bears fruit; if he has studied the children carefully and knows their needs, these unplanned moments can be used to help a child grapple with his deepest questions and most pressing concerns. Yet the subject must not get lost in digressions, for, like a mighty theme, the essence of the lesson must sound forth so that the class will develop clear concepts of the materials they have studied.

The presentation and review take, at most, one half of the main lesson. What do the students do in the remaining time? They work, thereby experiencing the subjects on another level. Herein lies the key to Waldorf education: something that has stirred the feelings and stimulated thoughts must be transformed into another level of experience—into deeds. And if they can be creative deeds, the child's experience will be enriched a hundredfold. In Waldorf schools the arts are not taught for their own sake; rather, they are taught because they allow a child to experience a subject on a level far deeper and richer than the intellectual level. The class teacher is fortunate in having all the arts at his disposal to involve the children more deeply in a subject. He must, however, first have schooled himself sufficiently in the arts so that he can lead the children in the artistic experience. He need not be an expert at drawing, but needs to have experienced the dynamic power of line and form; he need not be a theatrical director, but he needs to have developed beautiful, clear speech and gestures; he need not be a consummate artist in any medium, but he needs to have schooled his eye, ear, hand, and heart so that he can recognize the beautiful and help his students in their desire to achieve it. In our experience, it is the artistic experiences that leave lasting impressions in a student's life. Information can be gathered or retrieved, but the experience of the subjects through individual work and through the arts builds a foundation in the soul which will enrich all further learning and the whole of a student's life.

Through these methods, Waldorf teachers seek to transform teaching into an art. Yet the greater artistry lies in the transformation of the art of teaching into true education, into the schooling of capacities, into a preparation for life.

## Developing capacities: An education for the future

Waldorf teachers who hope to prepare students to be citizens in the next century must work to transform the teaching profession into an art of education. Is there a difference between teaching and educating? In my opinion there is, and if we examine the etymologies of these two words we may gain some sense of what this difference might be. The verb "to teach" derives from the Old English verb *taecan*, which meant to show, to point out, to instruct. This Old English verb has a modern English cognate in the word token, a sign, symbol, or mark. The verb "to educate" derives from the Latin *ex ducere* which means to lead out or lead forth. If one pursues this line of thought beyond the literal meanings of the words, one might see that the *teacher* is essentially one who shows, points out, or instructs. The *educator*, on the other hand, is one who leads forth that which lives in the child, or one who leads the child forth into life. The difference between these words may be academic, but the difference in approach between an ordinary teacher and a true educator is not. A teacher sees the child as a vessel which needs to be filled, a tabula rasa on which the lines of learning must be written; an educator sees the child as a being of unfolding capacities, who must be nurtured so that he may take his rightful place in life.

Waldorf teachers see their responsibility as that of preparing children for life—but for which aspects of life do we seek to prepare them? Should we prepare them to meet the "real world" of the present or of the future? Should we teach our students the skills which are needed in contemporary life or those which will be needed when the children reach maturity?

We live in a century of change. Improvements in technology—and especially in the field of communications—have so rapidly altered our way of life that we seem to have less and less in common with our forebears. How much more the world will change during our time and in the coming generations is beyond our power to speculate. We can be certain, however, that children now in school, who will be adults in the twenty-first century, will live in a world where much of what we experience today will be obsolete. We cannot prepare them for entering a new age by teaching them only of this one. Rather, we must prepare them by nourishing in them the ability to work with and adapt to whatever the future might bring. Of course students in Waldorf schools must develop up-to-date, in-depth knowledge about the subjects they study, and we certainly give them the skills and resources necessary for success in their future studies and careers, but if Waldorf schools are to prepare students for their lives in the next century, they must go beyond these immediate tasks of schooling and strive to educate capacities which can mature and can serve students in the unimagined and unimaginable situations of the future.

What capacities do we strive to nourish, to draw forth from our students? First and foremost, we work to foster the capacity to think clearly, logically, and creatively, and we work to guide the child towards self-knowledge. Secondly, we hope to engender the capacity to feel deeply, to be sensitive to the beauties, the joys, the sorrows of this world, to experience compassion for others. Finally, we try to cultivate the strength and willingness to act, to do what must be done, and to work not only for oneself, but for the benefit of all mankind and for the earth.

The education of these capacities is not only achieved through our rich curriculum and our teaching methods, but also through the attitude with which we, as teachers, approach the process of education itself. From the descriptions above it should be clear that we perceive education as a process of inner growth promoted by students' relationships with their teachers and peers, their exposure to our rich curriculum, and their work in the arts and in the practical spheres of life. Most graduates of Waldorf schools attest to the fact that the education they received made a vital difference in their lives. They recognize that this difference derived largely from the teachers' values, from the teachers' fundamental respect for the individuality of each child, and from the teachers' willingness to serve each child and meet his needs.

Ultimately, any form of education can only go as far as those individuals who practice it. The most profound philosophy, the most interesting curriculum, the most innovative teaching methods cannot succeed if the individuals who work in the school are not working on themselves. Whether in the preschool, elementary school, or high school, Waldorf education succeeds because the teachers try, consciously and constantly, to develop themselves, to transform themselves into self-aware, compassionate individuals who can translate their ideas into ideals and their ideals into reality. The rapid spread of Waldorf education in this century is more than a social fact; it is a testament to the power of an ideal and the striving of men and women who are working for the development of the human being, the transformation of society, and the renewal of the earth.

# Appendices

# Holistic Education Glossary

Holistic education is a comprehensive philosophy that finds expression in a variety of organized and unorganized movements, classroom methods, and approaches. The aim of this brief listing is to give a vivid impression of the diversity of holistic approaches and to suggest their interrelationships.

### Alternative education

This term is used loosely to mean any school or educational method that is significantly different from conventional, mainstream approaches. Many public "alternative schools" are simply more relaxed and student-centered programs for dissatisfied high school students who are considered to be "at risk" of dropping out. In the holistic context, alternative education refers more specifically to a school or learning center, public or private, that adopts a different style of education for *all* students on the basis of genuine philosophical disagreement with the goals and methods of mainstream education.

### Conflict resolution and mediation

Conflict resolution and creative problem-solving skills are advocated by a number of mainstream educational groups, and programs that train students to be mediators and peer counselors are increasingly popular even in public schools. This is a promising new field in public education. In holistic approaches, human relationships are a central concern, not secondary to academic concerns. Conflict resolution and interpersonal skills are an integral part of the holistic curriculum.

### Critical pedagogy

This is probably the most provocative and radical intellectual trend in the scholarly study of education. The writings of Paulo Freire, Ira Shor, Henry Giroux, Michael Apple, Stanley Aronowitz, and others apply a hard-hitting, left-inspired analysis to public educational theory and practice. Because most of the work of these writers is highly focused on economic and ideological factors, it is not truly holistic. However, as students of this school begin to integrate its critical cultural perspective with more spiritual, human-potential concerns, the result is a powerful holistic analysis. (See, in particular, *The Moral and Spiritual Crisis in Education* by David E. Purpel [1989], and "Realizing the Promise of

Humanistic Education . . ." by Lee Bell and Nancy Schniedewind, *Journal of Humanistic Psychology* [vol. 29, no. 2, 1989]).

### Developmentally appropriate curriculum

This concept draws upon empirical studies in psychology (especially the work of Jean Piaget) to demonstrate that children learn in different ways at different ages, and asserts that their natural development ought to be respected. Major national educational groups (e.g., the National Association for the Education of Young Children) and leading psychologists such as David Elkind have endorsed this approach; they argue that young children, in particular, should not be rushed into academics. Holistic theory has included this perspective since long before developmental psychology confirmed it: Jean-Jacques Rousseau and Johann Pestalozzi recognized the principles of human development, and Maria Montessori and Rudolf Steiner fashioned entire educational systems according to their deep understanding of, and respect for, the child's natural development.

### Global education

In the late twentieth century, it is becoming clear that the problems confronting humankind transcend national and cultural borders and that our survival depends on global cooperation. Many programs to explore cross-cultural and international perspectives are being developed and implemented in schools across the country. This is a positive step toward holistic education, because a holistic approach strongly emphasizes the interconnectedness of life on Earth. Peace education is an intrinsic aspect of a global education. A truly holistic global education program would teach cross cultural understanding for its own sake, not, for example, to give business people a competitive edge in the emerging world marketplace.

### Green education

For many years there have been programs in outdoor education, environmental education, nature study, and ecology—and they are all valuable. But, the green approach involves a more serious confrontation with the wasteful, destructive, consumer-driven habits of the modern age. Green teaching, exemplified by the Centre for Alternative Technology in Wales and the Institute for Earth Education in Warrenville, Illinois, strives to impart a deeper respect for the Earth and the interconnectedness of all life. Green education is thus global education in its truest sense. It includes a deep concern for peace, justice, and the struggles of "third world" cultures, because these are all part of a holistic appreciation for the Earth and its life.

### Humanistic education

In the 1960s and 1970s, the humanistic psychology movement (based on the work of Abraham Maslow, Carl Rogers, Fritz Perls, Rollo May, and others) offered a more dynamic and positive view of human nature than the dominant behaviorist and Freudian models. The application of this approach to the classroom presented mainstream education with a new array of concerns and skills: self-esteem, emotional health, personal values, human relations, and imagination and creativity. Humanistic education was often called "integrative," "affective," or "confluent" education, indicating the integration of feelings and intellect in the learning process. Holistic educators, from Pestalozzi on through the free school movement of the 1960s, have always been humanistic educators.

### Integrated day

About 1970, American educators enthusiastically adopted methods being pioneered by the British Infant Schools; known informally as the "open classroom," this approach was more technically called the integrated day. Children were free to work at their own rate, on projects, in various learning centers around the classroom or throughout the school. The classroom became more of a busy laboratory than a lecture hall. The integrated day experiment was rapidly dropped when teachers and students, unaccustomed to such freedom, couldn't seem to maintain discipline or improve test scores enough to satisfy conventional expectations. However, holistic educators have used the integrated day approach with much success (the Montessori method has refined it into an art) and tend to avoid having children sitting obediently in rows of desks. Currently, the integrated day is taught in the education program at Antioch/New England Graduate School in Keene, New Hampshire.

### Learning styles

Over the past twenty years, our understanding of how the brain functions and how people learn has expanded dramatically. We have discovered that individuals differ biologically in their preferences for, and receptivity to, environmental stimuli. A number of psychologists and educators have applied these research findings to the educational setting, and this has resulted in new methods that address individual learning styles and multiple intelligences. These approaches can be a powerful tool for encouraging the unique potentials of each learner. Although these approaches can contribute significantly to holistic education, often they are simply grafted onto traditional educational aims and assumptions and used to impart the conventional curriculum more efficiently, rather than to allow individuals to grow more freely from within.

### Montessori education

The Montessori method revolves around a "prepared environment"— using specially designed educational materials and allowing children freedom to concentrate on activities that serve their current developmental needs. This approach serves children from infancy through adolescence. Maria Montessori (1870-1952), a brilliant pioneer in educational theory and practice, was a medical doctor who observed children's physical and intellectual development with a trained scientific eye, but who also brought a deeply spiritual attitude toward education. Although this attitude is perhaps the real essence of her contribution, it is sometimes lost in application. Lacking this aspect, Montessori education may become rigid in practice and overly focused on intellectual development. There has been much debate within the international Montessori community over the extent to which the founder's original teachings may be modified or compromised—to meet the requirements of public education, for example.

### Progressive education

From the 1890s through the 1930s, a strong reform movement known as progressive education attempted to make significant changes in American schools. Based largely on the work of Francis W. Parker, John Dewey, and other innovative educators, progressive education emphasized the needs of the growing child by replacing traditional teaching methods with interdisciplinary, cooperative classroom projects and field trips. Social studies and the creative arts were especially emphasized. In the 1930s the progressive movement became split between "child-centered" educators and a more radical group of "social reconstructionists" who, responding to the Great Depression, believed that schools should model alternatives to America's competitive, individualistic economic system. The progressive education movement declined in the 1940s and was discredited by critics in the 1950s who sought a return to "basics" in education. But only recently, a new Network of Progressive Educators has emerged to rekindle the idealism of the earlier progressive education movement. At its best (that is, when it integrates the "child-centered" and "reconstructionist" perspectives), progressive education is an expression of the holistic approach.

### Rites of passage

In traditional cultures, significant transitions in a person's life are celebrated and supported by the community in rites of passage. Birth, adolescence, marriage, and death are treated as sacred times—as openings to new and potentially higher levels of experience. Modern, materialistic cultures focus almost exclusively on the social and economic aspects rather than on the inner, spiritual significance of these transitions. This is especially obvious with respect to the passage from childhood to adulthood, where our lack of meaningful rites of passage is probably a major source of many of our teenagers' difficulties. Some holistic educators attempt to re-create traditional rites of passage, such as the Native American Vision Quest, or seek to create new ones in order to support and affirm their adolescent students' "coming of age."

### Spirituality

Probably the single most essential characteristic of holistic approaches is their spiritual perspective. That is, holistic approaches are guided by a reverence for life—a deep appreciation for the natural, spontaneous unfolding of life. Spirituality may be expressed in traditional religious language and rituals, or it may be expressed in more empirical terms (e.g., transpersonal psychology); the important point is to see life and nature and the growth of every child as mysteries to be honored rather than as mechanistic systems to be regulated. When education is grounded in a spiritual perspective, external measures of success, such as grades and test scores, become far less significant, and the natural creativity, spontaneity, and imagination of childhood are given far greater respect and opportunity for expression. Spirituality may also be described as the desire for beauty, simplicity, humility, connectedness, and peace—an uncommon pursuit in a culture that values utility, profit, fame, competition, and winning.

### Transpersonal psychology

While humanistic psychology is concerned primarily with personal and interpersonal growth, transpersonal psychology studies the more mysterious realms of religious experience, intuition, and altered states of consciousness. Pioneers in this field, which today is becoming established as a serious and disciplined study of transcendent experience, included Carl Jung, William James, Abraham Maslow, and Roberto Assagioli. Its findings have been applied to education by people such as Thomas Roberts and the late Beverly-Colleen Galyean and have led to the use of guided imagery and meditation in the classroom. Transpersonal educators have found that such techniques contribute to academic success as well as emotional well-being. A particularly good account of transpersonal theory and its application to child development is *The Radiant Child* by Thomas Armstrong (1985).

### Waldorf education

Rudolf Steiner (1861-1925) was a philosopher/scientist/mystic who lectured and wrote on an astounding variety of subjects from medicine and agriculture to theology and education. He founded a movement called anthroposophy, which he considered to be a spiritual science— that is, an empirical, verifiable understanding of the inner workings of the human soul. In 1919 he founded the first Waldorf School as an application of anthroposophic principles to education. Today, there are more than 400 Waldorf schools around the world. Waldorf education goes far beyond the usual curriculum and seeks to connect the growing child to the ongoing cultural and spiritual evolution of humankind. The method makes extensive use of classical legends and folklore, and it incorporates the creative and dramatic arts in every facet of instruction. Waldorf teachers are trained to be extremely responsive to the unfolding personalities of each of their students by establishing a lasting, trusting relationship with them. To accomplish this goal, the teachers move up a grade with their classes each year between first and eighth grades. Based on Steiner's teachings, the Waldorf movement has been a consistent critic of premature academic work for young children. Unfortunately, to a large extent the movement tends to remain isolated from other educational movements, even from its potential holistic allies.

### Whole child

Basically, holistic education seeks to teach the whole child. This means that academic achievement is only one goal of education, that the social, emotional, physical, aesthetic, and spiritual aspects of the human personality need to be recognized as well. In modern society, "school" has been defined as the place where knowledge and facts are taught, where people are prepared for careers and to be useful citizens. Holistic educators assert, however, that this emphasis on intellect and vocation results in lopsided development of human potentials and that a complete redefinition of the school is needed.

### Whole language

Although it is primarily concerned with reading and writing instruction, the whole language approach is based on a holistic philosophy. Advocates of whole language argue that instruction should be child centered and meaning centered rather than teacher and curriculum centered. They believe that reading and writing should be learned in the same natural, spontaneous ways that earlier language skills (hearing and speaking) are acquired. Whole language has roots in previous educational approaches (including progressive education) but only in the past ten years has it taken a definite shape and begun to spread rapidly—even in mainstream education. There is a danger that it could become the latest popular trend, ultimately destined (like the integrated day approach), to be diluted and finally abandoned. But there is also a chance that its holistic approach may spread throughout the educational system, leading to a genuinely holistic education even in public schools. (Whether the essential spiritual element can be adopted remains to be seen.) The whole language movement is a fascinating development that bears watching.

# Holistic Education Reading List

## Background Readings on the Holistic Paradigm

Bateson, Gregory. *Steps to an Ecology of Mind* (New York: Ballantine, 1972).

Berman, Morris. *The Reenchantment of the World* (Ithaca, NY: Cornell University Press, 1981).

Bohm, David. *Wholeness and the Implicate Order* (London: Routledge & Kegan Paul, 1980).

Bohm, David and F. David Peat, *Science, Order and Creativity* (New York: Bantam, 1987).

Capra, Fritjof. *The Tao of Physics: An Exploration of the Parallels Between Modern Physics and Eastern Mysticism* (Boulder, CO: Shambhala, 1976).

Capra, Fritjof. *The Turning Point: Science, Society, and the Rising Culture* (New York: Simon & Schuster, 1982).

de Chardin, Teilhard. *The Phenomenon of Man* (1955) (trans. by Bernard Wall) (New York: Harper & Row, 1961).

Eisler, Riane. *The Chalice and the Blade* (New York: Harper & Row, 1987).

Ferguson, Marilyn. *The Aquarian Conspiracy: Personal and Social Transformation in the 1980's* (Los Angeles: Tarcher, 1980).

Fox, Matthew. *The Coming of the Cosmic Christ* (San Francisco: Harper & Row, 1988).

Harman, Willis. *Global Mind Change: The Promise of the Last Years of the Twentieth Century* (Indianapolis: Knowledge Systems, 1988).

Houston, Jean. *The Possible Human* (Los Angeles: Tarcher, 1982).

Huxley, Aldous. *The Perennial Philosophy* (New York: Harper, 1945).

Jantsch, Erich. *The Self-Organizing Universe* (New York: Pergamon, 1980).

Johnston, Charles M. *The Creative Imperative: A Four-Dimensional Theory of Human Growth & Planetary Evolution* (Berkeley, CA: Celestial Arts, 1986).

Lemkow, Anna F. *The Wholeness Principle: Dynamics of Unity Within Science, Religion and Society* (Wheaton, IL: Quest, 1990).

Mumford, Lewis. *The Transformations of Man* (New York: Harper, 1956).

Pearce, Joseph Chilton. *The Crack in the Cosmic Egg: Challenging Constructs of Mind and Reality* (New York: Julian, 1971).

Prigogine, Ilya and Isabelle Stengers. *Order Out of Chaos: Man's New Dialogue With Nature* (New York: Bantam, 1984).

Rifkin, Jeremy. *Entropy: A New World View* (New York: Viking, 1980).

Roszak, Theodore. *Where the Wasteland Ends: Politics and Transcendence in Postindustrial Society* (Garden City, NY: Anchor/Doubleday, 1973).

Roszak, Theodore. *Person/Planet: The Creative Disintegration of Industrial Society* (Garden City, NY: Anchor/Doubleday, 1978).

Schumacher, E.F. *Small is Beautiful: Economics as if People Mattered* (Abacus, 1974).

Schumacher, E.F. *A Guide for the Perplexed* (New York: Harper & Row, 1977).

Sheldrake, Rupert. *A New Science of Life* (Los Angeles: Tarcher, 1981).

Swimme, Brian. *The Universe is a Green Dragon* (Santa Fe, NM: Bear & Co., 1984).

Wilber, Ken. *Up From Eden: A Transpersonal View of Human Evolution* (Boulder, CO: Shambhala, 1983).

Wilson, Colin. *Introduction to the New Existentialism* (Boston: Houghton Mifflin, 1967).

## Holistic Educational Theory

Armstrong, Thomas. *The Radiant Child* (Wheaton, IL: Quest, 1985).

Armstrong, Thomas. *In Their Own Way* (Los Angeles: Tarcher, 1987).

LePage, Andy. *Transforming Education: The New 3 R's* (Oakland: Oakmore House, 1987).

Miller, John P. *The Holistic Curriculum* (Toronto: Ontario Institute for Studies in Education, 1988).

Miller, Ron. *What Are Schools For? Holistic Education in American Culture* (Brandon, VT: Holistic Education Press, 1990).

Montessori, Maria. *Spontaneous Activity in Education* (1917) (trans. by F. Simmonds) (New York: Schocken, 1965).

Naumburg, Margaret. *The Child and the World* (New York: Harcourt Brace, 1928).

Neef, Joseph. *Sketch of a Plan and Method of Education* (1808) (New York: Arno/New York Times, 1969).

Oliver, Donald W. and Kathleen W. Gershman. *Education, Modernity, and Fractured Meaning: Toward a Process Theory of Teaching and Learning* (Albany: SUNY Press, 1989).

Parker, Francis W. *Talks on Pedagogics* (1894) (New York: Arno/New York Times, 1969).

Pearce, Joseph Chilton. *Magical Child: Rediscovering Nature's Plan for Our Children* (1977) (New York: Bantam, 1980).

Pearce, Joseph Chilton. *Magical Child Matures* (1985) (New York: Bantam, 1986).

Purpel, David E. *The Moral & Spiritual Crisis in Education: A Curriculum for Justice & Compassion in Education* (Granby, MA: Bergin & Garvey, 1989).

Randle, Damian. *Teaching Green: A Parent's Guide to Education for Life on Earth* (London: Merlin, 1989).

Richards, M.C. *Toward Wholeness: Rudolf Steiner Education in America* (Middletown, CT: Wesleyan University Press, 1980).

Rogers, Carl. *Freedom to Learn* (Columbus: Merrill, 1969/1983).

Sloan, Douglas. *Insight-Imagination: The Emancipation of Thought and the Modern World* (Westport, CT: Greenwood, 1983).

Sloan, Douglas (ed.). *Toward the Recovery of Wholeness: Knowledge, Education and Human Values* (New York: Teachers College Press, 1984).

5891

## DATE DUE